1 MO̶N̶T̶H̶

FR̶EE̶

READING

at

www.ForgottenBooks.com

By purchasing this book you are
eligible for one month membership to
ForgottenBooks.com, giving you
unlimited access to our entire
collection of over 1,000,000 titles via
our web site and mobile apps.

To claim your free month visit:
www.forgottenbooks.com/free921749

ISBN 978-1-5278-6982-0
PIBN 10921749

TRAVELS AND DISCOVERIES

IN

NORTH AND CENTRAL AFRICA.

VOL. I.

LONDON:
Printed by SPOTTISWOODE & Co.
New-street Square.

TRAVELS AND DISCOVERIES

IN

NORTH AND CENTRAL AFRICA:

BEING A

JOURNAL OF AN EXPEDITION

UNDERTAKEN

UNDER THE AUSPICES OF H.B.M.'S GOVERNMENT,

IN THE YEARS

1849—1855.

BY

HENRY BARTH, Ph.D., D.C.L.

FELLOW OF THE ROYAL GEOGRAPHICAL AND ASIATIC SOCIETIES

&c. &c.

IN FIVE VOLUMES.

VOL. I.

SECOND EDITION.

LONDON:

LONGMAN, BROWN, GREEN, LONGMANS, & ROBERTS.

AFR.
B 282 n E (1) copy 1
L. Cabot Briggs Collection
9 February 1976

TO THE RIGHT HONOURABLE

THE EARL OF CLARENDON, K.G., G.C.B.

ETC. ETC. ETC.

HER MAJESTY'S SECRETARY OF STATE FOR FOREIGN AFFAIRS,

THESE VOLUMES,

CONTAINING AN ACCOUNT OF

TRAVELS AND DISCOVERIES IN NORTH AND CENTRAL AFRICA,

MADE UNDER HIS LORDSHIP'S AUSPICES,

ARE,

IN GRATEFUL ACKNOWLEDGMENT FOR MANY ACTS OF KINDNESS,

Dedicated,

BY HIS OBLIGED AND FAITHFUL SERVANT,

THE AUTHOR.

PREFACE.

On the 5th of October, 1849, at Berlin, Professor Carl Ritter informed me that the British Government was about to send Mr. Richardson on a mission to Central Africa, and that they had offered, through the Chevalier Bunsen, to allow a German traveller to join the mission, provided he was willing to contribute two hundred pounds for his own personal travelling expenses.

I had commenced lecturing at the University of Berlin on comparative geography and the colonial commerce of antiquity, and had just at that time published the first volume of my " Wanderings round the Mediterranean," which comprised my journey through Barbary. Having undertaken this journey quite alone, I spent nearly my whole time with the Arabs, and familiarized myself with that state of human society where the camel is man's daily companion, and the culture of the date-tree his chief occupation. I made long journeys through desert tracts;

A 4

I travelled all round the Great Syrtis, and, passing through the picturesque little tract of Cyrenaica, traversed the whole country towards Egypt; I wandered about for above a month in the desert valleys between Aswán and Kosér, and afterwards pursued my journey by land all the way through Syria and Asia Minor to Constantinople.

While traversing these extensive tracts, where European comfort is never altogether out of reach, where lost supplies may be easily replaced, and where the protection of European powers is not quite without avail, I had often cast a wistful look towards those unknown or little-known regions in the interior, which stand in frequent, though irregular, connection with the coast. As a lover of ancient history, I had been led towards those regions rather through the commerce of ancient Carthage, than by the thread of modern discovery; and the desire to know something more about them acted on me like a charm. In the course of a conversation I once held with a Háusa slave in Káf, in the regency of Tunis, he, seeing the interest I took in his native country, made use of these simple but impressive words: " Please God, you shall go and visit Kanó." These words were constantly ringing in my ears; and though overpowered for a time by the vivid impressions of interesting and picturesque countries, they echoed with renewed intensity as soon as I was restored to the tranquillity of European life.

During my three years' travelling I had ample opportunity of testing the efficacy of British protection; I experienced the kindness of all Her Britannic Majesty's consuls from Tangiers to Brúsa, and often enjoyed their hospitality. It was solely their protection which enabled me to traverse with some degree of security those more desert tracts through which I wandered. Colonel Warrington, Her Majesty's consul in Tripoli, who seems to have had some presentiment of my capabilities as an African explorer, even promised me his full assistance if I should try to penetrate into the interior. Besides this, my admiration of the wide extension of the British over the globe, their influence, their language, and their government, was such that I felt a strong inclination to become the humble means of carrying out their philanthropic views for the progressive civilization of the neglected races of Central Africa.

Under these circumstances, I volunteered cheerfully to accompany Mr. Richardson, on the sole condition, however, that the exploration of Central Africa should be made the principal object of the mission, instead of a secondary one, as had been originally contemplated.

In the meantime, while letters were interchanged

between Berlin, London, and Paris (where Mr.
Richardson at that time resided), my father, whom I
had informed of my design, entreated me to desist from my perilous undertaking, with an earnest-
ness which my filial duty did not allow me to resist;
and giving way to Dr. Overweg, who in youthful
enthusiasm came immediately forward to volunteer,
I receded from my engagement. But it was too late,
my offer having been officially accepted in London;
and I therefore allayed my father's anxiety, and
joined the expedition.

It was a generous act of Lord Palmerston, who
organized the expedition, to allow two foreign gentlemen to join it instead of one. A sailor was besides
attached to it; and a boat was also provided, in order
to give full scope to the object of exploration. The
choice of the sailor was unfortunate, and Mr. Richardson thought it best to send him back from Múrzuk;
but the boat, which was carried throughout the difficult and circuitous road by Múrzuk, Ghát, Aïr, and
Zínder, exciting the wonder and astonishment of all
the tribes in the interior, ultimately reached its destination, though the director of the expedition himself
had in the meanwhile unfortunately succumbed.

Government also allowed us to take out arms. At
first it had been thought that the expedition ought to
go unarmed, inasmuch as Mr. Richardson had made

his first journey to Ghát without arms. But on that occasion he had gone as a private individual, without instruments, without presents, without anything; and we were to unite with the character of an expedition that of a mission,—that is to say, we were to explore the country while endeavouring at the same time to establish friendship with the chiefs and rulers of the different territories. It may be taken for granted that we should never have crossed the frontier of Aïr had we been unarmed; and when I entered upon my journey alone, it would have been impossible for me to proceed without arms through countries which are in a constant state of war, where no chief or ruler can protect a traveller except with a large escort, which is sure to run away as soon as there is any real danger.

It may be possible to travel without arms in some parts of Southern Africa; but there is this wide dif-ference, that the natives of the latter are exclusively Pagans, while, along all those tracts which I have been exploring, Islamism and Paganism are constantly arrayed against each other in open or secret warfare, even if we leave out of view the unsafe state of the roads through large states consisting, though loosely connected together, of almost independent provinces. The traveller in such countries must carry arms; yet he must exercise the utmost discretion in using them. As for myself, I avoided giving offence to the men with whom I had to deal in peaceful intercourse, endeavouring to attach them to me by esteem and friendship. I have never proceeded onwards without leaving a sincere friend behind me, and thus being sure that, if obliged to retrace my steps, I might do so with safety.

But I have more particular reason to be grateful for the opinion entertained of me by the British Government; for after Mr. Richardson had, in March, 1851, fallen a victim to the noble enterprise to which he had devoted his life, Her Majesty's Government honoured me with their confidence, and, in authorizing me to carry out the objects of the expedition, placed sufficient means at my disposal for the purpose. The position in which I was thus placed must be my excuse for undertaking, after the successful accomplishment of my labours, the difficult task of relating them in a language not my own.

In matters of science and humanity all nations ought to be united by one common interest, each contributing its share in proportion to its own peculiar disposition and calling. If I have been able to achieve something in geographical discovery, it is difficult to say how much of it is due to English, how much to German influence; for science is built up of the materials collected by almost every nation, and, beyond all doubt, in geographical enterprise in general none has done more than the English, while, in Central Africa in particular, very little has been achieved by any but English travellers. Let it not, therefore, be attributed to an undue feeling of nationality if I correct any error of those who preceded me. It would be unpardonable if a traveller failed to penetrate further, or to obtain a clearer insight into the customs and the polity of the nations visited by him, or if he were unable to delineate the country with greater accuracy and precision, than those who went before him.

Every succeeding traveller is largely indebted to the labours of his predecessor. Thus our expedition would never have been able to achieve what it did, if Oudney, Denham, and Clapperton had not gone before us; nor would these travellers have succeeded so far, had Lyon and Ritchie not opened the road to Fezzán; nor would Lyon have been able to reach Tejérri, if Captain (now Rear-admiral) Smyth had not shown the way to Ghírza. To Smyth, seconded by Colonel Warrington, is due the merit of having attracted the attention of the British Government to the favourable situation of Tripoli for facilitating intercourse with Central Africa; and if at present the river-communication along the Tsádda or Bénuwé seems to hold out a prospect of an easier approach to those regions, the importance of Tripoli must not be underrated, for it may long remain the most available port from which a steady communication with many parts of that continent can be kept up.

I had the good fortune to see my discoveries placed on a stable basis before they were brought to a close, by the astronomical observations of Dr. Vogel*, who was sent out by Her Britannic Majesty's Government for the purpose of joining the expedition; and I have only to regret that this gentleman was not my companion from the beginning of my journey, as exact astronomical observations, such as he has made, are of the utmost importance in any geographical exploration. By moving the generally-accepted position of Kúkawa more than a degree to the westward, the whole map of the interior has been changed very considerably. The position assigned by Dr. Vogel to Zínder gives to the whole western route, from Ghát through the country of A'sben, a well-fixed terminating point, while at the same time it serves to check my route to Timbúktu. If, however, this topic be left out of consideration, it will be found that the maps made by me on the jour-

---

* Some details will be considered in a Memoir to be subjoined at the end of this work. It is to be hoped that Dr. Vogel's calculations themselves may be received in the meantime.

ney, under many privations, were a close approximation to the truth. But now all that pertains to physical features and geographical position has been laid down, and executed with artistic skill and scientific precision, by Dr. Petermann.

The principal merit which I claim for myself in this respect is that of having noted the whole configuration of the country; and my chief object has been to represent the tribes and nations with whom I came in contact, in their historical and ethnographical relation to the rest of mankind, as well as in their physical relation to that tract of country in which they live. If, in this respect, I have succeeded in placing before the eyes of the public a new and animated picture, and connected those apparently savage and degraded tribes more intimately with the history of races placed on a higher level of civilization, I shall be amply recompensed for the toils and dangers I have gone through.

My companion, Dr. Overweg, was a clever and active young geologist; but, unfortunately, he was deficient in that general knowledge of natural science which is required for comprehending all the various phenomena occurring on a journey into unknown regions. Having never before risked his life on a dangerous expedition, he never for a moment doubted that it might not be his good fortune to return home in safety; and he therefore did not always bestow that care upon his journal which is so desirable in such an enterprise. Nevertheless almost all his observations of latitude have been found correct, while his memoranda, if deciphered at leisure, might still yield a rich harvest.

One of the principal objects which Her Britannic Majesty's Government had always in view in these African expeditions was the abolition of the slave-trade. This, too, was zealously advocated by the late Mr. Richardson, and, I trust, has been as zealously carried out by myself whenever it was in my power to do so, although, as an explorer on a journey of discovery, I was induced, after mature reflection, to place myself under the protection of an expeditionary army, whose object it was to subdue another tribe, and eventually to carry away a large proportion of the conquered into slavery. Now, it should always be borne in mind that there is a broad distinction between the slave-trade and domestic slavery. The foreign slave-trade may, comparatively speaking, be easily abolished, though the difficulties of watching over contraband attempts have been shown sufficiently by many years' experience. With the abolition of the slave-trade all along the northern and south-western coast of Africa, slaves will cease to be brought down to the coast; and in this way a great deal of the mischief and misery necessarily resulting from this inhuman traffic will be cut off. But this, unfortunately, forms only a small part of the evil.

There can be no doubt that the most horrible topic connected with slavery is slave-hunting; and this is carried on not only for the purpose of supplying the foreign market, but, in a far more extensive degree, for supplying the wants of domestic slavery. Hence it was necessary that I should become acquainted with the real state of these most important features of African society, in order to speak clearly about them; for with what authority could I expatiate on the horrors and the destruction accompanying such an expedition, if I were not speaking as an eye-witness? But having myself accompanied such a host on a grand scale, I shall be able, in the third volume of my narrative, to lay before the public a picture of the cheerful comfort, as well as the domestic happiness, of a considerable portion of the human race, which, though in a low, is not at all in a degraded state of civilization, as well as the wanton and cruel manner in which this happiness is destroyed, and its peaceful abodes changed into desolation. Moreover, this very expedition afforded me the best opportunity of convincing the rulers of Bórnu of the injury which such a perverse system entails upon themselves.

But besides this, it was of the utmost importance to visit the country of the Músgu; for while that region had been represented by the last expedition as an almost inaccessible mountain-chain, attached to that group which Major Denham observed on his enterprising but unfortunate expedition with Bú-Khalúm, I convinced myself on my journey to A'da-máwa, from the information which I gathered from the natives, that the mountains of Mándará are entirely insulated towards the east. I considered it, therefore, a matter of great geographical importance to visit that country, which, being situated between the rivers Shárí and Bénuwé, could alone afford the proof whether there was any connection between these two rivers.

I shall have frequent occasion to refer, in my journal, to conversations which I had with the natives on religious subjects. I may say that I have always avowed my religion, and defended the pure principles of Christianity against those of Islám; only once was I obliged, for about a month, in order to carry out my project of reaching Timbúktu, to assume the character of a Moslim. Had I not resorted to this expedient, it would have been absolutely impossible to achieve such a project, since I was then under the protection of no chief whatever, and had to pass through the country of the fanatic and barbarous hordes of the Tawárek. But though, with this sole exception, I have never denied my character of a Christian, I thought it prudent to conform to the innocent prejudices of the people around me, adopting a dress which is at once better adapted to the climate and more decorous in the eyes of the natives. One great cause of my popularity was the custom of alms-giving. By this means I won the esteem of the natives, who took such a lively interest in my wellbeing that, even when I was extremely ill, they used to say, "'Abd el Kerím * shall not die."

I have given a full description of my preparatory excursion through the mountainous region round Tripoli; for though this is not altogether a new country, anyone who compares my map with that of Lyon or Denham will see how little the very interesting physical features of this tract had been known before, while, at a time when the whole Turkish empire is about to undergo a great transformation, it seems well worth while to lay also the state of this part of its vast dominions in a more complete manner before the European public.

Of the first part of our expedition there has already appeared the Narrative of the late Mr. Richardson, published from his manuscript jour-

* "'Abd el Kerím," meaning "Servant of the Merciful," was the name which I thought it prudent to adopt.

nals, which I was fortunately able to send home from
Kúkawa.   It is full of minute incidents of travelling
life, so very instructive to the general reader.   But
from my point of view, I had to look very differently
at the objects which presented themselves; and Mr.
Richardson, if he had lived to work out his memoranda himself, would not have failed to give to his
Journal a more lasting interest.   Moreover, my stay
in A'gades afforded me quite a different insight into
the life, the history, and geography of those regions,
and brought me into contact with Timbúktu.

Extending over a tract of country of twenty-four
degrees from north to south, and twenty degrees from
east to west, in the broadest part of the continent of
Africa, my travels necessarily comprise subjects of
great interest and diversity.

After having traversed vast deserts of the most
barren soil, and scenes of the most frightful desolation, I met with fertile lands irrigated by large
navigable rivers and extensive central lakes, ornamented with the finest timber, and producing various
species of grain, rice, sesamum, ground-nuts, in unlimited abundance, the sugar-cane, &c., together with
cotton and indigo, the most valuable commodities of
trade.   The whole of Central Africa, from Bagírmi
to the east as far as Timbúktu to the west (as will be
seen in my narrative), abounds in these products.
The natives of these regions not only weave their

own cotton, but dye their home-made shirts with their own indigo. The river, the far-famed Niger, which gives access to these regions by means of its eastern branch the Bénuwé, which I discovered, affords an uninterrupted navigable sheet of water for more than six hundred miles into the very heart of the country. Its western branch is obstructed by rapids at the distance of about three hundred and fifty miles from the coast; but even at that point it is probably not impassable in the present state of navigation, while, higher up, the river opens an immense highroad for nearly one thousand miles into the very heart of Western Africa, so rich in every kind of produce.

The same diversity of soil and produce which the regions traversed by me exhibit, is also observed with respect to man. Starting from Tripoli in the north, we proceed from the settlements of the Arab and the Berber, the poor remnants of the vast empires of the middle ages, into a country dotted with splendid ruins from the period of the Roman dominion, through the wild roving hordes of the Tawárek, to the Negro and half-Negro tribes, and to the very border of the South African nations. In the regions of Central Africa there exists not one and the same stock, as in South Africa; but the greatest diversity of tribes, or rather nations, prevails, with idioms entirely distinct.

The great and momentous struggle between Islamism and Paganism is here continually going on, causing every day the most painful and affecting results, while the miseries arising from slavery and the slave-trade are here revealed in their most repulsive features. We find Mohammedan learning engrafted on the ignorance and simplicity of the black races, and the gaudy magnificence and strict ceremonial of large empires side by side with the barbarous simplicity of naked and half-naked tribes. We here trace a historical thread which guides us through this labyrinth of tribes and overthrown kingdoms; and a lively interest is awakened by reflecting on their possible progress and restoration, through the intercourse with more civilized parts of the world. Finally, we find here commerce in every direction radiating from Kanó, the great emporium of Central Africa, and spreading the manufactures of that industrious region over the whole of Western Africa.

I cannot conclude these prefatory remarks without expressing my sincere thanks for the great interest shown in my proceedings by so many eminent men in this country, as well as for the distinction of the Victoria medal awarded to me by the Royal Geographical Society. As I may flatter myself that, by the success which attended my efforts, I have encouraged further undertakings in these as well as in other quarters of Africa, so it will be my greatest satisfaction, if this narrative should give a fresh impulse to the endeavours to open the fertile regions of Central Africa to European commerce and civilization.

Whatever may be the value of this work, the Author believes that it has been enhanced by the views and illustrations with which it is embellished. These have been executed with artistical skill and the strictest fidelity, from my sketches, by Mr. Bernatz, the well known author of the beautiful " Scenes in Æthiopia."

I will only add a few words relative to the spelling of native names, — rather a difficult subject in a conflux of languages of very different organization and unsettled orthography. I have constantly endeavoured to express the sounds as correctly as possible, but in the simplest way, assigning to the vowels always the same intonation which they have in Italian, and keeping as closely as possible to the principles adopted by the Asiatic Society. The greatest difficulty related to the "g" sound, which is written in various ways by the Africans, and puzzled even the Arabic writers of the middle ages. While the "k" in North Africa approaches the g in "give," it takes the sound of it entirely in the Central African languages. On this ground, although I preferred writing " Azkár," while the name might have been almost as well written " Azgár;" yet further into the interior the application of the g, as in " A'gades," " Góber," and so on, was more correct. The ع of the Arabs has been expressed, in conformity with the various sounds which it adopts, by á, ó and ú; the غ by gh, although it sounds in many words like an r; ج by j; the چ, which is frequent in the African languages, by ch.

The alphabet, therefore, which I have made use of is the following : —

Vowels.

a as in cat.
á   „   father.
ȧ (not English) not unlike a in dart.
e as in pen.
é like the first a in fatal
i as in it.
í   „   ravine.
o   „   lot.
ó   „   home.
ȯ (not English) not unlike o in noble.
u as in put.
ú   „   adjure, true.
u̇ not unlike oo in doom.
y, at the end of words, instead of i.

Diphthongs.

ai as i in tide (ay at the end of words).
oi (oy), as in noise.
au (aw), as ow in now.

Consonants.

b as in beat.
d   „   door.
f*   „   fan.

Consonants (continued).

g as in got.
j†   „   join.
k   „   keep.
l   „   leave.
m   „   man.
n   „   not.
ñ   „   the Spanish " campaña," like ni in companion, onion.
p*   „   pain.
r   „   rain.
s   „   son.
t   „   tame.
v   „   vain.
w   „   win.
y   „   yet.
z   „   zeal.

Double Consonants.

gh as in ghost, and the g in grumble.
ks as x in tax, excise.
kh as ch in the Scotch word loch.
th as in tooth.
ts as in Betsy.
ng as in wrong.

---

* p, ph, f, in many African languages, are constantly interchanged, the same as r and dh, r and l.

† No distinction has been made between the different sounds of j.

A few slight discrepancies in the spelling of names will, I trust, be excused, the printing having already commenced before I had entirely settled the orthography I would adopt.

St. John's Wood, London, HENRY BARTH, Ph. D.
May 1. 1857.

CONTENTS

OF

THE FIRST VOLUME.

CHAPTER I.

CHAP. II.

CHAP. III.

CHAP. IV.

CHAP. V.

CHAP. VI.

CHAP. VII.

CHAP. VIII.

---

* "The people of A'gades at that time (the last quarter of the last century) —though A'gades then belonged to the Cashna empire—were annually permitted to load their immense caravans with the salt of Bornou, from the salt lakes of Demboo" (the Tebu country ?), "the merchants of A'gades giving in return for the article a trifling price in brass and copper."—*Lucas, Proceedings of the African Association,* vol. i. p. 159.

III.

IV.

V.

VI.

VII.

LIST OF ILLUSTRATIONS

IN

THE FIRST VOLUME.

MAPS.

PLATES.

WOODCUTS.

TRAVELS AND DISCOVERIES

IN

AFRICA.

CHAPTER I.

FROM TUNIS TO TRIPOLI.

MR. RICHARDSON was waiting in Paris for despatches, when Mr. Overweg and I reached Tunis, by way of Philippeville and Bona, on the 15th of December, 1849; and having, through the kind interference of Mr. Ferrier the British vice-consul, been allowed to enter the town after six days' quarantine, we began immediately to provide ourselves with articles of dress, while in the meantime we took most interesting daily rides to the site of ancient Carthage.

Having procured many useful articles for our journey, and having found a servant, the son of a freed slave from Gober, we left Tunis on the 30th of December*, and passed the first night in Hammám el

---

* I cannot leave Tunis without mentioning the great interest taken in our undertaking, and the kindness shown to us, by M. le Baron Théis, the French consul.

Enf. Early next morning we followed the charming route by Krumbália, which presents a no less vivid specimen of the beauty and natural fertility of the Tunisian country than of the desolate state to which it is at present reduced. We then passed the fine gardens of Turki, a narrow spot of cultivation in a wide desolate plain of the finest soil; and leaving el Khwín to our right, we reached el Arbáin.

Both these places enjoy a peculiar celebrity with the natives. El Khwín is said to have been once a populous place; but nearly all its inhabitants were destroyed by a spring of bituminous water, which, according to tradition, afterwards disappeared. El Arbáin, the locality of the "forty" martyrs, is a holy place; and 'Ali, our muleteer, in his pious zeal, took up a handful of the sacred earth and sprinkled it over us. It is a most picturesque spot. Keeping then along the wild plain covered with a thick under-wood of myrtle, we beheld in the distance the highly picturesque and beautiful Mount Zaghwán, the Holy Mountain of the ancient inhabitants, which rose in a majestic form; and we at length reached Bir el buwíta, "the well of the little closet," at one o'clock in the afternoon. The "little closet," however, had given place to a most decent-looking whitewashed khán, where we took up our quarters in a clean room. But our buoyant spirits did not allow us long repose; and a quarter before eleven at night we were again on our mules.

I shall never forget this, the last night of the year

1849, which opened to us a new era with many
ordeals, and by our endurance of which we were to
render ourselves worthy of success.   There were,
besides ourselves, our servants, and our two muleteers,
four horsemen of the Bey, and three natives from
Jirbi.   When midnight came my fellow traveller
and I saluted the new year with enthusiasm, and with
a cordial shake of the hand wished each other joy.
Our Mohammedan companions were greatly pleased
when they were informed of the reason of our con-
gratulating each other, and wished us all possible
success for the new year.   We had also reason to be
pleased with them ; for by their not inharmonious
songs they relieved the fatigue of a long, sleepless,
and excessively cold night.

Having made a short halt under the olive-trees at
the side of the dilapidated town of Herkla, and taken
a morsel of bread, we moved on with our poor
animals without interruption till half an hour after
noon, when we reached the funduk (or caravanserai)
Sídi Bú Jàfer, near Súsa, where we took up our
quarters, in order to be able to start again at night,
the gates of the town being kept shut till morning.*

Starting before three o'clock in the morning, we
were exactly twelve hours in reaching El Jem, with .
the famous Castle of the Prophetess, still one of the

---

* The town presented quite the same desolate character which
I have described in my former journey, with the single exception
that a new gate had since been built. Several statues had been
brought from Medinet Ziyán.

most splendid monuments of Roman greatness overhanging the most shabby hovels of Mohammedan
indifference.   On the way we had a fine view, towards the west, of the picturesque Jebel Trutsa, along
the foot of which I had passed on my former wanderings, and of the wide, out-stretching Jebel Uselelt.

Another ride of twelve hours brought us, on the
3rd of January, 1850, to Sfákes, where we were obliged
to take up our quarters in the town, as our land-
journey was here at an end, and we were to procure a
vessel to carry us either direct to Tripoli, or to some
other point on the opposite side of the Lesser Syrtis.
The journey by land is not only expensive, particularly for people who are encumbered with a good
deal of luggage, as we then were, and very long and
tedious, but is also very unsafe, as I found from
experience on my former journey.   The island of
Jirbi, which forms the natural station of the maritime
intercourse between the regency of Tunis and that
of Tripoli, had been put under the strictest rules of
quarantine, rather from political considerations than
from those of health, all intercourse with the main-
land having been cut off.   It was therefore with great
difficulty that we succeeded in hiring a " gáreb " to
carry us to Zowára, in which we embarked in the
forenoon of Saturday the 5th of January.

During our two days' stay in Sfákes we made the
acquaintance of a Jew calling himself Baránes, but
who is in truth the Jew servant named Jacob who
accompanied Denham and Clapperton, and is several

times mentioned in the narrative of those enterprising
travellers as self-conceited and stubborn; yet he
seems to be rather a clever fellow, and in some way
or other contrives to be on the best terms with the
governor. He communicated to us many anecdotes
of the former expedition, and, among other things, a
very mysterious history of a Danish traveller in dis-
guise whom they met in Bórnú coming all the way
from Dar-Fúr through Wádáy. There is not the least .
mention of such a meeting in the journal of the expedition, nor has such an achievement of a European
traveller ever been heard of; and I can scarcely
believe the truth of this story, though the Jew was
quite positive about it.

The vessel in which we embarked was as miserable
as it could be, there being only a small low cabin
as high as a dog-kennel, and measuring, in its
greatest width, from six to seven feet, where I
and my companion were to pass the night. We
thought that a run of forty-eight hours, at the utmost,
would carry us across the gulf; but the winds in the
Lesser Syrtis are extremely uncertain, and sometimes
so violent that a little vessel is obliged to run along
the coast.

At first we went on tolerably well; but the wind
soon became unfavourable, and in the evening we
were obliged to cast anchor opposite Nekta, and, to
our despair, were kept there till the afternoon of
Tuesday, when at length we were enabled to go
forward in our frail little shell, and reached Méheres

— not Sídi Méheres, as it is generally called in the maps — in the darkness of night. Having made up our minds rather to risk anything than to be longer immured in such a desperate dungeon as our gáreb, we went on shore early on Wednesday morning with all our things, but were not able to conclude a bargain with some Bedowín of the tribe of the Léffet, who were watering their camels at the well.

· The majestic ruins of a large castle, fortified at each corner with a round tower, give the place a picturesque appearance from the seaside. This castle is well known to be a structure of the time of Ibrahím the Aghlabite. In the midst of the ruins is a small mosque. But notwithstanding the ruinous state of the place, and the desolate condition of its plantations, there is still a little industry going on, consoling to the beholder in the midst of the devastation to which the fine province of Byzacium, once the garden of Carthage, is at present reduced. Several people were busily employed in the little market-place making mats; and in the houses looms, weaving baracans, were seen in activity. But all around, the country presented a frightful scene of desolation, there being no object to divert the eye but the two apparently separate cones of Mount Wuedrán, far in the distance to the west, said to be very rich in sheep. The officer who is stationed here, and who showed us much kindness, furnishing us with some excellent red radishes of extraordinary size, the only luxury which the village affords, told us that not less than five hundred soldiers are quartered upon this part of the coast. On my former journey I had ample opportunity to observe how the Tunisian soldiery eat up the little which has been left to the peaceable inhabitants of this most beautiful, but most unfortunate country.

Having spent two days and two nights in this miserable place without being able to obtain camels, we resolved to try the sea once more, in the morning of the 11th, when the wind became northerly; but before the low-water allowed us to go on board, the wind again changed, so that, when we at length got under weigh in the afternoon, we could only move on with short tacks. But our captain, protected as he was by the Promontory of Méheres, dared to enter the open gulf. Quantities of large fish in a dying state, as is often the case in this shallow water when the wind has been high, were drifting round our boat.

The sun was setting when we at length doubled the promontory of Kasr Unga, which we had already clearly distinguished on the 8th. However, we had now overcome the worst; and when on the following morning I emerged from our suffocating berth, I saw, to my great delight, that we were in the midst of the gulf, having left the coast far behind us. I now heard from our raïs that, instead of coasting as far as Tarf el má (" the border of the water "), a famous locality in the innermost corner of the Lesser Syrtis, which seems to preserve the memory of the former connection between the gulf and the great Sebkha or Shot el Kebír (the "palus Tritonis "), he had been so bold as to keep his little bark straight upon the channel of Jirbi.

Our voyage now became interesting; for while we were advancing at a fair rate, we had a charming view of the mountain-range, which in clear contours extended along in the distance behind the date-groves on the coast, seen only in faint outlines. The western part of the chain is very low, and forms almost a group apart, but after having been intersected by a gap or " gate," the chain rises to greater elevation, being divided, as it would seem from hence, into three separate ranges enclosing fine valleys.

We had hoped to cross the difficult channel to-day; but the wind failing, we were obliged to anchor and await the daylight, for it is not possible to traverse the straits in the night, on account of their extreme shallowness. Even in the light of the following day, when we at length succeeded, our little bark, which drew only two or three feet, struck twice, and we had some trouble to get afloat again. On the conspicuous and elevated promontory the " Jurf," or " Tarf el jurf," stood in ancient times a temple of Venus, the hospitable goddess of the navigator. Here on my former journey I crossed with my horses over from the main to the island of Jirbi, while from the water I had now a better opportunity of observing the picturesque character of the rugged promontory. After traversing the shallow basin or widening, we crossed the second narrowing, where the castles which defended the bridge or " kantara," the " pons Zitha " of the Romans, now lie in ruins on the main as well as on the island, and greatly obstruct the passage, the difficulty of which has obtained celebrity from contests between Islam and Christianity in comparatively modern times.

Having passed safely through this difficult channel, we kept steadily on through the open sea ; and doubling Rás Mámúra, near to which our captain had a little date-grove and was cheerfully saluted by his family and friends, we at length entered the harbour of Zarzís, late in the afternoon of Sunday, and with some trouble got all our luggage carried into the village, which is situated at some distance.   For although we had the worst part of the land journey now before us, the border-district of the two regencies, with the unsafe state of which I was well acquainted from my former journey, and although we were insufficiently armed, we were disposed to endure anything rather than the imprisonment to which we were doomed in such a vessel as our Mohammed's gáreb.   I think, however, that this nine days' sail between Sfákes and Zarzís, a distance of less than a hundred and twenty miles, was on the whole a very fair trial in the beginning of an undertaking the success of which was mainly dependent upon patience and resolute endurance.   We were rather fortunate in not only soon obtaining tolerable quarters, but also in arranging without delay our departure for the following day, by hiring two horses and three camels.

Zarzís consists of five separate villages — Kasr Bú 'Alí, Kasr Mwanza, Kasr Welád Mohammed, Kasr Welád Saíd, and Kasr Zawíya: the Bedowín in the neighbourhood belong to the tribe of the Akára. The plantation also is formed into separate date-groves. The houses are in tolerable repair and neatly whitewashed; but the character of order and well-being is neutralised by a good many houses in decay. Near the place there are also some Roman ruins, especially a cistern of very great length; and at some distance is the site of Medinet Ziyán, of which I have given a description in the narrative of my former journey.

Besides the eight men attached to our five animals, we were joined here by four pilgrims and three Tripolitan traders; we thus made up a numerous body, armed with eight muskets, three blunderbusses, and fourteen pistols, besides several straight swords, and could venture upon the rather unsafe road to the south of the Lake of Bibán, though it would have been far more agreeable to have a few trustworthy people to rely on instead of these turbulent companions.

Entering soon, behind the plantation of Zarzís, a long narrow sebkha, we were struck by the sterile and desolate character of the country, which was only interrupted by a few small depressed localities, where a little corn was cultivated. Keeping along this tract of country, we reached the north-western corner of the Lake of Bibán, or Bahéret el Bibán, after a little more than eight miles. This corner has even at

the present day the common name of Khashm el kelb
(the Dog's Nose), while the former classical name of
the whole lake, Sebákh el keláb, was only known to
Tayyef, the more learned of my guides, who, without
being questioned by me, observed that in former times
towns and rich corn-fields had been where the lake
now is, but had been swallowed up by a sinking of
the ground.

The real basin has certainly nothing in common
with a sebkha, which means a shallow hollow, incrusted with salt, which at times is dry and at others
forms a pool; for it is a deep gulf or fiord of the sea,
with which it is connected only by a narrow channel
called Wád mtà el Bibán. The nature of a sebkha
belongs at present only to its shores, chiefly to the
locality called Makháda, which, indenting the country
to a great distance, is sometimes very difficult to
pass, and must be turned by a wide circuitous path,
which is greatly feared on account of the neighbourhood of the Udérna, a tribe famous for its highway
robberies. Having traversed the Makháda (which at
present was dry) without any difficulty, we entered
upon good arable soil, and encamped, after sunset,
at about half a mile distance from a Bedowín encampment.

Starting from here the following day, January 15th.
we soon became aware that the country
was not so thinly inhabited as we had thought; for numerous herds covered the rich pasture-grounds, while
droves of gazelles, now and then, attested that the in-

dustry of man did not encroach here upon the freedom
of the various orders of creation.   Leaving the path
near the ruins of a small building situated upon a
hill, I went with Tayyef and the Khalífa to visit the
ruins of a Roman station on the border of the Bahéra,
which, under the name of el Medaina, has a great
fame amongst the neighbouring tribes, but which,
with a single exception, are of small extent and bad
workmanship.   This exception is the quay, which is
not only of interest in itself, formed as it is of regularly-hewn stones, in good repair, but of importance
as an evident proof that the lake was much deeper in
ancient times than it is now.

Traversing from this spot the sebkha, which our
companions had gone round, we soon overtook them,
and kept over fine pasture-grounds called el Fehén,
and further on, Súllub, passing, a little after noon, a
group of ruins near the shore, called Kitfi el hamár.
At two o'clock in the afternoon, we had directly
on our right a slight slope which, according to the
unanimous statement of our guides and companions,
forms the mágttá, مقطّة, or frontier between the two
regencies*; and keeping along it we encamped an
hour afterwards between the slope and the shore,
which a little further on forms the deep gulf called
Mirsá Buréka.

* This point is not without importance, as a great deal of dispute has taken place about the frontier. Having on my former
journey kept close along the seashore, I have laid it down erroneously in the map accompanying the narrative of that journey.

Starting at an early hour, we reached, after a march of ten miles, the ruins of a castle on the sea-shore, called Búrj el Melha, to which those of a small village, likewise built of hewn stone, are joined, while a long and imposing mole called el Míná juts out into the gulf. Four and a half miles further on we reached the conspicuous hill on the top of which is the chapel of the saint Sídi Saíd ben Sálah, sometimes called Sídi Gházi, and venerated by such of the natives as are not attached to the Puritan sect of El Mádani, of which I shall speak hereafter. All our companions went there to say a short prayer.

Here we left the shore, and, having watered our animals near a well and passed the chapel of Sídi Saíd, close to which there are some ruins, we passed with expedition over fine meadows till we approached the plantation of Zowára, when, leaving Mr. Overweg and my people behind, I rode on with the Khalífa, in order to procure quarters from my former friend Saíd bú Semmín, who, as I had heard to my great satisfaction, had been restored to the government of that place. He had just on that very day returned from a visit of some length in the capital, and was delighted to see me again; but he was rather astonished when he heard that I was about to undertake a far more difficult and dangerous journey than my former one along the coast, in which he well knew that I had had a very narrow escape. However, he confided in my enterprising spirit and in the mercy of the Almighty, and thought if anybody was likely to do it, I was the man.*

January 17th.   We had now behind us the most dreary part of our route, having entered a district which in ancient times numbered large and wealthy cities, among which Sabratha stands foremost, and which even in the present miserable state of the country is dotted with pleasant little date-groves, interrupted by fine pasture-grounds. In the westernmost part of this tract, however, with the exception of the plantation of Zowára, all the date-groves, as those of Rikdalíye, Jemíl, el Meshíah, and Jenán ben Síl, lie at a considerable distance from the coast, while the country near the sea is full of seb-khas, and very monotonous, till the traveller reaches a slight ridge of sand-hills about sixteen miles east from Zowára, which is the border between the dreary province of that government and a more favoured tract belonging to the government of Bú-'Ajíla, and which lies a little distance inland. Most charming was the little plantation of Kasr 'Alaiga, which exhibited traces of industry and improvement. Unfortunately our horses were too weak and too much fatigued to allow us to visit the sites either of Sabratha or Pontes. The ruins of Sabratha are properly

---

* I will here correct the mistake which I made in my former narrative, when I said that Zowára is not mentioned by Arabic authors. It is certainly not adverted to by the more celebrated and older writers; but it is mentioned by travellers of the 14th century, especially by the Sheikh e' Tijáni.

called Kasr 'Alaiga, but the name has been applied to the whole neighbourhood; to the ancient Pontes seem to belong the ruins of Zowára e' sherkíyeh, which are considerable. Between them lies the pretty grove of Om el hallúf.

About four o'clock in the afternoon we traversed the charming little valley called Wadi bú-harída, where we watered our horses; and then following the camels, and passing Asermán with its little plantation, which is bordered by a long and deep sebkha, we took up our quarters for the night in an Arab encampment, which was situated in the midst of the date-grove of 'Ukbah, and presented a most picturesque appearance, the large fires throwing a magic light upon the date-trees. But there are no roses without thorns: we were unfortunately persuaded to make ourselves comfortable in an Arab tent, as we had no tent of our own; and the enormous swarms of fleas not only disturbed our night's rest, but followed us to Tripoli.

We had a long stretch the following day to reach the capital, which we were most anxious to accomplish, as we expected Mr. Richardson would have arrived before us in consequence of our own tedious journey; and having sent the Khalífa in advance to keep the gate open for us, we succeeded in reaching the town after an uninterrupted march of thirteen hours and a half, and were most kindly received by Mr. Crowe, Her Majesty's consul-general, and the vice-consul Mr. Reade, with whom I was already

acquainted. We were surprised to find that Mr.
Richardson had not even yet been heard of, as we
expected he would come direct by way of Malta.
But he did not arrive till twelve days after. With
the assistance of Mr. Reade, we had already finished
a great deal of our preparations, and would have
gladly gone on at once; but neither the boat, nor
the instruments, nor the arms or tents had as yet
arrived, and a great deal of patience was required.
However, being lodged in the neat house of the
former Austrian consul, close to the harbour, and
which commands a charming prospect, our time
passed rapidly by.

On the 25th of January Mr. Reade presented Mr.
Overweg and me to Yezíd Bashá, the present governor, who received us with great kindness and good
feeling. On the 29th we had a pleasant meeting
with Mr. Frederic Warrington on his return from
Ghadámes, whither he had accompanied Mr. Charles
Dickson, who on the 1st of January had made his
entry into that place as the first European agent
and resident. Mr. F. Warrington is perhaps the
most amiable possible specimen of an Arabianized
European. To this gentleman, whose zeal in the
objects of the expedition was beyond all praise, I
must be allowed to pay my tribute as a friend. On
setting out in 1850, he accompanied me as far as the
Ghurián; and on my joyful return in 1855 he received me in Murzuk. By the charm of friendship
he certainly contributed his share to my success.

CHAP. II.

In the Introduction I have given a rapid sketch of
our journey from Tunis, and pointed out the causes
of our delay in Tripoli.   As soon as it became apparent that the preparations for our final departure for
the interior would require at least a month, Mr. Overweg and I resolved to employ the interval in making
a preliminary excursion through the mountainous
region that encompasses Tripoli in a radius of from
sixty to eighty miles.

With this view, we hired two camels, with a
driver each, and four donkeys, with a couple of men,
for ourselves and our two servants, Mohammed Belál,
the son of a liberated Háusa slave, and Ibrahím,
a liberated Bagirmi slave, whom we had been fortunate enough to engage here; and through the Consul's influence we procured a shoush, or officer, to
accompany us the whole way.

Neither the instruments provided by Her Majesty's
Government, nor the tents and arms, had as yet
arrived.   But Mr. Overweg had a good sextant, and

VOL. I.   C

I a good chronometer, and we were both of us provided with tolerably good compasses, thermometers,
and an aneroid barometer.   Mr. Frederic Warrington,
too, was good enough to lend us a tent.

We had determined to start in the afternoon of
the 4th of February, 1850, so as to pass the first
night in Gargash; but meeting with delays, we did
not leave the town till after sunset.   We preferred
encamping, therefore, in the Meshíah, a little beyond
the mosque, under the palm-trees, little knowing at
the time what an opportunity we had lost of spending a very cheerful evening.

February 5th.   Soon after starting, we emerged from the
palm-groves which constitute the charm
of Tripoli, and continued our march over the rocky
ground.   Being a little in advance with the shoush,
I halted to wait for the rest, when a very peculiar
cry, that issued from the old Roman building on the
road-side, called "Kasr el Jahalíyeh," perplexed us
for a moment.   But we soon learnt, to our great surprise, not unmixed with regret, that it was our kind
friend Frederic Warrington, who had been waiting for
us here the whole night.   From the top of the ruin,
which stands on an isolated rock left purposely in
the midst of a quarry, there is a widely extensive
view.   It appears that, before the Arabs built the
castle, this site was occupied by Roman sepulchres.
A little further on we passed the stone of Sídi 'Arífa.
This stone had fallen upon the head of a workman
who was digging a well.   The workman, so runs the

legend, escaped unhurt; and at Sídi 'Arífa's word
the stone once more sprung to the surface.   Further
on, near the sea-shore, we passed the chapel of Sídi
Sálah, who is said to have drawn by magic to his
feet, from the bottom of the sea, a quantity of fish
ready dressed.

From this point our kind friend Mr. Frederic Warrington returned with his followers to the town, and
we were left to ourselves.   We then turned off from
the road, and entered the fine date-plantation of
Zenzúr, celebrated in the fourteenth century, as one of
the finest districts of Barbary, by the Sheikh e' Tijáni,
passing by a great magazine of corn, and a moulder-
ing clay-built castle, in which were quartered a body
of horsemen of the Urshefána.   Fine olive-trees pleas-
ingly alternated with the palm-grove, while the
borders of the broad sandy paths were neatly fenced
with the *Cactus opuntia.*   Having passed our former
place of encampment in Sayáda, we were agreeably
surprised to see at the western end of the plantation
a few new gardens in course of formation; for there
is a tax, levied not on the produce of the tree, but
on the tree itself, which naturally stands in the way
of new plantations.

Having halted for a short time at noon near the
little oasis of Sídi Ghár, where the ground was beautifully adorned with a profusion of lilies; and having
passed Jedaim, we encamped towards evening in the
wide courtyard of the Kasr Gamúda, where we were.

kindly received by the Kaimakám Mustapha Bey,
whom I was providentially destined to meet twice
again, viz. on my outset from, and on my final return
to, Fezzán. The whole plantation of Zawíya, of which
Gamúda forms a part, is said to contain a hundred
and thirty thousand palm-trees.

Ibrahim gave me an interesting account to-day of
Negroland. Though a native of Bagírmi, he had
rambled much about Mándará, and spoke enthusiastically of the large and strong mountain-town Karáwa,
his report of which I afterwards found quite true;
of the town of Míndif, situated at the foot of the
great mountain of the same name; and of Morá,
which he represented as very unsafe on account of
bands of robbers, — a report which has been entirely
confirmed by Mr. Vogel. Our chief interest at that
time was concentrated upon Mándará, which was
then supposed to be the beginning of the mountainous
zone of Central Africa.

Wednesday, While the camels were pursuing the
February 6th. direct tract, we ourselves, leaving our
former road, which was parallel to the sea-coast, and
turning gradually towards the south, made a circuit
through the plantation, in order to procure a supply
of dates and corn, as we were about to enter on
the zone of nomadic existence. The morning was
very fine, and the ride pleasant. But we had hardly
left the plantation, when we exchanged the firm turf
for deep sand-hills which were broken further on by
a more favoured soil, where melons were cultivated in

great plenty; and again, about four miles beyond the plantation, the country once more assumed a genial aspect. I heard that many of the inhabitants of Zawíya habitually exchange every summer their more solid town residences for lighter dwellings here in the open air. A little before noon we obtained a fine view over the diversified outlines of the mountains before us.

In the plain there are many favoured spots bearing corn, particularly the country at the foot of Mount Mámúra, which forms a very conspicuous object from every side. As we advanced further, the country became well inhabited, and everywhere, at some distance from the path, were seen encampments of the tribe of the Belása, who occupy all the grounds between the Urshefána and the Bú-'Ajíla, while the Urjímma, a tribe quite distinct from the Urghámma, have their settlements S.W., between the Nuwayíl and the Bú-'Ajíla. All these Arabs hereabouts provide themselves with water from the well Núr e' dín, which we left at some distance on our left.

The encampment near which we pitched our tent in the evening belonged to the chief of the Belása, and consisted of seven tents, close to the slope of a small hilly chain. We had scarcely pitched our tent when rain set in, accompanied by a chilly current of air, which made the encampment rather uncomfortable. The chief, Mohammed Chélebi, brought us, in the evening, some bazín; the common dish of the

Arab of Tripoli. We wanted to regale him with coffee, but, being afraid of touching the hot drink, and perhaps suspicious of poison, he ran away.

Thursday, February 7th. Continuing our march southward through the fine and slightly undulating district of el Habl, where water is found in several wells, at the depth of from fifteen to sixteen fathoms, we gradually approached the mountain-chain. The strong wind, which filled the whole air with sand, prevented us from obtaining a very interesting view from a considerable eminence called el Ghunna, the terminating and culminating point of a small chain of hills, which we ascended. For the same reason, when I and Ibrahim, after lingering some time on this interesting spot, started after our camels, we lost our way entirely, the tracks of our little caravan being totally effaced, and no path traceable over the undulating sandy ground. At length we reached firmer grassy soil, and, falling in with the path, overtook our people at the " Bír el Ghánem."

Hence we went straight towards the slope of the mountains, and after little more than an hour's march reached the first advanced hill of the chain, and began to enter on it by going up one of the wadis which open from its flanks. It takes its name from the ethel (*Tamarix orientalis*), which here and there breaks the monotony of the scene, and gradually widens to a considerable plain bounded by majestic ridges. From this plain we descended into the deep and rugged ravine of the large Wadi

Sheikh, the abrupt cliffs of which presented to view beautiful layers of red and white sandstone, with a lower horizontal layer of limestone, and we looked out for a well-sheltered place, as the cold wind was very disagreeable. The wadi has its name from its vicinity to the chapel, or zawíya, of the Merábet Bú-Máti, to which is attached a large school.

On setting out from this hollow we ascended the other side, and soon ob- _{Friday, February 8th.} tained an interesting view of the varied outlines of the mountains before us, with several half-deserted castles of the Arab middle ages on the summits of the hills. The castle of the Welád Merabetín, used by the neighbouring tribes chiefly as a granary, has been twice destroyed by the Turks; but on the occasion of nuptial festivities, the Arabs, in conformity with ancient usage, still fire their muskets from above the castle. The inhabitants of these mountains, who have a strong feeling of liberty, cling to their ancient customs with great fondness.

We descended again into Wadi Sheikh, which, winding round, crossed our path once more. The regular layers of limestone, which present a good many fossils, with here and there a layer of marl, form here, during heavy rains, a pretty little cascade at the foot of the cliffs. We lost much time by getting entangled in a branch of the wadi, which had no outlet, but exhibited the wild scenery of a glen, worn by the torrents which occasionally rush down the abrupt rocky cliffs. Having regained the direct road, we had to cross a third time the Wadi Sheikh at the point where it is joined by Wadi Ginna, or Gilla, which also we crossed a little further on. In the Jefára, or fertile zone along the coast, the monotony of the palm-groves becomes almost fatiguing; but here we were much gratified at the sight of the first group of date-trees, which was succeeded by others, and even by a small orchard of fig-trees. Here, as we began to ascend the elevated and abrupt eastern cliffs of the valley, which at first offer only a few patches of cultivated plateau, succeeded further on by olive-trees, a fine view opened before us, extending to the S.E. as far as the famous Roman monument called Enshéd e' Sufét, which is very conspicuous. Having waited here for our camels, we reached the first village, whose name, " Ta-smeraye," bears, like that of many others, indubitable proof that the inhabitants of these mountainous districts belong originally to the Berber race, though at present only a few of them speak their native tongue. These people had formerly a pleasant and comfortable abode in this quarter, but having frequently revolted against the Turks, they have been greatly reduced, and their villages at present look like so many heaps of ruins.

Having passed some other hamlets in a similar state of decay, and still going through a pleasant but rather arid country, we reached the oppressor's stronghold, the " Kasr el Jebel," as it is generally called, although this part of the mountains bears the special name of Yefren. It lies on the very edge of the steep rocky cliffs, and affords an extensive view over the plain. But though standing in a commanding position, it is itself commanded by a small eminence a few hundred yards eastward, where there was once a large quadrangular structure, now in ruins.

The castle, which at the time of our visit was the chief instrument in the hands of the Turks for overawing the mountaineers, contained a garrison of four hundred soldiers. It has only one bastion with three guns, at the southern corner, and was found by Mr. Overweg to be 2150 feet above the level of the sea. The high cliffs inclosing the valley are most beautifully and regularly stratified in layers of gypsum and limestone; and a man may walk almost round the whole circumference of the ravine on the same layer of the latter stone, which has been left bare, — the gypsum, of frailer texture, having been carried away by the torrents of rain which rush violently down the steep descent. From the little eminence above mentioned, there is a commanding view over the valleys and the high plain towards the south.

After our tent had been pitched, we received a visit from Háj Rashíd, the Kaimakám or governor, who is reckoned the second person in the Bashalík, and has the whole district from Zowára as far as Ghadámes towards the S.W., and the Tarhóna towards the S.E., under his military command. His salary is 4600 mahhbúbs annually, or about 720*l.* He had previously been Basha of Adana, in Cilicia; and we indulged, to our mutual gratification, in 'reminiscences of Asia Minor.

Saturday, February 9th. Early in the morning I walked to a higher eminence at some distance eastward from the castle, which had attracted my attention the day before. This conspicuous hill also was formerly crowned with a tower or small castle; but nothing but a solitary rustic dwelling now enlivens the solitude. The view was very extensive, but the strong wind did not allow of exact compass observations. While my companion remained near the castle, engaged in his geological researches, I agreed with our shoush and a Zintáni lad whom I accidentally met here, and who on our journey to Fezzán proved very useful, to undertake a longer excursion towards the west, in order to see something more of this interesting and diversified slope of the plateau.

I was anxious to visit a place called Ta-gherbúst, situated on the north side of the castle, along the slope of a ravine which runs westward into the valley; accordingly, on leaving the site of our encampment, we deviated at first a little northwards. Ta-gherbúst is said to have been a rich and important place in former times. Some of its inhabitants possessed as many as ten slaves; but at present it is a heap of ruins, with scarcely twenty-five inhabited houses. From hence, turning southward, we descended gradually along the steep slope, while above our heads the cliffs rose in picturesque majesty, beautifully adorned by scattered date-trees, which, at every level spot, sprung forth from the rocky ground, and gave to the whole scene a very charming character.   A fountain which gushed out from a cavern on a little terrace at the foot of the precipice, and fed a handsome group of date-trees, was one of the most beautiful objects that can be imagined.

The Turks, two years ago, made a small path leading directly down from the castle to this fountain, which supplies them with water.   After sketching this beautiful spot while the animals were watering, we followed a more gradual descent into the valley of el Ghasás, which here with a rough level widens to a plain, while its upper or southern part, called Wadi Rumíye, forms a very narrow and picturesque ravine. We then continued our march in a westerly direction, having on our right the plain extending, with slight undulations, towards the sea, and on our left the majestic offshoots of the plateau jutting into the plain like vast promontories, with a general elevation of two thousand feet. This grand feature is evidently due to the waters which, in ancient times, must have rushed down the slope of the plateau in mighty streams. At present, the chief character of the country is aridity. On asking my guide whether great torrents are not still occasionally formed along those ravines strong enough to reach the sea, he replied, that once only — forty-four years ago — such a torrent was formed, which, passing by Zenzúr, gave a red colour to the sea as far as the Island of Jirbi. He also informed me that, in general, all the waters from the ridge joined the Wadi Haera.*

On our left, in the valley Khalaifa, a group of date-trees, fed by an abundant spring called ʿAín el Wua-níye, forms a conspicuous and interesting object; while, in general, these valleys or ravines exhibit, besides small brushwood, only trees of the siddre, (*Rhamnus nabeca*), jári, and batúm tribe. The batúm-tree (*Pistacia Atlantica*) produces the fruit called

---

* I can scarcely believe this to be correct; for all the water descending from the Jebel Yefren evidently joins the little wadi which runs on the east side of Zowára (Zowára el Gharbíye). I am sure that he spoke of the torrents descending from the Ghurián, which, without doubt, join the Wadi Haera, and, if very exuberant, will reach the sea at Zenzúr.

Drawn by M. Rippon delt.t from Nature

MALI MOUNTAINS.

On stone by M. Picken & Co. Lith. Printers to the Queen.

gatúf, which is used by the Arabs for a great variety
of purposes.   Small brushwood or gandul, also, and
various sort of herbage, such as sebót, shedíde, and
sháde, enliven the ground.

As we advanced, we changed our direction gradually to the south-west, and entered the mountainous
region.   On our right there extended far into the
plain a steep narrow promontory, which had served
as a natural fortress to the mountaineers in the last
war with the Turks; but no water being found near
it, its occupants were soon reduced to extremities.
Having gone round the last promontory on our left,
we entered the picturesque valley " Welád 'Alí," once
adorned with orchards and groves of date-trees, but
at present reduced to a desolate wilderness, only a
few neglected fig-trees and scattered palms still remaining to prove how different the condition of this
spot might be.   After we had commenced our ascent
along the side of the ravine, in order to return upon
the level of the plateau, we made a short halt near a
cluster of about eighty date-trees, where I made the
sketch of the accompanying view.   But the ascent
became extremely steep, especially near the middle of
the slope, where the water, rushing down in cascades,
has laid bare the limestone rock, and formed a sort of
terrace.   Here, on the east side of the cascade, is a
spring in a well, called 'Aín el Gatár mtá Welád 'Alí.
On both of the summits overlooking the slope are two
villages of the Riaina, the eastern one a little larger
than the other, but at present not containing more

than about thirty stone-built cottages. In both we tried in vain to buy a little barley for our cattle, as we knew not whether, at our halting-place for the night, we might be able to obtain any; but we: got plenty of dried figs for ourselves. This slope, with its ravines and valleys, might certainly pro-, duce a very considerable quantity of fruit; and in this respect it resembles in character that of the so-called Kabylia in Algiers. The rearing of fruit-trees seems to be a favourite occupation of the Berber race, even in the more favoured spots of the Great Desert.

Continuing our march on the summit of the plateau, we reached the village Kasr Shellúf, which exhibited far greater opulence, as it had escaped being ran-. sacked by the Turks in the last war. Most probably in consequence of this circumstance, its inhabitants are more hospitably disposed than those of Riaina: but the cave or cellar in which they wanted to lodge me, had nothing very attractive for a night's quarters, so that I urged my two companions onward. Having continued our south-westerly direction for awhile, and passed another village, we thought it safer to turn our steps eastwards, and took the direction of the zawíya or convent situated on the summit of the promontory; but when we reached it, just after dusk, the masters or teachers of the young men, who are sent to this holy place for education, refused to admit us for the night, so that we were obliged to go on and try to reach one of the five villages of Khalaifa. At length, after a very difficult descent down the steep rocky slope in the dark, we succeeded in reaching the principal village, and, after some negotiation, occasioned by the absence of the Kaid Bel Kásem, who is chief of the Khalaifa as well as of the Wuërje, we at length obtained admission, and even something to eat, my companions (rather against my will) representing me as a Turk.

Our route on leaving the village was very pleasant, winding round the sloping Sunday, February 10th. sides of several ravines, among which that formed by the rivulet Wuaníye, and adorned with date-trees, was the most beautiful.   Ascending gradually, we reached again the level of the plateau, and obtained an extensive prospect, with the remarkable monu- ment Enshéd e' Sufét as a conspicuous and attrac- tive landmark in the distance. The elevated level had a slight undulation, and was clothed with halfa (*Cynosurus durus*) and gedím. However, we did not long continue on it, but descended into the well-irri- gated valley Rumíye, which is extremely fertile, but also extremely unhealthy, and notorious for its fevers. The beauty of the scenery, enlivened as it is by a considerable torrent foaming along the ravine, and feeding luxuriant clusters of palm, pomegranate, fig, and apricot trees, surpassed my expectation.

Having kept awhile along this picturesque ravine, we ascended its eastern side, and then followed the very edge of the steep, directly for the castle; but before reaching our tent we were obliged to cross a deep branch of the ravine.   There was some little activity to-day about the castle, it being the market-day; but the market was really miserable, and the Turkish troops, exercising outside the castle, could ill supply the want of national welfare and prosperity. If a just and humane treatment were guaranteed to these tribes, even under a foreign rule, the country might still enjoy plenty and happiness. Most of the tribes westward from the Riaina—namely, the Zintán, .who formerly were very powerful, and even at present hold some possessions as far as Fezzán, the Rujbán, the Fissátu, the Weládd Shebel, the Selemát, the Arhebát, the Harába, the Génafíd, the Kabáw, and the Nalút, belong to the Berber race. With regard to the westernmost of these tribes, M. Prax on his way to Tuggúrt, has obtained some new information.

After a friendly parting from the Kaimakám, we broke up our encampment near the kasr, in the afternoon, in order to continue our tour eastward along the varied border of the plateau, under the guidance of a faithful black servant of the governor, whose name was Barka. Having passed several smaller villages, we reached Um e' Zerzán, a considerable village, situated on a round hill in the midst of a valley, ornamented with fine olive-trees, and surrounded by fine orchards. Um e' Zerzán is well known among the mountaineers as a centre of rebellion. The whole neighbourhood is full of reminiscences of the late war, and about two miles in the rear of the village are the remains of strong walls

called el Mataris, behind which the Arabs made some
stand against the Turks.   Having passed a solitary
rustic dwelling surrounded with a thriving olive-
plantation, we reached the ruins of a castle or village
from which the Roman sepulchre, known among the
Arabs by the name Enshéd e' Sufét, burst suddenly
upon our view.

After an extremely cold night on this   Monday,
high rocky ground, the thermometer in   February 11th.
the morning indicating only 5° above freezing-point,
with the dawn of day I mounted the hill opposite
to the monument, commanding an extensive view.*
It was a level tableland, uninterrupted by any higher
eminence; but the landscape seemed to me highly
characteristic, and I made a sketch of it.

Upon this hill there was formerly a castle built of
hewn stone.   The foundation-walls, which are still
traceable, show that it faced the east, the eastern
and the western sides measuring each 57 ft. 8 in., the
northern and southern, not more than 54 ft.   On the
eastern side there was a strong outwork protecting
the gate, and measuring 16 ft. 11 in. on the north
and south sides, and 12 ft. 1 in. on the east side, where
there was a large gate 9 ft. 1 in. wide.   This outwork
juts off from the castle at 17 ft. 6 in. from the south
corner.   It was evidently a Roman castle; but after the
dominion of the Romans and Byzantines had passed

---

* Mr. Overweg, who made a hypsometrical observation by boiling water, found the elevation of this spot just the same as that
of Mount Tekút, viz. 2800 feet.

away, the Berbers appear to have strengthened it
by adding another outwork on the west side, not,

however, in the same grand style as the Romans,
but with small irregular stones, putting bastions to
the corners, and surrounding the whole castle with
considerable outworks on the slope of the hill.

The Roman castle has been swept away; but the
Roman sepulchre is still preserved, with almost all
its architectural finery, and is still regarded by the
surrounding tribes with a certain awe and reverence.*

---

* In El Bekri's time (11th century) all these Roman monuments hereabout were still the objects of adoration. "De nos
jours encore, toutes les tribus berbères qui habitent aux environs
offrent à cette idole des sacrifices, lui adressent des prières pour
obtenir la guérison de leurs maladies, et lui attribuent l'accroisse-
ment de leurs richesses."—*Notices et Extraits*, vol. xii. p. 458.

It was most probably the sepulchre of a Roman commander of the castle in the time of the Antonines;

hence, in my opinion, the name Sufét, by which the
natives have distinguished it.   It is certainly not
a Punic monument, though it is well known that the
Punic language was generally spoken in several towns
of this region much later than the second century
after Christ.   The style of its architecture testifies
that it belongs to the second century; but no inscription remains to tell its story.

This interesting monument is situated on an eminence a little less elevated than that on which the
castle is built, and south-westward from it.   Its
whole height is about 36 ft.   The base or pedestal
measures 16 ft. 8¾ in. on the W. and E., and 16 ft.
N. and S.   Its elevation varies greatly from E. to W.,
on account of the sloping ground, the eastern side
measuring 3 ft. 2 in., the western 5 ft. 7 in.   In the
interior of this base is the sepulchral chamber, measuring 7 ft. 1 in. from N. to S., and 6 ft. 6 in. from E.
to W., and remarkable for the peculiar construction of
the roof.   Upon this lowest part of the base
rises a second one 15 ft. 9 in. W. and E.,
14 ft. 3¾ in. N. and S., and 2 ft. 1 in. high;
and on this a third one, measuring 14 ft.
7½ in. W. and E., 13 ft. 10¼ in. N. and S., and 1 ft.
7 in. in height.   Upon this base rose the principal
part of the monument, 13 ft. 7 in. high, and measuring
at its foot 13 ft. 11½ in. W. and E., decorated at the
corners with pilasters, the feet of which measure 1 ft.
1¾ in., and the shaft 9¾ in.   The moulding is handsomely decorated.   Upon this principal body of the
monument is constructed the upper story, about 10

feet high, decorated with pilasters of the Corinthian order.   On the south and west sides the walls are plain; but on the east side they are ornamented with a bow window enclosed with pilasters of the same order, and on the north side with a plain window running up the whole height of the body.   Inside of this chamber stood, probably, the statue of the person in whose honour the monument was erected.   The upper compartment has a plain moulding about four feet high, and surmounted by a cornice.

The material of this interesting monument is a very fine limestone, which under the influence of the atmosphere has received a vivid brownish colour, almost like that of travertine.   It was taken from a quarry, which extends all round the monument, and is full of caverns now used by shepherds as resting-places when they tend their flocks hereabouts.

Our camels had already gone on some time before we parted from this solitary memorial of Roman greatness; and after a little distance we passed the ruins of another Roman fort called Hanshír Hámed. The country hereabouts, forming a sort of bowl or hollow, and absorbing a great deal of moisture, is very fertile, and is also tolerably well cultivated; but after a while it becomes stony.   Having here passed a village, we reached a beautiful little valley, the head of the Wadi Sheikh, which is irrigated by two springs, that feed a splendid little orchard with all sorts of fruit.   Here lies Swédna, a considerable village spreading over the whole eminence, and known

on account of the murder of Mohammed Efendi.   As
the valley divides into two branches, we followed the
main wadi, and afterwards crossed it, where it
formed a pretty brook of running water.   We then
wound along a narrow valley overgrown with halfa
and sidr, and, changing our direction, took the road
to Kikla.   The valley soon became decked with
olives, which gradually formed a fine plantation.
This is the chief branch of industry of the inhabitants, the ground being rather stony, and not so fit
for grain.   The district of Kikla contains numerous
villages, all of which suffered much from the last
war, when a great number of people were slaughtered, and their dwellings ransacked, by the Turks.*
Several of these villages lay in small hollows, or on
the slope of ravines, and exhibited rather a melancholy appearance.   After some delay, we resumed
our easterly direction towards Rabda, and soon came
to the spot where the elevated ground descends
abruptly into the deep and broad valley called Wadi
Rabda, over which we obtained an interesting view.
To the left the slope broke into a variety of cones
and small mounts, among which the Tarhóna—" the
mill," so called from a mill that stood formerly on
its summit — is remarkable for its handsome shape;

---

* These villages are as follows :—Bú-Jáfet, Amsír, Welád
Bú-Síri, El Abaiyát, Welád Músa, Welád Naam, Welád 'Amrán,
Ghurfa, Welád Sí-Ammer, El Khodhúr, Nsú, Takbán, Welád Saíd,
Gujíla (consisting of four separate villages), Jendúba, Welád Bú-
Músi, Msaidu, El Fratsa, Shehésh, Negúr, and El Makhrúg.

while in front of us rose an almost perpendicular cliff of limestone, on a turn of which, in a very commanding position, lies the village Jáfet, enclosed, and naturally defended on every side by a deep ravine. Here we commenced our descent, which took us a whole hour; on the middle of the slope we passed a kiln for preparing gypsum. At length we reached the side valley, which joins the main wadi on the west. It was ornamented with a few solitary date-trees, and the beautifully shaped slopes and cones of the Tarhóna were just illuminated by a striking variety of light and shade. The soil, a fertile marl, remained uncultivated. Gradually we entered the main valley, a grand chasm of about two miles in width, which has been formed by the mighty rushing of the waters down* the slope of the plateau. In its upper part it is called Wadi Kérdemín, in its lower part Wadi Sert. The industry of man might convert it into a beautiful spot; but at present it is a desolate waste, the monotonous halfa being the only clothing of the ground.

The eastern border presents a perpendicular rocky cliff about 1500 feet high, on the brink of which lies the village Misga. The western border consists of a cluster of detached mounts and rocks. Among these a black cone, which attracted Mr. Overweg's attention, was found on examination to be pure

---

* Compare what Captain Lyon narrates with regard to the valley of Beniulíd, p. 61. of his Narrative.

basalt, with certain indications of former volcanic
action.   From beyond this remarkable cone, a mount
was visible crowned with a castle.   As we proceeded,
the valley became enlivened by two small Arab encampments.   Here we gradually obtained a view of
the date-grove of Rabda, which, from the foot of the
steep eastern cliffs, slopes down into the bottom of
the valley, and is overtopped, in the distance, by
the handsome bifurcated Mount Manterús.   But
Rabda was too far off to be reached before sunset;
and we encamped in the wadi, near a group of five
tents inhabited by Lasába or el Asába Arabs, whose
chief paid us a visit and treated us with bazín, but
declined tasting our coffee, probably thinking, with
his fellow chief the other day, that we were in the
service of the Turks, and wanted to poison him.   All
the people of these regions regard strangers with
suspicion.

Tuesday,
February 12th.   Soon after we had started we entered
upon cultivated ground,—the first trace of
industry we had seen in this spacious valley.   The
eastern cliffs formed here a wide chasm, through
which a lateral valley joined the Wadi Sert.   On the
southern slope of this valley lies the Kasr Lasába,
from which a torrent that came forth from it, and
crossed our route, presented a refreshing spectacle.
Emerging gradually from the valley, we obtained
an extensive view over the plain called el Gatís.
Westward, as far as the well called Bír el Ghánem,
little was to be seen which could gladden the eye

of the husbandman. Towards the north-east the
level is broken by a small range of hills, the culminating points of which, called el Guleát and
Mámúra, rise to a great elevation. Beyond this
range the plain is called Shefána, the country of the
Ur-shefána.

At nine o'clock we reached the fine date-grove of
the westernmost village of Rabda. It is fed by a
copious spring, which arrested our attention. Following it up to trace its source, we were greatly surprised to find, in the heart of some date-trees, a basin
fifty feet in length, and about thirty in breadth, in
which the water was continually bubbling up and
sending forth a considerable stream to spread life
and cheerfulness around. The water gushed up at
a temperature of 72° Fahrenheit, while that of the
air was only 52°. Besides dates, a large quantity of
onions is produced in this fertile spot. The village
itself was in former times the residence of Hamíd, a
powerful Arab chieftain, who at one time ruled the
whole mountainous district, but was obliged to yield
to the Turks, and lives at present about Bení-Ulíd,
where I had to deal with him on my home-journey
in 1855.

The groves of the two villages of Rabda are not
far apart. On the north-eastern side of the village
are seven holy chapels called el Hararát. The
eastern village lies upon a hill, over a hollow, in
which spreads a date-grove, likewise fed by a spring
called 'Aín Rabda e' sherkíyeh. On crossing a brook

we obtained a view of the Jebel Shehésh, which, attached to the Tahóna, stretches a long way westward, and even el Gunna was seen faintly in the distance. Thus we approached gradually the interesting bicorn of the dark-coloured Jebel Manterús, which we were bent on ascending. Alighting at the foot of the mount, near the border of a deep channel, we sent the camels on, but kept the shoush and our guide back to wait for us. It took me twenty-five minutes to reach the eastern and higher summit, on which there is the tomb of a merábet, a holy shepherd called Sídi Bú-Máza; but I was disappointed in my expectation of obtaining a great extent of view, the cone of Mount Tekút and other mountains intervening. Towards the south only, a peep into the Wadi el 'Ugla, bordered by high cliffs, slightly rewarded me for my trouble; and the mount itself is interesting, as it exhibits evident traces of volcanic action.

I had reached the western lower cone in descending, when I met my companion in his ascent, and, being anxious to overtake the camels, I started in advance of him, accompanied by the guide, along the Wadi el 'Ugla. But my companions did not seem to agree as to the path to be pursued; and my guide, overlooking on the rocky ground the footsteps of the camels, which had taken the direct path to the Kasr Ghurián, wanted to take me by the wadi, and, instead of ascending the eastern cliffs of the ravine, kept along it, where, from being narrow and rocky—the

mere bed of a torrent,—it widens to a pleasant, cultivated, open valley, with rich marly soil, and adorned
with an olive-grove. On a hill in the centre lies the
first village of the district Ghurián.

We had begun to leave the principal valley by a
lateral opening, when the shoush, overtaking us, led
us back to the more northern and more difficult but
shorter path which our camels had taken. The
ascent was very steep indeed; and the path then
wound along the mountain-side and across ravines,
till at length we reached the olive-grove which surrounds the Kasr Ghurián; but in the dark we had
some difficulty in reaching it, and still more in finding our companions, who at length, however, re-
joined the party. In order to obtain something to
eat, we were obliged to pay our respects to the
governor; but the Turks in the castle were so suspicious that they would scarcely admit us. When at
last they allowed us to slip through the gate in single
file, they searched us for arms; but the governor
having assured himself that we had no hostile intention, and that we were furnished with a letter
from the basha, sent a servant to procure us a lodging
in the homestead or housh of a man called Ibrahim,
where we pitched our tent. It was then nine o'clock;
and we felt quite disposed to enjoy some food and
repose.

We paid a visit to the governor, who, Wednesday,
as well as the aghá, received us with February 13th.
the civility usual with Turks, and, in order to do

us honour, ordered the garrison, consisting of 200 men, to pass in review before us. They were good-looking men and well conditioned, though generally rather young. He then showed us the magazines, which are always kept in good order, for fear of a revolt, but will be of no avail so long as the command rests with ignorant and unprincipled men. It is built on a spur of the tableland, commanding on the south and south-west side the Wadi Rummána and the highroad into the interior. Towards the north the lower hilly ground intervenes between it and Mount Tekút.

Having returned to our quarters, we started on foot a little after mid-day, on an excursion to Mount Tekút, which, from its elevation and its shape, appeared to us well worth a visit. Descending the slope by the " trík tobbi," a road máde by the Turks, we reached the eastern foot of the mountain, after an hour and a half's expeditious march through the village Gwásem, and olive-groves, and over a number of subterranean dwellings. My companion went round to the south side in search of an easier ascent. I chose the cliff just above us, which, though steep, indeed, and difficult on account of scattered blocks and stones, was not very high. Having once climbed it, I had easier work, keeping along the crest, which, winding upwards in a semicircle, gradually led to the highest point of the mountain, on the north side, with an absolute elevation of about 2800 feet. On the top are the ruins of a chapel of

Sí Ramadhán, which, I think, is very rarely visited.
The crest, which has fallen in on the S. E. side,
encloses a perfectly circular little plain, resembling
an amphitheatre, and called Shábet Tekút.   The
mount appears evidently to have been an active vol-
cano in former times, yet my companion declared the
rock not to be pure basalt.   The view was very extensive, and I was able to take the angles of several
conspicuous points.   After we had satisfied our curiosity, we descended along the northern slope, which
is much more gradual, being even practicable for
horses, and left the " Shábet " by the natural opening.   Thence we returned along the path called Um
e' Nekhél, which passes by the Roman sepulchre described by Lyon in general terms*, and situated in a
very conspicuous position.

Accompanied by the shoush, I made an Thursday,
excursion in a south-westerly direction. February 14th.
The villages, at least those above the ground, are
generally in a wretched condition and half deserted;
still the country is in a tolerable state of cultivation,
saffron and olive-trees being the two staple articles
of industry.   Passing the little subterranean village
of Shuëdíya, we reached the Kasr Teghrínna, originally a Berber settlement, as its name testifies, with
a strong position on a perfectly detached hill.   At
present the kasr, or the village on the hill-top, is
little more than a heap of ruins, inhabited only by a

* Lyon's Narrative, p. 30.

few families. At the northern foot of the hill a
small village has recently been formed, called Menzel
Teghrínna. On the west and east sides the hill is
encompassed by a valley with a fine olive-grove, beyond which the Wadi el Arbä stretches westwards;
and it was by this round-about way that my guide
had intended to take me from Wadi el 'Ugla to Kasr
Ghurián. Protected by the walls, I was able to take
a few angles; but the strong wind which prevailed
soon made me desist.

From this spot I went to the villages called Ksúr
Gamúdi. These once formed likewise a strong place,
but were entirely destroyed in the last war, since
which a new village has arisen at the foot of the
rocky eminence. A few date-trees grow at the N.
foot of the hill, while it is well known, that the palm
is rare in the Ghurián. As I was taking angles
from the top of the hill, the inhabitants of the village
joined me, and manifested a friendly disposition, furnishing me readily with any information, but giving
full vent to their hatred of the Turks. As the most
remarkable ruins of the time of the Jahalíyeh — or
the pagans, as the occupants of the country before
the time of Mohammed are called, — they mentioned
to me, besides Ghirze, a tower or sepulchre called
Metuïje, about two days' journey S.E.; Beluwár,
another tower-like monument at less distance; and
in a S.W. direction 'Amúd, a round edifice which has
not yet been visited by any European.

The valley at the foot of the Ksúr Gamúdi is watered

by several abundant springs, which once supplied
nourishment for a great variety of vegetables; but
the kitchen-gardens and orchards are at present neglected, and corn alone is now cultivated as the most
necessary want. The uppermost of these springs,
which are stated to be six in number, is called Sma
Rháin — not an Arabic name. Beyond, towards the
south, is Jehésha, further eastward Usáden, mentioned by Lyon, with a chapel, Géba with a chapel,
and, going round towards the north, Shetán, and
further on Mésufín. The country beyond Kuléba, a
village forming the southern border of the Ghurián,
is called Ghadáma, a name evidently connected with
that of Ghadámes, though we know the latter to be
at least of two thousand years' standing.

Continuing our march through the valley N. E.,
and passing the village Bú-Mát and the ruined old
places called Hanshír Metelíli and Hanshír Jamúm*,
we reached the ruins of another old place called
Hanshír Settára, in the centre of the olive-grove.
The houses, which in general are built of small
irregular stones, present a remarkable contrast to
a pair of immense slabs, above ten feet long and
regularly hewn, standing upright, which I at first
supposed to be remnants of a large building; but
having since had a better opportunity of studying
this subject, I concluded that they were erected, like

* I will only mention, that the name "Hanshír" is evidently the
same word with the "Hazeroth" of the Hebrew wanderers.

the cromlechs, for some religious purpose. On the road back to our encampment, the inhabitants of Gamúdi, who were unwilling to part company with me, gave vent to their hatred against the Turks in a singular way. While passing a number of saffron-plantations, which I said proved the productiveness of their country, they maintained that the present production of saffron is as nothing compared to what it was before the country came into the impious hands of the Osmanlis. In former times, they said, several stems usually shot forth from the same root, whereas now scarcely a single sample can be found with more than one stalk,—a natural consequence of the contamination or pollution (nejes) of the Turks, whose predominance had caused even the laws of nature to deteriorate. In order to prove the truth of this, they went about the fields and succeeded in finding only a single specimen with several stems issuing from the same root.

Passing the subterranean villages of Suayeh and U'shen, and further on that called Housh el Yehúd, which, as its name indicates, is entirely inhabited by Jews, we reached our encampment in the housh of Ibrahím. The subterranean dwellings which have been described by Captain Lyon *, seem to me to have originated principally with the Jews, who, from time immemorial, had become intimately connected with

* The name of this part of the mountains has, I think, been erroneously brought into connexion with these caves. For, from the word ghár, غَار, the regular and only plural 'orm besides

ing adopted
v as they
egions
long

adopted

KARA SU OGUZ H

the Berbers, many of the Berber tribes having adopted
the Jewish creed; and just in the same way as they
are found mingling with the Berbers in these regions
— for the original inhabitants of the Ghurián belong
entirely to the Berber race — on friendly terms, so
are they found also in the recesses of the Atlas in
Morocco.

I then went to see the market, which is held every
Thursday on the open ground at the east side of
the castle, close to the northern edge of the ridge.
Though much better supplied than that near Kasr
Jebel, it was yet extremely poor; only a single camel
was offered for sale. This results from the mistrust
of the inhabitants, who, in bringing their produce to
the great market at Tripoli, are less exposed to vexa-
ations than here. When taking leave of the Kaimakám, we found the whole castle beset by litigants.
I saw in the company of the governor the chief of
the Haj caravan, the Sheikh el Rakeb, of whose
grand entrance into the town I had been witness.
The agbá, wanting to show us their little paradise,
accompanied us into the Wadi Rummána, which, in a
direction from S.E. to N.W., winds along the southern
foot of the ridge on which the castle is situated.
Though it looks rather wild and neglected, it is a
charming retreat for the leisure hours of a governor

أغوار is غِيرَان. E' Sheikh e' Tijāni certainly (Journal Asiatique,
série v. tom. i. p. 110.) calls it expressly by this name, غِيرَان. But
we see from Ebn Khaldúm (t. i. p. 275. transl.) that Ghurián was
the name of a tribe.

of a place like this. It is irrigated by a very powerful spring issuing from the limestone rock in a
channel widened by art, and then dividing into
several little rills, which are directed over the terraces
of the slope. These, of course, have been raised by
art, and are laid out in orchards, which, besides the
pomegranates which have given their name to the
valley, produce sferéj (sfarájel) — the Malum Cy-
donium — of an excellent quality, figs, grapes, and
almonds. A path, practicable even for horses, leads
down from the castle to the spring. Before I left this
charming spot, I made a sketch of the valley, with
the castle on the cliffs, which is represented in the
accompanying plate.

CHAP. III.

FERTILE MOUNTAIN REGION RICH IN ANCIENT REMAINS.

IT was past three in the afternoon of Thursday, February 14th, when we started from the dwelling of our host, in order to pursue our route in a south-easterly direction. We were agreeably surprised to see fine vineyards at the village called Jelíli; but the cultivation of olive-trees seemed almost to cease here, while the country became quite open, and afforded an unbounded prospect towards the distant southern range, with its peaks, depressions, and steep slopes. But the fine olive-grove of Sgáif proved that we had not yet reached the limit of this useful tree. We were just about to descend the slope into the broad valley called Wadi Rán, when, seeing darkness approaching and frightened by the black clouds rising from the valley, together with a very chilly stream of air, we began to look seriously about for some secure shelter for the night. To our right we had a pleasant little hollow with olive-trees; but that would not suffice in such weather as was apparently approaching, and we therefore descended a little along the cliffs on our left, where our shoush knew that there were caverns called Merwán. Scarcely had we pitched our tent on the little terrace in front of these, when the rain began to pour down, and, accompanied with snow, continued the whole night.

When we arose next morning, the whole country was covered with snow about an inch deep, and its natural features were no longer recognisable. Placed on the very brink of a bank partly consisting of rocky ground, with many holes, partly of marly soil and accordingly very slippery, we could not think of starting. At half-past six, the thermometer stood at 34° Fahr. Fortunately our tent, which had been fitted by Mr. Warrington for every kind of weather, kept the wet out. The caverns were very irregular excavations, used by the shepherds as temporary retreats, and full of fleas. The snow did not melt till late in the afternoon, and the rain fell without intermission the whole night.

February 16th. In the morning the bad weather still continued, but the cold was not quite so severe. Tired as we were of our involuntary delay in such a place, we decided upon starting; but it was difficult to get our half-frozen people to go to work. At length we set out, accompanied by an old man whom we hired as guide, on the deep descent into Wadi Rán. The soil was often so slippery that the camels could scarcely keep their feet; and we were heartily glad when, after an hour and a quarter's descent, we at length reached stony ground, though still on the slope. Here the valley spread out before us to the right and left, with the village Usíne, in-

habited by the Merábetín Selahát, situated on the top
of a hill, and distinguished for the quality of its
dates, which are of a peculiar kind, short and thick
with a very broad stone, — while at the foot of the
western heights another village was seen, and on the
top of them the castle Bústam. Here the great valley
is joined by a smaller ravine, called Wadi Nkhal, with
a small village of the same name. We crossed two
paths leading to Bení Ulid, passing by Wadi Rán,
which went parallel to our course on the right, and
where there are two springs and a date-grove, while
to the left, we obtained a view of Sedi-úris, situated
on a cone overtowering the northern end of Wadi Ko-
minshát. We then approached closely the steep glen
of Wadi Rán, and, after some turnings, crossed the
small rivulet which flows through it, and, a little
further on, recrossed it. Then, traversing the valley called Wadi Marníyeh, we entered a fine fertile
plain surrounded on all sides by heights, among
which the Kelúba Naáme was conspicuous on our
right.

But the camels found the marly soil, fully saturated as it was with rain, very difficult, especially
after we had entered the "Shábet Sóda." For this
reason, also, we could not think of following the direct
path, which leads over the hills. At the western end
of the shábet are the villages Deb Bení 'Abbás and
Suadíyeh, with olive-groves. All the waters of the
district are carried into Wadi Rán, which joins the
Wadi Haera.

The country begins to exhibit decidedly a volcanic character, and from all the heights rise bare basaltic cones, while the lower part is covered with halfa. This character of the country seems to have been well understood by the Arabs, when they gave to these basins, surrounded by basaltic mounts, the name "Shàbet," which we have already seen given to the crater of the Tekút. Here, at a short distance on our left, we passed "another Shàbet," distinguished as "el A'khira."

At length we found an opening through the hilly chain on our right, behind an indented projection of the ridge called "Sennet el O'sis," and then suddenly changed our course from N.E. to S.E. As soon as we had made the circuit of this mount, we obtained a view of the highest points of the Tarhóna, and directed our course by one of them, Mount Bíbel, which is said to be sometimes visible from Tripoli. Tales of deadly strife are attached to some localities hereabouts; and, according to our guide, the torrent which we crossed beyond Wadi Rwéra poured down, some years ago, a bloody stream. But at present the scene wants life, the Kasr Kuséba, situated on the apex of a cone, being almost the only dwelling-place which we had seen for five hours. Life has fled from these fertile and pleasant regions; and the monotonous character which they at present exhibit necessarily impresses itself on the narrative of the traveller.

At length, after having entered the gorges of the mountains, we reached the encampment of the

Merábetín Bú-'Aáisha, and pitched our tent at a short
distance from it. These people have considerable
herds of camels and sheep; as for cattle, there are
at present very few in the whole regency of Tripoli,
except in the neighbourhood of Ben-gházi. Their
chief, 'Abdallah, who lives in Tripoli, is much respected. The valleys and plains hereabouts, when
well saturated with rain, produce a great quantity
of corn, but they are almost entirely destitute of
trees. Having been thoroughly drenched to-day by
heavy showers, we were in a very uncomfortable
condition at its close.

About an hour before sunrise, when   Sunday.
the thermometer stood at 41°, I set   February 17th.
out to ascend an eminence north from our tent,
which afforded me an excellent site whence to take
the bearings of several prominent cones. After my
return to the tent, we started together in advance
of the camels, that we might have time to ascend
the broad cone of Jebel Msíd, which had arrested
our attention. We soon passed a well, or rather
fountain, called Bír el 'Ar, which gives its name to
some ancient monument (" sanem," or idol, as it is
called by the Arabs) at a little distance, and which
the guide described as a kasr tawíl Bení Jehel,
" a high fortress of the Romans." The country was
varied and pleasant, and enlivened, moreover, by
flocks; but we saw no traces of agriculture till
we reached the well called Hasi el abiár, beyond ·
which we entered upon a volcanic formation. As

we ascended along a small ravine, and entered another irregular mountain-plain of confined dimensions, we found the basalt in many places cropping out on the surface. The more desolate character of the country was interrupted in a pleasant way by the Wadi Nekhél, which has received its name from the number of palm-trees which grow here in a very dwarfish state, though watered by a copious spring. Following the windings of another small valley, we reached a plain at the foot of Mount Msíd, while on the right a large ravine led down from the heights. Here we commenced our ascent of the cone; and on the slope of the mountain we met with large pillars similar to those which I had seen in the ruins of Hanshír Settára. The pillars succeeded each other at regular distances up the slope, apparently marking the track to be followed by those ascending for religious purposes. The ascent was very gradual for the first twelve minutes; and twelve minutes more brought us to its summit, which was crowned with a castle of good Arabic masonry of about the thirteenth century. Its ruined walls gave us a little protection against the very strong blasts of wind; but we found it rather difficult to take accurate angles, which was the more to be regretted as a great many peaks were visible from this beautifully-shaped and conspicuous mount.

It was a little past noon when we pursued our journey from the western foot of this once holy

mount *, and, turning its southern side, resumed
our north-easterly direction. We then soon came
to the " Wadi hammám," which forms here a wider
basin for the brook running along it towards Mejenín, so as to produce a pleasant and fresh green
spot. Having watered our animals, we entered a
plain from which detached basaltic hillocks started
up; and some ruins of regularly-hewn stones, scattered about, bore testimony that the Romans had
deemed the place worthy of fixed settlements. A
small limestone hill contrasts handsomely with these
black basaltic masses, among which the Leblú, the
highest summit of a larger group to our right, is
particularly remarkable. At the foot of the Jebel
Jemmà was an encampment of the Welád 'Alí; but
I cannot say in what degree they are connected with
the family which has given its name to the valley
in the Yefren. From this side in particular, the
Jebel Msíd presents the form of a beautiful dome,
the most regular I remember to have ever seen. It
seems to rise with a proud air over its humbler
neighbours. Having then passed a continuous
ridge of cones stretching S.S.E., and cleared the
basaltic region, we entered a wide plain covered
with halfa, and, cutting right across it, we reached
the fertile low plain Elkeb, where another encampment of the Welád 'Alí excited the desire of our
people to try their hospitality for our night's quar-

* The ancient character of this mountain is most probably indicated by its present name " Msíd."

ters; but some distance to the left two enormous
pillars were to be seen standing upright, and thither
we repaired.   Here I had an opportunity of accurately investigating a very peculiar kind of ancient
remains, giving a clue, I hope, to the character of the
religion of the early inhabitants of these regions,
though it seems impossible to give a satisfactory
explanation respecting all the details of their structure.

It consists in a pair of quadrangular pillars
erected on a common basis, which is fixed into
the ground, and measures 3 ft. 1$\frac{6}{12}$' in length, and
2 ft. 10' in width.   The two pillars which measure
2 feet on each side, being 1 ft. 7$\frac{2}{10}$' asunder, are 10

feet high.   The western pillar has three quadrangular holes on the inside, while the corresponding holes in the eastern pillar go quite through ; the lowest hole is 1 ft. 8' above the ground, and the second 1 ft. $\frac{1}{2}$' higher up, and so the third above the second.   The holes are 6 in. square.

Over these pillars, which at present lean to one side, is laid another enormous stone about 6 feet $6\frac{1}{2}$ inches long, and of the same width as the pillars, so that the whole structure bears a surprising resemblance to the most conspicuous part of the celebrated Celtic ruins at Stonehenge * and other ruins in Malabar †, about the religious purpose of which not the least . doubt remains at present.   But besides these, there are other very curious stones of different workmanship, and destined evidently for different purposes ; some of them are large, flat, and quadrangular, very peculiarly worked, and adapted, probably, to sacrifices. One of them is three feet in length and breadth, but with a projection on one side, as is represented in the woodcut, and 1 ft. 2' high.   On the surface of this stone, and parallel to its sides, is carved a channel $4\frac{8}{10}$ inches broad, forming a quadrangle ; and from this a small channel branches along the projecting part.   Several stones of similar workmanship lie about.   There is also the remnant of an enormous stone 3 feet $7\frac{1}{2}$ inches at the back and across, but rounded off at the corners, looking like a solid

---

* See especially the Plate No. 7. in Higgins's " Celtic Druids."
† See Plate No. 39. in Higgins's work.

throne, excepting that on the upper side there is an excavation measuring 1 ft. $3\frac{2}{10}$ in. at the back, $9\frac{6}{10}$ inches on the front, and 1 ft. $1\frac{2}{10}$ in. across, and about 10 inches deep, with a small opening. This stone looks very peculiar, and probably formed an altar.

These ruins are certainly very remarkable. Any one who looks at them without prejudice or preconceived opinion, will be impressed with the belief that they belonged to a place of worship; though how this peculiar structure could be adapted to religious purposes, I will not undertake to decide. It is well known, that the most ancient idols were mere pillars or stones, not only of a round or conical shape, as symbols of the procreative power of nature, but even of a square form. It is also well known, from the example of the columns in On or Heliopolis, of the two celebrated columns, Yakín and Boäz, in front of the temple in Jerusalem, and from that of the two pillars of the Phœnician Hercules in Gades, that the power of the Deity was often represented by a pair. A pair of massive columns or pillars, covered with a similarly massive impost, may well serve to represent symbolically the firmness and eternity of the cosmical order, while the name of the chief deity of the pagan Berbers, 'Amún, may possibly have the original meaning of " the Founder, Supporter." But I will not enter here into such conjectures; I will only say that my distinct impression on the spot was, that the structure was a rude kind of sun-dial, combining the vertical with the horizontal principle. That it could not be intended as a common doorway, even if it were connected with another building, is evident from the narrowness of the passage; but it may have had the purpose of serving as a sort of penitential or purgatory passage in consecrating and preparing the worshippers *, previous to their offering sacrifices, by obliging them to squeeze themselves through this narrow passage, the inconvenience of which was increased by the awful character attributed to this cromlech. Even in Christian and Mohammedan countries religious ordeals of a similar kind are not unknown; and a very analogous custom in the celebrated mosque of Kairowán may well have its origin in the older pagan practice of the aborigines. However this may be, the religious character of the whole structure can scarcely be doubtful, from the nature of the flat stone, the channel in which was certainly intended to carry off the blood of the victim.†

It must strike the observer, in regarding these ruins, that while they are so rude in principle, their style of execution evidently bears traces of art; and I think it not improbable that the art may be ascribed to Roman influence. We shall further on see another specimen of these curious pillars combined

---

* Compare what Higgins says, p. lx., in describing the Constantine tolmen in Cornwall.

† From this plain example it might seem that the flat stone in Stonehenge was intended for a similar purpose.

with the ground-plan of an almost regular Roman temple. But from whatever quarter this artistical influence may have proceeded, there cannot be the least doubt that the character of the structure is, on the whole, not Roman, but indicates quite another race ; and if we take into regard what I have just said about the influence of art visible in this structure, and that such influence could scarcely proceed from any other quarter than that of the Carthaginians or the Romans, we must attribute these remains to the Berber race, who, during the historical period, were the exclusive possessors of these inland regions. Analogous structures have been found, however, not only in England and Ireland on the one side, and in several parts of India, principally in the Nilgherries, on the other, but also in Circassia, Southern Russia, on the South Arabian coast, and in the Somali country. This analogy might certainly be explained by a similarity of principle in the simple religious rites of rude people ; but there may be also in these curious remains a confirmation of the theories of Sir Henry Rawlinson respecting the wide extension of the Scythians. But while, with regard to other tribes, from the Dravidian group in Southern India to the Celtic in Ireland, such a connexion of origin seems to be confirmed by analogy of language, there exist but very few points of analogy between the Berber and the Central Asiatic languages, except by means of the Coptic. In every respect, however, it may be better to call such remains by the general

name of Scythian than by that of Druidical, which
certainly can be justified only with regard to the
north-west of Europe.

These remarkable ruins are at a short distance
from the foot of a fortified hill, which is crowned
with ancient fortifications of hewn stone, to which
are added later works of small stones.   Other ruins
of cut-stone buildings lie about; and on an eminence
at a little distance eastward is a small castle belonging to the earlier times of the Arabs, while on the
highest top of the hilly chain behind the Arab encampment, and which is called Gábes, are likewise
ruins.   The ruins of a whole village, partly built of
regularly-cut stone, and even exhibiting the ornament of a column, were found the next morning near
our encampment, which our people had placed on the
slope of the hills bordering the plain towards the
north-east.

All these ruins are evident proofs that the fertile
plain Elkeb, and the adjoining one, called Mádher,
were once well cultivated and thickly inhabited.
Their situation is very favourable, as the direct road
from Tripoli to Bení Ulíd and Sókna, by way of the
valley Melgha, passes close by.   We had here descended to an average height of about one thousand
feet above the level of the sea.

During the night there was heavy rain,
which lasted till morning, and delayed our   February 18th.
starting till rather late.   After about a mile and a
half's march, we ascended a little from the plain to the

undulating pastures of the Dháhar Tarhóna, which soon became enlivened by the tents and herds of the Megaigera, and where I was glad to see at length a few cows. The ground, though scantily covered with herbage, was dotted with *Tulipa sylvestrie*, which my companion called balúdt, though this name is generally understood to signify the ash-tree. Our guide from Meruán informed me here that the water of this district takes its course not towards the north, as might be expected, but towards the south-east, running from hence to Temásla, on this side of Bení Ulíd, thence into the Wadi Merdúm, and thence into Wadi Sófejín, which, as is well known, descends towards Tawárgha. A little further on we left, on a small eminence to the left, another hanshír surrounded by cultivated ground. It had been an inconsiderable place, built chiefly of small stones; but even here two enormous pillars or slabs were to be seen standing in the midst of the rubbish. There were two holes in each of these pillars, going quite through, and widening on one side.

At half-past nine o'clock, when passing the Hanshír Bú-Trehébe, at a distance of more than two miles on our left, we had a fine retrospective view of the various peaks of the Ghurián range, while on our left a lower range approached more and more, with two summits rising from it to a greater elevation. About noon we passed another site, called Hanshír Suwán, where are the remains of a large castle, with an inner and outer fortification, built of small stones, but in a very neat and regular style. The country, chiefly owing to the murkiness of the sky, had begun to assume a very sombre character, and was crossed by stripes of red sand, which, however, affords the best soil for the growth of the pumpkin; but in the after-noon it improved greatly, showing fine pasture-ground and ample corn-fields, and, among the ruins of ancient times, the rare example of a well-proportioned and neatly-worked Ionic capital, which I found at the border of a ravine.   Further on, upon a detached low rock, which had been hewn into rectangular walls, and surrounded with a ditch, were seen ruins of cut stone, very similar in appearance to those of Kasr Ja-halíyeh, near Gargash.   We at length found traces of living beings, in an Arab encampment situated in a green hollow, where we learnt that the Kaïd or governor of Tarhóna, whose residence we were in search of, was at present encamped near the spring called 'Aín Shershára.

The country gradually assumes a more diversified aspect, agreeably succeeding its former monotony. A considerable mountain-range, with manifold crags, peaks, and ravines, approaches from S.S.W., and, turning N.E., presents an insurmountable barrier to an advance in that direction, while the plain sweeps nicely in a concave towards its foot; but it is quite bare and desolate, and only now and then is seen a poor remnant of the large olive-grove, consisting, according to the statement of our shoush, of 10,000 trees, which Bey 'Abd Allah, in Masráta, my host on my former journey, had ventured to plant here five years ago. My people maintained, whether correctly or not I cannot say, that the strong gales which prevail in this plain did not allow the young olive-tree to thrive. I think the failure is due rather to the character of the inhabitants, who, unaccustomed to this branch of culture, have not paid the necessary attention to the young trees.

Having passed a small wadi, we came in sight of the encampment of the governor, which stretched out in front of us in a well-chosen situation at the southern foot of a small cone. A Turkish officer's green tent, pitched a little in advance, was surrounded by several smaller ones, while another group of twelve Bedwín tents, in a higher position up the slope of the mount, contained the household. The governor received us in a very friendly but rather affected manner, which seemed peculiar to him, and might even be thought becoming in a man who has assisted his country's foes in exterminating all the members of his family, formerly one of the foremost in the country. His friends, who try to represent him as an honest man, say that he was forced to the deed, after having once entered into Turkish service. This man, Bel Kásem el Lohéshi Mahmúdi, has since played a conspicuous part in the present revolution ; for he it was who led the Turkish force last year against Ghóma, his near relative but most bitter enemy, who, having been a prisoner in Trebizond for many years, suddenly made his escape from thence during the Russian war, and, issuing from the Tunisian frontier, appeared in Jébel Yefrén   El Lohéshi was routed, and taken prisoner, and, according to the first report, slain by the successful rebel.   When we visited El Lohéshi, he had occupied his new post only for the last year, having been before governor of the Jebel.   During all the period he had been in Tarhóna, he assured us he had not moved his encampment from this place; which I can well understand, as it is a very pleasant spot.   His principal business, of course, consists in collecting the tithes, in registering which he was busily employed. He knew very little of the province under his government; and it was to other men that I had to look for information.

Having pitched our tent near that of the governor, we proceeded to make ourselves acquainted with the locality, and, a few paces north from our encampment, stumbled upon the famous brook called 'Aín Shersher, or 'Aín Shershára, which, proceeding from the junction of three springs, forms here a cascade of about twenty-five feet over the firm calcareous rock.   Running west a short distance, it then turns north and, breaking through the mountain-slope in a deep picturesque glen, takes the direction of the Wadi Ramle, which, however, it only reaches during great floods.

It seems as if this pleasant spot had already been a favourite residence in the Roman times, as is amply shown by the fine ruins of a large building of hewn

stone, which the torrent has rent asunder and scattered on both sides.   From this place, ascending the
side of a very wild ravine, we reached the height
which overlooks the Bedwín encampment, and on the
morning of the following day made a more distant
excursion to the mount called Bú-tawíl, about three
miles north, which was represented to us as affording a very distant prospect, and the name of which
seemed to promise more than ordinary elevation.

As to the view we were rather disappointed; yet
we were well repaid for our trouble from the character of the country traversed, and the unex-
pectedly pleasing aspect of the terrace spread out
at the western foot of the mountain, which must
have formed a favourite retirement in the time of
the Romans, so literally strewn is it with the ruins
of buildings of hewn stone.   In descending it, about
300 feet below the summit, we first came to a
Roman tomb, 8 ft. 7 in. long, and 7 ft. 9 in. broad,
rising in two stories, the lower being about ten
feet high from the base to the moulding, and ornamented with pilasters at the corners.   A little further
on, to the west, was another tomb, just on the
brink of the slope into the valley below; but it has
been destroyed, and at present the chief interest
attaches to a monumental stone, which most probably stood upright on its top, and fell down when
the monument went to pieces, so that it now lies in
a merely casual position on the floor of the sepulchre,
which has been repeatedly rifled by greedy hands.

This stone is 7 ft. 2 in. long, and has on one side, in high relief, the figure of a man, of natural size, clothed in a toga.   The workmanship is good, and certainly not much later than the time of Severus. Close at hand are other ruins lying about; and further west are several groups of buildings.   Three olive-trees and a palm-tree adorned this beautiful retired spot.

Having returned to our encampment, I and my companion resolved to separate for a few days, Overweg wishing to examine the neighbourhood of the 'Aín Shershára for geological purposes, while I was rather bent upon executing the original plan of our route all round the mountain-range.   We agreed to meet again at the castle called Kasr el Jefára in the plain or jefára near the sea-shore.   We borrowed another tent from the governor for Mr. Overweg during his stay at this place, while I procured a horse-man, with whom, together with Ibrahím, our shoush, and one of the camel-drivers, I was ready for starting an hour before noon; for the heat of the sun was not much to be dreaded at this season of the year. Overweg accompanied me as far as Kasr Dóga.*

Winding along narrow ravines, after about one mile's march we passed, on an eminence to our right,

* The principal tribes living in the district Tarhóna are the Hhamadát, the Drahíb, Welád Bú-Síd, Welád Bú-Márah, Marghána, Welád 'Alí, W. Yusuf, Megaigerah, Firján, W. Me-háda, W. Bú-Sellem, Naáje, Máta, Khwárish, Gerákta, Bú-Sabn, Shefátra, Welád Hámed, Erhaimíyeh.

another specimen of large pilasters with an impost, and ruins of buildings of large square stones close by. After much winding, we cleared the narrow channel ascending the hills, which were covered with halfa; but here too there was not a single tree to be seen, and my guide said that there were no olive-trees in the Tarhóna except in Máta, a place situated between Mount Bú-tawíl and Kasr Jefára, from which the tribe Máta derives its name. I have noticed before, as remarkable, the three olive-trees near Bu-tauwíl. It was about one o'clock in the

afternoon when we came in sight of the Roman monument called Kasr Dóga; and its brown colour. almost induced us to conclude that it was of brick; but on approaching nearer, we found that it was built of hewn stone. We were astonished at the grand dimensions of the monument, as it appeared evident that it was originally a mere sepulchre, though in after times blocked up by the Arabs, and converted into a castle.

The front of the monument faces the south with ten degrees of deviation towards the west. The whole body of the building, rising upon a base of three steps, measures 47 ft. 6 in. in length, and 31 ft. 4 in. in breadth. The entrance or portal, equidistant from both corners, was 12 ft. 6 in. wide; but it has been entirely blocked up with hewn stone, so that it is now impossible to get into the interior of the monument without great labour, and only a glimpse can be obtained of a kind of entrance-hall of small dimensions. Of the interior arrangement, therefore, nothing meets the view; but on the top of the solid mass of building, rising to a height of 28 ft. 10 in., the ground-plan of the third story, which has been demolished to obtain materials for closing the entrance, is distinctly visible. Here the vestibule measures 10 ft. 10 in., the wall of the interior chamber or cell being adorned with two columns, which are no less than 3 ft. 10 in. apart: the inner room itself measures 22 ft. 4 in. in length within the walls. The monument, although more massive than beautiful, is a fair proof of the wealth of this district in ancient times. Opposite to it, on a limestone hill of considerable elevation, is another specimen of the cromlech kind in good preservation, besides other ruins.

In the hollow at the S.E. side of the sepulchre there
are six deep and spacious wells sunk in the rock.

Here my companion left me, and I continued my
route alone, passing through a well-cultivated tract,
till I reached an encampment of the Welád Bú-Sellem,
where we pitched our tent.   Here I met a cousin of
Haj 'Abd el Hádi el Meráyet, who had once been
master of half the Tarhóna district, but was made
prisoner by the Turks, and sent to Constantinople.
This man also reappeared on the stage last year.

Wednesday, We set out early in the morning, the
February 20th. country continuing flat as far as the
chapel of Sídi 'Alí ben Sálah, which, standing on a
hill, is a conspicuous object for many miles round.
At a short distance from this chapel, I observed the
ruins of a castle built of large square stones taken
from older buildings; it measures 42 feet in every
direction, and exhibits a few bad but curious sculptures, among others an ass in relief.   Around are
the ruins of a small village, and flat stones of immense size, similar in workmanship to those described
above, but no upright pillars.

Beyond the chapel of the saint the country became
more hilly, and after some time we entered a ravine
joining the Wadi Gedéra, which exhibited the remains of three broad and firmly-constructed dikes,
crossing the ravine at the distance of about 800
yards from each other.   They were built of small
stones, and were evidently intended to exclude the
water from the lower part of the valley.   Another

eight hundred yards below the innermost dike, the ravine widens out into a fine verdant hollow, stretching from west to east, and provided with several wells. On a detached hill rising in the midst of this basin, is situated the Kasr Dawán, built partly of older materials of hewn stone, partly of small stones, and probably of the same age as the dikes. The whole floor of the basin is strewn with ruins; and a considerable village seems to have extended round the castle: where the ground was free from stones, it was covered with ranunculuses. Altogether, this spot was interesting — the stronghold of a chieftain who appears to have had energy and foresight, but whose deeds are left without a record.

As soon as we emerged from this ravine the whole character of the country changed, and through a pleasant valley we entered a wider plain, bordered in the distance by a high range of mountains, among which the Jébel Msíd, crowned with a zawíya or convent, is distinguished by its height and its form. It is rather remarkable, and of the highest interest as regards the ancient history of the civilization of these regions, that the two most conspicuous mountains bordering Tarhóna, one on the west, the other on the east side, should bear the same name, and a name which bears evident testimony to their having been places of worship in ancient times. Both of them have grandeur of form; but the western one is more regularly dome-shaped.

The fine pasturage which this plain affords to the

cows of the Mehédi enabled their masters to regale us with fine fresh sourmilk, which interrupted our march very pleasantly. On the site of an ancient village, near the margin of a small torrent, I found the following curious specimens of upright pilasters, together with the impost, remarkable for their height as well as for the rough sculp-ture of a dog, or some other animal, which is seen on the higher part of one of them. About 700 yards beyond the torrent called Ksaea, we had on our right a large building of hewn stone about 140 yards square, besides six pairs of pilasters together with their imposts; but some of them are lying at present on the ground. These structures could never have been intended as doors or passages; for the space between the upright stones is so narrow, that a man of ordinary size could hardly squeeze his way through them. Other ruins are on the left.

Here we entered the mountain chain which forms the natural boundary between the district of Tarhóna and that of Meselláta, and at the present time sepa- rates scenes of nomadic life from fixed settlements. The highest part of the chain round the Jébel Msíd remained on our left, while the heights on the right decreased in elevation. The chain has little

breadth; and we had hardly reached its crest when
the country that presented itself to our view had
quite a different appearance from that just left behind, presenting among other objects the castle of
Meselláta, surrounded by an olive-grove. In this
spot ancient sites and modern villages with stone
houses are intermixed, while thick olive-groves enliven the whole, and constitute the wealth of the
inhabitants.

Having passed a village called Fatír, lying in a
ravine that runs S.W., we soon descried, in a hollow
at the southern foot of the Kasr S̈aade (a small
ancient fortress), the first olive-plantation and the
first orchards belonging to Meselláta. From this
place onward they succeed each other at short intervals. Having passed a small eminence, with a
fine olive-grove in the hollow at its foot, we entered
the beautiful and well-inhabited plain of Meselláta.
Here a great deal of industry was evinced by the
planting of young cuttings between the venerable old
olive-trees, or ghúrs Faraón as the Arabs call them.
My shoush affirmed that the inhabitants of Meselláta are the most industrious and diligent people
in the whole regency, taking good care of their
plantations, and watering them whenever they need
it. The whole country has here a different character from that of Tarhóna, the naked calcareous
rock protruding everywhere, while in Tarhóna the
plains generally consist of clayey soil. This district
is only about one thousand feet above the sea, while

the average height of the Jebel (Yefrén) and the
Ghurián is about two thousand feet. Here the olives
had been collected a month ago; in the former districts they remained still on the tree.

Cheered by the spectacle of life and industry
around us, we continued our pleasant march, and
having crossed an open space of rough rocky ground
filled with cisterns, we reached the castle of Meselláta, an edifice of little merit, built with square stones
from old ruins, and lying at the northern end of the
village Kúsabát, which properly means " the Castles."
While my people were pitching my tent behind the
castle, on the only spot which would allow of the
pegs being driven into the ground, I went to pay a
visit to Khalíl Aghá, who resided in the castle; but
I found it to be so desolate and comfortless that I
left it immediately, taking with me the sheikh Mesáud
and a shoush named Ibrahím Tubbát, in order to view
the Kalá or Gellàh, a very conspicuous object, visible
even from the sea. Keeping along the western side
of the village, which consists of from 300 to 400
cottages* built of stone, and occupies a gentle slope
towards the south, the highest point of which, near
the mosque, is 1250 feet† above the level of the
sea, we reached a pleasant little hollow adorned with
gardens, which being fenced with hedges of the Indian

* The quarter of the village nearest to the castle is principally
inhabited by Jews.

† The elevation of this place was determined by Lieutenant
(now Rear-Admiral) Smyth, in 1819.

fig-tree, rendered the spot extremely picturesque. From hence we ascended the naked calcareous eminence, from the top of which the fortress overlooks a great extent of country. Going round its demolished walls, from east to west, I was able to descry and to take the bearings of a great number of villages belonging to the district of Mesellàta, some of them peeping out of olive-groves, others distinguishable only by the smoke rising up from them.

The fortress itself is evidently a work not of Mohammedans, but of Europeans, and was most probably constructed by the Spaniards in the first half of the 16th century. It is built in the form of a triangle, one side of which, running N.W. and S.E., measures about 108 yards; another, running E.N.E. and W.S.W., measures $78\frac{1}{2}$ yards, and the third, S. 5 W. and N. 5 E., $106\frac{1}{2}$ yards. At the corner between the first and the second wall, is a polygonal bastion; between the second and third a round bastion, and a small one also between the third and the first wall. Descending from the fortress, I went with Mesàúd through the village, the dwellings of which are built in a much better style than is usual in the regency. It is also stated that, in comparison with the rest of the country, its inhabitants enjoy some degree of wealth, and that the market is well supplied.

I rose at an early hour, in order to continue my route, and entered a very pleasant country, rendered more agreeable in appearance by the fineness of the morning. Winding along

Thursday, February 21st.

through hilly slopes covered with luxuriant corn-
fields and wide-spreading olive-trees, we reached at
half-past eight o'clock an interesting group of ruins
consisting of immense blocks, and amongst them
one like the flat quadrangular stones represented
above, but having on its surface, besides the little
channel, a large hole; also a block of extraordinary
dimensions, representing a double altar of the curious
massive sort described above. Close to these remarkable ruins, in a fine corn-field, is a small castle,
situated upon a natural base of rock, in which subterranean vaults have been excavated in a very
regular way. Towards the south, at the distance
of about half an hour's march, the large castle of
Amámre rises into view. We then reached the fine
plantation of Rumíyeh, while on a hill to the left lie
other scattered ruins.

We met a good many people going to the Thursday
market at Kúsabát. Further on, near another little
grove, we found a small encampment of the Jehawát,
a tribe which claims the possession of this whole district. We then passed a castle irregularly built of
large square stones about twelve yards square. Having
crossed a hollow, we obtained a good view over the
country, in which the "Merkeb Sáid-n-'Alí (the most
advanced spur of this chain towards the coast) formed
a distinguished point, while we had already reached
the last low breaks of the mountain-country towards
the east. Meanwhile the greater dimensions of the
ruins remind the traveller that he is approaching the

famous remains of Leptis. I found here, a little to
the right of our path, near a Bedwín encampment, the
ruins of a temple of large proportions, called Sanem
ben Hamedán, and of rather curious arrangement,
the front, which faces the north and recedes several
feet from the side-walls, being formed by double
ranges of enormous stones standing upright — they
can scarcely be called pilasters,—while the inner part
is ornamented with columns of the Ionic order. The
whole building is about 40 paces long, and 36 broad;
but the architectural merit of its details is not sufficient to repay the trouble of exact measurements.
About a thousand yards further on, to the east, are
the ruins of another still larger monument, measuring
about 77 paces in every direction, and called by the
Arabs Kasr Kerker. It has several compartments
in the interior—three chambers lying opposite to the
entrance, and two other larger ones on the east side.
Nearly in the middle of the whole building, there is a
large square stone like those mentioned above, but
having on one of its narrow sides a curious sculpture
in relief.

The camels having been allowed to go on, I
hastened after them with my shoush as fast as
my donkey could trot, and passed several sites of

ancient villages or castles, and numerous fine hollows
with luxuriant olive-trees. I scarcely ever remember to have seen such beautiful trees. The country
continues undulating, with fertile hollows or depressions. We reached the camels at Wadi Lebda, which
I found perfectly dry.

Close to our left we had cultivated ground and
ruins. Near the sea-shore, the spacious and pleasant
site of Leptis spread out on the meadow-land, while
a little further on rose a small ridge, on the top
of which is situated the village Khurbet Hammám.
After we had passed a pleasant little hollow, the plain
became for a while overgrown with thick clusters of
bushes; but on reaching the plantation of Swail, an
almost uninterrupted line of villages stretched along
the sáhel (sea-shore) amid corn-fields and groves of
olive and date-trees. According to my shoush, a great
deal of corn is cultivated also in the valleys behind
this plain; and numerous well-trodden paths were
seen leading from the sahel into the hilly country
on its southern side. After plentiful rains, this part
of the plain is inundated by the waters of the Wadi
Bondári, which is called after the general name of
the low range bordering the plain. Having passed
several little villages of the sáhel, and paid my due
tribute of veneration to " el Dekhéle " (the oldest
and tallest palm-tree in the whole district), a little
before five o'clock in the afternoon I reached the
village called Zawíya Ferjáni, where we pitched our
tent in the stubble-field near a date-grove, and rested

from our pleasant day's march, experiencing hospitable treatment from our hosts.*

The country hereabouts is regarded as tolerably healthy, but 'Abd e' Saáde, a village a little further eastward, has suffered greatly from malignant fevers, which are attributed to the unwholesomeness of the waters of the Wadi Kúám, as I noticed on my former journey †; hence the population has become rather thin, and industry has declined. At some distance from the wadi, cultivation ceases entirely, and, instead of groves and gardens, a wide and wild field of disorder and destruction meets the eye. This rivulet, which is identical with the Cinyps, was in great vogue with the ancients, who knew how to control and regulate its occasional impetuosity. Immense walls, which they constructed as barriers against destructive inundations, remain to testify to their activity and energy. Of these one group, forming a whole system of dikes, some transverse, some built in the form of a semi-circle, is seen near the spot, where a beautiful subterranean aqueduct

---

* The inhabitants of the Sáhel in general, and those of Zliten and Masráta in particular, are more attached to the Turks than almost any other tribe of the regency; they would rather be subjected to a foreign power, than suffer oppression from their own brethren the Gedádefa and other tribes in the valleys of the interior. Hence, in the revolution in 1855, they remained faithful to the Turks; and a good many of them were killed in the first battle between the Turks and the rebel chief Ghóma.

† Wanderings along the Coasts of the Mediterranean, vol. i. p. 317.

which supplied Leptis issues from the wadi; another enormous wall, 650 yards long, and from 4 to 4½ yards thick, stands about three quarters of a mile higher up the valley. But with the details of all these works, though to me they appeared so interesting that I measured them with tolerable exactness, I will not detain the reader, but shall hasten to carry him back to Tripoli.

Having started in the afternoon from the mouth of the wadi, I re-entered Zawíya 'Abd el Ferjáni from the rear, but finding that my people had gone on to Leptis, I followed them, after a little delay, by the way of Wadi Súk, where every Thursday a market is held ("Súk el khamís," a name applied by Captain, now Rear-Admiral, Smyth to the neighbouring village), and then over the open meadow-plain, having the blue sea on my right, and came up with my people just as they were about to pitch my tent at the foot of an enormous staircase leading to some undefined monument in the eastern part of the ancient city of Leptis.

February 23rd.
During the forenoon I was busily employed in a second investigation of some of the ruins of Leptis, which have been so well described and illustrated by Admiral Smyth. Near the small creek called Mirsá Legátah, and a little east of the chapel of the Merábet ben Shehá, a small castle has been lately built by the Turks, about a hundred paces square. It has quite a handsome look with its pinnacles and small bastions.

Leaving the site of this celebrated city, we proceeded early in the afternoon, through a diversified hilly country, till we reached the high hill or mount of Merkeb* Saíd-n-'Alí, which is visible from a great distance. This I ascended in order to correct some of my positions, particularly that of el Gelláh in Mesellata, but found the wind too violent. Passing an undulating country, over-grown with the freshest green, and affording ample pastures to the herds of numerous Arab encampments, I pitched my tent near a small dowar of the Bení Jehem†, who treated us hospitably with sour milk and bazín.

The country continued varied, hill and dale succeeding each other; but beyond February 24th.
Kasr Aláhum (an irregular building of a late age), it became more rough and difficult, especially near the steep descent called Negási. Soon after this we descended into the plain, not far from the seashore, where we crossed several flat valleys. From the Wadi Bú Jefára‡, where a small caravan going from Zlíten to the town overtook us, a monotonous plain, called Gwaea mta Gummáta, extends to the very foot of the slope of Mesellata.. Having traversed the desolate

* Merkeb means here " the high seat."

† This tribe does not seem habitually to frequent this district, the indigenous name of which is Khoms. The principal tribes of this stock, named to me, were as follows: viz. the Sambára, the Shuwaig, Ziadát, Legáta, Shekhátra, Drúga, Argúb Jehawát, and Swaid.

‡ Smyth's Benzbárah, which he seems to have confounded in some degree with Wadi Terúggurt.

zone called el Míta mt'a Terúggurt, whence may be descried the " úglah" near the shore, the residence of my old friend the sheikh Khalífa bú-Ruffa, we reached the broad and rock-bound valley Terúggurt itself, probably the most perfect wadi which this part of the coast exhibits. To my great satisfaction I met Overweg at the Kasr Jefára.

K. Jefára is also called Karabúli, from the name of a Mamlúk who, in the time of Yusuf Basha, built here a sort of convent or chapel. It is rather a " funduk," or caravanserai, than a " kasr," or castle, and the gates are always left open; but its situation is important, and it is the residence of a judge or kaíd. A battle between Ghóma and the Turks was fought in 1855 at no great distance from it. The country around is a monotonous plain, enlivened only by three small clusters of palm-trees towards the north. The following morning we proceeded, and encamped on the eastern side of Wadi Raml. On Tuesday we returned to Tripoli well satisfied with our little excursion, and convinced that the Regency of Tripoli is not by any means so poor and miserable as it is generally believed to be.

Longitude East from Greenwich

London, Longman & Co.

CHAP. IV.

MEANWHILE the instruments provided by Government had arrived, and proved in general well adapted for their purposes.* But the tents and arms had not yet reached us; and I thought it better to provide a strong, spacious, and low tent, which, even after the Government tents arrived, did not prove superfluous, although perhaps rather too heavy. All tents intended for travellers in hot climates should be well lined, and not high. Those which we received were quite unfit for the country whither we were going, and while they were so light that they could hardly withstand a strong blast of wind, they scarcely excluded the sun, particularly after a little wear and

---

* Unfortunately the minimum and maximum thermometers were so deranged that Mr. Overweg was unable to repair them. We had no barometer, and the only aneroid barometer with which we had been provided, and which had been under the care of my companion, was damaged on our first excursion; so that nothing was left to us but to find the elevation of places by the boiling-point of water. I will here mention, for the use of future travellers, that I always wore not only my azimuth, but even my chronometer in my belt, and found this an excellent precaution against accidents of any kind.

tear. All the tents ought also to have top-ropes, which can alone secure them in a tornado such as are common in those climates. Mr. Richardson was soon obliged to provide himself with another tent, so that in the course of our journey we had altogether five tents, but generally pitched only two, or, where we encamped for a greater length of time, four.

Mr. Overweg and I sustained a heavy loss in the secession of our black servant Ibrahím, who might have proved of great service to us in the interior, as he spoke the Bórnu and Bagrímma languages, and had himself wandered about a good deal in those little-known districts between Mándará and Bagírmi. But he declared that he could not remain in our service along with our servant Mohammed ben Belál, the son of a liberated Góber slave, who was a very clever but unscrupulous and haughty fellow, and bore the character of a libertine. But another cause of detention was the protest of his wives, who would not allow him to go unless he divorced them. We tried every means of settling the matter, but without success; so that we had only two servants, one of whom, Mohammed e' Zintáni, the lad I have mentioned before, would certainly not go further than Fezzán.

At length all was ready for our outset, except the boat, which caused Mr. Richardson a great deal of trouble, as it had been divided in Malta into two pieces instead of four. I proposed that we should pitch our tents for some days at 'Aín Zára, in order that we might be duly seasoned for our long journey.

I would advise every traveller, who would calculate upon all the means of ensuring success, to adopt a similar course. A few days' stay in his tent will familiarize him with the little store which is henceforward to form his principal, if not his only resource, and will enable him to bear the heat of the sun with ease.

It was late in the afternoon of the 24th of March, 1850, when Overweg and I, seated in solemn state upon our camels, left the town with our train, preceded by the consul, Mr. Crowe, in his carriage, by Mr. Reade, and by Mr. Dickson and his family, of whom we took a hearty leave under the olive-trees near Kasr el Haeni. We then continued our route, and in fine moonlight pitched our tent on the border of 'Aín Zára.

This locality takes its name from a broad swampy hollow or depression to the south, thickly overgrown with reeds and rushes. At present no one lives in it; the wells are filled up with earth, and the date-trees, cared for by nobody, are partly overwhelmed by the sand which has accumulated in large mounds. Still it is an attractive spot, having just a little of cultivation and a little of sandy waste. A few olive-trees spread their fresh cool shade over a green meadow, forming a very pleasant resting-place. It was at this very spot that, in August 1855, on my joyful return, I again met Mr. Reade the vice-consul, and passed a night there.

Here we remained encamped till Friday the 29th.

In the afternoon of the 27th, Mr. Frederic Warrington, who wished to escort us for a few days, came out, accompanied by the American consul Mr. Gaines, and brought us the satisfactory news, that on the following Friday Mr. Richardson would move from the town, and that we should meet him at Mejenín. I and my countryman required eight camels for our luggage, besides the two which we rode ourselves, and which were our own. I should have preferred having a donkey for myself, as it would have enabled me to go with ease wherever I liked; but in Tripoli there are no donkeys strong enough for such a journey, and a horse, including the carriage of barley and water for him, was too expensive for the means then placed at my disposal. But I had been so fortunate as to procure an excellent Arab camel of the renowned breed of the Bú-Saef, which was my faithful companion as far as Kúkawa; and Mr. Warrington had made me a present of a handsome Ghadamsi saddle or basúr, with pillows and Stambúli carpet, so that I was comfortably mounted.

Friday, March 29th. After a great deal of trouble (the camel-drivers and our men being as yet unaccustomed to our unwieldy luggage), we at length succeeded in making a start. After leaving the olive-trees and the little palm-grove of 'Aín Zára, we very soon entered deep sand-hills, which sheltered us from the strong wind; and after more than two hours we came upon pasture-grounds, which furnished our camels with a variety of herbs

and gramineæ, such as the shâde, the shedíde, and
various others unknown to me. The progress of an
Arab caravan (where the camels march each after
its own inclination, straying to the right and to the
left, nipping here a straw, and there browsing on a
bush) must be rather slow in districts where the
stubborn animal finds abundance of food. This way
of proceeding is extremely tedious and fatiguing to
the rider; and to obviate it the Tawárek, the Téb,
and the people in the interior fasten all the camels
one behind the other. Owing to our slow progress,
the sun was almost setting when we overtook Mr.
Warrington, who had pitched his tent on a fine pasture-ground near Bir Sbaea. The last hour and a
half's ride from the well Jenáwa lay along well-
cultivated and flourishing corn-fields extending along
the narrow wadi of Mejenín*, and intermingled with
a rich profusion of flowers, principally the beautiful
blue " khobbés."

Having indulged for some hours in the   Saturday,
quiet enjoyment of a fine morning and an   March 30th.
open green country, I went with the shoush to look
after Mr. Richardson's party. After an hour's ride
through luxuriant corn-fields, and pasture-grounds
enlivened by the horses of the Turkish cavalry, we
found Mukni, the sailor, and all Mr. Richardson's
baggage; but he himself had not yet come up. I

* The place probably derives its name from the *Ruta tuber-
culata,* " Mejníneh."

could not persuade the people to remove to our encampment; so I returned, after having paid a visit
to the binbásha of the cavalry, who had been stationed here for the last seventeen years. He had
contrived to procure himself a cool retreat from the
sultry hours, by forming a regular tank, about two
feet and a half square, in the midst of his tent, and
keeping it always full of water.

In the afternoon I made a long excursion with my
Zintáni through the plain, beyond the chapel of Sidi
Bargúb, in order to buy a sheep; but though the
flocks were numerous, none of the shepherds would
sell, as pasturage was abundant and everyone had
what he wanted. In 1846, when I first visited the
regency, the people were starving, and selling their
camels and everything they possessed to procure
food.

Foggy weather indicated that rain was
approaching; and just in time Mr.
Richardson with his party arrived, and pitched his
enormous lazaretto tent opposite our little encampment. Mr. Reade also had come from the town,
in order to settle, if possible, the misunderstand-
ing with our servant Mohammed, and see us off.
It is an agreeable duty for me to acknowledge the
many services which this gentleman rendered us
during our stay in Tripoli. Our whole party was
detained here the following day by the heavy rains;
and Overweg and I were happy to get hold of the
black servant of the ferocious pseudo-sheríf mentioned

Sunday,
March 31st.

by Mr. Richardson, when that troublesome fellow was sent back to town, as we were much in want of another servant.

We fairly set out on our expedition. The country became more diversified as _{April 2nd.} we approached the defile formed by the Bátes and Smaera, two advanced posts of the mountain-chain, while the varied forms of the latter, in high cones and deep abrupt valleys, formed an interesting background. But the country hereabouts is cultivated with less care than Wadi Mejenín; and the ground being more stony, presents of course more obstacles than the latter, while both districts are inhabited by the same tribes, viz. the Urgáat and the Akára. Even here, however, in the circle formed by the surrounding heights, was a fine extent of plain covered with corn-fields. Just at the entrance of the pass there is a well, where the road divides; and after a little consultation, we took the western branch, as our people feared that on the eastern we should not find water before night. Changing, therefore, our direction, we seemed awhile to keep off entirely from the mountain-range till we reached the wide but very rugged and rocky Wadi Haera, which it was our object to reach at this spot, in order to fill our water-skins from the pools formed by the rains. The wadi, indeed, looked as if it sometimes bore in its floods a powerful body of water; and a considerable dike had been constructed in the early times of the Arabs, extending for two hundred paces from

the wadi eastward; but it has fallen to ruin, and
the path leads now through the breach.

Resuming our march, after a good deal of delay,
we turned sharp off towards the mountains, and at
an early hour encamped on a very pleasant spot
adorned with numerous sidr-trees (*Rhamnus Nabeca*);
but instead of enjoying it in quiet, Overweg and I
felt disposed to direct our steps towards a hill called
Fulíje, about half an hour's walk eastward, which
promised to be a convenient point for obtaining correct angles of the prominent features of the chain,
and proved to be so in reality. Having executed this
task, therefore, we returned to our companions well
satisfied, and spent the evening in the comfortable tent
of Mr. Warrington. We had now reached the slope
of the chain, where some of our people supposed that
the boat would cause difficulties; but it could not
well do so after being cut into quarters, which fitted
to the sides of the camels rather better than the large
quadrangular boxes. The most troublesome parts were
the long oars and poles, which caused the camel
much exhaustion and fatigue, by constantly swaying
backwards and forwards.

The ground, soon after we had started the next
morning, became stony, and, at three miles' distance,
very rugged and intersected by a number of dry
watercourses. The landscape was enlivened not only
by our own caravan, composed of so many hetero-
geneous elements, but also by some other parties who
happened to be coming down the slope: first, the

Kaimakám of the Jébel, then a slave caravan, consisting of about sixty of these poor creatures, of
whom the younger, at least, seemed to take a cheerful
interest in the varied features of the country.   The
Wadi Bú Ghelán, where the ascent commences, is
here and there adorned with clusters of date-trees.   In
about an hour the first camels of our party reached the
terrace of Bení 'Abbás; and till the whole had accomplished the ascent, I had leisure to dismount from my
tractable Bú-saefi, and to sit down quietly under a fine
olive-tree near the chapel of the Merábet Sámes,
watching them as they came up one by one, and
cheered by the conviction that the expedition was
at length in full train.   The country was here hilly,
and the path often very narrow and deeply cut in
the marly soil.   Further on, Overweg and I, together with our shoush, turned off a little to the right
from the great caravan-road, and, passing through
fine corn-fields interspersed with flowers of different
kinds, reached the village Gwásem, lying at a short
distance from the eastern foot of Mount Tekút, where
we were treated with sour milk by a friend of our
companions.   When we had overtaken our caravan,
I found time to pay a visit to the Roman sepulchre *, and ascertained that the base measured 24 ft.
in every direction, the principal body of the monument, containing the sepulchral chamber, having
fallen in entirely.   From this point we began to

* See above, p. 45.

ascend the second terrace, and reached the level of the plateau at two o'clock in the afternoon. The country had now a much more interesting appearance than when I was here two months before, being at present all covered with green corn. Having started in the direction of the castle, we descended, a little before reaching it, along the shelving ground towards Wadi Rummána, and encamped on the spot where the troups usually bivouac.

Here we remained the following day, when, in order to settle formally the demands of our camel-drivers, we had all our things accurately weighed by the officials of the castle. The little market did not grow busy till ten o'clock. The chief articles for sale were three head of cattle, one camel, some sheep and goats, a few water-skins, some barley, a few eggs, and sandals; but at noon it was moderately thronged. In the afternoon we paid a visit to several subterranean dwellings, but were disappointed in not getting access into an entirely new structure of this kind, formed of a much harder sort of clay. Our cheerful friend Mr. Warrington, in order to treat our party before he separated from it for a length of time which nobody could foresee, got an immense bowl of kuskus prepared, seasoned in the most savoury manner; and our whole party long indulged in the remembrance of this delicate dish as a luxury beyond reach. The site of our encampment was most pleasant: below us the wadi, rich with varied vegetation; while towards the north the

Tekút, with its regularly-shaped crater towering proudly over the lower eminences around, formed a most interesting object.

Though busy at an early hour, we did not get off till late; for many things were still to be settled here. We separated from Mr. Warrington; and of the three travellers I was the only one whom he was ever to see again.

Our path was at first very winding, as we had to turn round the deep indentation of the Wadi Rummána, after which it took a straighter course, passing through several villages, with their respective olive-groves, till we reached Bu Sriyán, where the cultivation of the olive-tree ceased entirely for some distance, and the country became more open. Here we made another considerable deviation from our southerly direction, and followed a wide valley with much cultivated ground. Having reached the village Sémsa, situated upon an eminence to our right, we turned off eastward into a very pleasant ravine with an olive-grove, and then began the steep ascent towards the height Kuléba*, which forms the passage over this southern crest of the plateau. While the camels in long rows moved slowly onwards, with their heavy loads, on the narrow and steep rocky path, I, allowing my camel to follow the rest, ascended directly to the village, which is situated round the

---

* "Kuléba," or "kelúba," is a term of frequent occurrence in these districts for a high mountain-top. In some respects it seems to be identical with the term "thníye," used in other districts.

eastern slope, and is still tolerably well inhabited, although many a house has fallen to ruin; for it has a considerable extent of territory; and owing to its situation as the southernmost point of Ghurián, the inhabitants are the natural carriers and agents between the northern districts and the desert. On the highest crest, commanding the village, there was formerly a castle; but it has been destroyed by the Turks.

Having descended a little into the barren valley, we encamped, at two o'clock in the afternoon, on the slope of the western hills, near the last scanty olive-trees, and not far from the well, from which we intended to take a sufficient supply of water to last us till we reached Mizda. While our people, therefore, were busy watering the camels and filling our water-skins, Overweg and I, accompanied by two of the inhabitants of the village, who had followed us, ascended a conspicuous mount, Jebel Toëshe, the highest in the neighbourhood, on the top of which a village is said to have existed in former times. We took several angles; but there is no very high point about Mizda which could serve as a landmark in that direction.

Saturday, April 6th. The country through which we were marching, along irregular valleys, mostly of limestone formation, exhibited scattered patches of corn for about the first three miles, after which almost every sign of cultivation suddenly ceased, and the " Twél el Khamér," stretching from N.W. to S.E., about two miles distant on the right, formed, as it were, the northern boundary of the naked soil. On its slope a few trees of the kind called radúk by the Arabs were seen from the distance. We then entered desolate stony valleys, famous for the bloody skirmishes which are said to have once taken place there between the Urfilla and the Welád Bú Séf, in the time of 'Abd el Jelíl. Refreshing, therefore, was the aspect of Wadi Ranne, which, extending from E. to S.W., was overgrown with green herbage, and had two wells.

A little beyond, near the hill, or rather slope, called Sh'abet el Kadím, the latter part of which name seems, indeed, to have some reference to antiquity, we found the first Roman milestone, with the inscription now effaced; but further on, Mr. Overweg, who went on foot and was far behind the main body of our caravan, succeeded in discovering some milestones with inscriptions, which he regretted very much not being able to show to me. Hereabouts commences the region of the batúm-tree, which, with the fresh green of its foliage, contributes a good deal to enliven and adorn some favoured spots of this sterile, gravelly tract. To the left of our path were some remarkable basaltic cones, starting up from the calcareous ridge. The ground was strewn with numerous flint-stones. About four o'clock P.M. I went to look at a curious quadrangular and regularly-hewn stone, three feet in breadth and length, but only eight inches thick, which was standing

upright at some distance from the caravan. It was
evidently meant to face the west; but no trace of
an inscription was to be seen. About a mile further
on we encamped at the foot of the western chain,
which rose to a height of about 300 feet, and formed
a narrow cleft with the eastern chain, which at this
point closes upon it. In this corner (which collects
the humidity of two valleys), besides several batúm-
trees, a little corn had been sown. Panthers are
said to be numerous in this region.

The next day we directed our march towards the
pass, crossing the dry beds of several small torrents,
and a broader channel bordered by plenty of batúm-
trees. After an hour's march, we had reached the
summit of the pass, which now began to widen, the
heights receding on each side, and a more distant
range bounding the view. We found in the holes
of the rocky bottom of Wadi Mezummíta, which
we crossed about half-past eight, several pools of
rain-water, affording us a most refreshing drink;
but it was quite an extra treat, owing to recent
heavy rains which had fallen here, for in general
the traveller cannot rely on finding water in this
place. The ground becoming very stony and rugged,
our progress was excessively slow — not above
half an English geographical mile in seventeen
minutes. The hills on our right displayed to the
view regular layers of sandstone. Another long
defile followed, which at length brought us to a
plain called Wadi Lilla, encompassed by hills, and

offering several traces of former cultivation, while
other traces, further on, bore testimony to the industry of the Romans.   A small herd of goats, and the
barking of a dog, showed that even at present the
country is not wholly deserted.   In our immediate
neighbourhood it even became more than usually
enlivened by the passage of a slave-caravan, with
twenty-five camels and about sixty slaves, mostly
females.

After having passed a small defile, we at length
emerged into the north-west branch of the valley of
Mizda, called here Wadi Udé-Sheráb, the channel of
which is lined with a considerable number of batúm-
trees.   Crossing the stony bottom of this plain, after
a stretch of three miles more we reached the western
end of the oasis of Mizda, which, though my fancy
had given it a greater extent, filled me with joy at
the sight of the fine fields of barley, now approaching
maturity — the crop, owing to the regular irrigation,
being remarkably uniform — while the grove of date-
trees encompassed the whole picture with a striking
and interesting frame.   So we proceeded, passing
between the two entirely-separated quarters, or villages, distinguished as the upper, " el fók," and the
lower, " el utah," and encamped on the sandy open
space a little beyond the lower village, near a well
which formerly had irrigated a garden. People going
to Tripoli encamp at the other end of the oasis, as
was done by a caravan of Ghadamsi people with
slaves from Fezzán, on the following day.

Mizda, most probably identical with the eastern
" Musti kome " of Ptolemy, appears to have been an
ancient settlement of the indigenous inhabitants of
North Africa, the Berbers, and more particularly of
a family or tribe of them called " Kuntarár," who
even at present, though greatly intermixed with
Arabs, have not entirely forgotten their Berber idiom.
The oasis lies in the upper part of Wadi Sófejín, or
rather a branch of it, stretching out from S.W. to
N.E., which has in some parts a great breadth. The
natural advantage, or productive principle, of the
locality seems to lie in the circumstance that the
humidity carried down by the Wadi Sheráb is here
arrested by a hill, and absorbed by the clayey soil.
This hill is of a lengthened form, and consists entirely of gypsum. From its summit, which affords the
best prospect of the whole locality, I made a view
of the western village; while from a more elevated
height further west, called Madúm, I made the accompanying sketch of the whole locality.

The wells have little depth, and the water is drawn
to the surface by means of oxen; but there being at
present only three specimens of this precious animal
in the place, the wells are far from being made use of
to the extent which is practicable and has been once
practised, as may be concluded from the pillars which
extend to a considerable distance on the plain. The
town, as I said, consists of two distinct quarters or
villages, of which the western one, situated at the
eastern foot of the hill, is by far the larger; it is

..., most probably ... with the ...;
"Maci kome" of Ptolemy, appears to have been an
ancient settlement of the indigenous inhabitants of
North Africa, the Berbers, and more particularly of
a ... tribe of them called "Kuntarir," who
..., though ... mostly intermixed with
Arabs ... recently ... their Berber idiom.
The ... the upper part of Wadi Sofejin, or
... back of it, stretching out from S.W. to
... in some parts a great breadth. The
... the ... productive principle, of the
... in the circumstance that the
... down by the Wadi Sherds is here
... and ... by the clayey soil.
This ... of a ... form, and consists
... From its summit, which affords ...
... prospect of the ... locality, i ... a ...
of the ... villages; while from a more elevat..
height ... west, called Madum, i made the
... sketch of the whole locality.
The wells have little depth, and the water ...
... of ...; but there ...
... of this ...
in the ... far from being ...
to the ... is practicable and ...
... secluded from the pillars ...
... distance on the plain.
... of two distinct quarters
... of which ... are situated
... of the hill is by ... larger

built exactly in the character of the ksúr of the
Algerian Sahara, with high round towers decreasing

a little in width towards the upper part, and furnished with several rows of loopholes. The wall,
purposely built with a great many salient and re-
tiring angles, is in a state of decay, and many of
the houses are in ruins; but the village can still
boast a hundred full-grown men able to bear arms.
The chief of this village always resides in it, while
that of the other generally lives at some distance
under tents. The circumference of the village, together with the palm-grove attached to its eastern
side, and consisting of about 200 trees, is 2260 paces.

The lower or south-eastern village, the circumference of which is 600 paces, is separated from the

itself is on the general level of the plateau; but we obtained a fine view over the sea of heights surrounding the broad valley and the several tributaries of which it is formed. Night was setting in, and we returned to our tent.

Having heard our Zintáni make frequent mention of an ancient castle with numerous sculptures, and situated at no great distance, I resolved to visit it, and set out tolerably early in the morning of the 9th of April, accompanied by the Arab and one of our shoushes.

We had first to send for one of our camels, which was grazing at about three miles' distance, in the sandy bottom of the wadi S.E. from our encampment. It was only on this occasion that I became aware of the exact nature of the valley of Mizda, and its relation to the Wadi Sófejín; for we did not reach this latter wadi until we had traversed the whole breadth of the sandy plain, and crossed a mountain-spur along a defile called Khurmet bu Mátek, at the distance of at least eight miles from our encampment. This is the famous valley mentioned, in the 11th century, by the celebrated Andalusian geographer El Bekrí[*], and the various produce of which the Arabs of the present day celebrate in song:—

rás-há e' ttín ú merjín
ú wost-há bazín
ú ghár-há ájín.

[*] There cannot be the least doubt that this valley is meant in the passage cited in "Notices et Extraits," vol. xii. p. 453.; compare Journal Asiatique, série v. tom. i. 156.

Figs and olive-trees adorn its upper part, which is said to stretch out as far as Erhebát, a district one day and a half beyond Zintán; barley is cultivated in its middle course, while wheat, from which the favourite dish 'ajín is made, is grown chiefly in its lower part near Tawárgha. The valley seems worthy of better fortune than that to which it is reduced at present; for when we marched along it, where it ran S. 20 W. to N. 20 E., we passed ruins of buildings and water-channels, while the soil exhibited evident traces of former cultivation. I listened with interest to the Zintáni, who told me that the valley produced an excellent kind of barley, and that the Kuntarár, as well as the people of Zintán, his countrymen, and the Welád Bú-Séf, vied with each other in cultivating it, and, in former times at least, had often engaged in bloody contests for the proprietorship of the ground. When I expressed my surprise at his joining the name of his countrymen with those of the other tribes hereabouts, he gave me the interesting information that the Zintán had been the first and most powerful of all the tribes in this quarter before the time of the Turks, and held all this country in a state of subjection. Since then their political power and influence had been annihilated, but they had obtained by other means right of possession in Mizda as well as in Gharíya, and still further, in the very heart of Fezzán, by lending the people money to buy corn, or else corn in kind, and had in this way obtained the proprietorship of a great number of the date-trees, which were cultivated and taken care of by the inhabitants for a share of the produce. Formerly the people of Zintán were in possession of a large castle, where they stored up their provisions; but since the time of the Turkish dominion, their custom has been to bring home the fruits of their harvests only as they want them. In Wadi Sháti we were to meet a caravan of these enterprising people.

While engaged in this kind of conversation we entered a smaller lateral valley of Wadi Sófejín, and reached the foot of a projecting hill on its western side, which is crowned with a castle. Here it was

that I was to find marvellous ancient sculptures and drawings; but I soon perceived that it would be

as well not to cherish any high expectations. The
castle, as it now stands, is evidently an Arab edifice
of an early period, built of common stones hewn with
some regularity, and set in horizontal layers, but not
all of the same thickness. It forms almost a regular
square, and contains several vaulted rooms, all arranged with a certain degree of symmetry and regularity. But while we pronounce the main building
to be Arab, the gateway appears to be evidently of
Roman workmanship, and must have belonged to
some older edifice which the Arab chieftain who
built this castle probably found in the place,— a conjecture which seems to be confirmed by several ornamental fragments lying about.

It is a pity that we know so little of the domestic
history of these countries during the period of the
Arab dynasties, though a step in advance has been
made by the complete publication of Ebn Khaldún's
history; else we should regard with more interest
these relics of their days of petty independence. This
castle, as well as another, the description of which I
shall subjoin here, though it was visited some days
later, is called after a man named Khafáji 'Aámer,
who is said to have been a powerful chief of great
authority in Tunis no less than in Tarábolus (Tripoli).*

* For this statement there may be, indeed, some historical
foundation. We know that, from the year of the hejra 724 (1323
A. D.) till the year 802 (1399), there reigned in Tripoli a dynasty of
the Beni 'Aámer (Haji Khalfa's Chronological Tables, p. 167.),

The other ruin, related to this one as well by name
as by the style of its workmanship — but in many

respects more interesting, having been evidently once
a place of Christian worship — stands on a narrow
and detached neck of rock in the Shàbet Um el Kharáb, and, from its whole plan, appears to have been
originally and principally a church about forty-three
feet square, sufficiently large for a small congregation,
and with more art and comfort than one can easily
suppose a Christian community in these quarters ever

who most probably were related to the dynasty of the same name
which for a long time maintained its dominion over Tripolis in
Syria.

to have possessed. Hence greater interest attaches
to this building than it would otherwise deserve. It

closes with a plain apsis, in which there are two
openings or doorways leading into an open room
stretching behind it and the side-naves, and is divided
into three naves, the middle one of which is eight
paces, and the lateral ones six and a half, wide. The

naves are divided from one another by columns with
differently-ornamented capitals supporting arches, all
in the so-called round style of architecture. I made

purposely a sketch of two different capitals, in order
to show their designs; and I think they are very
characteristic. But it is curious to observe that the
walls also appear to have been originally painted on
stucco, though at present but a small piece of it remains near the corner; hence I conclude that the
date of the painting was later than that of the erec-
tion of the church.

The front of the building has suffered in some
degree from the depredations of the Arabs, who are
said to have carried away a great many sculptures
from this place—as much, indeed, a man from Mizda
would have made me believe, as fifty-five camel-loads.
However exaggerated this statement may be, it is
evident that the whole layer over the entrance was
originally covered with ornamental slabs, while now
only two remain to the left of the doorway; and
these, though in the same style of sculpture as the
capitals, would rather seem to have been taken from
another edifice. There are many debatable points
involved in the consideration of this building. The
first fact clearly shown is the existence of a Christian
community or a monastery in these remote valleys,
as late as the 12th century at least, under the protection of a powerful chief; and this is not at all
improbable, as we know that Mohammed expressly
ordered that zealous priests and monks should be
spared, and as we find so many monasteries in
several other Mohammedan countries. That it was
not merely a church, but a monastery, seems plainly

indicated by the division into apartments or cells, which is still clearly to be seen in the upper storey.

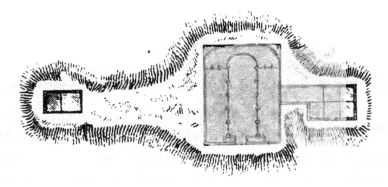

Attached to the north side of the church was a wing containing several simple apartments, as the ground-plan shows; and on the south corner of the narrow ridge is a small separate tower with two compart-ments.   Near this ruin there is another, which I did not visit, called Ksaer Labayed mtà Derayer, while a third, called Ksaer el Haemer, has been destroyed.

CHAP. V.

We lost the best part of the morning, our
April 11th. men not being able to find their camels,
which had roamed over the whole wadi. Our road
was almost the same as that by which I had returned
the previous day; and we encamped in the Wadi
Sófejín, on a spot free from bushes. From this place,
accompanied by the Zintáni, I visited, the next morning, the castle or convent in Shábet Um el kharáb,
which I have described, and thence struck across the
stony plateau in order to overtake our caravan. It
was a desolate level, rarely adorned with humble
herb or flower; and we hastened our steps to reach
our companions. Here I heard, from the Zintáni,
that his father came every year about this season,
with his flocks, to the valleys east of our road, and
that he would certainly be there this year also. He
invited me to go thither with him, and to indulge
in milk to the extent of my wishes; as for myself, I
declined, but allowed him to go, on condition that
he would return to us as soon as possible.

Even after we had overtaken the caravan, the
country continued in general very bare; but we
passed some valleys affording a good deal of herbage,

or adorned with some fine batúm-trees. About five
o'clock P. M. we encamped in Wadi Talha, not far
from a Roman castle or tower on a hill to our left.
On visiting the ruin, I found it built of rough stones

without cement, being about twenty feet square in
the interior, with rounded corners, and with only
one narrow gate, towards the east. But this was
not the only remnant of antiquity in the neighbourhood, for in front of us, on the plateau, there appeared something like a tower of greater elevation;
and proceeding early the next morning, when our
people had only begun to load, to examine it, I
found it to be a Roman sepulchre, originally consisting apparently of three stories; but of these only
the base and the first story remain, while the stones

belonging to the upper one are now scattered on the
ground, and show that it was ornamented with small
Corinthian columns at the corners. Even in the
most desolate spot, everything left by the Romans
has a peculiar finish. The first story, being all that
at present remains, measures 5 ft. 4 in. on the east
and west, and 5 ft. 9 in. on the north and south sides.
Not far from this sepulchre are the ruins of another
one, of which, however, nothing but the base remains,
if, indeed, it was ever completed. By the time my
drawing was finished, the caravan had come up.

I then passed several detached cones, the steep
precipitous sides of which, formed by the breaking
away of the strata, looked like so many castles, and
traversing Wadi Marsíd, reached the camels. They
marched to-day at a very good rate, the quickest we
had as yet observed in ordinary travelling—namely,
half a mile in twelve minutes, making a little less
than 2½ miles an hour; but we afterwards found that
this had now become our usual rate, whereas before
reaching Mizda we had scarcely ever exceeded 2 miles
an hour. The loads of the camels, of course, had
been heavier in the beginning; but this can hardly
be the only reason of the difference. The greater
dreariness of the country, and the impulse of our
camel-drivers and their beasts to get to their homes,
must be taken into account. I must here observe
that Overweg and I measured our rate repeatedly,
with a chain provided by Government, although it
was a very fatiguing labour, and injurious to our

dignity in the eyes of our people. Gradually the day grew very uncomfortable, a hot west wind driving the sand into our faces, and totally obscuring the sky. Keeping along the Wadi Téroth, sometimes more than a mile wide, we had on our left a broad mount, rising first with a gradual ascent, but in its upper part forming a steep and lofty wall called el Khaddamíyeh. Here too, according to the information of my faithful Arab, there is said to be a Roman sepulchre. Having passed a small defile, and crossed another valley, we had other Roman ruins on our right, a castle as it seemed, and near it something like a sepulchre; but the sand-storm hardly allowed us to look, still less to go in that direction.

At three o'clock in the afternoon we turned off to the west into Wadi Tagíje, and encamped near the bed of a torrent eight feet deep, which amply testifies that, at times, a considerable stream is formed here, a fact confirmed by the fresh and luxuriant herbage springing up in many parts of the valley among thick bushes and brushwood. Nor was it quite desolate even now; for the flocks of the Welád Bú-Séf were seen, and their tents were said to be not far off. The upper part of the valley is called el Khurrub.

This hot day proved a *dies ater* to my Arab, who had gone to visit his family. Having brought his old father with him, together with a goat, as a present, and a skin of milk, he unluckily arrived too late in the morning at our last night's encampment. He then sent his father back with the goat, and

began to follow us in the hope of soon overtaking
the caravan; but he was obliged to march the whole
intensely hot day without water, and he could not
drink the milk in the skin, which became quite hot,
so that he suffered greatly, and arrived in a very
exhausted state.

The fine herbage procured us a whole day's rest,
as the camel-drivers were in no haste to bring up
their camels. Not knowing this, but yet convinced
that we should not start at an early hour, as the well
was at some distance, and following the information
received from the Zintáni, who was himself too lame
to accompany me, I had taken my gun and pistols at
an early hour in the morning, and gone in the direction of the valley to look after a monument. After
nearly two hours' march I distinguished something
like a high pillar, and, proceeding straight towards
it, found it to be one of the richest specimens of this
kind of monument bequeathed to us by antiquity,
and an indisputable proof that these regions, now so
poor, must have then supported a population sufficiently advanced in taste and feeling to admire works
of a refined character.

The monument rises, upon a base of three steps
and in three stories, nearly to a height of forty-eight
feet. The base contains a sepulchral chamber 4 ft.
10½ in. long, and 4 ft. ⅛ in. broad, with three niches,
one on the north, and two on the east side. This
side was the principal face of the monument, forming its most ornamented part. The first story mea-

sures at its base on the E. and W. sides 5 feet 5⅜
inches, and on the N. and S. sides 4 feet 10⅛ inches:

it consists of six layers of stones, on the lowest of which is represented a pair of wild animals, probably panthers, with their forelegs or paws resting upon a sepulchral urn, as if they were watching it; on the next layer above is seen the handsome bust of a young female; two layers intervene without sculpture; and the fifth is ornamented on all the four sides with hunting-scenes. The frieze on every side is formed by four rosettes; but that on the north side has some additional decoration, the second rosette on that side, from the east, exhibiting a group of centaurs, and the fourth a cock. Upon this part of the frieze is a garland of clusters of grapes; then follows the moulding.

In the second story the third layer forms the sill and lower part of a false door very richly ornamented, and on the fifth layer a pair of genii hold a coronal over the door of the sepulchre, a representation which seems to intimate Christian ideas. Above it a niche contains the busts of a man and his wife; but on the north side an elderly woman occupies a niche with her bust, probably in her character as proprietress of the single sepulchral niche of the tomb below. Above is an ornament with two bunches of grapes; and then follows the frieze, of the common Ionic order. The moulding is surmounted by a pyramidal roof about 12 feet high, which has lost its summit; otherwise the whole monument, with the exception of the sepulchral chamber, which has been broken up in search of treasures, is in the best state of preservation, notwithstanding its very slender proportions,—a circumstance very remarkable, after a lapse of at least more than sixteen centuries. No wonder that the natives of these regions now regard these tall sepulchral monuments, so strange at present in this land of desolation, as pagan idols, and call them "sanem;" for I myself, when alone in front of the monument in this wide, solitary valley, and under the shadow of the deep, precipitous side of a plateau adjoining the Khaddamíye on the east, felt impressed by it with a certain degree of awe and veneration.

My sketch being finished, I was still attracted to a greater distance up the valley by something which seemed at first to be another monument; but it was only a mark fixed by the Arabs, and served but to lengthen my march back, which was more slow, as the heat had set in. But I was well satisfied with my morning's work; and my companions were greatly astonished when they saw the sketch. In the afternoon I made with Overweg another excursion in the opposite direction, when after an hour's march we ascended a height and obtained a most interesting view over this singular tract, which seems to be the fragmentary border of a plateau torn and severed by ravines and precipices, so that only wall-like cliffs, rising like so many islands out of a sea of desolation, indicate its height. A high craggy ridge towards the west, with precipitous pinnacled walls, looked like a castle of the demons. Just in a ravine on the border of this wild scene of natural revolutions, my companion had the good luck to find some very interesting fossils, particularly that beautiful specimen which after him has been called Exogyra Overwegi; but our zeal had carried us too far, and it grew dark as we commenced our return, so that we had some difficulty in groping our way back to our encampment, where we arrived weary and fatigued, after having caused our people a good deal of apprehension.

We were roused from our refreshing sleep as early as two o'clock after midnight; but this was a mere sham of our camel-drivers, who feigned making up for the loss of yesterday, and after all we did not get off early. Our road carried us from wadi to wadi, which were generally separated from each other by a defile, occasionally presenting some difficulty of passage. We left a castle of Roman workmanship, as it seemed, in the distance to the left, and further on to the right a slight stone wall called Hakl el Urínsa, dating from the petty wars between the Arab tribes. We had already passed a few small ethel-bushes; but now we came to a most venerable-looking old tree called Athelet Sí Mohammed fí Useát, spreading out its weatherbeaten branches to a considerable distance: under this I sat down quietly for a while, waiting for our people, who were still behind. The caravan at length came up; and continuing our march, we soon passed on our right hand the chapel of a great Merábet of the Welád Bú-Séf, called Si Rashedán. The Welád Bú-Séf in general enjoy great authority with the other tribes for their

April 14th.

sanctity of life and purity of manners; they allow no
stranger to come near their villages, but pitch a tent
for him at a distance, and treat him well.   The person at present most distinguished among them for
learning seems to be an old man named Sídi Bú-bakr,
who exercises great influence, and is able to grant
serviceable protection to travellers in time of war.

The Welád Bú-Séf are remarkable for the excellent
breed of their camels, which they treat almost as
members of their families. It is curious that this
tribe, intent upon right and justice, has waged war
incessantly from ancient times with the Urfílla, the
most warlike and violent of the tribes of these regions.
It is difficult to make out whether they are related
to the Welád Bú-Séf of the western part of the desert,
who are likewise distinguished by their peculiar manners, but who it seems would scruple, on religious
grounds, to call a man 'Abd e' Nebí (Slave of the
Prophet), which is the name of the ancestor of the
Eastern Bú-Séf.

Emerging from a defile, upon high ground, early in
the afternoon, we obtained a view over Wadi Zemzem,
one of the most celebrated valleys of this part of North
Africa.   It runs in general from W. to E.N.E., and
is furnished with a great many wells, the most famous
of which are El Abiadh, Oméla, Nákhala, Urídden,
Halk el Wadi, and, a little further down, Téder.   In
half an hour we encamped in the valley, full of herbage and with a goodly variety of trees.   A caravan
coming from the natron-lakes, and carrying their

produce to Tripoli, was here encamped. I could not withstand the temptation of ascending, in the afternoon, a projecting eminence on the south side of the valley, which was broken and rent into a great variety of precipices and ravines ; but its summit, being on a level with the plateau, did not afford me such a distant view as I had expected. The cliff was formed of strata of marl and gypsum, and contained many fossil shells.

Monday, April 15th. As soon as we left the bottom of the valley, the path, which became rugged and stony, led up the southern cliffs, went round the east side of the conspicuous promontory, and then continued to wind along between the slopes of the higher level of the plateau. A hill, distinguished from among the surrounding heights by the peculiar shape of its cone, has here received the significant name Shúsh el ábíd — the Slaves' Cap. A little further on, the roads separate, that to the left leading along the principal branch of the valley to the little town Gharíya, while the eastern goes to the well Taboníye.

One might suppose that in a desolate country like this, and just at the entrance into a desert tract of great extent, the caravans would gladly avail themselves of those abodes of life which still exist : but this is not the case ; they avoid them intentionally, as if a curse were attached to them, and those places, of course, fall every day more and more into decay. After a little consultation, the path by Taboníye was thought preferable, and we took it. The rough and

stony character of the country ceased, and we gradually entered a fine valley, called Wadi Tolágga,
richly clothed with a variety of trees and bushes,
such as the sidr, the ethel, the ghurdok, and several
others.   After meeting here with a caravan, we caught
the gladdening and rare sight of an Arab encampment, belonging to the Urínsa, and obtained some
milk.   Without crossing any separation or defile, but
always keeping along the same valley, we approached
the well Taboníye.   But near it the vegetation is less
rich; the soil is intermixed with salt, and covered
with a peculiar kind of low tree called by the present
inhabitants of the country, frò,—a term which in
pure Arabic would only mean "a branch."

While our people were busily employed pitching
the tents, I went at once to examine a monument
which, for the last hour of our march, had stood as a
landmark ahead of us.   I reached it at the distance
of a mile and a quarter from our encampment, over
very stony and rugged ground.   It was well worth
the pains I had taken; for, though it is less magnificent than the monument in W. Tagíje, its workmanship would excite the interest of travellers, even
if it were situated in a fertile and well-inhabited
country, and not in a desolate wilderness like this,
where a splendid building is of course an object
of far greater curiosity.   It is a sepulchre about
twenty-five feet high, and rising in three stories of
less slender proportions than the monument above
described, and is probably of a later period.   The

accompanying sketch will suffice to give an exact idea of it.

Near this is another sepulchre, occupying a more

commanding situation, and therefore probably of older date, but it is almost entirely destroyed ; and a third one in an equally ruinous state, but of larger proportions than either, is seen further S.E. These monuments serve to show that the dominion of the Romans in these regions was not of momentary duration, but continued for a length of time, as the different styles of the remains clearly prove. It may be presumed that no common soldier could pretend to the honour of such a tomb ; and it is probable that these sepulchres were destined to contain the earthly remains of some of the consecutive governors or officers stationed at the neighbouring place, which I shall soon describe.

Like a solitary beacon of civilization, the monument rises over this sea-like level of desolation, which, stretching out to an immense distance south and west, appears not to have appalled the conquerors of the ancient world, who even here have left behind them, in " lithographed proof," a reminiscence of a more elevated order of life than exists at present in these regions.

The flat valley below, with its green strip of herbage, stretches far into the stony level; and beyond, north-eastwards, the desolate waste extends towards Gharíya.

I returned to the encampment, which meanwhile had sprung up on the open space round the well, and was anxious to quench my thirst with a draught of the precious liquid; but the water was rather salt,

and disagreed with me so long as I continued to use
it,—that is, for the next seven days. That we might
make good use of our leisure hours, all three of us
went the next day to Gharíya, or rather Gharíya el
gharbíya—*i. e.* western, to distinguish it from the
more distant eastern place of the same name.

Cheerfully as we set forward, we were heartily
glad when, after a three hours' march, we saw the
northern tower of the place become visible over the
monotonous stony plain, the wide and unbounded
expanse of which seemed to indicate something above
a single day's excursion. After having also descried
the half-ruined dwellings of the village, we were

eagerly looking out for the palm-grove, when we
suddenly reached the brink of a deep ravine, in

which, on our left, the fresh green plantation started forth, while all around was naked and bare. We crossed the ravine, leaving the grove on our left, and ascended the opposite cliffs towards the ruined cluster of miserable cottages, when, having traversed the desolate streets, we encamped outside the Roman gate, the massive and regular architecture of which formed a remarkable contrast to the frail and half-ruined structures of the village. We were greatly astonished to find such a work here.*

It has but little resemblance to the Roman castle or station at Bonjem, such as it is seen in Captain Lyon's drawing †; for while the latter represents a single gateway flanked by two quadrangular towers, the building at Gharíya consists of three archways, flanked by towers with receding walls. The two smaller gateways have been almost entirely filled with rubbish; the upper layer likewise is gone, and only those stones which form the arch itself are preserved, the centre stone above the principal arch, bearing the inscription " PRO.AFR.ILL." (provincia Africæ illustris), encircled by a coronal, while that above the eastern side-gate is ornamented with a large sculpture, the lower part of which it is difficult

---

* A copy of my drawing of this interesting monument, of its ground-plan, and of the inscription, was sent by me to Dr. Patrick Colquhoun in May, 1850; and a short and learned treatise on it was published by John Hogg, Esq., in the Transactions of the Royal Society of Literature, vol. iv. new series.

† Capt. Lyon's Travels, p. 67.

to make out distinctly, except the trace of a chariot and a person in curious attire following it *, while the upper part represents two eagles in a sitting posture, with half-extended wings, holding a coronal, and at each end a female genius, in a flying posture, stretching out a larger and a smaller coronal. Besides this, and a few Berber names †, there is no inscription now on the building; but an inscription found in another place, which I shall soon mention, and which was probably originally placed over the small archway on the right ‡, seems to leave no doubt that this fortification dates from the time of Marc. Aurel. Severus Antoninus §, and if not built in the years between 232 and 235 after Christ, at least was then in existence.

As the ground-plan, which is here subjoined, evi-

---

* This might represent the subjugated nation or prince.

† Among these the following names can be made out with certainty, leaving only the short vowels, which are not expressed, in some doubt. Umaghmaghdúmer or úmaghem ghedúmer, Múthemaghem. besmeter. ménmenýr. The letters underlined are not certain. It is scarcely necessary to say that these inscriptions were made upon the building at a latter period, and that Mr. Hogg was wrong when, taken them for Punic, and thinking that I had overlooked "the most remarkable portions of this remain," he believed them to be taken from some older Punic building.

‡ This is a very probable conjecture of Mr. Hogg.

§ Although the name ANTONINO has suffered a little in the inscription, yet copying it, as I did, without any prejudice, I found sufficient traces of the letters composing this name; and I hardly think that I have been mistaken. If so, it is a curious and remarkable instance of this title, which Severus Alexander is said to have refused. See Gibbon, vol. i. p. 289.

dently shows, this is not by itself a complete building, and could only afford quarters to a very limited

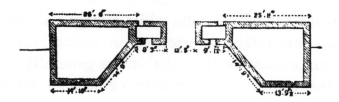

number of soldiers acting as a guard : in fact it can
only be the well-fortified entrance into the Roman
station ; but of the station itself I was unable to
discover any traces, though a great quantity of
stones from some building lie scattered about in the
village.   The only ancient building which I was able
to discover, besides the gate, was a cistern at the
N.W. corner of the wall, near the slope into the
wadi, which is here very precipitous.   It was probably 60 ft. long, for at 30 ft. there is an arch
dividing it ; but one half of it, except a space of
about 8 ft., has been filled with rubbish : its breadth
is 5 ft. 3½ in.   Perhaps the whole fortification was
never finished ; the inner edge of the stones would
seem to intimate that not even the gateway received
its entire ornament.

While I was busy making a drawing of the ruins,
Overweg, who, in order to measure the elevation of
the place by boiling water, had directed his steps to a
rising ground at some distance north of the village,
which was crowned with a tower, sent to inform me
that on the tower was a large Roman inscription,

which he was unable to make out; and as soon as I had finished my sketch I went thither. It is a round Arab tower, only two large ancient stones having been made use of as jambs, while a large slab, covered with an inscription, is used as an impost, owing to which circumstance the inhabitants generally regard even the tower as a Christian or Roman building. The inscription, which was evidently taken from the fortified station, is $32\frac{7}{12}$ in. long, and $15\frac{1}{8}$ in. high, and consists of nine lines. It has been read and interpreted by Mr. Hogg in the following manner.

I(mperatori) Caes(ari) M. Aurelio Severo Alexandro* P(atri) P(atriæ) P(i)o Felici Aug(usto) Et pagus et senatus et castr(um) [or castrum munitum] et municipium . . . . d. d.; poni curavit Severianæ P. Nero situs vexillationis leg(ioni)s IV. S(cythicæ) [or legionis XXI. Victricis Severianæ] dec(urio) Maurorum e(t) solo (o)pere (e)andem vexillationem instituit.

"To the Emperor Caesar M. Aurelius Severus, Father of his Country, Pious, Happy, Augustus, the district, the senate, the camp, and free town of . . . dedicate (this). . . . . P. Nero Decurion of the Moors, caused the station of the Severian regiment (horse) of the 21st Legion, Victorious, Severian, to be established; and he instituted by his own act the same regiment."

Though in this interpretation many words are very uncertain, it is clear from it—as it is more than probable that the inscription was taken from the former monument—that here was the station of a squadron of horse, or rather of an *ala sociorum;* but at the same time we have to regret that the name of the place is among the words entirely

* See note, p. 128.

effaced. I, however, think it extremely improbable that it was a municipium. I will here only add, that this direct western road to Fezzán and Jerma was not opened before the time of Vespasian, and received then the name " (iter) præter caput saxi," most probably on account of its crossing the mountain-chain near the coast at its steepest part.[*]

As for the tower, or nadhúr, it was evidently erected in former times in order to give timely notice when a band of freebooters — "el jésh" (the army), as they are called here—was hovering around the solitary village; for this seems to have been the chief cause of its destruction, the Urfílla being said to have been always watching and lying in ambush round this lonely place, to attack and rob small parties coming from or going to it; they are said even to have once captured the whole place. The consequence is, that it has now scarcely thirty male inhabitants able to bear arms, and is avoided by the caravans as pestilent, the water, they say, being very unwholesome. The small remnant of the inhabitants have a very pale and ghastly appearance, but I think this is owing rather to the bad quality of their food than to that of the water. In former times it is said to have been celebrated on account of a merábet of the name of Sidi Mádi.

* Plinius H. N. l. v. c. 5.: " Ad Garamantas iter inexplicabile adhuc fuit. Proximo bello, quod cum Œensibus Romani gessere auspiciis Vespasiani Imperatoris, compendium viæ quatridui deprehensum est. Hoc iter vocatur *Præter caput saxi.*"

As soon as I had sufficiently examined the ruins and the village, I hastened to the bottom of the ravine. The contrast between the ruined hovels of the village, perched on the naked rock, and the green, fresh plantation, fed by a copious supply of water, is very great. Thick, luxuriant, and shady clusters are here formed, principally around the basin filled by the spring, which rushes forth from beneath a rock, and gives life to the little oasis; its temperature I found, at half-past one o'clock P.M., $70\frac{1}{2}°$ Fahr., while that of the air was 70°. The number of the date-trees, though small, is nevertheless larger than in Mizda, and may be nearer to 350 than to 300. The water of the ravine after a heavy fall of rain joins the Wadi Zemzem, the principal valley of this whole district, which together with Wadi Sófejín and Wadi Beï', carries all the streams collected hereabouts to the sea.

Such is the character of Gharíya el gharbíya, uniting, even in its present state of decay, great historical interest with that attaching to a conspicuous and remarkable feature in the country. Whether her eastern sister, Gharíya e' sherkíya, awakens an equal or a still greater interest, it is difficult to say; but it seems to have quite the same elements of attraction as the western place, namely, a date-grove and Roman ruins. I had a great desire to visit it; but that was not possible, as we were to start next day from Taboníye.

According to our Zintáni, the path leading to it

from the western village first lies over the hammáda, then crosses a ravine called Wadi Khatab, leads again over the plateau, crosses another wadi, and at length, after about ten miles, as it seems, reaches the ravine of Gharíya e' sherkíya* stretching from W. to E., the grove, of about the same extent as in the other oasis, being formed at the N. and W. bases of the rocky height upon which the place stands. At the side of the village there is, he said, a large Roman castle, far larger than that in the western one, of about eight or ten feet elevation at present, but without an arched gateway of that kind, and without inscriptions. On the east side of the eminence are only a few palms, and on the south side none. The village is distinguished by a merábet called Bu-Sbaeha. Neither from the Zintáni nor from anybody else did I hear that the inhabitants of these two solitary ksúr are called by the peculiar name Waringa; I learnt it afterwards only from Mr. Richardson's statement†, and I have reason to think that the name was intended for Urínsa.

We returned by a more northern path, which at first led us through a rather difficult rocky passage, but afterwards joined our path of yesterday. Overweg and I had no time to lose in preparing for our journey over the hammáda, or plateau, while Mr.

* It is scarcely necessary to mention that Mr. J. Hogg has been greatly mistaken in identifying this place with Ghirza, which lies at a great distance.

† Vol. i. p. 40.

Richardson was obliged, by the conduct of the ill-provided and ill-disciplined blacks who accompanied him, to follow us by night. We therefore got up very early next morning, but lost a good deal of time by the quarrels among our camel-drivers, who were trying, most unjustly, to reserve all the heavy loads for the camels of the inexperienced Tarki lad 'Alí Karámra, till they excited his indignation, and a furious row ensued. This youth, though his behaviour was sometimes awkward and absurd, excited my interest in several respects. He belonged to a family of Tawárek, as they are called, settled in Wadi el Gharbi, and was sent by his father to Tripoli with three camels, to try his chance of success, although members of that nation, with the exception of the Tinýlkum, rarely visit Tripoli. He was slender and well-formed, of a glossy light-black complexion, and with a profile truly Egyptian; his manners were reserved, and totally different from those of his Fezzáni companions.

At length we were under way, and began gradually to ascend along the strip of green which followed the shelving of the plateau into the valley, leaving the Roman sepulchre at some distance to our right. The flat Wadi Lebaerek, which is joined by Wadi Shák, was still adorned with gattúf and rétem. It was not till we had passed the little hill called Lebaerek, and made another slight ascent, that we reached the real level of the terrible Hammáda; the ascent, or shelving ground, from Taboníye to this

point being called el Mudhár mtà el Hammáda, and
the spot itself, where the real Hammáda begins, Bú-
safár, a name arising from the obligation which
every pilgrim coming from the north, who has not
before traversed this dreaded district, lies under, to
add a stone to the heaps accumulated by former
travellers.

But, notwithstanding all the importance attached
to the dreary character of this region, I found it far
less naked and bare than I had imagined it to be.
To the right of our path lay a small green hollow, of
cheerful appearance, a branch of which is said, probably with some degree of exaggeration, to extend
as far as Ghadámes; but the whole extent of the
Hammáda is occasionally enlivened with small green
patches of herbage, to the great relief of the camel.
And this, too, is the reason why the traveller does
not advance at a rate nearly so expeditious as he
would expect. In the latter part of our preceding
journey we generally had made almost as much as
two and a half miles an hour; but we scarcely got
over two on this level open ground. Of course, the
wider the space the wider the dispersion of the
straggling camels; and much time is lost by un-
steady direction. At the verdant hollow called Garra
mtà e' Nejm the eastern path, which is called Trík el
mugítha (*via auxiliaris*), and passes by the village of
Gharíya, joined our path.

At Wadi Mámúra I first observed the little green
bird generally called asfír, but sometimes mesísa,

which lives entirely upon the caravans as they pass along, by picking off the vermin from the feet of the camels. In the afternoon we observed, to our great delight, in the green patch called el Wueshkeh, a cluster of stunted palm-trees. Hereabouts the camel-drivers killed a considerable number of the venomous lizard called bu-keshásh; and the Tarki in particular was resolute in not allowing any which he saw to escape alive. After a moderate march of little more than ten hours and a half, we encamped in a small hollow called, from a peculiar kind of green bush growing in it, el Jederíya. A strong cold wind, accompanied by rain, began to blow soon after we encamped. The tent, not being sufficiently secured, was blown down in the night; and we had some trouble in pitching it again.

Continuing our march, we passed, about ten o'clock in the morning, a poor solitary talha-tree bearing the appellation of el Duhéda. Further on we found truffles, which in the evening afforded us a delicious truffle-soup. Truffles are very common in many parts of the desert; and the greatest of Mohammedan travellers (Ebn Batúta) did not forget them in relating his journey from Sejelmása to Waláta, in the middle of the 14th century.* The sky was very dark and hazy; and the moon had an extraordinary "dára," or halo. We slept this night without a tent, and felt the cold very sensibly.

* Journal Asiatique, 1843, série iv. tom. i. p. 189.

The march of the following day was a little enlivened by our meeting with two small caravans: the first, of five camels; the second, belonging to Ghadámsi people, and laden with ivory, of fifteen. With the latter was also a woman, sitting quite comfortably in her little cage. Shortly after half-past one o'clock in the afternoon, we had reached the highest elevation of the Hammáda, indicated by a heap of stones, called, very significantly, Rejm el erhá, 1568 feet above the level of the sea. We encamped soon after, when a very heavy gale began to blow from N. N. W., driving the swallows, which had followed our caravan, into the tent and the holes formed by the luggage; but the poor things found no protection, for our tent, which was light and high-topped, was blown down again during the night, while a heavy rain accompanied the storm, and we as well as our little guests were left awhile without shelter, in a very uncomfortable situation.

April 19th.

We started rather late the following morning, entering now upon the very dreariest part of the Hammáda, called el Hómra. So far there had been only one track over this stony plateau; but in the afternoon a path, called Msér * ben Wáfi, branched off towards the left. This path, which leads to the eastern parts of Wadi Sháti, formed formerly the common road to Fezzán, the road by way of el

* The name Msér, being pure Arabic, testifies to its antiquity; for at present no Arab hereabouts would call a track or path by this name. It is properly the journey itself.

Hasi being considered as too insecure, on account of the robberies of the Urfílla. Hence the latter is still called the new road, " Trík el jedíd." Richardson, who had had enough of the inconveniences of travelling by night, easily got in advance of us this morning, after our short march of yesterday, and had advanced a good way by daytime. We were therefore anxious to come up with him ; and on our way we encountered a heavy shower of rain before we pitched our tent.

Sunday, April 21st. The whole caravan being once more united, the increased variety of our own party relieved a good deal of the feeling of monotony arising from the desolate character of the country through which we travelled. After marching about seven miles, we arrived at the greenest and largest hollow of the Hammáda, called Wadi el Alga, which we ought to have reached yesterday, in order to be able to get this day as near the well as possible.

As it was, when we encamped in the afternoon, we had still a long day's march before us, and therefore the next day, from general impulse, in order to make sure of our arrival at the well, we started at an early hour, keeping the caravan together by repeated shouting. After a march of about twelve miles, we reached the first passage leading down from the Hammáda and called Tníe* Twennín ; but it was too

---

* Tníe, or rather thníye, ثَنِيّة is a classical and still popular Arabic expression for a winding pass over high ground or up a hill.

steep and precipitous for our rather heavily laden caravan, and we had to continue till we reached the Tníe el 'Ardha, a little after eleven o'clock, when we began to descend from the plateau along a rough winding pass. The sandstone of which it is formed presented to us a surface so completely blackened, not only in the unbroken walls of the ravine, but also in the immense blocks which had been detached from the cliffs, and were lying about in great confusion, that at first sight anybody would have taken it for basalt; but when the stones were broken, their real nature became apparent. Over this broad layer of sandstone, which in some places covered a bed of clay mixed with gypsum, there was a layer of marl, and over this, forming the upper crust, limestone and flints.

After a winding course for an hour, the narrow ravine, shut in by steep, gloomy-looking cliffs, began to widen, and our direction varied less; but still the whole district retained a gloomy aspect, and the bottom of the valley was strewn with masses of black sandstone, while the country ahead of us lay concealed in a hazy atmosphere, which did not admit of an extensive view. Eager to reach the well, the caravan being scattered over a great extent of ground, we three travellers, with one of the shoushes, pushed on in advance, the south wind driving the sand, which lay in narrow strips along the pebbly ground, into our faces. We cherished the hope of finding a cool little grove, or at least some shade, where we might recline at ease after our fatiguing march; but, to our great disappointment, the sand became deeper, and nothing was to be seen but small stunted palm-bushes. But even these ceased near the well, which was dug in the midst of the sandy waste, and had once been protected by an oval-shaped building, of which nothing but crumbling ruins remained.

It was a cheerless encampment after so fatiguing a march; but there was at least no more fear of scarcity of water, for the well had an abundant supply. No name could be more appropriate to this place than el Hasi (the well). There is no need of any discriminating surname; it is "the Well"—the well where the traveller who has successfully crossed the Hammáda may be sure to quench his own thirst and that of his animals. But it is not a cheerful resting-place, though it is the great watering-place on this desert road, as he has to cross the fearful " burning plain " of the Hammáda before he reaches the spot.* There are several wells hereabouts, which might easily supply with water the largest caravan in an hour's time; for the water is always bubbling up, and keeps the same level.

The well at the side of which we had encamped·is rather narrow and deep, and therefore inconvenient for a large party; but it is, though slightly, pro-

---

* El hammáda is a very common name in North Africa for a stony level plain; but it is generally accompanied by a surname. The name is mentioned and explained by Ebn Khaldún, vol. ii. p. 358., trans. M. de Slane.

tected by the ruins around against the wind, which
is often very troublesome, and was particularly so on
the evening of our arrival.   Formerly there was here
a sort of fortified khan, such as is very rarely seen in
these parts, built by the tribes of the Notmán and
Swaíd*, in order tc protect their caravans against the
pillaging parties of the Urfílla, originally a Berber
tribe.   This building consisted of simple chambers,
twenty, as it seems, in number, lying round an oval
court which has entrances from north and south.
It is thirty paces long by sixteen wide, the centre
being occupied by the well, which, as it is dug in the
sandy soil, bears the general name Hasi.   It has a
depth of five fathoms; and its temperature was found
to be 71⅔° Fahr.   The quality of the water, in comparison with that of Taboníye, was very good.   The
elevation of this place was found by Overweg to be
696 feet; so that we had descended from the highest
point of the Hammáda 742 feet.

As it was, we felt heartily glad when our steady
and heavy Tripolitan tent being at length pitched,
we were able to stretch ourselves without being
covered with sand.   All the people were greatly fatigued, and required repose more than anything else.
Out of regard to the men as well as to the camels,
we were obliged to stay here the following day,
though the place was comfortless in the extreme,

* The Swaíd were formerly a very powerful tribe in Algeria,
and are often mentioned by Ebn Khaldún.   In vol. i. pp. 94. 101.
their subdivisions are enumerated.

and did not offer the smallest bit of shade. The accompanying sketch, which I made this day of the place, with the slope of the Hammáda in the background, will give but a faint idea of its desolate character. Scarcely any of our places of encampment on the whole journey seemed to me so bad and cheerless as this. If I had had an animal to mount, I would have gone on to a cluster of three or four date-trees, which are said to be at the distance of about three miles west from the well, and belong to the people of Zintán, to enjoy a little shade; but our camels were too much distressed.

CHAP. VI.

THERE are three roads from el Hasi: the westernmost called Trík e' duésa, after a small cluster of palm-trees; the second, called Trík e' safar, stony and more desolate than the former, but half a day shorter; and the third, or eastern, leading directly to Bírgen. When we at length left our uncomfortable encampment at el Hasi, our camel-drivers chose the middle road, which proved to be dismal and dreary. But the first part of it was not quite so bad, the appearance of granite among the rocks causing a little variety, while tamerán and shíah clothed the bottoms of the valleys; and we had a single specimen of a beautiful and luxuriant batúm-tree. When, however, we began to enter the region of the sand-hills, intermixed with rocky ridges and cliffs, the character of the country became desolate in the extreme.

Wednesday, April 24th.

We travellers, being in advance, chose our resting-place for the first night near a high rocky mass called el Medál, against the wish of the camel-drivers, who would rather have encamped in the Shábet e' talha, further on. The summit of the rocky eminence afforded a very interesting prospect over this singular district; and our younger shoush discovered, lower down, some scrawled figures. He came running up to inform me of his discovery; but it was of no interest, a cow and a sheep being the only figures plainly recognizable. The Fezzáni people come hither in spring, when the rain-water collects in the cavities of the rocks, and stay some months, in order to allow the camels to graze on the young herbage, which then shoots up here in profusion. Ben Sbaeda during such a stay here had lost a son, near whose tomb the camel-drivers said a prayer, or zikr, early the next morning.

Thursday, April 25th. Continuing our march, we soon came to the Shàbet e' talha, the bottom of which is clothed with the brushwood called arfísh, and with the rétem, or broom. Further on, when we came upon the higher rocky ground, the country grew more sterile, though we were so fortunate as to catch two gazelles. Black masses of sandstone jutted out on all sides, and gave a wild air to the desolate region through which we were passing. The sterile character of the scene underwent no change till next morning, when, on advancing about a mile and a half, we came to the Wadi Siddre, which was enlivened by a few talha-trees. A narrow defile led us from this place to the Wadi Boghár, whence we entered another defile. Mid-day was past, when we obtained a distinct view of the date-grove in Wadi Sháti*, and the

* So the name is generally pronounced, the correct form being Shiyáti, "the rent."

high sand-hills which border the valley on the south.
Towards the north it was rather open, and we
hastened on to escape from the hot desert through
which we were marching; but a good while elapsed
before we reached the border of the valley, which on
this side abounded in herbage.   After a mile and a
half we reached the first wild palm-trees, thriving in
separate and casually-formed groups.   Then followed
a belt of bare black ground, covered with a whitish
crust of salt.   The town, on the top of a broad terraced rock, seemed as far off as ever.   But I urged
on my Bú-Séfi along the winding path over the hard
ground; Richardson and Overweg followed close behind, while the camel-drivers had fallen back to exchange their dirty costume for one more decent.   At
length we reached the north-western foot of the picturesque hill, and chose our camping-ground beyond
the shallow bed of a torrent between the date-trees
and the corn-fields, near the largest fountain, — a very
agreeable resting-place, after the dreary desert which
we had traversed.

We had felt tired so long as the place was yet
ahead of us; but we had no sooner reached it than
all fatigue was gone, and Overweg and I, under the
guidance of a mállem, went forth to view the interesting features of the locality.   It is certainly a
very rare spectacle in this quarter of the world, to
see a town on the top of a steep terraced hill in the
midst of a valley, and occupying an advantageous
position which might be supposed to have given the

... at times.
... de place till
... spirits ...
... should ...
... of the School
... the ... having
... necessity
... enough
... new place
... ... who ...
... water-line, and
... no next order

... gates. Crossing it, we
... streets of the old town
... ... fundated, ...
... is ... above th.
... of the ... interesting view
... the walk, with its arcl ... tures,
... in ... place of ...
... ... great
... distances
... ... the high ...
... ... on the ... th. The thick
... ... whitish ... ...
... s which in others it ... rely
... perhaps, towards ... any slope
... in the town ... up
... ... caverns which
... ... and which we

interesting only on account of the oval-shaped form in which they have been excavated, as they are neither remarkable for dimensions nor for regularity; their general shape is this: A larger group of caverns has been made in a detached rocky eminence, upon which at present the cemetery is situated; but it is only seventy-two feet in length, and its ground-plan is far from being regular.

From this place I went through the adjoining grove, which, with a little more care, might easily become a very beautiful plantation; for there are a great many wells of very little depth, and the water is led through the channels with slight trouble. Our encampment in the beautiful moonlight, with not a breath of wind to disturb the tranquillity of the scene, was pleasant in the extreme, and we all felt much delighted and greatly restored.

Early on Sunday morning, after having finished my sketch of the village on the hill, with our encampment in the foreground, I took a walk all round the scattered groups of the plantation, which must have suffered a great deal from 'Abd el Jelíl, even though the number of 6000 trees, which he is said to have cut down, be an exaggeration. Towards the east side the salt crust is still thicker than on the west, and is very unpleasant for walking. I found here that, in addition to wheat and barley, much amára was cultivated in the garden-fields, besides a few figs; but I saw no grapes. Several families were living here outside in light huts or sheds made of palm-branches, and seemed to enjoy some degree of happiness. At the south-east end of the plantation rose a hill also formed of marl, and very similar to that on which the town is situated. The names of the villages along the valley, proceeding from west to east, are the following: after E'deri, Témesán; then Wuenzerík, Berga (a couple of villages distinguished as B. el foka and B. el utíyah), Gúta, Turut, El Ghurda, Meheråga, Agár, Gógam, Kosaer Sellám, Támezawa, Anerúya, Zeluáz, Abrák, Gíreh, Debdeb, and Ashkiddeh. The valley has two kaíds, one of whom, 'Abd el Rahmán, resides at present in Temesán, while the residence of the other, 'Agha Hassan e' Rawi, is in Támezawa. Meheråga seems to be the most populous of the villages. Abrák has the advantage of a school.

April 28th. We left our picturesque encampment in order to commence the passage over the sand-hills which separate the shallow "rent" of Wadi Shiyáti from the deeper valley the Wadi el Gharbi, the great valley *par excellence*. It is rather singular that even the higher ground, which is elevated about fifty feet above the bottom of the valley, is entirely covered with a crust of salt. Having traversed this, we began the ascent of the sand-hills, which in several favoured spots present small clusters of palm-trees, which too have their proprietors. Mukni, the father of Yusuf, Mr. Richardson's interpreter, is said to have killed a great many Welád Slimán hereabouts.

The most considerable of the depressions or hollows in the sand, which are decked with palm-trees, is the Wadi Shiúkh, which afforded in truth a very curious spectacle,—a narrow range of palm-trees half-buried between high sand-hills, some of them standing on the tops of hillocks, others in deep hollows, with the head alone visible. At length, after a good deal of fatigue, we encamped in Wadi Góber, another shallow cavity between sand-hills with brackish water and a few palm-trees. Here our camel-drivers themselves possessed a few trees, and, of course, were more interested in the inspection of their own property than in starting at an early hour the next day.

When we resumed our march we found our work more difficult than before, the sand-hills assuming a steepness most trying for the camels, particularly at the brink of the slopes. We were several times obliged to flatten away the edges with our hands, in order to facilitate the camels' ascent. I went generally a little in front, conducted by Mohammed ben Sbaeda, one of our camel-drivers, who, from the moment we had entered Fezzán, had exchanged the quarrelsome character by which he had made himself disagreeable to us, for very obliging and pleasing manners, and was anxious to give me every information. He told me that this belt of sand extended in a south-west and north-east direction from Dwésa as far as Fukka, a place, according to

him, five days' march on this side of Sókna. He
added, that however high and steep we might think
these sand-hills, they were nothing in comparison
with those in the direction of the natron-lakes; but,
in making this remark, I think he wanted to excuse
himself and his companions for taking us this long
way round by the west. He knew that it was our
desire to visit the natron-lakes, and that our direct
way to Murzuk led by those lakes, while their object
was to take us to their native village Ugréfe. Mohammed stated that each district in Fezzán has its
own peculiar dialect; and he contended that, while
the inhabitants of Wadi Sháti speak a good sort of
Arabic, similar to that spoken in Mizda, the people
of the great wadi (Wadi el Gharbi) make use of a
corrupt dialect.

Meanwhile the caravan remained very far behind,
and we thought it prudent to wait for them in Wadi
Tawíl, particularly as the path divided here. It was
so hot that my camel, when I let it loose to browse
a little, would not touch anything. When the other
camel-drivers at length came up, there was a dispute
as to the path to be followed; but the truth was,
that while there could be no doubt about the direct
road to Murzuk, some of the camel-drivers wished to
take us to Ubári. But at length the other party, interested only in carrying us westward as far as
Ugréfe, which was a great deal out of our route,
got the upper hand, and we left the road to Ubári,
which passes only two wadis, or hollows, called

Tekúr and 'Uglah, both with bad water, to the west, and followed the road to Ugréfe.

About four o'clock in the afternoon we encamped in the Wadi Mukméda, near the sand-hills bordering its southern side, under the shade of a wild palm-bush. Close to it was very good water only two feet below the surface; but as the hole had only just been made, it contained much sulphuretted hydrogen. The following day we crossed several smaller valleys with a few palm-trees (but a larger grove adorned the Wadi Jemál), all belonging to one of our camel-drivers of the name of Bú-Bakr. He also possessed here a magazine, built of bricks, and probably several centuries old, but entirely covered with sand, where he had deposited forty camel-loads of dates. They were of the kind called tefsirt, of very large size and exquisite taste, and were eagerly devoured by our people. After having refreshed ourselves for a moment, we went on, having just before us the very steepest ascent that occurs on the whole road. I was obliged to dismount from my beautiful Bú-Séfi in order to get him over it. This ridge being once behind us, we were told that all the "wár" was over; there were, however, still a few "difficult passes" before us. In the Wadi Gellah, which we next crossed, we found the footsteps of a flock of sheep and of a single camel, which latter animal finds plenty of food in this sandy district, and, at the shallow well in Wadi 'Uglah, is able to quench its thirst without the assistance of man. Thence we descended into Wadi Tigidéfa, where we encamped near a couple of palm-trees, the only ones in the wadi ; a copious well of very good water was near them, overshadowed by a thick cluster of palm-bushes. It was altogether a very satisfactory camping-ground, except that it swarmed with camel-bugs, as such places in the desert generally do.

Wednesday,   With a general impulse of energy, we
May 1st.   started this morning at a very early hour, twenty minutes past two o'clock in the morning, in order to get out of the sands, and to arrive in " the Wadi." After seven hours' constant march, we at length got a fine view of the steep cliffs which enclose the Wadi on the south side, and which contrasted marvellously with the white sand-hills in the foreground ; for, stretching out in a horizontal dark line which faded away at each end, they exhibited an illusive picture of a lake spread out before us in the remote distance. The cool east wind, which had blown in the morning, and promised a fine day, changed, as is very common in these regions, towards noon into a hot south wind, and made us very uncomfortable and susceptible of the fatigue of a long march, particularly as the distance proved much greater than we had expected. Indeed it was not till nearly two o'clock in the afternoon, that Mr. Richardson and I, who were much in advance of the caravan, reached the border of the Wadi, and shortly afterwards the well Moghrás, at the foot of two tall palm-trees, where we found a woman with two neatly dressed

children.   They belonged to the Azkár-Tawárek,
who, leaving their miserable abodes, migrate to these
more fertile districts, where they build themselves
light cottages of palm-branches, and indulge in a
patriarchal life, breeding camels and rearing sheep.
Near almost every village in the Wadi, outside the
palm-grove, in the bare naked bottom of the valley,
these poor people form a sort of suburb of frail
huts ; but nevertheless they keep up family ties
with their brethren near Ghát, and respect in some
degree the authority of the chief Nakhnúkhen.   That
this state of things might become very unfavourable
to Fezzán in an outbreak of hostilities between the
Turks and the Tawárek, is obvious; I shall have
occasion to say more on this subject further on.
A belt of saline incrustation, of more than half a mile
in breadth, runs through the middle of the valley,
forming a line of demarcation between the separate
palm-groups and the continuous grove.

On reaching this grove we soon caught sight of
the famous village Ugréfe, the residence of our
camel-drivers, which was to them the grand point
of attraction, and in truth the only cause of our
taking this westerly route.   It consisted of about
thirty light and low dwellings made of clay and palm-
branches, and lay near an open space where we were
desired to encamp; but longing for shade, we went a
little further on, and encamped near two splendid
ethel-trees (*Tamarix orientalis*), the largest I ever
saw before I reached E'geri.   When the camels came

up and the tents were pitched, the encampment
proved most agreeable.

Early next morning I was again in motion, roving
over the plantation, and was very much pleased with
its general character. The corn, which was a fine
crop, was just ripe and about to be harvested; and
close to our camping-ground two negro slaves were
employed in cutting it, while three or four negresses
carried it away to the stores. The negroes were
powerful young fellows; the women were rather
ugly, excepting one, who had a very handsome
figure, and by coquettish demeanour tried to make
herself more attractive. All of them accompanied
their work with singing and wanton movements,

and gave distinct manifestations of the customs of
this district, which is notorious for the familiarity of
its female inhabitants with the large caravans of pilgrims who annually pass through the Wadi on their
way to or from Mekka.   The fields are watered from
large holes or wells, which are sunk through layers
of variegated marl.

Being anxious to visit Old Jerma, and to convince myself of its identity with the Garama of the
Romans, I hired a miserable little donkey, and,
accompanied by the stupid young son of Sbaeda, set
out on an exploring expedition into the eastern
part of the valley.   Keeping in general along the
southern border of the plantation, and having on my
right the precipitous rocky cliff, of from 300 to 400
feet elevation, I went on slowly till I reached the
south-west corner of Jerma kadím, fortified with a
quadrangular tower built of clay, and exhibiting a
very curious arrangement in its interior.   The whole
circumference of the town, which was deserted long
ago, is about 5000 paces.   Here, near the town, there
are no Roman ruins whatever, but the remains of
several large and strong towers built of clay are to
be seen a little further on; and being unable to make
out the sepulchre described by Dr. Oudney*, I was
obliged to go to Tawásh, the village inhabited by
the Merabetín.   It is divided into three distinct parts,

* Excursion to the Westward of Mourzuk, p. xlvii., Denham
and Clapperton.

a Tarki village, consisting of huts of palm-branches, an outer suburb of scattered dwellings built of clay, and a small quadrangular place of very regular shape, surrounded by earthen walls, and furnished with two gates, one on the east, and the other on the west side, and regular streets crossing at right angles. Having here obtained a guide from Háj Mohammed S'aídi, a wealthy man and the owner of almost all our camels, I started for the Roman monument, situated in the wide opening of the southern recess. I found it in tolerably good preservation, and without delay made a sketch of it, as it seemed to me to be an object of special interest as the southernmost relic of the Roman dominion. It is a remarkable fact, that several years before the beginning of our era the Romans should have penetrated as far as this place; and that their dominion here was not of a merely transitory nature, this monument seems clearly to show. It is only one story high, and seems never to have been loftier. This is evidently characteristic of the age in which it was built; and I am persuaded that it is not later than the time of Augustus. Those high steeple-tombs which I have described above, seem not to have come into fashion before the middle of the 2nd century after Christ.* The base measures 7 ft. 9½ in. on the west and east sides, and at least

---

* Lucius Balbus Gaditanus, the conqueror of Cydamus (Gha-dámes) as well as of Garama (Jerma), celebrated his triumph in the year 18 B.C. or A.U. 735. (Plin. N. H. l. v. c. 5.; Velleius Patercul. ii. 51.; Strabo, iii. 169.; Marmor Capitolin.) The names

7 ft. 4 in. on the other two sides, including a spacious
sepulchral chamber or burial-room; but while the

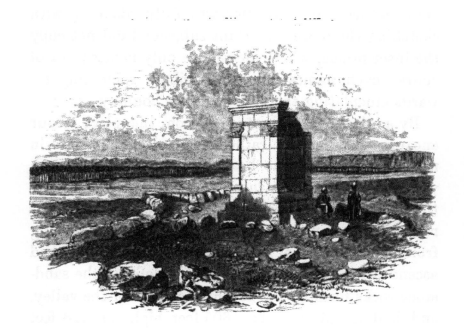

base forms almost a quadrangle, the sides of the principal structure are of very different dimensions, measuring not more than 5 ft. 8½ in. on the north and
south, and 7 ft. on the west and east sides.   It is
adorned with pilasters of the Corinthian order.   The
whole monument is covered with Tfínagh or Berber
writing, which was not only intelligible to me, but

and pictures of the other nations and towns, which Balbus carried
in his triumph (Plinius, l. c.), were evidently a mere show, comprising, most probably, all the information which he had been able
to obtain of the interior.

also to our young camel-driver 'Ali Karámra, whose family lives in this part of the wadi, in a homely little dwelling of palm-leaves. However, as the writing was very careless, and my time was fully taken up with sketching the more important subjects, I did not copy the inscriptions, which indeed are only names; but of course even names might contribute something towards elucidating the history of the country.

By a direct path I returned from this place to our encampment, and felt rather fatigued, having been in motion during all the heat of the day. The south wind still increased in the evening; and we could distinctly see that it was raining towards the longed-for region whither we were going, while we had nothing from it but clouds of sand. Overweg, meanwhile, had ascended in the morning the highest cliff of the sandstone rocks forming the southern border of the valley, and had found it to be 1605 feet high, or 413 feet above the ground at our encampment.

Friday, May 3rd. Having heard, the day before, in the village of the Merábetín, that Háj Mohammed, the owner of our camels, ordered the boy who was with me to tell Sbaeda, his father, that they should not start before this evening, I was not surprised at our camel-drivers not bringing the camels in the morning. It was almost four o'clock in the afternoon when Overweg and I at length pushed on, entering the extensive grove of New Jerma, — a miserable place, which, being entirely shut in by the palm-grove, is almost deserted. The grove, however, exhibited a very interesting aspect, all the trees being furnished with a thick cluster of palm-bush at their roots, while the old dry leaves were left hanging down underneath the young fresh crown, and even lower down the stem, not being cut off so short as is customary near the coast. But picturesque as the state of the trees was, it did not argue much in favour of the industry of the inhabitants; for it is well-known to Eastern travellers that the palm-tree is most picturesque in its wildest state. Beyond the town the grove becomes thinner, and the ethel-tree predominates over the palm-tree; but there is much palm-bush.

We entered another grove, which stretches far northward into the valley, its produce being, according to our camel-drivers, entirely reserved for the poor. Having passed Tawásh, with its little grove, we entered the fine plantation of Brék, enlivened by the bleating of sheep and goats. Here, in the small fields where corn is cultivated, the ground is thickly incrusted with salt and soda. We at length encamped near the grove of Tewíwa, close to the village of the same name, and to the north side of the Merábet Sídi e' Salám.

The next morning, while the camels were loading, I visited the interior of the village. The walls have given way in several places, and the whole made the impression of a half-deserted place ; but the little kasbah, which is never wanting in any of these towns, was in tolerable condition. One of the inhabitants, on being asked why the village was so much decayed, told me that a torrent had destroyed a great portion of it nine years ago, in consequence of which the greater part of its population had dispersed abroad, only about twenty families now remaining. But this is the condition of nearly all the places in Fezzán; and it can be partially accounted for only by supposing that many of the male inhabitants go off to Negroland, to avoid being made soldiers. A very extensive grove belongs to Tewíwa; but the plain between the village and the rocks is rather open, only a few patches of corn-field being scattered thereabouts. Three vast and detached buttresses, which jut out from the cliffs into the plain, give a very picturesque appearance to the groves and villages which we passed on our route.

We were just proceeding in the best manner, when a halt was ordered, from very insufficient reasons, a little south from the village Tekertíba, where we were to pass the heat. Meanwhile I ascended a ridge of rocks which, a little further down, crossed the valley from the southern border. The ridge was a narrow, steep, wall-like cliff, which afforded a very interesting view of the end, or rather beginning, of the fertile Wadi, which was close at hand.

From the highest point of the ridge I descended northwards, crossing a small defile, which is formed between the two rocky buttresses to the north and south, the latter being the more considerable. Along it runs a path, connecting the two valleys. Here I obtained a view of the fresh green valley on the one

side, and the destructive sand-hills on the other, and
directed my steps to the plantation, where young
people were busily engaged in drawing water from
the large pond-like wells.   The beams, by means of
which the water is drawn up, require to be strongly
constructed, the whole of the khattár having a height
of from sixty to eighty feet.   These draw-wells are
always placed in pairs; and a couple of miserable
asses, partners in suffering, do all the work.   The
young male labourers all wore straw-hats, and had
an energetic appearance.

The northern border of the plantation is now
menaced by the approach of the sand-hills, which
have already overwhelmed the last range of palm-
trees.   There is a curious tradition in Tekertíba,
that from the highest peak of the cliffs bordering
the valley on the south side, a rivulet or brook, issuing from a spring, runs down into the valley un-
derground.   There were, it is related, originally
several canals or stream-works leading down to this
subterranean aqueduct; but they have been all filled
up.   The village itself, on the south border of the
plantation, is tolerably large, but is inhabited by only
forty families at the utmost, though it is the most
populous place in the valley next to Ubári.

· By the exertion of much energy, I at length succeeded in the afternoon in getting our little caravan
again under way; and we left the Great Wadi
through the defile, which appears to have been once
defended by walls, and, having crossed some irregular

depressed plains, encamped at seven o'clock in the evening in a wadi with a moderate supply of herbage. Starting on the following morning, at an early hour, we soon emerged into a more open level, beautifully adorned with fine talha-trees, and having with difficulty dragged on our camel-drivers, who shortly afterwards wanted to encamp in Wadi Resán, we entered a dreary wilderness, from which we did not emerge till we arrived at the plantation of Aghár, where we encamped.

Monday, May 6th.   All the people were eager to reach to-day the first great station of our journey; but owing to the straying of some of the camels, we were unable to start quite as early as we wished. The country in general was very sterile, presenting only a few small date-groves, which we passed at greater or less distance, and at length, when we reached the plantation of Múrzuk itself, we were far from finding in it that picturesque and refreshing character which we had admired in the palm-groves of the Wadi. These had formed a dense beautiful shade and fine groups; while the plantation of Múrzuk was scattered about in thin growth, so that it was scarcely possible to determine exactly where it began or where it ended. Thus we reached the wall of the town, built of a sort of clay glittering with saline incrustations; and going round the whole western and northern sides, which have no gate wide enough for a caravan, we halted on the eastern side of the town, not far from the camp of the pilgrims who were returning from Egypt to Marocco and Tawát, till Mr. Gagliuffi came out of the town, and brought us in.   Mr. Richardson had arrived about an hour before us.   I was lodged in a cool and airy room on the N.E. corner of Mr. Gagliuffi's house, which had within the court a very pleasant half-covered hall.   Mr. Gagliuffi treated us with all possible hospitality, and did all in his power to render our stay in the town agreeable.

CHAP. VII.

UNFORTUNATELY our stay in Múrzuk seemed likely to
become a very long one, as the chiefs from Ghát,
who were to take us under their protection, were not
yet sent for; the courier with our letters, to which
was added a missive from the acting governor, promising perfect security to the chiefs, did not set out
till the 8th of May. No doubt, in order to visit Aïr,
a country never before trodden by European foot, with
any degree of safety, we wanted some powerful protection; but it was very questionable whether any of the
chiefs of Ghát could afford us such, while the sending
for them expressly to come to Múrzuk to fetch us
would, of course, raise their pretensions very high,
and in the same degree those of other chiefs whose
territory we should enter hereafter. Be this as
it may, this mode of procedure having been once
adopted, the question arose, whether all three of us
should proceed to Ghát; and it was decided, the very
next day after our arrival, that the director of the
expedition alone (Mr. Richardson) should touch at
that place, in order to make, if possible, a treaty with
the chiefs in that quarter, while Mr. Overweg and I
were to proceed with the caravan by the southern

route directly to the well Arikím, and there to await Mr. Richardson.

Providentially, a man had been sent to act as mediator between us and the countries to which we were about to direct our steps. He had been recommended to us in the very strongest terms by Hassan Bashá, the former governor of Fezzán, whom we had frequently seen in Tripoli, and who knew something about the men of influence and authority in Negroland. This man was Mohammed Bóro, who, with the title Serki-n-turáwa, "Lord of the Whites," resided generally in A'gades, but had also a house and many connections in Sókoto, and at present was on his home-journey from a pilgrimage to Mekka. It was a great pity that Mr. Gagliuffi, H. M.'s agent and our host, influenced I know not by whom, greatly underrated the importance of this man, and treated him with very little consideration. He was represented to us as an intriguer who, besides, arrogated to himself much more consequence than he was really entitled to — a man, in short, whose friendship was scarcely worth cultivating, at least not at any sacrifice.

Mohammed Bóro called upon us on the 8th of May at Gagliuffi's house. He was an elderly, respectable-looking man, wearing a green bernús over white under-clothes. He could speak but little Arabic, but received Mr. Gagliuffi's empty and rather ironical assurances, that the whole welfare and success of the expedition were placed in his (Mohammed Bóro's) hands, with a continual strain of "el hamdu lilláhi"'s. In his company were his eldest son and another man of Asben. He afterwards sent us some gúro, or kola-nuts, of which he seemed to have a great stock, and which he also sold in the market. Gagliuffi sent him, as an acknowledgment, a very lean sheep, which, with a small loaf of sugar, was all he got from us in Múrzuk. Instead of gaining his friendship, this treatment served only to irritate him, and was productive of some very bad consequences for us. This interesting person will appear in his true character and importance in the course of this narrative.

The appearance of Múrzuk is rather picturesque; but its extreme aridity is felt at once; and this feeling grows stronger on a prolonged residence.* Even in the plantation which surrounds it there are only a few favoured spots where, under the protection of a deeper shade of the date-trees, a few fruit-trees can be cultivated, such as pomegranates, figs, and peaches. Culinary vegetables, including onions, are extremely scarce; milk, except a little from the goats, is of course quite out of the question.

The town lies in a flat hollow, " Hófrah," which is the appropriate native name of the district, but never-

* I will here only remark, that the degree of heat observed here by Captain Lyon, which has astonished and perplexed all scientific men, is not the real state of the atmosphere, but evidently depended upon the peculiar character of the locality where that enterprising and meritorious traveller had placed his thermometer.

theless at the considerable elevation of 1495 ft., surrounded by ridges of sand; and in this hollow lies scattered the plantation, without the least symmetry of arrangement or mark of order. In some places it forms a long narrow strip extending to a great distance, in others a detached grove, while on the southeast side of the town the desert approaches close to the walls in a deep inlet. Towards the east a little grove apart forms as it were an advanced post. The densest and finest part of the grove is towards the north, where also are the greatest number of gardens and fields in which wheat, barley, gédheb (or rather kédheb), and a few vegetables, are cultivated with much labour. In the same quarter also the greatest number of cottages are to be found, including huts (large and small) made of palm branches,—the former consisting of several apartments and a small courtyard, the latter having generally only one room of very narrow dimensions.

In the midst of this plantation lies Múrzuk. It is situated so as not to face the cardinal points, but with a deviation from them of thirty degrees, the north side running N. 30° E., S. 30° W., and so on : it is less than two miles in circumference. The walls, built of clay, with round and pointed bastions, but partly in bad repair, have two gates, the largest on the east, and the other on the west side. There is only a very small gate on the north side, and there is none towards the south. This quarter of the town has been greatly contracted by 'Abd el Jelíl, as the remains of the old wall of the time of Muknî clearly show; but the town is still much too large for its scanty population, which is said now to amount to 2800, and the greatest part of it, especially in the quarters most distant from the bazar, is thinly inhabited and half in ruins. The characteristic feature of the town, which shows that it has more points of relation with Negroland than with the lands of the Arabs, is the spacious road or "dendal" stretching out from the eastern gate as far as the castle, and making the principal part of the town more airy, but also infinitely more exposed to the heat.

The bazar, of course, is the most frequented part of the town. It lies nearly half-way between the east and west gates, but a little nearer to the former, and affords, with its halls of palm-stems, a very comfortable place for the sellers and buyers. The watch-house at the east end of the bazar, and almost opposite Mr. Gagliuffi's house (from the terrace of which the accompanying view was taken), is ornamented with a portico of six columns, which adds to the neat appearance of this quarter of the town. The kásbah is the same as in Captain Lyon's time, with its immense walls and small apartments; but the outer court has been much improved by the building of a barrack or kishlah, which now forms its northern portion. It is a large quadrangular building, with a spacious esplanade in the interior, around which are arranged the principal apartments. The building is said to be capable of containing 2000 men, though at present

... ... me of M... ...part,
... ...ch ... ... to its
... ... new to ar...n...
... ...p.....n... ...
... the baz... ...airly
... ... The ...arac...asi... fea-
...ca sh...ws ...hat it has ...ore points
... ... N...... ...n with the lanus of
... ...sp... ... ...dendal" stretch-
...n th... ... ...s far ... ...astle, and
... ...e town ...re air, but
... ...h ...t.
... ...t... ...equ...s...d ...
... ...way betw...n the east
... ...eau...r to the former, and
....st...ns, ...v...ry comfortable
pl... to... ...he sellers...... ...ary rs. The wat...h-house at
th... east ...nd of the ...... and almost ...ppos...e ...ir.
....n...'s ...use ... ...the terrace of wh...h ...e accom-
... ...w... ...n', 's ornamented w...h ...orti...
... ...dds ...o ...ne nea... ap...earanc...
...n... ...he ka...ah ...s the same
... ...ith ...ts immense walls
... ...ut...r court ...as ...een
....ng of a barra...r dish-
... .ther... portion. It ...s a
...r...rang...... ... ...ng, ...ith ... ...acious espla-
...h...nte...... ...orn... ...hich ...e arranged the
... ...s s...id ...o ...e
... . men, ...hough ...t ...resent

there are but 400 in the garrison, who are well lodged and fed.

The accompanying sketch of a ground-plan will give a tolerably exact idea of the whole character of the town.

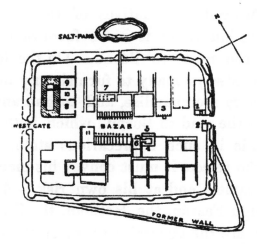

1 Custom-house.
2. Guard-house.
3. Watch-house.
4. Mr. Gagliuffi's house.
5. Garden.
6. House of the agent of Bórnu.

7. Mosque.
8. First courtyard of kásbah.
9. Kiahlah.
10. Staircase leading to the upper apartments.

With regard to commerce, the condition of Múrzuk is very different from that of Ghadámes. The latter is the residence of wealthy merchants, who embark all their capital in commercial enterprises, and bring home their own merchandise. But Múrzuk is rather the thoroughfare than the seat of a considerable commerce, the whole annual value of imports and exports amounting, in a round sum, to 100,000 Spanish dollars; and the place, therefore, is usually in great

want of money, the foreign merchants, when they
have sold their merchandise, carrying away its price
in specie, — the Mejábera to Jálo, the Tébu to Bílma
and Bórnu, the people of Tawát and Ghadámes to
their respective homes. Few of the principal merchants of Múrzuk are natives of the place. The
western or Sudán route is more favourable to commerce than the route to Bórnu. On the latter the
Tawárek are always ready to furnish any number of
camels to carry merchandise, and to guarantee their
safety, while the road to Bórnu, which is the nearest
for Múrzuk, is in such a precarious state, that the
merchant who selects it must convey his merchandise
on his own camels and at his own risk. As for the
routes through Fezzán, the Hotmán, the Zwáya, and
the Megésha are the general carriers of the merchandise; while, on the route to Sudán, the conveyance
at present is wholly in the hands of the Tinýlkum.

As soon as Gagliuffi learned distinctly the plan of
our expedition, he made an agreement with these
people to take our things as far as Selúfiet; and they
were anxious to be off. After much procrastination,
they fixed upon the 6th of June for taking away
the merchandise with which we had been provided
here. We were to follow on the 12th; but the
luggage not being ready at an early hour, our final
departure was fixed for the 13th.

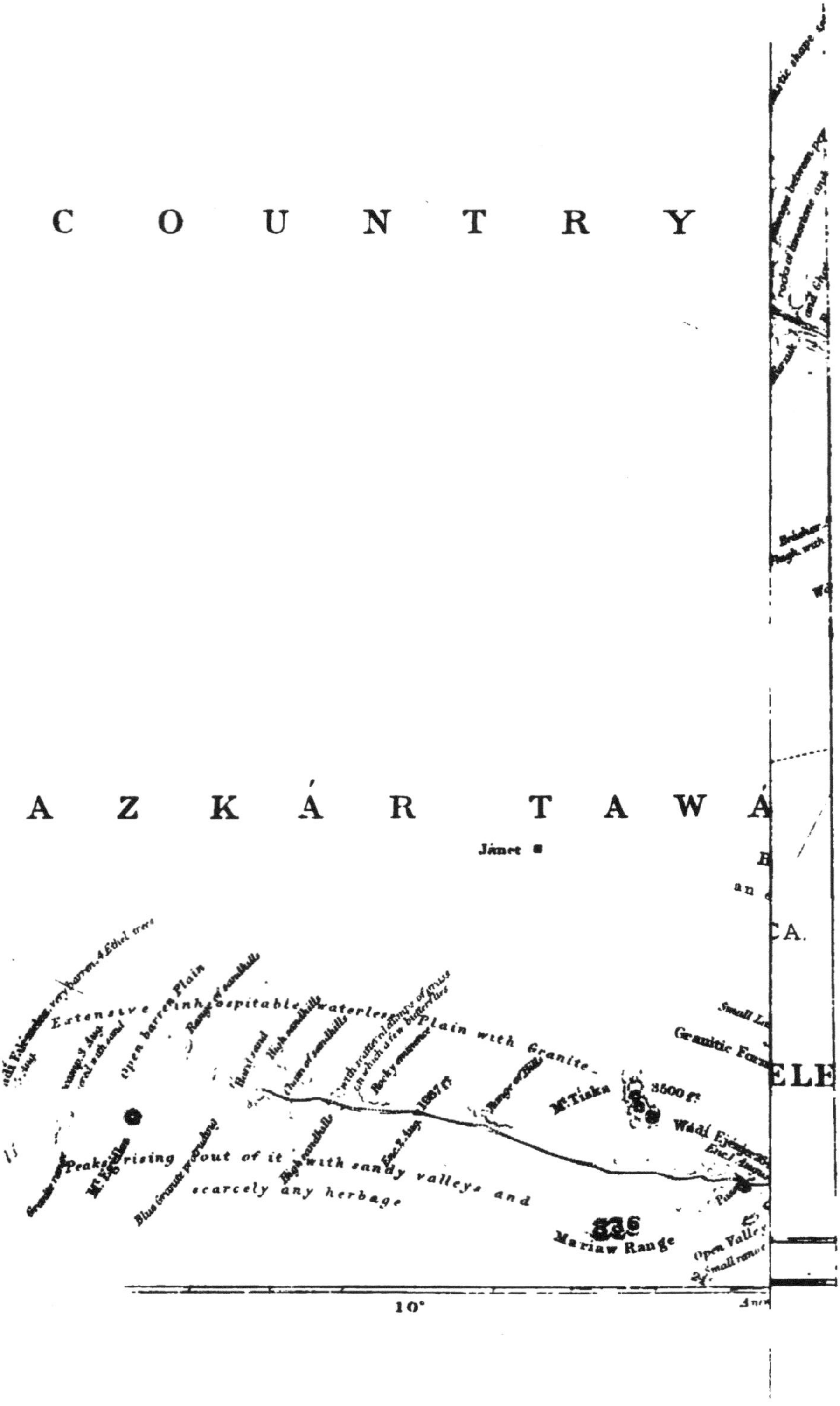

COUNTRY
AZKÁR TAWÁ
Jánet
Extensive
inhospitable waterless Plain with Granite
Peaks rising out of it with sandy valleys and
scarcely any herbage
Open barren Plain
Range of sandhills
High sandhills
Rocky eminence
1987 ft
Range of Hills
Mt. Tiska
3500 ft
Granitic Form
Small La
Mariaw Range
Open Valley
Small range
CA.
ELE
10°

ACCOMPANIED by Mr. Gagliuffi, the Greek doctor, and the Bin-básha, we left Múrzuk by the western gate. My parting from Mr. Gagliuffi was cordial. He had received us and treated us hospitably, and had shown an earnest desire to further our proceedings, and to secure if possible the success of our expedition; and, if in his commercial transactions with the mission he did not neglect his own advantage, we could not complain, though it would have been infinitely better for us if we had been provided with a more useful sort of merchandise.

In leaving the town we kept, in general, along the same path by which we had first entered it, and encamped during the hot hours of the day in the scanty shade afforded by the trees of Zerghán, the well close by affording us delicious draughts of cool water, not at all of that brackish insipid taste which is common to the water of Fezzán. We had started in the belief that we should find our luggage in O'm el hammám; but in this place we learned from the poor ragged people who come occasionally hither to take care of the trees, that it was gone on to Tigger-urtín.

Not knowing, however, the road to the latter place, we took the path to O'm el hammám, and encamped about seven o'clock in the afternoon a little north of it.

O'm el hammám is a half-decayed and deserted village, built of clay, which is strongly incrusted with salt, the inhabitants at present living entirely in huts made of palm-branches. The plantation being intermixed with a large number of ethel-trees (*Tamarix orientalis*), and interspersed with gardens, exhibited a more varied aspect than is generally the case with these groves ; and having pitched our tent near a large ethel-bush, we felt very comfortable, especially as we had the good luck to obtain a few eggs, which, fried with plenty of onions, made a very palatable supper.

Next morning we directed our course to Tigger-urtín, making almost a right angle towards the north, and crossing a desolate plain incrusted with salt, after we had left the fine plantation of O'm el hammám. Having reached the village of our camel-drivers, which consists entirely of huts of palm-branches, we looked long in vain for a tolerable camping-ground, as the strong wind filled the whole air with sand. At length we pitched our tents a few paces south from the well. It was an extremely sultry and oppressive day, and the wind anything but refreshing.

In the afternoon we went to pay our compliments to Mohammed Bóro, who had left Múrzuk several days before us. He informed us that he had consumed all his provisions, and that he would have left to-day

for Tasáwa, in order to replenish his stores, if he
had not seen us coming.   We consoled him with the
intimation that we hoped our whole party would be
soon ready for starting, and sent him a quantity of
dates and corn.

The next day I went roving through the valley,
which a little further to the N.W. was much prettier,
and had several fine clusters of palm-trees; but the
most picturesque object was the old village, built of
clay, now entirely in decay, but surrounded by a
dense group of fine date-trees.   Subjoined is a sketch
of it.

At the south-west end of the grove also is a little
village, likewise deserted.   Here I met a Felláta or
Pullo slave, a full-grown man, who, when a young lad,

had been carried away from his native home, somewhere about Kazaure, and since then had been
moiling and toiling here in this half-deserted valley,
which had become his second home. He told me
that fever had driven away the old inhabitants of
the village long ago, after which the Tinýlkum seem
to have taken entire possession of it, though it is
remarkable that its name seems rather to belong to
the Berber language, its original form being Tigger-
odén (ŏdē means the valley), which has been changed
into the more general form Tigger-urtín. The whole
valley, which makes a turn towards the south-west,
is full of ethel-bush, and affords shelter to a number of doves. Groups of palm-trees are scattered
about.

In the morning I took a walk round the
village of the Tinýlkum, which exhibited
some lively and interesting scenes. All the men
were saying their prayers together upon a sand-hill
on the north side of the principal cluster of cottages,
while the women were busy in getting ready the
provisions for the long journey about to be undertaken by their husbands, and the children were playing among them. About fifty or sixty huts were
lying hereabouts, most of them formed into groups;
others more detached. Some of them had pointed
roofs, while others were flat-roofed; but all of them
had a neat and orderly appearance. Besides camels,
which constitute their principal wealth, as by means
of them they are enabled to undertake those long

June 16th.

annual journeys to Sudán, they possess a good many
sheep.   Two of our camel-drivers, Ibrahím and
Slimán, whom I shall have occasion to mention repeatedly, together with their mother and sister, were
in possession of a flock of about 200 head, which they
were sending to the fine pasture-grounds of Terhén
in Wadi Berjúsh.   Besides the latter valley, the
Tinýlkum also use the valley Táderart as their chief
pasture-grounds.

On the E.N.E. side of the village rose a hill
about 100 feet high, and affording a fine view
over the valley-plain.   From its highest summit,
where a niche for prayers has been laid out with
stones on the ground, it stretches from east to west,
and forms a kind of separation in the flat valley,
limiting the ethel-tree to its western part, all the sand-
hills in the eastern prolongation being covered with
palm-bushes, which, from a distance, have the appearance of a thick grove.   Descending from this hill
northwards, I came to the handsomely-decorated
sepulchre of Háj Sálemi, the brother of the sheikh,
who resides in Múrzuk, and further on met a party
of Tinýlkum *en route* for the wadi, where numbers
of them are residing.   Another division dwells about
Sebhha; but the whole body of the tribe comprises
from 350 to 400 families, which are united by the
closest bonds, and act as one body — " like meal "
(to use their own expression) " falling through the
numerous holes of a sieve into one pot."   About
noon arrived the pilgrim-caravan of the Tawáti,

which had been long encamped near Múrzuk, on
their way home; it had been this year only 114
persons strong, with 70 muskets, while sometimes
it musters as many as 500 persons. Their chief,
or sheikh el rákeb, was an intelligent person of the
name of 'Abd el Káder, a native of Timímun, who
had been leader of the caravan several times. They
encamped at no great distance from us on the open
ground.

Being obliged to buy another camel for myself (in
order to be able to mount our servant Mohammed el
Túnsi on a camel of our own, the Tinýlkum being
very particular about their beasts, and not liking to
see a man often mounting them), I bought, in the
afternoon, a fine tall méheri from Háj Mohammed, for
69 Fezzán riyals or 55 Spanish dollars.

June 17th.   I made a longer excursion along the
eastern part of the wadi, which here, where
it is lower and collects more humidity, is adorned
with some beautiful wild groups of palm-trees left
quite to themselves; the valley extends towards
Wadi Ghodwa, which it joins. Keeping on in that
direction, I came to a poor hamlet called Márhhaba
inhabited by a few families, who bitterly complained
of their poverty. Here was formerly a village built
of clay, and a large spacious castle about sixty-five
paces square. All is now deserted; and only a
small part of the available ground is under culture,
forming about six or seven small fields. The same
picture is met with all over Fezzán, where the only

places exhibiting to the eye some degree of life and prosperity are Sokna and Murzuk. The population of this wide expanse of country falls short of even sixty thousand souls.

The heat of the day had already set in, when I returned to the tents, where I was extremely rejoiced to see the different members of our caravan collecting at last, so as to afford a fair prospect of our soon setting out for unknown and more interesting regions. There had arrived Mohammed el Sfaksi, a man with whom Mr. Gagliuffi had entered into a sort of partnership for a commercial journey to Negroland, and whom he had supplied with a tolerable amount of merchandise; and in the afternoon came the boat. The following day Yusuf Mukní, Mr. Richardson's interpreter, came with the rest of the luggage, so that gradually everything fell into its right place, and nothing was now wanting but the Tawárek chiefs to set our whole body in regular motion. We therefore procured a load of dates from Aghár, and, getting everything ready, roused our spirits for the contemplation of novelties and the encountering of difficulties; for the latter could certainly not be wanting where the former were at hand.

While the greater part of the caravan took the direct road to the well Sháraba, Mr. Overweg and I, with the remainder, chose the road to Tessáwa, or, rather more accurately, Tasáwa; but though our party formed but a small body of people, yet it presented a very animated spectacle.

Wednesday, June 19th.

The lazy Arab mode of letting the camels go singly, as they like, straggling about right and left, strains and fatigues the traveller's attention; but his mind is stimulated and nerved to the contemplation of great distances to be traversed when he sees a long line of camels attached one to the other, and led by a man at a steady pace without any halt or interruption. As for myself, riding my own méheri, I was quite at liberty to go before or fall behind, just as the circumstances of the road called for observation, or presented something worthy of attention.

Having passed some tolerably-deep sand-hills accumulated in the wadi, we obtained a sight of an advanced spur of the plantation of Aghár to our left, when the ground became firm, and the country more open. Then, keeping along the southern border of the principal plantation, we passed the village and our former camping-ground, and having left further on some deserted villages and a few scattered huts of palm-leaves, still inhabited, a little on one side, about noon we again entered a sandy region with a few detached palm-groups. Here I observed a specimen of a very rare sort of bifurcated or divided palm-tree (not the dúm, which is generally so) with two distinct tufts hanging down on the opposite sides: this is the only specimen I ever saw. We then passed the village of Tasáwa*, which, with its clay walls and

* This is evidently a Central African name, and appears to belong to the original black population of Fezzán. But it seems

towers, looks much more considerable from afar than it appears when viewed from among the deserted houses within it; still it is one of the more wealthy and important places of the country. A little beyond it we encamped on the open sandy ground, when, as our small tent had by mistake gone on in advance, and our large tent was too bulky to be pitched for one night's rest, we contrived a very tolerable airy shade with our carpets.

We had scarcely made ourselves comfortable, when we received the joyful news that Hatíta, with two sons of Sháfo, had just arrived from Ghát, and were about to call on us. Their arrival of course had now become a matter of the utmost importance, as Mr. Richardson had made his mind up not to start without them, though it might have been clear, to every one well acquainted with the state of things in the interior, that their protection could not be the least guarantee for our favourable reception and success in the country of Aïr or Asben, inhabited and governed by an entirely distinct tribe. And, on the other hand, the arrival of these chiefs made our relation to Mohammed Bóro extremely disagreeable, for, after waiting so long for us, he now clearly saw that Mr. Gagliuffi, in declaring that we relied entirely on him for our success, while we were in fact placing ourselves wholly at the disposal of the chiefs of Ghát,

---

to stand in some sort of relationship to Asáwa, the name of one of the original seats of the Auràghen.

was only trifling with him.   He therefore flew into a
violent passion, threatening openly before the people
that he would take care that we should be attacked
on the road by his countrymen; and these were not
empty threats.

After a hot day followed a very fine evening, with
a beautifully-clear moonlight; and cherishing the fervent hope that, with the assistance of the Almighty,
I should succeed in my dangerous undertaking,
I lay down in the open encampment, and listened
with hearty sympathy to the fervent prayers of the
Tinýlkum, which in melodious cadence, and accompanied with the sound há, há, sometimes in a voice of
thunder, at others in a melancholy unearthly plaint,
were well adapted to make a deep impression upon
the mind, the tall palm-trees forming majestic groups,
and giving a fanciful character to the landscape in
the calm moonlight.

It is a remarkable fact that, while the Mohammedan
religion in general is manifestly sinking to corruption along the coast, there are ascetic sects rising up
in the interior which unite its last zealous followers
by a religious band.   The particular sect to which
belong the Tinýlkum, who in general are Máleki, has
been founded by Mohammed el Médani, who established a sort of convent or oratory (zawíya) near
Masráta, and endowed it with a certain extent of
landed property, from the produce of which he fed
many pilgrims.   The best feature of this creed is the
abolition of the veneration of dead saints, which has

sullied in so high a degree the purity of Íslám.   Mohammed el Médani is said to have died a short time
ago; but his son continues the pious establishment.*
It is a sort of freemasonry, and promises to make a
great many proselytes.   I am not one of those who
think it a sign of progress when Mohammedans become indifferent to the precepts of their religion, and
learn to indulge in drinking and such things; for I
have not given up my belief that there is a vital
principle in Islám, which has only to be brought
out by a reformer, in order to accomplish great
things.

In Tasáwa also reside a few Tinýlkum, who, however, have been intimately intermixed with the
Arabs, while the others in general keep their blood
pure, and do not intermarry with the people of Fezzán.

Having assured ourselves that, owing to the arrival
of the Tawárek chiefs, we should have to make some
stay here, we determined to pitch our large tent early
the next morning, while the chiefs had a long dispute
with Mohammed e' Sfaksi, the subject of which I
must relate, as it throws some light on the history
and the present state of this country.   The northern
Tawárek, when they occupied the country round
Ghát, established a sort of tribute, or gheráma, to be
paid by merchants passing through their territory,
and on payment of which the trader should be no

* From what Major Burton says in his "Pilgrimage," vol. ii.
p. 290., it would appear that Mohammed Ibn 'Abdallah e' Snúsi,
which is his full name, is still living.

further molested, but enjoy full protection. At that
time the Masráta—a section of a very powerful
Berber tribe—had made, as we shall see, a colonial
settlement in A'gades, and, owing to their great
power, commercial activity, and near connection with
the Tawárek, were considered wholly exempt from
any tribute, while the inhabitants of Tunis, who
seem to have excited the jealousy or hostility of the
great lords of the desert, were subjected to the
highest personal exaction, viz. ten dollars a head.
Now Gagliuffi's partner was a native of Sfákes; but
having long resided in Masráta, he insisted upon
being free from tribute, like the inhabitants of the
latter place: but our friends were not to be cheated
out of their right, and made him pay as a Tunisian.

Having settled this little business, they came to us.
There were Hatíta Inek (the son of) Khóden of the
Manghásatangh, Utaeti (the eldest son of Sháfo), a
younger son of the latter, and several more. The
first, who had enjoyed the friendship of Captain Lyon,
behaved throughout like a man well acquainted with
Europeans; but Utaeti conducted himself like a strict
Tarki, neither showing his face, nor speaking a single
word. Hatíta expressed the wish that we should not
proceed until he returned from Murzuk, where he
assured us he would remain but a very short time;
and we engaged to do our best to keep back the
camel-drivers, who were but little inclined to stay
here long.

In consequence of this state of things, I determined

to return to the town, in order to ascertain the terms entered into between the parties; and accordingly, starting at five in the evening, and resting a few hours after midnight in Zerghán, I reached Murzuk on Friday morning at seven o'clock. I found that Mr. Gagliuffi had been very ill during the hot weather of the last few days; but to-day he was fortunately a little better.

Having waited in vain for the chiefs the whole of Saturday, we received a visit from them on Sunday, when they appeared in the finery with which they had been dressed by Mustapha Bey, but would not come to any terms; and it was not till Monday, when they took up their residence in the house belonging formerly to Mukni, but now to the Wakíl of Borno, that they concluded an arrangement. The sum which they then received would have been moderate, had they undertaken to see us safe under the protection of Annur, the chief of the Kél-owí. I urged, with Mr. Gagliuffi, the necessity of having a written copy of the agreement; but to this the chief would not listen, and thus confessed that there was really no distinct contract, as we had been given to understand, to the effect that Utaeti should not leave us till he had committed us to the care of the chief Annur.

This business being concluded, I was in great haste to return to Tasáwa; and starting immediately afterwards, at one o'clock in the afternoon, arrived at our tent a little before midnight. Our tent, indeed, was still there; but all the Tinýlkum (Músa alone excepted), and all our things, were gone on, and Overweg and I were obliged to follow the next day without waiting for Mr. Richardson.

Accordingly, on the 25th of June we left Tasáwa, and after having crossed some sand-hills, entered upon harder soil, with ethel-bushes crowning the little hills, —the whole scene making the impression that a considerable current of water had at one period flowed along here and carried away the soil, which had once extended to the top of the hills. The whole district, which is a narrow and very long strip of land, affording a little herbage for cattle and sheep, bears the name of Wadi Aberjúsh, or Berjúsh, and soon exhibits a more pleasant character; the encircling borders increase a little in height, while the sand ceases and a great deal of herbage begins to cover the soil. But after about another hour's march, we entered upon pebbly ground like that of the Hammáda, and continued descending through a bare country till we reached the well Sháraba, where we encamped a little to the north, near a talha-bush. It is an open well, only three feet below the surface of the ground, which here forms a very remarkable hollow, almost six hundred feet below the level of Murzuk, but nevertheless contains water only for two or three months in the year. It is, however, evident that in case of heavy rains a large pond or lake must be temporarily formed here by the torrent, which, sweeping along Wadi Berjúsh, finds no outlet.

Towards evening the locality was enlivened for a short time by a small slave-caravan, led by Mohammed Trumba or 'Akerút, an active, energetic man, whom I met several times in the course of my travels, and incurred some obligation towards him, as it was he who, on my setting out from Zinder to Timbúktu in the beginning of 1853, brought me a supply of one thousand dollars, without which I could scarcely have succeeded in my undertaking. He had come in only sixty-five days from Zinder, and thirty-three from Asben, having been obliged to pursue his journey as fast as possible, because, owing to the expedition of the Kél-owí against the Welád Slimán, provisions were very scarce in Asben. He estimated the number of fighting men who had gone on that expedition at seven thousand, and stated that the Tawárek were acting- in concert with the Dáza, a tribe of Tébu, whose real name is Búlgudá. He stated that E' Núr (or Annur, as the name is pronounced), the chief of the Kél-owí, was at present in Tasáwa (that is to say, the town of that name on the borders of Negroland), but would soon return to Asben. He confirmed the report of plenty of rain having fallen in the desert, in consequence of which the wells were full; but he begged me to beware of the cold during the nights, which he represented as very intense. He had twenty-three female slaves with him and only five camels, and hastened on to Tasáwa, in order to obtain dates for his famished people.

Wednesday, June 26th. Owing to the camels having strayed, it was very late when we left our encampment, and entered a sort of flat valley, from which we ascended to a higher level. From this we obtained a distant glance, towards the W.S.W., of the ruins of a fortress called Kasr Sháraba, the history of which, as it is connected with the struggles of yore between the Tebu and the inhabitants of Fezzán, would be full of interest, if it could be made out distinctly. Towards noon the country wore a more genial aspect, being adorned with several groups of palm-trees. We had to go round a rather steep hill, about 350 feet high, from the summit of which I obtained an interesting view over the desert. The whole country presented a very irregular structure, and scarcely allowed the continuous line of the Wadi Berjúsh to be traced by the eye, hills of considerable height and black pebbly tracts succeeding each other. Over such a desert we continued our march until, late in the afternoon, we reached a spot where the sight of a true wadi, full of herbage and bordered by a strip of talha-trees, gladdened our hearts, and we encamped. It was a pleasant open ground; and the night being cool and refreshing, we felt very much invigorated when we rose the next morning to continue our march.

The talha-trees continued; but the herbage was principally limited to resú, an herb which has a very strong taste, and is not relished by camels for any length of time. The green strip took an irregular, winding course, sometimes approaching the sand-hills

which we had always on our left at a certain distance,
sometimes keeping more to our right; and Músa, our
grave but cheerful camel-driver, dwelt in terms of the
highest praise on the great superiority of this wadi,
which he said is joined by as many as a hundred
smaller branches.   It evidently forms the natural
highroad between Fezzán and the western desert, and
about a month ago must have exhibited a more varied
aspect, enlivened as it then was by a considerable
torrent sweeping along it.   In the afternoon we saw
several spots where the eddying stream had formed
itself a bed about five feet deep, and had turned
up the ground all around; the crust of mire which
covered the bed of the torrent had not yet dried.
We encamped on a pleasant spot called Hamáwa,
without pitching our tents, so delighted were we to
enjoy the fresh air of the desert.   Here we were joined
by a man from Tasáwa, who wanted to seize a debtor,
who had attached himself to Bóro's party in order to
make his escape into Sudán—a practice very common
with the people of Fezzán.

By repeated measuring with our chain, we had found
that, on tolerably even ground, our ordinary rate as
the Tawárek travel was half an English geographical
mile in thirteen minutes.   It is the general custom
of these people, who do not allow their camels to feed
on the march, to leave them the whole night on the
pasture, and not to fetch them till morning, for which
reason they never start very early, and often at a
rather late hour.

Friday,
June 28th. About an hour after we had begun our march along the line of green herbage, we came to a temporary well called Ahitsa*, containing very fine rain-water, but only for a period of about two months in the year.   Having filled two of our water-skins, we continued our march, and soon, to our great joy, got sight of two white tents belonging the one to Mohammed Bóro, the other to Mohammed e' Sfaksi, and pointing out to us the encampment of the caravan. It had been pitched on open ground, in the midst of the strip of green herbage, and surrounded with a rich border of talha-trees.   The place offered good pasture for the camels; and a small encampment of other Tinýlkum not belonging to our caravan, but merely pasturing their camels and goats here, had been formed near the trees.   The whole presented an animated picture.   Our camel-drivers are said to possess, in the sand-hills bordering this valley on the south side, considerable stores of dates and corn, and to have taken from thence their supplies for the road. The whole character of this landscape appeared to me so peculiar that, the following morning before we started, I made a sketch of it from the elevated stony ground to the north of the channel, which here ex-hibited evident traces of a small waterfall formed by the heavy rains.   Stones had been laid here in the form

---

* The commencing vowel-sound "a" is generally inaudible, at least by a strange ear, if the word be not very distinctly spoken; but nevertheless it is characteristic of these Tawárek names.

of a circle, as a place of prayer.   The whole valley
was about four miles broad; the locality is called
Tesémmak.

When we started next morning, we formed a

tolerably large party, with sixty-two camels, which
were arranged in four strings, one of which consisted of thirty-three animals, each fastened to the
tail of the preceding one.   The valley was enlivened
by a small herd of gazelles, which Overweg and I
tried for a moment to pursue.   Having passed a
well called Tafiyúk, at a place where the sand-hills
jut out into the valley, we encamped about half an
hour beyond, near another well containing rain-water
for a short time of the year, and called Em-éneza.
Two branches of the wadi unite here; and distinct

traces of the great force of the last torrent remained in the broken condition of the ground.

Here we remained encamped for the two following days, in order to allow Mr. Richardson and the Azkár chiefs to come up. I spent the time sometimes writing and studying, at others roving about or musing while seated on some elevated rocks at the border of the rising ground. Músa was our constant visitor, and gave us all the information required, though he was not very intelligent. There had been some small differences between us and our camel-drivers, who, though in other respects not uncouth or uncivil, had, from religious principles, sometimes assumed a rather hostile position towards us. We now effected a general reconciliation; and there was every reason to believe that we should go on well with them.

Tuesday, July 2nd. Being informed that our companions were near, we moved on a little, and at length got out of the eternal Wadi Aberjúsh, with all its little side-branches, which are divided from the main wadi by a gently rising ground covered with black pebbles. Then after a little we reached the Wadi Eláwen, forming a broad depression running from the north, where it is joined by several branch channels descending from the plateau towards the sand-hills on the south, and encamped on its western side, between tall sebót shooting up from the sandy ground, and near some fine talha-trees. We soon discovered, to our great delight, that only two hundred paces above our encampment the floods, descending from the higher ground in two large branches, and carrying down with them bushes and brushwood in abundance, had formed a pond at present about 100 feet long and 50 feet broad, which contributed greatly to enliven the district. All the world was bathing and playing about the water; and flights of thirsty birds, of the kinds *Numida* and *Pterocles*, were hovering about, watching a favourable moment to come in for their share. Everywhere in the bottom of the valley there was water at a little depth; and we obtained excellent potations from a well dug by our people close below our tents.

About five o'clock in the afternoon we were at length joined by Mr. Richardson and the chiefs of the Azkár; but the unsatisfactory way in which the business had been concluded with these chiefs in Murzuk, led to a break up sooner even than I had suspected. The next evening Hatíta summoned us to a divan, and declared distinctly that he required a month's time to make the necessary preparations for the journey to Aïr. Hence it would be necessary for us to separate from the caravan, and, taking our luggage with us to Ghát, to hire or buy other camels there. In reply to this unjust and absurd demand, we declared that we had no other choice but to follow the direct Sudán road in the company of the caravan, and that it was our firm intention at any rate not to lose more than seven days in Ghát. Hatíta having left us rather dissatisfied at our decision, our servants, who would gladly have idled away one or two months

in Ghát as they had done in Murzuk, insolently told
us that we were very much mistaken in thinking
that the road to Aïr was in any degree open to us,
for it would first be necessary to send a courier to
ask the permission of the chiefs of that country to
enter it, and we must wait for the answer.

While remaining firm in our resolution, we of course
consented to go to Ghát, and tried at the same time
to come to some final arrangement with our camel-
drivers, promising them a small allowance for every
day they should wait for us.   They at length promised
to spend ten days on the way to Arikím, a well three
days' march south from Ghát, where they would wait
six days, and then go on directly to Aïr.   Attacking
the old chief, therefore, on his weakest side, we sent
him word the next morning, that, as we had but
little money with us, he would not succeed in getting
anything of value from us, if he should try to keep us
in Ghát for any length of time; and I insisted, with
Yusuf Mukni, upon the dishonesty of the chief's
conduct, in trying to make an entirely new bargain
after he had got all he demanded.   His answer was
satisfactory; and with the fervent hope that we should
not be baffled in our attempt to discover new regions
and new tribes of men, we left the further develop-
ment of the affair to time.

While these disputes were going on, I employed
my leisure hours in roving about our encampment,
in different directions, up and down the valley.   The
eastern of the two branches, which by their junction

form the valley, was peculiarly rich in herbage, and commanded by a hill starting up from the plateau, which afforded a very interesting view around, though this was almost surpassed by the prospect from a mound a little to the W.S.W. of our tent.   The lower part of the valley was more diversified by numerous branches, which joined it on the S.E. side.   One of these, which was bordered by high ridges of sandstone, was evidently a favourite play-ground of the gazelles, the fresh footmarks of which chequered its sandy bottom like a net.   Pursuing this direction, I approached the sand-hills which form the southern border of this whole district.

Fatigued by my long walk, I was the more able in the evening to do full justice to our supper, which was diversified by a variety of birds that had been shot in the course of the day near the pond.

CHAP IX.

SINGULAR SCULPTURES IN THE DESERT. — THE MOUNTAIN-PASS.

June 5th. WE had to separate from the Tinýlkum, and from our luggage, without having any certainty as to where and when we might overtake them. The chiefs of Ghát, too, had started in advance. The country had been rising all the way from Wadi Sháraba, which seems to form the lowest point in this whole region; and we ascended to-day very considerably. Pushing on in advance of our little troop, and passing a small caravan, which was laden with provisions and merchandise belonging to the pilgrim-caravan of the Tawáti, I soon came up with Hatíta and his companions. They were civil and kind; but the old friend of the English, who had an eye to a new marriage with some pretty Amóshagh girl some forty or fifty years younger than himself, gave me sundry expressive hints that I should spare him something of my outfit, — either a pair of pistols, or a carpet, or a bernús, or any other little article. My refusal in nowise rendered him uncivil. While he was riding by my side, I took the opportunity of making a slight sketch of him,—his English gun, the gift of some previous traveller, forming a striking contrast to his large shield of antelope-hide, ornamented with a cross. Having crossed another valley of some extent, we descended into Wadi

Elghom-udé (the Valley of the Camel), which, richly clothed with herbage, forms an inlet in the stony plateau from north to south, and has a very cheerful aspect. The encampment, spread over a great extent of ground, formed quite an ethnographical museum, comprising as it did six distinct small caravan-troops from different parts of Africa, and even of Europe.

A splendid morning, cool and fresh. We were happy to meet a small caravan coming *Saturday, June 6th.* from Sudán, which brought us some important pieces of news: first, that they had come to Ghát in the company of five men belonging to the family of A'n-nur (the chief of the Kél-owí), who, after a short stay, would return to their country; and secondly, that the expedition of the Kél-owí had returned from Kánem, after having totally annihilated the Welád Slimán. They brought with them seventeen slaves, among whom were fifteen females, one with a

very engaging countenance. After less than three
miles' march, our companions looked about in the
Wadi Telísaghé for a camping-ground. The valley
proved of more than ordinary interest. It was
hemmed in by steep cliffs of rock, and adorned with
some fine talha-trees. With no great reluctance we
followed the Tawárek chiefs, who kept along its
steep western border, and at length chose the camping-
ground at a spot where a western branch joins the
principal wadi. Scarcely had we pitched our tents,
when we became aware that the valley contained
some remarkable sculptures deserving our particular
attention.

The spot where we had pitched our tents afforded
a very favourable locality for commemorating any
interesting events; and the sandstone blocks which
studded it were covered with drawings representing
various subjects, more or less in a state of preservation. With no pretensions to be regarded as finished
sculptures, they are made with a firm and steady
hand, well accustomed to such work, and, being cut
to a great depth, bear a totally different character
from what is generally met with in these tracts.

The most interesting sculpture represented the
following subject, the description of which I am unfortunately able at present to accompany with only
an imperfect woodcut, as the drawing which I made
of it on the spot was forwarded by me to England to
Mr. Birch, the celebrated Egyptian archæologist, and
seems to have been mislaid.

TELMAGHRE

The sculpture represents a group of three individuals of the following character and arrangement: —

To the left is seen a tall human figure, with the head of a peculiar kind of bull, with long horns turned forward and broken at the point; instead of the right arm he has a peculiar organ terminating like an oar, while in his left hand he carries an arrow and a bow — at least such is the appearance, though it might be mistaken for a shield: between his legs a long tail is seen hanging down from his slender body. The posture of this figure is bent forward, and all its movements are well represented.   Opposite to this curious individual is another one of not less remarkable character, but of smaller proportions, entirely human as far up as the shoulders, while the head is that of an animal which reminds us of the Egyptian ibis, without being identical with it. The small pointed head is furnished with three ears, or with a pair of ears and some other excrescence, and beyond with a sort of hood (which, more than any other particular, recalls the idea of Egyptian art), but it is not furrowed; over the fore part of the head is a round line representing some ornament, or perhaps the basilisc. This figure likewise has a bow in its right hand, but, as it would seem, no arrow, while the left hand is turned away from the body.

Between these two half-human figures, which are in a hostile attitude, is a bullock, small in proportion to the adjacent lineaments of the human figure, but chiselled with the same care and the same skilful hand, with the only exception that the feet are omitted, the legs terminating in points, a defect which I shall have occasion to notice also in another sculpture. There is another peculiarity about this figure, the upper part of the bull, by some accident, having been hollowed out, while in general all the inner part between the deeply-chiselled outlines of these sculptures is left in high relief. The animal is turned with its back towards the figure on the right, whose bow it seems about to break. The block on which it was sculptured was about four feet in breadth and three in height. It was lying loose on the top of the cliff.

No barbarian could have graven the lines with such astonishing firmness, and given to all the figures the light, natural shape which they exhibit. The Romans, who had firmly established their dominion as far as Garama, or Jerma, might easily have sent emissaries to this point and even further; but the sculptures have nothing in them of a Roman character. Some few particulars call to mind the Egyptian sculptures.   But on the whole it seems to be a representation of a subject taken from the native mythology, executed by some one who had been in intimate relation with the more advanced people on the coast, perhaps with the Carthaginians.   Be this as it may, it is scarcely doubtful that the subject repre sents two divinities disputing over a sacrifice, and that the figure at the left is intended for the victor.

On the cliff itself there is another sculpture on a large block which, now that the western end is broken off, is about twelve feet long and five feet high.   The surface of the block is quite smooth, protected as it has been, in some degree, by the block above, which projects considerably; nevertheless the sculpture has suffered a good deal.   It bears testimony to a state of life very different from that which we are accustomed to see now in these regions, and illustrates and confirms Saint Augustine's * statement, that the ancient kings of this country made use of bulls for their conveyance.   It represents a dense group of oxen in a great variety of positions, but all moving towards the right, where probably, on the end of the stone which is now

---

* Augustin. Op. vol. xvi. p. 526. ed Bassan. : — "Garamantum regibus tauri placuerunt."

broken off, the pond or well was represented from which the beasts were to be watered. Some of these bulls are admirably executed, and with a fidelity which can scarcely be accounted for, unless we suppose that the artist had before his eyes the animals which he chiselled. My sketch gives only a faint idea of the design, which is really beautiful. The only defect, as I have already remarked above, is in the feet, which, from some reason or other, have been negligently treated.

If we consider that the sculpture described is close to a watering place on the high road to Central Africa, we are reduced to the conjecture, that at that time cattle were not only common in this region, but even that they were the common beasts of burden instead of the camel, which we here look for in vain. Not only has the camel no place among these sculptures, but even among the rude outlines which at a much later period have been made on the blocks around, representing buffaloes, ostriches, and another kind of birds, there are no camels; and it is a well-known fact that the camel was introduced into the western part of Northern Africa at a much later period.[*]

There was a similar group on another block of this interesting cliff, but too much effaced to allow the particulars to be distinguished; but the figure of an  ass among the oxen was quite clear, as well as that of a horse, which was, however, ill-drawn. Not far off, Overweg found another sculptured stone representing, as the annexed sketch shows, an ox jumping through or falling into a ring or hoop, which I should suppose to have an allegorical meaning, or to represent a sacrifice, rather than, as Mr. Richardson thought, to represent any games of the circus.   There was a circle regularly laid with large blocks of rock, at the south-western slope of the cliff: these, I should suspect, belong to the same period as the sculptures before mentioned.

* See my Wanderings along the Shore of the Mediterranean, vol. i. p. 5. ff.

It is, however, to be remarked, that even now, when the quantity of water all over the ancient world has certainly decreased a great deal, oxen are sometimes used on this Sudán road by way of Ghát soon after the rains. I have been assured that in 1847 or 1848 the well-known Tebu Háj Abérma travelled with oxen from Kanó as far as Ghát, about the time of the 'Aíd el kebír,—that is to say, in the month of December,—the oxen being watered every second day.

To a later period belong innumerable inscriptions in Tefínagh, with which the cliffs on the other side of the valley and overhanging the waterpond are covered. These are mere scribblings, and are interesting merely as they serve to render evident, by contrast, the superior merit and age of the adjacent sculptures. It appeared to me remarkable, that on this side, where the water now principally collects, not a single drawing should be seen ; and I formed the conclusion that in more ancient times the water collected on the other side.

The valley is formed by the junction of two branches coming from the north, of which the western is the more considerable, being joined by some smaller wadis. Just at the place of our encampment it changed its direction, and extended from W. to E., having run in its upper course from N.W. to S.E. After the junction, the valley runs from N. to S., and loses for a moment almost the character of a wadi, while running over pebbly ground ; but it soon becomes once more well-bordered and adorned with fine groups of talha-trees, and in some places exhibits a river-bed eight feet deep, and still wet. Near a shepherd's cave there was a very luxuriant tree, under whose shade I lay down. Towards evening the pilgrim-caravan of Háj 'Abd el Káder, which had delayed so long in the wadi, arrived. The whole valley resounded with the cries of the men and their camels, who were all eagerly pressing towards the pond at the foot of the steep cliffs.

Fortunately we had already laid in a supply of water ; else we should not have been able to obtain any fit to drink.

Owing to the camels having strayed to a great distance, we started at a late hour, still leaving the Tawárek chiefs behind, who wanted to settle some business with the Tawáti, and for this purpose had changed their dirty travelling-dress for showy caftans and bernúses. We ascended the higher level, and continued along it, crossing some small beds of watercourses overgrown with herbage, till, after a little more than four miles, we had to descend into a deep and wild ravine which led us to a vale. Having again ascended, we then came to the wide and regular valley called Erazar-n-Hágarné, bordered by steep cliffs from 150 to 200 feet high, and richly clothed with herbage. Following the windings of this large wadi, which evidently has received its name from the circumstance that the Hogár or Hágara pasture their camels chiefly hereabouts, we reached the point where it is joined by the valley called A'man sémmedné, and encamped near a fine talha-tree in order to allow Hatíta to come up. This valley has its name from the cold water which at times descends from the plateau in floods, of which the deeply-worn channel bears evident traces ; it is joined at this place by an important branch-valley and several smaller ravines.

When the heat of the sun began to decline, I took a walk through the valley; and being attracted by

a circle laid out very regularly with large slabs like
the opening of a well, I began to ascend the steep
cliffs opposite the mouth of the valley of A'man sémmedné, rising to a height of about 500 feet, and
which, as I clearly saw, had been repeatedly ascended.
The cliffs are here, as is usual in this formation,
broken into regular strata ; and steep flat blocks
standing upright give them an imposing appearance.
My search here, however, led only to the discovery
of the well-chiselled form of a single bullock, in
exactly the same style as that in Wadi Telísaghé,
though it had suffered a little from its exposed situation ; but the whole appearance of the locality shows
that in former times it contained more of this kind.
On the plain above the cliffs is another circle regularly laid out, and, like the many circles seen in
Cyrenaica and in other parts of Northern Africa,
evidently connected with the religious rites of the
ancient inhabitants of these regions. Quartz pebbles
were scattered about this part of the valley.

Our people meanwhile had been busy laying in
provision of dry herbage for the next marches, during
which we were told our camels would scarcely find
anything to feed upon ; and our Tawárek friends,
when they at length arrived for their supper, did the
same.

Monday,
July 8th.   The caravan of the Tawáti having
passed by our encampment at an early
hour, we followed betimes, having an interesting
day's march before us. For the first three miles we

still kept along the large valley, into which masses of sand had been driven down from the plateau by the strong east winds: further on it became dry and bare. To this succeeded an irregular knot of hollows and plains between the sides of the plateau, which in some places formed imposing promontories and detached buttresses, all on one and the same level. We then began to ascend along a sort of broad valley, which gradually assumed a regular shape, and bore the name of Tísi. The slope of the plateau was shaped into regular strata, the uppermost of which form steep precipices like the walls of a castle; the lower ones slope down more gradually. Here we discovered ahead of us, at the foot of the southern slope, the encampment of the pilgrim-caravan, who were resting during the heat of the day. We continued our march, always ascending, till a little after noon we reached the edge of the pass, a perfect watershed, of more than 2000 feet elevation, descending more gradually towards the east as far as the well of Sháraba, while towards the west it formed a steep precipice, passable only along a most interesting gully cut into it by the water towards the Valley of Ghát. The higher level, which rises above the pass about 300 feet, seems to be considerably depressed in this place, where it collects large floods of water, such as could alone cut the remarkably wild passage through the sandstone cliffs which we were about to descend: it is called Ralle.

The first part of it was more rough than wild, and

the cliffs of the sandstone rather rugged and split
than precipitous and grand; but after half an hour's
descent it bore evident traces of the waters that
descend from the heights, and which being here collected into one mighty stream, with enormous power,
force their way down through a narrow channel.
The defile was here encompassed by rocky walls
about a hundred feet high, half of which consisted of
sandstone, while the other half was formed by a thick
deposit of marl; and a little further down it was not
more than six feet wide, and the floor and the walls
were as smooth as if they had been cut by the hand
of man; but the course of the defile was rather
winding and not at all in a straight line, forming
altogether a pass easily to be defended by a very
small power, and affording the Tawárek a stronghold
against any designs of conquest on the side of the
Turks, although it does not form the frontier, but is
regarded as entirely belonging to Fezzán. At the
narrowest point Tawárek, as well as Arab travellers
had recorded their names.

Where the channel began to widen, there were
some curious narrow gaps or crevices on both sides,
the one to the right, with its smooth rounded surface,
bearing a great similarity to the famous Ear of Dio-
nysius in Syracuse. The walls contained strata of
chalk and ironstone; and Overweg found here some
interesting petrifactions. The crevice to the left was
less deep, and rather resembled a cell or chamber.

Having here waited some time for the boat to

come up, we started together, but had still to get
through two more narrow passes of the wadi, and
at four o'clock in the afternoon entered another
very narrow defile, the steep cliffs forming it being
covered with inscriptions. At length, after a descent of altogether four hours, we emerged into
the open plain some 600 feet below, and had a
wide view of the high precipitous cliffs of the plateau, stretching out in several buttresses into the
plain, which is interrupted only by detached hills.
Amongst these was a rather remarkable one upon
a terrace-like base, and opening with three caverns
towards the roadside.   Ascending the terrace, I
found the westernmost of the caverns vaulted, as if
by art, in the shape of a large niche, but it was a
little filled with sand; I found, however, no inscriptions nor anything but four round holes, about nine
inches in diameter, hollowed out in a slab on the
terrace in front of the cavern.   Beyond this hill,
where Hatíta told us that he had once passed the
heat of the day with 'Abd Allah (Clapperton) and the
tabíb (Oudney), the country is quite open towards
the north.   About sunset we encamped in the deep
Erazar-n-Tése; there were a few talha-trees and some
herbage.

The following day our route lay over the dreary
plain, where nothing but the varied form of the rocky
buttresses projecting from the plateau into the plain
interrupted the monotony of the prospect.   Near
the slope the country seems a little less desolate; and

the valley Támelelt, which extends between two of the promontories, has even a great reputation among the natives. In the afternoon we entered a sandy region, when we began to ascend gradually till we reached the summit of the sand-hills. We then continued on the higher level, where chalk protruded to the surface. After a long march we encamped on stony ground, covered only with a scanty growth of sebót.

On the 10th we descended a good deal from this higher ground. At first the descent was gradual; but beyond the valley In-kássewa, which running through high rocky ground is not so poor in herbage, we descended about two hundred feet by steep terraces, having before us the peculiarly serrated crest of the Akakús, and in front of it some lower offshoots covered with sand. The bottom of the plain was a broad and entirely naked level with hard calcareous soil, surrounded by irregular half-decayed hilly ridges. It forms the boundary between Fezzán and the country of the Hogár. The character of the country underwent no change till we reached the valley Telíga, where, at an early hour in the afternoon, we encamped near a group of talha-trees, not far from the well, and remained for the next two days at an elevation of 1435 feet.

The valley is very shallow, now and then interrupted by some sand-hills and adorned with some fine specimens of the ethel-tree, while broad strips of herbage cover the more favoured spots. It runs

N. W., nearly parallel with the range of the Akakús, which remained at a distance of three miles. It joins the valley Ilághlaghén, which again unites with the Titábtarén ; and this valley runs towards a favoured spot called Sérdales, which we were unfortunately prevented from visiting, as Hatíta thought we should be annoyed by the begging propensities of the people. Copious springs, from which the whole locality takes the name of el Awenát, irrigate and fertilize the soil, and support a village of about the same size as Tigger-odé, inhabited by about a hundred families, while in the gardens corn, melons, and ghédeb are produced in tolerable quantity. The water of the springs is said to be warm. We saw a party of Hágara from that place, who called on our friends; they were fine men and neatly dressed.

The water of our well was not very good; from being at first discoloured, it gradually acquired a taste like that of ink, and when boiled with tea became entirely black. Late in the evening our best and most steady servant, Mohammed from Gatrón, was wounded, but whether stung by a scorpion or bitten by a snake he knew not, and was much alarmed. We applied spirits of hartshorn to the wound; but he was very ill for the next twenty-four hours, and totally disabled, so that we were obliged to bind him on the camel during the next day's march.

There had been much talk for some days to the effect that we travellers, to- Saturday, July 13th.

gether with Hatíta, should take the nearer, but more
difficult, road to Ghát across the range, while our
luggage should go by the longer, but smoother, road
round the mountains; but it was at length decided
that we should all go by the longer road, and none
but the Sfaksi, who was anxious to overtake the
caravan as soon as possible, took the more difficult
path, which, for geological observations, might have
proved the more interesting. Going sometimes on
pebbly, at others on sandy ground, after five miles
we reached the shallow valley, Ilághlaghén, running
from east to west, and handsomely overgrown with
bushes; and after another stretch of about the same
length, we entered the range of mountains, consisting of remarkably cragged and scarred rocks, with
many narrow defiles. Altogether it presented a very
curious spectacle.

When the rocks assumed a smoother appearance,
we suddenly descended into a deep ravine, which, at
the first glance, appeared to be of a volcanic nature;
but, on closer inspection, all the black rocks composing these dismal-looking cliffs, proved to consist
of sandstone, blackened by the influence of the atmosphere: further on it was disposed in regular strata
very much like slate. The western and highest part
of the range seems to consist of clay-slate. The
valley changed its character in some degree after its
junction with a side-valley called Tipérkum, which
bears distinct marks of great floods occasionally descending along its channel from the mountains.

Here we collected some firewood, as we were told that further on we should find none, and then entered a defile or glen with an ascent of about a hundred feet above the bottom of the valley. Beyond this the scene grew more open, and irregular plains, interrupted by steep buttresses, succeeded each other.

At half-past four o'clock in the afternoon we had gradually begun to change our direction from N.W. by W. to S. The valley was bordered by a deep chasm and craggy mountain to the right, and a range of grotesque promontories towards the left, the slope of which was broken into a variety of terraces, with several cones rising from them. At length turning round the edge of the mountain-range, we entered the broad valley of Tánesóf, having before us the isolated and castellated crest of mount I'dinen, or Kasr Jenún, and on our left the long range of the Akakús, beautifully illuminated by the setting sun, and forming a sort of relief in various colours, the highest precipitous crest, with its castles and towers, being white, while the lower slope, which was more gradual and rugged, disclosed regular strata of red marl. Towards the west the valley, about five miles broad, was bordered by sand-hills, whence the sand was carried by the wind over its whole surface. We ourselves encamped at length on sandy soil without the least herbage, while at the distance of about two miles a strip of green was seen running along the valley.

Starting at an early hour the next day, we kept along the broad barren valley straight for the Enchanted Castle, which the fanciful reports of our companions had invested with great interest. Notwithstanding, or perhaps in consequence of, the warnings of the Tawárek not to risk our lives in so irreligious and perilous an undertaking as a visit to this dwelling of the demons, I made up my mind to visit it, convinced as I was that it was an ancient place of worship, and that it might probably contain some curious sculptures or inscriptions. Just at noon the naked bottom of the valley began to be covered with a little herbage, when, after another mile, beyond a depression in the ground which had evidently at one time formed a considerable waterpond, talha-trees and ethel-bushes broke the monotony of the landscape, while between the sand-hills on our right a broad strip of green was seen, coming from the westernmost corner of the I'dinen. Keeping still on for about five miles, we encamped in the midst of a shallow concavity of circular shape, surrounded by herbage, and near a large mound crowned by an ethel-tree. At some distance S. E. we had the well Táhala, the water of which proved very good.

As it was too late to visit the I'dinen to-day, I sat down in the shade of a fine talha, and made the subjoined sketch of it.

In the evening we received a visit from two men belonging to a caravan laden with merchandise of Ghadamsíyin (people of Ghadámes), which was said

SKETCH OF THE I'DINEN.

to have come, by the direct road through the wadi, in thirty days from Tripoli.

P 5

This was a *dies ater* for me. Overweg and I had determined to start early in the morning for the remarkable mountain; but we had not been able to obtain from the Tawárek a guide to conduct us from thence to the next well, whither the caravan was to proceed by the direct road. Hatíta and Utaeti having again resisted all our solicitations for a guide, I at length, determined as I was to visit the mountain at any cost, started off in the confidence of being able to make out the well in the direction indicated to me. By ill-luck, our provision of zummíta (a cool and refreshing paste on which we were accustomed to breakfast) was exhausted the day before, so that I was obliged to take with me dry biscuit and dates, the worst possible food in the desert when water is scarce.

But as yet I needed no stimulus, and vigorously pushed my way through the sand-hills, which afforded no very pleasant passage. I then entered a wide, bare, desolate-looking plain, covered with black pebbles, from which arose a few black mounds. Here I crossed the beginning of a *fiumara* richly overgrown with herbage, which wound along through the sand-hills towards the large valley-plain. It was the abode of a beautiful pair of maraiya (*Antelope Soemmeringii*), which, probably anxious for their young ones, did not make off when roused by my approach, but stopped at a short distance, gazing at me and wagging their tails. Pursuing my way over the pebbly ground, which gradually rose till it was broken up by a considerable ravine descending from the western part of the mount, I disturbed another party of three antelopes, which were quietly lying down under the cover of some large blocks. At last I began to feel fatigued from walking over the sharp-pointed pebbles, as the distance proved to be greater than I had originally imagined; and I did not seem to have got much nearer to the foot of the Enchanted Mountain. In fact it proved that the crest of the mount formed a sort of horseshoe, so that its middle part, for which I had been steering all the time, in order to gain a depression which seemed to afford an easy ascent, was by far the remotest. I therefore changed my course and turned more eastward, but only met with more annoyance, for, ascending the slope which I hoped would soon convey me to the summit, I suddenly came to the steep precipice of a deep ravine, which separated me from the crest.

Being already fatigued, the disappointment, of course, depressed my spirits, and I had to summon all my resolution and energy in order to descend into the ravine and climb the other side. It was now past ten o'clock; the sun began to put forth its full power, and there was not the slightest shade around me. In a state of the utmost exhaustion I at length reached the narrow pinnacled crest, which was only a few feet broad, and exhibited neither inscriptions nor sculptures. I had a fine prospect towards the S.W. and N.E.; but I looked around in vain for any traces of our caravan. Though exposed to the full rays of the sun, I lay down on my high barbacan to seek repose; but my dry biscuit or a date was quite unpalatable, and being anxious about my little provision of water, I could only sip an insufficient draught from my small water-skin.

As the day advanced I got anxious lest our little band, thinking that I was already in advance, might continue their march in the afternoon, and, in spite of my weakness, determined to try to reach the encampment. I therefore descended the ravine, in order to follow its course, which, according to Hatíta's indications, would lead me in the direction of the well. It was very hot; and being thirsty, I swallowed at once the little water that remained. This was about noon; and I soon found that the draught of mere water, taken upon an empty stomach, had not at all restored my strength.

At length I reached the bottom of the valley. Hatíta had always talked as if they were to encamp at no great distance from the mountain; yet, as far as I could strain my view, no living being was to be seen. At length I became puzzled as to my direction, and, hurrying on as fast as my failing strength would allow, I ascended a mound crowned with an ethel-bush, and fired my pistols; but I waited in vain for an answer: a strong east wind was blowing dead against me. Reflecting a moment on my situation, I then crossed the small sand-hills, and, ascending another mound, fired again. Convinced that there could be nobody in this direction, at least

at a moderate distance, I bethought myself that our
party might be still behind, and, very unluckily, I
kept more directly eastward.

The valley was here very richly overgrown with
sebót; and to my great delight I saw at a distance
some small huts attached to branches of the ethel-
tree, covered on the top with sebót, and open in
front. With joy in my heart I hastened on towards
them, but found them empty; and not a living being
was to be seen, nor was there a drop of water to be
got.

My strength being now exhausted, I sat down on
the naked plain, with a full view before me of the
whole breadth of the wadi, and with some confidence
expected the caravan. I even thought, for a moment,
that I beheld a string of camels passing in the distance.
But it was an illusion; and when the sun was about
to set, not being able to muster strength enough to
walk a few paces without sitting down, I had only to
choose for my night's quarters between the deserted
huts and an ethel-tree which I saw at a little distance.
I chose the latter, as being on a more elevated spot,
and therefore scrambled to the tree, which was of a
respectable old age, with thick tall branches, but
almost leafless. It was my intention to light a fire,
which promised almost certain deliverance; but I
could not muster sufficient strength to gather a little
wood. I was broken down and in a feverish state.

Having lain down for an hour or two, after it became quite dark I arose from the ground, and, looking

around me, descried to my great joy a large fire S.W.
down the valley, and, hoping that it might be that of
my companions, I fired a pistol, as the only means of
communicating with them, and listened as the sound
rolled along, feeling sure that it would reach their
ears; but no answer was returned. All remained
silent. Still I saw the flame rising towards the sky,
and telling where deliverance was to be found, without
my being able to avail myself of the signal. Having
waited long in vain, I fired a second time—yet no
answer. I lay down in resignation, committing my
life to the care of the Merciful One; but it was in
vain that I tried to sleep, and, restless and in a high
fever, I tossed about on the ground, looking with
anxiety and fear for the dawn of the next day.

At length the long night wore away, and dawn
was drawing nigh. All was repose and silence ; and
I was sure I could not choose a better time for trying
to inform my friends, by signal, of my whereabouts.
I therefore collected all my strength, loaded my pistol
with a heavy charge, and fired — once — twice. I
thought the sound ought to awaken the dead from
their tombs, so powerfully did it reverberate from
the opposite range and roll along the wadi ; yet no
answer. I was at a loss to account for the great
distance apparently separating me from my companions, who seemed not to have heard my firing.

The sun that I had half longed for, half looked
forward to with terror, at last rose. My condition,
as the heat went on increasing, became more dread-

ful; and I crawled around, changing every moment
my position, in order to enjoy the little shade afforded
by the leafless branches of the tree. About noon
there was of course scarcely a spot of shade left—
only enough for my head,—and I suffered greatly
from the pangs of thirst, although I sucked a little of
my blood till I became senseless, and fell into a sort of
delirium, from which I only recovered when the sun
went down behind the mountains. I then regained
some consciousness, and crawled out of the shade of
the tree, throwing a melancholy glance over the plain,
when suddenly I heard the cry of a camel. It was
the most delightful music I ever heard in my life;
and raising myself a little from the ground, I saw a
mounted Tarki passing at some distance from me,
and looking eagerly around. He had found my footsteps in the sandy ground, and losing them again on
the pebbles, was anxiously seeking traces of the direction I had taken. I opened my parched mouth, and
crying, as loud as my faint strength allowed, "áman,
áman" (water, water), I was rejoiced to get for
answer "íwah! íwah!" and in a few moments he
sat at my side, washing and sprinkling my head,
while I broke out involuntarily into an uninterrupted
strain of "el hamdu lilláhi! el hamdu lilláhi!"

Having thus first refreshed me, and then allowed
me a draught which, however, I was not able to enjoy,
my throat being so dry, and my fever still continuing, my deliverer, whose name was Músa, placed me
upon his camel, mounted himself in front of me, and

brought me to the tents.   They were a good way off.
The joy of meeting again, after I had been already
despaired of, was great; and I had to express my
sincere thanks to my companions, who had given
themselves so much trouble to find me.   But I could
speak but little at first, and could scarcely eat anything for the next three days, after which I gradually
recovered my strength.   It is, indeed, very remarkable how quickly the strength of a European is broken
in these climes, if for a single day he be prevented
from taking his usual food.   Nevertheless I was able
to proceed the next day (the 17th), when we kept
more towards the slope of the Akakús, and here passed
a broad lateral valley, rich in herbage, called A'dar-n-
jelkum, after which we descended about a hundred
feet from the pebbly ground into sandy soil forming
a sort of valley called Ighelfannís, and full of ethel-
trees and sebót.   In such a locality we encamped
two hours after noon, near splendid ethel-trees; but   .
the strong north-easterly wind, enveloping ourselves
and baggage in thick clouds of sand, banished all
enjoyment.

Thursday,   We continued our march with the sure
July 18th.   expectation of soon reaching Ghát*, the
second great station on our journey.   The valley after

---

* If I were to give the real native sound, I should write Rhát
rather than Ghát; and it is only from fear lest I might offend the
ear of the English reader, that I abstain from following this principle.   The ghain of the Arabs has a double sound, sometimes as
gh, at others as rh, and the latter prevails entirely in this part of
Africa; and I do not see why we should not express this differ-

some time became free from ethel-trees, and opened a
view of the little town, situated at the north-western
foot of a rocky eminence jutting out into the valley,
and girt by sand-hills on the west. Its plantation
extends in a long strip towards S.S.W., while another
group, formed by the plantation and by the noble-
looking mansion of Háj A'hmed, appears towards the
west.   Here we were joined by Mohammed Sheríf, a
nephew of Háj A'hmed, in a showy dress, and well
mounted on a horse; and we separated from Hatíta
in order to take our way round the north side of the
hill, so as to avoid exciting the curiosity and im-
portunity of the townspeople.   But a good many
boys came out of the town, and exhibited quite an
interesting scene as they recognized Yakúb (Mr.
Richardson), who had visited this place, on his former journey.   Many people came out to see us, some
offering us their welcome, others remaining indifferent spectators.

Thus we reached the new plantation of Háj A'hmed
the governor, as he is called, of Ghát, and found, at
the entrance of the out-building, which had been destined for our use, the principal men of the town, who
received us with great kindness and politeness.   The
most interesting among them was Háj A'hmed himself, a man of grave and dignified manners, who,
although a stranger to the place, and a native of
Tawát, has succeeded, through his address and his

ence. For the same reason I should prefer writing Sonrhay, and
not Songhay, or Sunghay.

mercantile prosperity, in obtaining for himself here an almost princely position, and has founded in reality a new town, with large and splendid improvements, by the side of the old city. His situation as governor of Ghát, in reference, and in some degree in opposition, to the Tawárek chiefs, is a very peculiar one, and requires, on his part, a good deal of address, patience, and forbearance. I am convinced that when we first arrived he did not view us with displeasure, but, on the contrary, was greatly pleased to receive under his roof a mission of Her Britannic Majesty's Government, with whose immense influence and power, and the noble purpose of whose policy, he was not entirely unacquainted; but his extraordinary and precarious situation did not allow him to act freely, and besides I cannot say that he received from us so warm an acknowledgment as his conduct in the first instance seemed to deserve.

Besides him, the chief parties in our first conversation were his nephew A'hmed Mohammed Sheríf (the man who came to meet us), a clever but forward lad, of pleasant manners—whom in the course of my travels I met several times in Sudán,—and Mohammed Káfa, a cheerful good-humoured man.

Our quarters, of which the accompanying woodcut gives the ground-plan, were certainly neither airy nor agreeable; but the hot sand-wind which blew without made them appear to us quite tolerable.

CHAP. X.

THE INDIGENOUS BERBER POPULATION.

THERE can be no doubt that even Fezzán, in ancient times, had a population entirely different from that dwelling near the coast; but the original black inhabitants of that country have been swept away, or mixed up entirely with the Arabs, who seem to have invaded this country not earlier than the 15th century of our era, for in Makrizi's time Fezzán was still a Berber country.* But few names now remain which evidently bespeak a Central African origin, such as those terminating in *awa*, as Tasáwa or Tessáwa (a town already mentioned by Edrísi†), Portukawa, and others.

* Makrizi, Hamaker Specim. Categ. p. 206. بلد فزان
واهلها بربر. El Bekri, p. 455., already mentions Benu-Khaldín, besides the Fezzánab, as inhabitants of some places. On the same page this diligent author says expressly that the town of Zawíla was on the border of Negroland. We shall see, in the second volume, that all this country constituted part of the Empire of Kánem; indeed, from what El Bekri says, p. 457., it appears that even within twenty years after the great and unfortunate immigration of the Arab tribes into Barbary, two tribes, the Hadrámis and the Sehámis, had taken possession of Wadán. But we shall see that the Negroes regained this place at a later period.

† Edrísi, ed. Jaubert, vol. i. p. 113. Edrísi deserves attention when he says that the Negroes called Tessáwa " Little Jerma ;" that is to say, they attached to it a celebrated name, as if it were another capital of the country.

But in the country of Ghát, which we have now entered, the case is very different; for here the former state of things has not been so entirely altered as not to leave some unmistakable testimonies behind it.

All the original population of North Africa appear to have been a race of the Semitic stock, but who, by intermarriage with tribes which came from Egypt, or by way of it, had received a certain admixture. The consequence was, that several distinct tribes were produced, designated by the ancients as Libyans, Moors, Numidians, Libyphœnicians, Getulians, and others, and traced by the native historians to two different families, the Beránes and the Abtar, who, however, diverge from one common source, Mazigh or Madaghs. This native wide-spread African race, either from the name of their supposed ancestor, Ber, which we recognize in the name Afer, or in consequence of the Roman term *barbari*, has been generally called Berber, and in some regions Shawi and Shelluh. The general character and language of these people seem to have been the same, while the complexion alone was the distinguishing point of difference.

How far southward the settlements of this North African race originally extended, it is difficult to say; but it may be gathered, even from ancient writers, that they did not extend to the very border of the naked desert, and that they were bounded on the south by a region occupied by Æthiopian races,—

an observation which is confirmed by the present
state of things. Wárgela evidently belonged originally to the dominion of the Blacks, as well as
Tawát. The Berbers seem in general to have kept
within their borders till driven from their native
seats by the Arabs : for they had been mildly treated
by the former conquerors of the country (the Phœ-
nicians, the Romans, Vandals, and Byzantines), and
they appear even to have partly embraced Christianity*; but this, of course, was just another
principle of opposition between them and their
Mohammedan conquerors, and a great proportion of
them were evidently obliged to retire into the more
desolate regions in their rear. The exact time when
this happened we are not able to determine.

In the western part of the desert this transmigration
commenced before the time of Islam; but in the
central part of Barbary the flight of the Berbers
seems to have been connected with that numerous
immigration of Arab families into North Africa,
which took place in the first half of the 11th
century, in the time and at the instigation of A'hmed
ben 'Alí el Jerjeráni, who died in A.H. 436, or

---

* Procop. de Ædificiis, vi. 4.; Joann. Abb. Chronic. p. 13. (respecting the Mauri pacati, but especially the important tribe of
the Lewátah); Abu 'l Hassan, Annales Regg. Maur., ed. Tornberg,
pp. 7. 15. 83. (respecting the Western Berbers); El Bekri, Notices
et Extraits, &c., vol. xii. p. 484.; E'bn Khaldún, tom. i. p. 209., le
Baron de Slane, and *passim*.

1044–5 of our era.* The fugitives pushed forward in several great divisions, which it is not essential here to enumerate, as, with a few exceptions, they have become extinct. It seems only necessary to advert here to the fact, that of all the reports handed down to us by the ancient Arab historians and geographers respecting the different Berber nations existing in the desert, the name of Tárki, or Tawárek, by which they are at present generally designated, occurs only in E'bn Khaldún †, under the form Tarká or Táriká; and after him Leo Africanus is the first who, in mentioning the five great tribes, names one of them Terga.‡ This name, which has been given to the Berber inhabitants of the desert, and which Hodgson § erroneously supposed to mean

---

* A few authors make this momentous event, which plunged North Africa into a series of misfortunes, happen a few years later, under El Yezúri. — Leo Africanus, ed. Venezia, 1837, l. i. c. 21.: " Ma quando la loro (degli Arabi) generazione entrò nell' Africa, allora con guerra scacciò di là i Numidi ; e ella si rimase ad abitar ne' diserti vicini ai paesi de' datteri, e i Numidi andarono a far le loro abitazioni ne' diserti che sono propinqui alla Terranegra."

† E'bn Khaldún, vol. i. p. 235. Arab. text, vol. ii. p. 64. transl. De Slane ; vol. i. p. 260. Arab. text, vol. ii. p. 105. transl. In both passages the name is written تاريكا and it is to be noted that this name was borne by a clan which dwelt nearest to the Arab tribe of the Beni Solaim. The great General Tárek E'bn Zíyad, who was a Berber from the tribe of the Ulhassa, seems to have received his name Tárek from the same source as the Berber clan Táriká received theirs.

‡ El Bekri certainly mentions (Notices et Extraits, vol. xii. p. 623.) وادى ترقا ; but this has nothing to do with the tribe.

§ Hodgson, Notes on Northern Africa, p. 23. The word which

"tribe," is quite foreign to them. The truly indigenous name by which these people call themselves, is the same by which they were already known to the Greeks and Romans, and which was given to their ancestors by E'bn Khaldún and other Arabic writers, viz. Amázigh, Mázigh, Mazix, Masix, Mazys, Mazax, and even Maxitanus in the singular form. The general form now used in these regions is Amóshagh* in the singular, Imóshagh in the plural, and Temáshight in the neutral form. This is the native name by which the so-called Tawárek† designate their whole nation, which is divided into several great families. And if the reader inquires who gave them the other name, I answer, with full confidence, the Arabs; and the reason why they called them so was probably from their having left or abandoned their religion, from the verb تَرَكَ, "tereku dínihum;" for, from evidence which I have collected elsewhere, it seems clear that a great part of the Berbers of the desert were once

means tribe is written طَارِقَة; and this is an Arabic, and not a Berber word.

* The ز and ش (sh) in Berber names are often confounded. Thus they say Ikázkezan, Ikáshkeshan; A'gadez, E'gedesh.

† The name is written by the Arabs promiscuously with the ك and with the ق, but oftener with the كّ; and the name is so pointedly Arabic that besides the plural form توارك another form is used, الـتـاركـيـون. Sultan Bello says properly, وكان هذه ·التوارك من بقايا البربر الذى انتشروا ايام افريقية

Q 2

Christians (they are still called by some Arabs "the Christians of the desert"), and that they afterwards changed their religion and adopted Islám; notwithstanding which they still call God "Mesí," and an angel "anyelús," and have preserved many curious customs which bear testimony to their ancient creed.

I said that the regions into which the Berbers had thus been obliged to withdraw, had been formerly occupied by Ethiopian or, as we may rather call them, sub-Libyan tribes. But who were these tribes? We have here to do only with the region about Ghát, reserving the other districts of the desert for future discussion as we advance in our journey. This region, as well as the whole country southward, including Aïr, or rather A'sben, was anciently inhabited, I think, by the Góber race. But the Hogár, or Azkár, who now occupy this country, do not seem to have been its first conquerors, but to have found another race, nearly related to themselves, in possession of it.

The tribe which now possesses the country, the Imóshagh or Tawárek of Ghát, are generally called Azkár or Azgár; but they are named also Hogár, or Hágara, though the latter name is very often employed to denote another tribe. Upon this point, also, we have received full and credible information from E'bn Khaldún, who tells us* that the name Hogár was

* E'bn Khaldún, vol. i. p. 275. transl. De Slane.

formed from that of Hauwára, and served to designate that section of the great Berber tribe which
had retired into the desert about Gógó; and it is
very remarkable that the Hogár were described just
about the same time, in those same regions, by the
traveller E'bn Batúta.* Hogár therefore seems to be
the more general name, while Azkár serves to designate a section of this tribe. However, this name
also appears to be an ancient one, being mentioned
already by Edrísi (A.H. 453)† as the name of a tribe
evidently identical with that of which we are speaking,
the settlements of which he indicates as being distant
twelve days' journey from Tasáwa, and eighteen from
Ghadámes. It is mentioned about a century later
by E'bn Sáíd‡ as dwelling in the same place. The

---

* Journal Asiatique, série iv. tom. i., 1843, p. 238. هڪّار.
This is the usual form, Hogár, although Hágara, with the second
vowel short, seems to have no less pretension to correctness.

† Edrisi, trad. Jaubert, i. pp. 113. 116. It is very probable,
indeed, that this tribe is already mentioned as early as the 4th
century, under the form of 'Αυξωριανοί, and in connection with the
Μάζυες, which is nothing else but the general name of the whole
tribe, Imóshagh, by Philostorgius (Hist. Eccles. xi. viii.), who represents them as making incursions into Egypt. Under the form
Ausuriani ('Αυσουριανοί), the same tribe is several times mentioned
by Synesius, the bishop of Cyrene, who expressly represents them
as mounted upon camels. Whether they are identical with the
Austoriani of Ammianus Marcellinus is less certain. For this
hint I am indebted to Mr. Cooley.

‡ E'bn Sáíd, mentioned by Abu 'l Fedá, ed. Reinaud, tom. i.
(texte Arabe), p. 125., in the corrupted reading ازكان; trad.
vol. ii. p. 177.

Tinýlkum Ibrahim was of opinion that Azkár means that section of the Hogár who had remained (at some period unknown to us) "faithful to the established authority." But this interpretation of the name, if we consider the early period at which it occurs, does not seem quite probable; and I suspect that those may be right who give to the name a more general meaning.

At present the Azkár form but a small part of the population of the country which they rule, namely, the region inclosed between the desert bordered by Wadi Talíya in the east, the valleys Zerzúwa and A'fara in the west, the well of Asíu towards the south, and Nijbertín towards the north, and are not able to furnish more than about five hundred armed men. In fact, they form a warlike aristocracy of five families, divided into thirty divisions or fayas, each of which has an independent chief. The names of the five families are Urághen, I'manang, I'fogas, Hadánarang, and Manghássatang. The Urághen or Aurághen, meaning the " Yellows," or " golden " (in colour), who seem to have once formed a very powerful family*, and have given their name to one of the principal dialects of the Tarkíye or Temáshight, are at present much dispersed, many of them living among the Awelímmiden on the northern shore of the Isa or Niger, where I shall have more to say about

* The Aurághen are evidently identical with the Aurígha, one of the seven principal clans of the Beránes.

them. Even among the Azkár they still form the
most important division, and count at least a hundred
and fifty full-grown men. A large body of them is
settled in and about the valley of Arikím, on the
direct road from Murzuk to Sudán, and about fifty
miles to the south of Ghát. Their original abode is·
said to have been at a place called Asáwa, to the
south of Irálghawen. But the tribe that formerly
possessed the greatest authority, and which on this
account is still called Amanókalen, or the sultan
tribe, is that of the I'manang, who are at present
reduced to extreme poverty, and to a very small
number, said not even to reach ten families. But
they have still a very large number of Imghád under
their command. Their women are celebrated for
their beauty. They are most of them settlèd in the
valley of Díder. The third division of the Azkár, to
which Hatíta, the friend of the English, belongs, are
the Manghássatang, or Imaghássaten, whose leather
tents are generally pitched in the Valley of Zerzúwa,
on the road from Ghát to Tawát, about six days'
journey from the former.*

* In order to point out clearly the situation of these valleys, I
here subjoin a short itinerary of the road from Ghát to Zerzúwa,
and thence to E'geri.

In going from Ghát westwards to Tawát, you reach, after four
or five hours, the place Fiyút; on the second day you sleep in
Idú ; on the third, in A'tser-n-táshelt; on the fourth, in Azákkan
temanókalt ("the royal plain"); on the fifth, in Ihór-hayen; after
which, on the sixth day, you arrive in Zerzúwa. (This part of
the itinerary varies a little from the itinerary from Ghát to Tawát,

The three clans, or "tiyúsi," which I have mentioned, constitute at present, strictly speaking, the family of the Azkár; the other two divisions, viz. the I'fogas and the Hadánarang, having separated from the rest, and broken in some way the national bond ·which formerly united them with the others.   One of them, the I'fogas, are scattered over the whole desert, some having settled among the Kél-owí at a place called Tórit, on the road to Damerghú; another section dwells in the more favoured valleys to the east of Mabrúk; while a small portion of this tribe remains in the territory of the Azkár, where they have their abode in the valley of A'fara, about halfway between Ghát and Tawát.   The second of these tribes, viz. the Hadánarang, is settled in a place called A'demar, not far from the southern frontier of the territory of the Azkár, in the midst of the Imghád. They are, to some extent at least, migratory freebooters; and to them belonged those robbers who, soon after we had fortunately got out of their clutches, murdered two Tebu merchants on the road from Air to Ghát, carrying away their whole caravan, with no less than thirty-three slaves.

I was assured by Hatíta that there were not less than thirty subdivisions of the larger clans, called

given by Mr. Richardson in his first journey.)   Going thence to E'geri, in a direction east from south, you encamp on the first night in Téni; on the second, in Tin-túzist; on the third, in Adómar; on the fourth, in Aderár; on the fifth, in Díder; and on the sixth arrive in E'geri.

"faya," in Temáshight; but I could only ascertain
the names of four of them: viz. the Izóban and the
Okéren, living in the Wadi Iráraren, and probably
belonging to one and the same family (I believe
the I'manang); the Degárrab, probably a section
of the Hadánarang, living in a place called Tárat
together with some Imghád; and finally the Ihiyáwen
or Ihéwan, a portion of whom dwell in Titarsén,
while another section has settled near Tasáwa in
Fezzán, forming the last link of the chain which
connects the Imghád and the Azkár. Another
link is formed by the Makéresang, who, like the
former, submit to the authority of the chief Nakhnúkhen; then follow the Ifélelen, who are settled in
Tasíl with the Imghád. The least degenerate of
these half-caste tribes, who hold a middle place between the Imóshagh and the Imghád, or between the
free and the servile, is said to be the section of the
Mateghílelen, now settled in the Wadi el Gharbi, in
Fezzán, while their kindred certainly belong to the
Imghád. This is the best proof that the name A'mghi
does not express national descent, but social condition. Another section or tribe loosely connected
with the Azkár, but not regarded as noble, although
as strict ascetics they are much respected, and are
enabled to carry on almost undisturbed the commerce
between Fezzán and Negroland, are the Tinýlkum,
of whom I have already had occasion to speak repeatedly. At present they are settled partly in the
valley Tigger-odé, where their chief the Háj 'Alí

resides, partly in Wadi el Gharbi and around Tasáwa ; but their ancient seats were to the south of Ghát, and even in the town of Ghát itself, they having been called in to decide the quarrel between the former inhabitants of that place, the Kél-tellek and the Makamúmmasen.

As I said above, the ruling class of the Ázkár constitutes by far the smaller part of the popula- tion of the country, while the great mass of the population of these regions consists of a subject or degraded tribe called Imghád, or, in the Arabic form, Merátha or even Metáthra. This I formerly considered to be a gentile name ; but I found after- wards that it is a general epithet used by all the different tribes of the Imóshagh to denote degraded tribes. The singular form of the name is A′mghí*, which is the counterpart of Amóshagh, as it means "servile," while the latter means "free." The Im- ghád of the Ázkár differ a great deal from the ruling tribe, particularly the women ; for while the Imóshagh are tolerably fair, a great many of the former are almost black, but nevertheless well made, and not only without negro features, but generally with a very regular physiognomy, while the women, at least in their forms, approach more to the type of the negro races. But as for their lan-

* امغي pl. امغاد The change of the غ into the ر in the Arabic form of the name shows to what extent the sound of the r prevails in the African pronunciation of this letter. The final d has re- placed n.

guage, I must confess that I am not able to decide with confidence whether it sprang originally from a Berber dialect or the Háusa language *: many of the people, indeed, seem to be bilingual; but by far the greater part of the men do not even understand the Háusa language. I am persuaded that they were originally Berbers who have become degraded by intermixture with the black natives.

The Imghád of the Azkár, who altogether form a numerous body, being able to furnish about 5000 armed men, are divided into four sections, — the Batánatang or Ibétnaten, the Fárkana or Aférkenén, Segígatang, and Wárwaren, which latter name, I think, very naturally calls to mind the Latin "Barbari," a name which, according to some ancient authors, belonged to certain tribes of Northern Africa†, and may fairly explain the origin of the name Berber, though it is to be remarked that "war," a syllable with which a great number of Berber names begin, seems to signify "man." Of these four divisions the last three seem to live principally in and around the small town of Bárakat, a few miles south of Ghát, and in and around Jánet or Yánet, about thirty miles

---

* Hatíta told us expressly that, if any of the Imghád should trouble us we should say, "bábo." Now "bábo" is neither Arabic nor Temáshight, but the Háusa word for "there is none."

† Hippolytus, Lib. Generat. (p. 101. in the second volume of the Chronicon Paschale, ed. Bonn.), enumerates among the African tribes "Afri qui et Barbares;" and in Itinerar. Antonini, p. 2., the Macenites Barbari are mentioned. Varvar is a Sanscrit word of very general meaning.

S.S.W. from E'geri. Neither the population of the town of Ghát nor that of the town of Bárakat is at present formed by these Imghád; but I should suppose that in former times they were also the privileged inhabitants of Ghát itself, which at present is occupied by a very mixed race, so well described by the late Mr. Richardson. These two favoured spots of the desert seem to be left entirely to these people as tenants, on condition that they take care of the plantations and of the gardens, and gather the fruit, of which they are bound to give a portion to their masters. Some of the noble Imóshagh, indeed, seem to have a great many of these people at their disposal. The Batánatang or Ibétnaten, reside principally in a valley called Tesíli, while another section of them have their abode amongst the Hogár, in a district called Tehellahóhet, on the road from Asíu to Tawát. A portion of the last tribe (viz. the Fárkana or Afér-kenén) dwell in a valley called Tárat, about a day's journey north-west from Nghákeli.

Besides these four great divisions, there are many other sections of the Imghád. The names of these, as far as they became known to me, are as follows:— the Dik-Surki, settled in the territory of the Azkár in a place called E'dehi; the Kél-n-tunín, living in Aderár; the Amatghílelen*, who have their abode in the same spot; the Kél-áhenet, living in Hágara; the

---

* This clan is evidently related to the Mateghílelen mentioned above, p. 233., as settled at present in the Wadi el Ghárbi.

Akeshemáden, in the valley called Atúl; the I'kelan, who have their dwelling-places in Zerzer; the Kél-ghafsa, in I'fak; the Kél-ífis, in Temághaset; and finally, the Ijrán.

The ruling race of the Imóshagh subsists entirely on the labour of this depressed class, as the old Spartans did upon that of the Lacedæmonians, but still more upon the tribute or gheráma which, as I mentioned above, they raise from the caravans—a custom already mentioned by Leo Africanus.[*] Without some such revenue they could not trick themselves out so well as they do, though when at home in their "tekábber" they live at very little expense, particularly as they are not polygamists. The Imghád are not allowed to carry an iron spear nor to wear a sword, which is the distinction of the free man, nor any very showy dress. Most of them may be regarded as settled, or as "Kél," that is to say as the constant, or at least as the ordinary, inhabitants of a given place; and this indeed, it seems, is even to be said of a great many of the Azkár themselves, who seem to hold a middle place between the nomadic and the settled tribes. The consequence is, that many of them do not live in leather tents, or "éhe," but in round conical huts called tekábber, made of bushes and dry grass.

The town of Ghát (the favoured locality of which

---

[*] L. i. c. 20.: "Ma le carovane che passano per li diserti loro, sono tenute di pagare ai lor principi certa *gabella*."

... might be ... or have attracted a settlement at a very ... mentioned by any Arabic writer except the traveller E'bn Batúta in the 14th century, and seems never to have been a large place, being now ... is a small town of about 250 houses, but nevertheless of considerable commercial importance, which would become infinitely greater if the jealousy of the Tawáti would allow the opening of the direct road from Timbúktu, which seems to be under the special protection of the powerful chief Gemáma.

The view from the rocky hill, which ... its greatest elevation just over the town, and, together with a ... of ... few Berber and Arabic inscriptions ... to the ... traveller, proved far less expensive and ... than that from a sand-hill a little distance eastward from the house of Háj A'hmed. I ascended this little hill in the afternoon of the 22nd, and, screened by an ethel-bush, made the accompanying sketch of the whole oasis, which I hope will give a tolerably good idea of this interesting ... the separate strips of palm-trees, the wide ... valley, bordered by the steep slope of the ... with its regular strata of marly slate and its ... crest of sandstone; the little town on the left, at the foot of the rocky hill, contrasting with the few and frail huts of palmbranches scattered about here and there; the noble and spacious mansion of the industrious Háj A'hmed in the foreground, on the northern side of which lies the ... dwelling assigned to us. When descend-

ing from this hill towards the south, I was greatly
pleased with the new improvements added by Háj
A'hmed to his plantation. The example of this
man shows how much may be achieved by a little
industry in these favoured spots, where cultivation
might be infinitely increased. In the southernmost
and most recent part of the plantation a large basin,
about 100 ft. long and 60 ft. broad, had been formed,
receiving a full supply of water from the northern
side of the sand-hills, and irrigating kitchen-gardens
of considerable extent. Thus the wealthy governor
makes some advance every year; but, unfortunately,
he seems not to find many imitators.

Our negotiation with the Tawárek chiefs might
have been conducted with more success, if a letter
written by Her Majesty's Government to the chief
Jabúr had not been produced at the very moment
when all the chiefs present were ready to subscribe the
treaty. But their attention was entirely distracted
from the object in view. This letter made direct
mention of the abolition of the slave-trade; hence
it became a very difficult and delicate matter, especially as Mr. Richardson's supplies of merchandise
and presents at that moment were entirely in the
hands of the merchant Háj Ibrahím, who, even if
liberal enough to abstain from intrigue against admit-
ting the competition of English merchants, would
be sure to do all in his power to prevent the abolition of the slave-trade.

It was a serious undertaking to enter into direct

negotiation with these Tawárek chiefs, the absolute masters of several of the most important routes to Central Africa.* It required great skill, entire confidence, and no inconsiderable amount of means, of which we were extremely deficient. To this vexation let there be added the petulant and indiscreet behaviour of our servants, who were exasperated by the sufferings of the Ramadhán during the hottest season of the year, and were too well aware of the insufficiency of our means to carry out the objects of our mission; and the reader will easily understand that we were extremely glad when, after repeated delays, we were at length able to leave this place in the pursuance of our journey.

* Jackson was the first who pointed out the importance of entering into direct negotiation with the Tawárek.

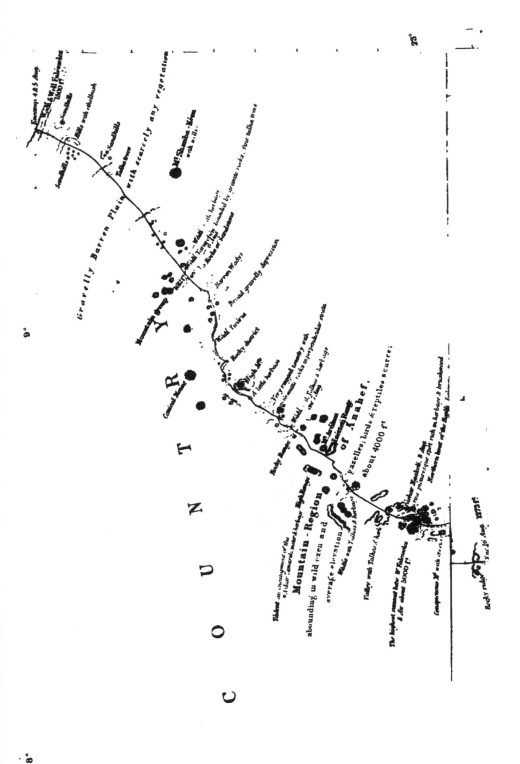

CHAP. XI.

CROSSING A LARGE MOUNTAIN-RIDGE, AND ENTERING ON THE OPEN GRAVELLY DESERT.

ON the morning of the 26th of July I once more found myself on the back of my camel, and from my elevated seat threw a last glance over the pleasant picture of the oasis of Ghát. There is an advanced spur of the plantation about two miles south from the town, called Timéggawé, with a few scattered cottages at its southern end. Having left this behind us, we came to the considerable plantation of I'berké, separated into two groups, one on the west, and the other on the east side, and kept along the border of the western group, which forms dense clusters, while that to the east is rather thin and loosely scattered. The town of Bárakat, lying at the foot of a sandy eminence stretching north and south, became now and then visible on our right, glittering through the thinner parts of the plantation.

Being prepared for a good day's march, as not only the Tinýlkum were reported to have left Arikím several days ago, but as even the little caravan of Kél-owí, with whom we had made arrangements for protection and company on the road, was a considerable way in advance, we were greatly asto-

nished when ordered to encamp near the scattered
palm-trees at the extreme eastern end of the plantation.   Utaeti, who had accompanied us all the way
from Ghát on foot, chose the camping-ground.   Mr.
Richardson, who had been behind, was not less
astonished when he found us encamped at so early
an hour.   But our camels, which seemed to have
been worked during our stay at Ghát, instead of
being allowed to recover their strength by rest and
pasture, were in great want of some good feeding; and
there was much aghúl (*Hedysarum Alhajji*) about
our encampment.   Towards noon we were visited by
several Hogár, or rather Azkár, who proved a little
troublesome, but not so much so as the townspeople,
who caused us a great deal of annoyance, both during
the evening and on the following morning, and gave
us some idea of what might await us further on.

Being annoyed at our delay here, I accompanied
two of Mr. Richardson's people and the young son
of Yusuf Mukní, who wished to go into the town
to buy a fowl.   We were followed by two men
from among the townspeople, who wanted to extort
a present from me, and one of whom, by bawling
out the characteristic phrase of his creed, made
me fear lest he might succeed in exciting all
the people against me.   The town was distant
from our encampment a mile and a quarter; and
having once reached its wall, I determined to
enter it.   The town, or ágherim, forms a tolerably-
regular quadrangle, on an open piece of ground at

the eastern foot of the sandy eminence, and is enclosed by a wall (agadór), built of clay, about five-
and-twenty feet high, and provided with quadrangular towers. We entered it by the eastern gate,
which, being defended by a tower, has its entrance
from the side, and leads first to a small court with a
well, from which another arched passage leads into
the streets. Here several women, of good figure
and decently dressed, were seated tranquilly, as it
seemed, enjoying the cool air of the afternoon, for
they had no occupation, nor were they selling anything. Although I was dressed in a common blue
Sudán shirt, and tolerably sunburnt, my fairer complexion seemed to alarm them; and some of them
withdrew into the interior of the houses crying "lá
ílah." Still I was not molested nor insulted by the
people passing by; and I was pleased that several of
them courteously answered my salute. They were
apparently not of pure Berber blood. It appeared
that a good many of the inhabitants had gone to their
date-groves to look after the harvest, as the fruit was
just about to ripen; hence the place, though in
good repair, and very clean, had a rather solitary
appearance. There is no commerce in this place as in
Ghát, the whole wealth of the inhabitants consisting
in their plantations. Yet they are said to be better
off than the population of Ghát, who are exposed to
great and continual extortions from the Tawárek
on account of their origin, while the people of Bárakat

enjoy certain privileges.   The houses were all two
or three stories high, and well built, the clay being
nicely polished.   A few palm-trees decorate the interior of the town.   It is of still more diminutive
size than Ghát, containing about two hundred houses;
but it is built with great regularity.

Having stuck fast awhile in a lane which had no
thoroughfare, we at length got safely out of the little
town of Bárakat by the south gate.   It has, I believe,
four gates, like Ghát.   On this side of the town,
inside of the walls, stands the mosque, a building of
considerable size for so small a place, neatly whitewashed, and provided with a lofty minaret.

Leaving the town, we took a more southern and
circuitous road than that by which we had come, so
that I saw a good deal of the plantation.   The soil
is for the most part impregnated with salt; and the
wells have generally brackish water.   There was much
industry to be seen, and most of the gardens were
well kept; but the wells might easily be more numerous, and only a small quantity of corn is cultivated.
The great extent to which dukhn, or Guinea corn
("éneli" in Temáshight*), or *Pennisetum typhoïdeum*,
is cultivated here, as well as near Ghát, in proportion
to wheat or barley, seems to indicate the closer and
more intimate connection of this region with Negroland. Some culinary vegetables also were cultivated;
and some, but not many, of the gardens were care-

* This word " éneli " occurs in the Travels of Ebn Batúta.

fully fenced with the leaves of the palm-tree. The grove was animated by numbers of wild pigeons and turtle-doves, bending the branches of the palm-trees with their wanton play; and a good many asses were to be seen. Cattle I did not observe.

But far more interesting were the scenes of human life that met my eyes. Happiness seemed to reign, with every necessary comfort, in this delightful little grove. There was a great number of cottages, or tekábber, built of palm-branches and palm-leaves, most of them of considerable size, and containing several apartments; all of them had flat roofs. They are inhabited by the Imghád, or Merátha. A great many of the men seemed at present to be busy else-where; but these lightly-built straggling suburbs were full of children, and almost every woman carried an infant at her back. They were all black, but well formed, and infinitely superior to the mixed race of Fezzán. The men wore in general blue shirts, and a black shawl round the face; the women were only dressed in the túrkedi, or Sudán-cloth, wound round their body, and leaving the upper part, including the breasts, uncovered. They understood generally nothing but Temáshight; and only a few of them spoke the Háusa language. The men were nearly all smoking.

Having returned to our tent from this pleasant ramble, I did not stay long in it, but stealing off as secretly as possible, I walked to the eastern side of the valley, which is here locked up by the steep slope of the Akakús range. The plain on this side, being much interrupted by hills crowned with ethel-trees, does not afford a distant prospect. In this quarter, too, there are a few scattered gardens, with melons and vegetables, but no palm-trees.

In the evening we were greatly annoyed by some Imghád; and between one of them and our fiery and inconsiderate Tunisian shushán a violent dispute arose, which threatened to assume a very serious character. We were on the watch the whole night.

Friday, July 26th. Having waited a long time for Utaeti, we at length started without him, passing on our right a beautiful palm-grove, with as many as ten thousand trees, while our left was bordered by scattered gardens, where the people were busy in the cool of the morning irrigating the corn and vegetables, with the assistance of Sudán oxen. They came out to see us pass by, but without expressing any feeling, hostile or otherwise. After a mile and a half the plantation ceased, at the bed of a torrent which contained a pond of rain-water collected from the higher rocky ground, which here terminates. Further on we passed another small channel, overgrown with bushes, and remarkable for nothing but its name, which seems plainly to indicate that this country originally belonged to the Góber or Háusa nation, for it is still called Korámma, a word which in the Háusa language denotes the bed of a torrent. To this watercourse particularly, the general designation was most probably assigned because in its further progress it widens very considerably, and in some degree appears as the head of the green bottom of the Valley of Ghát.

But a more luxuriant valley, from three to four miles broad, begins further on, rich in herbage, and full of ethel-trees, all crowning the tops of small mounds. Here we encamped near a pond of dirty rain-water, frequented by great flocks of doves and water-fowl, and a well called I'zayen, in order to wait for Utaeti. The well was only about three feet deep, but the water brackish and disagreeable. Our friend came at length, and it was then decided to march during the night, in order to reach the Kél-owí; we therefore left our pleasant camping-ground about half-past nine in the evening, favoured by splendid moonlight. So interesting was the scene, that, absorbed in my thoughts, I got considerably in advance of the caravan, and, not observing a small path which turned off on the right, I followed the larger one till I became conscious of my solitary situation, and, dismounting, lay down in order to await my companions. Our caravan, however, had taken the other path, and my fellow-travellers grew rather anxious about me; but my camel, which was evidently aware of the caravan ahead of us, would not give up this direction, which proved to be the right one, and after I had joined the caravan we were obliged to return to my former path.

Here we found the small Kél-owí caravan encamped in the midst of a valley well-covered with herbage,

near the well Karáda. Our new companions were
perfect specimens of the mixed Berber and Sudán
blood, and, notwithstanding all their faults, most
useful as guides. It was two hours after midnight
when we arrived; and after a short repose we started
again tolerably early the next morning.

For the first hour we kept along the valley, when
we began to ascend a narrow path winding round the
slope of a steep promontory of the plateau. The
ruins of a castle at the bottom of the valley formed
an object of attraction.

The ascent took us almost an hour, when the defile
opened to a sort of plateau with higher ground and
cones to the left. After another ascent four miles
further on, over a rocky slope about 180 ft. high and
covered with sand, we encamped at an early hour, as
the heat was beginning to be felt, in a valley with
sidr-trees and grass, called Erázar-n-A'keru.

A large basin of water, formed by the rains in a
small rocky lateral glen joining the large valley on
the west side, afforded a delightful resting-place to
the weary traveller. The basin, in which the negro
slaves of our Kél-owí swam about with immense
delight, was about 200 ft. long and 120 ft. broad, and
very deep, having been hollowed out in the rocks by
the violent floods descending occasionally from the
heights above. But on a terrace about 200 ft. higher
up the cliffs, I discovered another basin of not more
than about half the diameter of the former, but likewise of great depth. All along the rocky slope between

these two basins, cascades are formed during heavy rains, which must render this a delightfully refreshing spot.

We soon emerged from the valley, and entered a district of very irregular cha- Sunday, July 28th. racter, but affording herbage enough for temporary settlements or encampments of the Imghád, whose asses and goats testified that the country was not quite uninhabited. Some people of our caravan saw the guardians of these animals,—negroes, clad in leather aprons. Against the lower part of the cliffs, which rise abruptly on all sides, large masses of sand have accumulated, which, as in the case of the upper valley of the Nile, might induce the observer to believe that all the higher level was covered with sand, which from thence had been driven down; but this is not by any means the case.

I had a long conversation this morning with the Tawáti ʿAbd el Káder, who had come with the pilgrim-caravan as far as Ghát, and, together with another companion, had attached himself to the Kél-owí, in order to go to A'gades. He was a smart fellow, of light complexion and handsome countenance, but had lost one eye in a quarrel. He was armed with a long gun with a good English lock, of which he was very proud. He had, when young, seen the Ráís (Major Laing) at Tawát, and knew something about Europeans, and chiefly Englishmen. Smart and active as this fellow was, he was so ungallant as to oblige his young female slave, who was at once his mistress, cook, and servant, to walk the whole day on foot, while he generally rode.

A little after noon we encamped in the corner of a valley rich in sebót, and adorned with some talha-trees, at the foot of cliffs of considerable height, which were to be ascended the following day.

Monday, July 29th. We began our task early in the morning. The path, winding along through loose blocks on a precipitous ascent, proved very difficult. Several loads were thrown off the camels; and the boat several times came into collision with the rocks, which, but for its excellent material, might have damaged it considerably. The whole of the cliffs consisted of red sandstone, which was now and then interrupted by clay-slate, of a greenish colour. The ascent took us almost two hours; and from the level of the plateau we obtained a view of the ridge stretching towards Arikím, the passage of which was said to be still more difficult. Having successively ascended and descended a little, we then entered a tolerably-regular valley, and followed its windings till about noon, when we once more emerged upon the rugged rocky level, where Amankay, the well-travelled búzu or mulatto of Tasáwa, brought us a draught of deliciously cool water, which he had found in a hollow in the rocks. Here our route meandered in a very remarkable way, so that I could not lay aside my compass for a moment; and the path was sometimes reduced to a narrow crevice between curiously-terraced buttresses of rocks.

The ground having at length become more open, we encamped about a quarter past three o'clock in a small ravine with a little sprinkling of herbage.

Here we had reached an elevation of not less than 4000 feet above the sea, — the greatest elevation of the desert to be passed, or rather of that part of Africa over which our travels extended. The rugged and bristling nature of this elevated tract prevented our obtaining any extensive views. This region, if it were not the wildest and most rugged of the whole desert, limiting vegetation to only a few narrow crevices and valleys, would be a very healthy and agreeable abode for man; but it can only support a few nomadic stragglers. This, I am convinced, is the famous mountain Tántanah, the abode of the

Azkár* mentioned by the early Arabic geographers, although, instead of placing it to the south-west of Fezzán, they generally give it a southerly direction. I am not aware that a general name is now given to this region.

But this highest part of the table-land rather forms a narrow " col" or crest, from which, on the following morning, after a winding march of a little more than three miles, we began to descend by a most picturesque passage into a deeper region.   At first we saw nothing but high cones towering over a hollow in the ground; but as we advanced along a lateral wadi of the valley which we had entered, the scenery assumed a grander aspect, exhibiting features of such variety as we had not expected to find in this desert country. While our camels began slowly to descend, one by one, the difficult passage, I sat down and made the accompanying sketch of it, which will convey a better idea of this abrupt cessation of the high sandstone level, with the sloping strata of marl where it is suc-ceeded by another formation—that of granite, than any verbal description would do.

The descent took us two hours, when we reached the bottom of a narrow ravine about sixty feet broad, which at first was strewn with large blocks carried down by occasional floods, but a little further on, had a floor of fine sand and gravel.   Here the valley is joined by a branch wadi, or another ravine, coming from the north.   Near the junction it is tolerably

* See above, p. 229.

.... to the early Arabia geographers, ... placing it to the south-west of .... give it a southerly direction. .... that a general name is now given ....

.... part of the table-land rather forms .... from which, on the following .... march of a little more than .... traversal by a most picturesque .... region. At first we saw nothing .... save a hollow in the ground; .... a lateral wadi of the valley .... scenery assumed a grander .... scenes of such variety as we .... to find in this desert country. While our camels began slowly to descend, one by one, the difficult passage, I sat down and made the accompanying sketch of it, which will convey a better .... of this abrupt cessation of the high sandstone .... with the sloping strata of marl where it is succeeded by another formation—that of granite, than .... description would do.

The descent took us two hours, when we reached the bottom of a narrow ravine about sixty feet broad, which at first was strewn with large blocks carried down by occasional floods, but a little further on, had a floor of fine sand and gravel. Here the valley is .... by a branch wadi, or another ravine, coming .... the north. Near the junction it is tolerably

wide; but a few hundred yards further on, it narrows between steep precipitous cliffs looking almost like walls erected by the hand of man, and more than a thousand feet high, and forms there a pond of rain-water. While I was sketching this remarkable place, I lost the opportunity of climbing up the wild ravine. The locality was so interesting that I reluctantly took leave of it, fully intending to return the following day with the camels when they were to be watered; but, unfortunately, the alarming news which reached us at our camping-ground prevented my doing so. I will only observe that this valley,

which is generally called E'geri, is identical with the celebrated valley Amáis or Máis, the name of which became known in Europe many years ago.

A little beyond the junction of the branch ravine the valley widens to about one hundred and fifty feet, and becomes overgrown with herbage, and ornamented with a few talha-trees, and after being joined by another ravine exhibits also colocynths, and low but wide-spreading ethel-bushes, and, what was more interesting to us, the àshur (or, as the Háusa people call it, "tunfáfia," the Kanúri "krunka," the Tawárek "tursha"), the celebrated, wide-spread, and most important *Asclepias gigantea*, which had here truly gigantic proportions, reaching to the height of twenty feet; and being just then in flower, with its white and violet colours it contributed much to the interest of the scene. Besides, there was the jadaríyeh, well known to us from the Hammáda, and the shià or *Artemisia odoratissima*, and a blue crucifera identical, I think, with the damankádda, of which I shall have to speak repeatedly.

Having gone on a little more than three miles from the watering-place, we encamped; and the whole expedition found ample room under the wide-spreading branches of a single ethel-tree, the largest we had yet seen. Here the valley was about half a mile broad, and altogether had a very pleasant character.

I was greatly mortified on reflecting that the uncertainty of our relations in the country, and the precarious protection we enjoyed, would not allow me to visit Jánet, the most favoured spot in this mountainous region; but a great danger was suddenly announced to us, which threatened even to

drive us from that attractive spot. An expedition
had been prepared against us by the mighty chieftain Sídi * Jáfel ínek (son of) Sakertáf, to whom a
great number of the Imghád settled thereabouts are
subject as bondmen or serfs.

Upon the circumstances of this announcement and
its consequences, which have been fully detailed by
the late Mr. Richardson, I shall not dwell, but will
only observe that this transaction made us better acquainted with the character of each of our new friends.
There were three principal men in the Kél-owí caravan with which we had associated our fortunes, A'n-
nur (or properly E' Núr), Dídi, and Fáraji. A'nnur
was a relative of the powerful Kél-owí chief of the
same name, and, in order to distinguish him from
the latter, was generally called A'nnur karamí, or the
little A'nnur. He was of agreeable prepossessing
countenance and of pleasing manners, but without
much energy, and anything but warlike. Dídi and
Fáraji were both liberated slaves, but of very different appearance and character. The former was
slim, with marked features indicating a good deal of
cunning; the latter was a tolerably large man, with

* The appellative Sídi appears to be an honourable distinction
among the Hogár; and the messenger who brought us this news
generally called the chieftain of whom he spoke only by this
name Sídi. This is also the name by which Sultan Shafo's
father is generally called. The whole tribe of the Urághen seems
even to have the surname Síd-azkár. To what extent this name
Sídi is abused in Timbúktu, I shall have occasion to observe in
the further course of my travels.

broad coarse features which well expressed his character, the distinguishing trait of which was undis-
guised malice. When a new demand was to be put
forth, Fáraji took the lead, and, with an impudent
air, plainly stated the case; Dídi kept back, assisting
his companion underhand; and A'nnur was anxious
to give to the whole a better appearance and to soothe
our indignation.

The whole affair having been arranged, and the
stipulation being made, that in case the direct road
should become impracticable our Kél-owí were to lead
us by a more eastern one, where we should not meet
with anyone, we started in good spirits on the morning of the first of August, and soon emerged from
the valley by a southern branch, while the surrounding cliffs gradually became much lower and
flatter. Here we observed that granite had superseded
the sandstone, appearing first in low bristled ridges
crossing the bottom of the valley in parallel lines
running from W.N.W. to E.S.E., and gradually occupying the whole district, while the sand, which before
formed the general substance of the lower ground, was
succeeded by gravel. Our path now wound through
irregular defiles and small plains enclosed by low
ridges of granite blocks, generally bare, but in some
places adorned with talha-trees of fine fresh foliage.
The whole country assumed quite a different aspect.

Our day's journey was pleasantly varied by our
meeting with the van of a large caravan belonging to
the wealthy Fezzáni merchant Khweldi, which had

separated in A'ír on account of the high prices of provisions there.   They carried with them from forty to fifty slaves, most of them females, the greater part tolerably well-made.   Each of our Kél-owí produced from his provision-bags a measure of dates, and threw them into a cloth, which the leader of the caravan, a man of grave and honest countenance, had spread on the ground.   A little before noon, we encamped in a sort of wide but shallow valley called Ejénjer, where, owing to the junction of several smaller branch-vales collecting the moisture of a large district, a little sprinkling of herbage was produced, and a necessary halting-place formed for the caravans coming from the north, before they enter upon the naked desert, which stretches out towards the south-west for several days' journey.   The camels were left grazing the whole night, in order to pick up as large a provision as possible from the scanty pasture.

We entered upon the first regular day's march since we left Ghát.   After a stretch August 2nd. of nine miles, an interesting peak called Mount Tiska, rising to an elevation of about 600 feet, and sur-rounded by some smaller cones, formed the conspi-cuous limit of the rocky ridges.   The country became entirely flat and level, but with a gradual ascent, the whole ground being formed of coarse gravel; and there was nothing to interrupt the monotonous plain but a steep ridge, called Mariaw, at the distance of about five miles to the east.

The nature of this desert region is well understood

by the nomadic Tawárek or Imóshagh, who regard the Mariaw as the landmark of the open uninterrupted

desert-plain, the "ténere;" and a remarkable song of theirs, which often raised the enthusiasm of our companions, begins thus: —

" Mariaw da ténere nís" (We have reached Mariaw and the desert-plain).

The aspect of this uninterrupted plain seemed to inspire our companions; and with renewed energy we pursued our dreary path till after sunset, when we encamped upon this bare gravelly plain, entirely destitute of herbage, and without the smallest fragment of wood for fuel; and I was glad to get a cup of tea with my cold supper of zummíta. Even in these hot regions the European requires some warm food or beverage.

The next morning, all the people being eager to get away from this dreary spot, every small party started as it got ready, without waiting for the rest, in order to reach as soon as possible the region of

the sand-hills, which we saw before us at the distance
of a little more than five miles, and which promised
to the famished camels at least a slight repast. Herbage was scattered in bunches all about the sides of
the sand-hills; and a number of butter- and dragon-
flies greatly relieved the dreary scene. After a while
the sand-hills ranged themselves more on both sides,
while our road led over harder sandy soil, till the
highest range crossed our path, and we began to
ascend it, winding along its lower parts. Granite,
lying a few feet under the surface, in several spots
chequered the sand, tinged with a pretty blue.

A little after mid-day we emerged from the sand-
hills, and entered a plain from two to three miles
wide, bounded on both sides by sand-hills, and were
here gratified with the view of shifting lakes which
the mirage set before our eyes. Then followed
another narrow range of sand-hills, succeeded by a
barren open plain, and then another very considerable bank of sand, leaning on a granite ridge. After
a steep ascent of forty-five minutes, we reached the
highest crest, and obtained an extensive prospect over
the country before us—a desert-plain interspersed by
smaller sand-hills and naked ledges of rock, and
speckled with ethel-bushes half overwhelmed by sand,
at the foot of a higher range of sand-hills. For sand-
hills are the landmark of Afalésselez; and the verse
of the desert-song celebrating Mariaw as the landmark of the open gravelly desert-plain, is succeeded by

s 2

another celebrating the arrival at Afalésselez and its sand-hills: —

" In-Afalésselez da jéde nís."

Having long looked down from this barbican of sand, to see whether all was safe near that important place whence we were to take our supply for the next stretch of dry desert land, we descended along the south-western slope, and there encamped.

After a march of little more than four miles the next morning, we reached the well Falésselez, or Afalésselez. This camping-ground had not a bit of shade; for the few ethel-bushes, all of them starting forth from mounds of not less than forty feet eleva: tion, were very low, and almost covered with sand. Besides, the gravelly ground was covered with camels' dung, and impurities of a more disagreeable nature; and there was not a bit of herbage in the neighbourhood, so that the camels, after having been watered, had to be driven to a distance of more than eight miles, where they remained during the night and the following day till noon, and whence they brought back a supply of herbage for the next night.

But, notwithstanding its extraordinary dreariness, this place is of the greatest importance for the caravan-trade, on account of the well, which affords a good supply of very tolerable water. At first it was very dirty and discoloured; but it gradually became clearer, and had but little after-taste. The well was five fathoms deep, and not more than a foot and a half wide at the top, while lower down it widened considerably.   It is formed of the wood of the ethel-tree.   The temperature of the water, giving very nearly the mean temperature of the atmosphere in this region, was 77°.

. After the camels had gone, our encampment became very lonely and desolate, and nothing was heard but the sound of ghussub-pounding.   The Kél-owí had encamped at some distance, on the slope of the sand-hills.   It was a very sultry day — the hottest day in this first part of our journey, — the thermometer, in the very best shade which we were able to obtain, showing 111°·2 heat, which, combined with the dreary monotony of the place, was quite exhausting.   There was not a breath of air in the morning; nevertheless it was just here that we remarked the first signs of our approaching the tropical regions, for in the afternoon the sky became so thickly overcast with clouds, that we entertained the hope of being refreshed by a few drops of rain.   In the night a heavy gale blew from the east.

Next day came Utaeti.   On his fine méheri, enveloped as he was in his blue Sudán-cloth, he made a good figure.   The reply which he made, when Mr. Richardson asked him how his father had received the present of the sword which H. B. M.'s Government had sent him, was characteristic: the sword, he said, was a small present, and his father had expected to receive a considerable sum of money into the bar-

gain.   He informed us also that, by our not coming
to Arikím, we had greatly disappointed the Tawárek
settled thereabouts.

Tuesday,   The sand-hills which we ascended after
August 6th.   starting were not very high; but after a
while we had to make another ascent.   Sometimes small
ridges of quartzose sandstone, setting right across our
path, at others ethel-bushes, gave a little variety to
the waste; and at the distance of about eight miles
from the well, singularly-shaped conical mounts began
to rise.   The eastern road, which is a little more circuitous, is but a few hours' distance from this; it
leads through a valley at the foot of a high conical
mount with temporary ponds of rain-water, and herbage called Shambakésa, which about noon we passed
at some distance on our left.

In the afternoon we came in sight of a continuous
range of heights ahead of us.   The whole region exhibited an interesting intermixture of granite and
sandstone formation, white and red sandstone protruding in several places, and the ground being strewn
with fragments of granite and gneiss.   Passing at one
time over gravel, at another over rocky ground strewn
with pebbles, we encamped at length in a sort of shallow valley called Taghárebén, on the north side of a
very remarkable mass of curiously-shaped sandstone
blocks, heaped together in the most singular manner,
and rising altogether to a height of about 150 feet.
On inspecting it more closely, I found that it consisted of four distinct buttresses, between which large

masses of loose sand had collected, the sandstone being
of a beautiful white colour, and in a state of the
utmost disintegration.

After a weary day's march, the camping-ground
adorned as it was with some fine talha-trees, and surrounded with small ridges and detached masses of
rock, on which now depended the beauty of the scene,
cheered our minds, and fitted us for another long
day's work. Soon after we started, the ground became
rugged and stony, and full of ridges of sandstone,
bristling with small points and peaks. In this wild
and rugged ground, our people amused themselves and
us with hunting down a lizard, which tried to escape
from the hands of its pursuers in the crevices of the
rocky buttresses. Then followed broad shallow valleys,
at times overgrown with a little herbage, but generally very barren; winding along them we turned
round a larger cluster of heights which seemed to
obstruct our route. Bare and desolate as the country
appears, it is covered, as well as the whole centre of
the desert, with large herds of wild oxen (*Antilope
bubalis*), which rove about at large, and, according
as they are more or less hunted, linger in favoured
districts or change their haunts. Our men tried to
catch them, but were unsuccessful, the animal, clumsy
and sluggish as it appears, climbing the rocks with
much more ease than men unaccustomed to this sort
of sport, and, owing to the ruggedness of the ground,
being soon lost sight of.

At five o'clock in the afternoon the heights on our

left rose to a greater elevation, as much as 1000 feet, bristling with cones, and formed more picturesque masses. Resting on the spurs of the mountain-range was a peculiar knot of cliffs, ridges of rocks, and isolated perpendicular pillars, through which our road led with a gradual ascent till we reached the highest ground, and then descended into a shallow valley furnished with a tolerable supply of herbage and a few talha-trees, some of which, with their young leaves, soon attracted the attention of the famished camels. The poor animals were left grazing all night, which recruited their strength a little. These long stretches were fatiguing both for man and beast; and they were the more trying for the traveller, as, instead of approaching by them in long strides the wished-for regions to the south, there was scarcely any advance at all in that direction, the whole route leading to the west.

Thursday, August 8th. After a mile and a half's march the country became more open and free, and those ridges of granite rock which had been characteristic of the region just passed over ceased; but ahead of us considerable mountain-masses were seen, the whole mountainous district, in which the long range called Isétteti is conspicuous, being named A'nahef. After a march of about ten miles, a path branched off from our road towards the west, leading to a more favoured place, called Tádent *, where the

* In Mr. Richardson's Journal, vol. i. p. 194., this place has

moisture collected by the mountain-masses around
seems to produce a richer vegetation, so that it is the
constant residence of some Azkár families; it is distant from this place about sixteen miles. Here some
advanced heights approach the path, and more talha-
trees appear; and further on the bottom of the fiumara was richly overgrown with bú rékkebah (*Avena
Forskalii*), grass very much liked by the camels, and
which we had not observed before on our route.
The country ahead of us formed a sort of defile, into
which I thought we should soon enter, when suddenly, behind the spur of a ridge projecting into the
plain on our left, we changed our direction, and
entering a wide valley inclosed by two picturesque
ranges of rocks, we there encamped.

The valley is called Nghákeli, and is remarkable
as well on account of its picturesque appearance
as because it indicates the approach to a more
favoured region. Besides being richly overgrown
with luxuriant herbage of different species, as sebót,
bú rékkebah, shiá, and adorned with fine talha-trees,
it exhibited the first specimens of the *Balanites
Ægyptiaca* (or " hajilíj," as it is called by the Arabs,
" áddwa" by the Háusa people), the rope-like roots of
which, loosened by the torrent which at times sweeps
along the valley, grew to an immense length over

been confounded with Janet, the name having been probably
written in the MS. " Tanet," a form used also by Mr. Overweg,
and which seems to be verified.

the ground. I walked up the valley to a distance of two miles. Compared with the arid country we had been travelling over latterly, it made upon me just the same impression which the finest spots of Italy would produce on a traveller visiting them from the north of Europe. The Kél-owí had chosen the most shady talha-tree for a few hours' repose; and I sat down a moment in their company. They gave me a treat of their palatable fura, or ghussub-water, the favourite (and in a great many cases the only) dish of the Absenáwa.

In the evening Mr. Richardson bought from some sportsmen a quantity of the meat of the wadán, or (as the Tawárek call it) aúdád (*Ovis tragelaphos*), an animal very common in the mountainous districts of the desert, and very often found in company with the wild ox. As for myself, I kept my tent, filling up from my memorandum-book my last day's journal, and then, full of the expectation that we were now about to enter more pleasant regions, lay down on my hard couch.

DANGEROUS APPROACH TO ASBEN.

THERE had been much talk about our starting at midnight; but, fortunately, we _{Friday, August 9th.} did not get off before daylight, so that I was able to continue my exact observations of the route, which was now to cross the defile observed yesterday after-noon, which already began to impart quite a charac-teristic aspect to the country. There were some beautifully-shaped cones rising around it, while be-yond them an uneven tract stretched out, crowded with small elevations, which gradually rose to greater height; among them one peak, of very considerable elevation, was distinguished by its graceful form,

and seemed worthy of a sketch. Attached to it was a lower rocky range, with a very marked horizontal crest, while running parallel to our path were small ledges of gneiss. After a march of seven miles and a half, we ascended a considerable range of rugged eminences, from the crest of which we followed a steep descent into an uneven rocky tract intersected by several shallow beds of torrents; and then, just as the heat began, we reached the valley of Arókam, where we encamped at about half an hour's distance from the well, and opposite to a branch-wadi through which lay our next day's route. In the afternoon I climbed the highest of the cones rising above the cliffs, but without obtaining any distant prospect.

Saturday, August 10th.   The active buzu Amankay, who early in the morning went once more to the well in order to fill a few water-skins, brought the news that a considerable caravan, consisting chiefly of Aníslimen or Merabetín from Tintaghodé, had arrived at the well the evening before, on their road to Ghát, and that they protested against our visiting their country, and still more against our approaching their town. Notwithstanding the bad disposition of these people towards us, I managed to induce one of them, who visited our encampment, to take charge of letters addressed by me to Háj Ibrahim, in Ghát, which I am glad to say arrived safely in Europe. Amankay reported to us that on his way to the well he had observed a small palm-tree.

We started rather late in the morning, entering
the branch-wadi, which proved to be far more considerable than it seemed, and rich in talha-trees.   In
this way we kept winding along several valleys, till,
after a march of three miles, we ascended and crossed
a very interesting defile, or a slip in the line of elevation, bordered on both sides by a terraced and indented slope, the highest peaks of the ridge rising
to not less than a thousand feet, while their general
elevation was about six hundred feet.   Mr. Overweg

recognised this as gneiss.   Close beyond this defile,
at the foot of mounds of disintegrated granite, we
encamped, to our great astonishment, a little after
eight o'clock in the morning; but the reason of this
short march was, that our companions, on account
of the arrival of the caravan above mentioned, did
not choose to stop at our former encampment, else

they would have rested there to-day. In the afternoon a high wind arose, which upset our tent.

Sunday,   After a march of little more than two
August 11th. miles over an irregular tract of granite, in a
state of great disintegration, intersected by crests of
gneiss, we obtained from a higher level an interesting
view over the whole region, and saw that beyond the
hilly ground of broken granite a large plain of firm
gravelly soil spread. out, surrounded by a circle of
higher mounts.. Then followed a succession of flat
shallow valleys overgrown with sebót and talha-trees,
till the ridges on the right and left (the latter rising
to about 800 feet) approached each other, forming a
sort of wider passage or defile. The spur of the
range to the left with its strongly marked and indented crest, formed quite an interesting feature.

Beyond this passage we entered a bare gravelly
plain, from which rose a few detached mounts,
followed by more continuous ranges forming more
or less regular valleys. The most remarkable of
these is the valley Aséttere, which, in its upper
course, where it is called A'kafa, is supplied by the

famous well, Tajétterat*; but as we were sufficiently supplied with water from Arókam, and as the well Aísalen was near, we left it on one side.

We encamped at length in a valley joined by several branch-vales, and therefore affording a good supply of herbage, which the Kél-owí were anxious to collect as a supply for the journey over the entirely bare tract to Asíu. As for ourselves, one of our servants being utterly unfit for work, we could not lay in a supply. We had been rather unfortunate with this fellow; for having hired him in Múrzuk, he was laid up with the guineaworm from the very day that we left Ghát, and was scarcely of any use at all. This disease is extremely frequent among people travelling along this route; Amankay also was suffering from it, and at times became quite a burden. It attacked James Bruce even after his return to Europe; and I always dreaded it more than any other disease, during my travels in Central Africa; but fortunately, by getting a less serious one, which I may call sore legs, I got rid of the causes which I am sure, when acting in a stronger degree, produce the vena.

About sunset I ascended the eastern cliffs, which are very considerable, and from the highest peak, which rose to an elevation of more than 1200 feet above the bottom of the valley, obtained an extensive view. The whole formation consists of granite, and

* The two names Aséttere and Tajétterat are apparently derived from the same root.

its kindred forms of mica, quartz, and felspar. The bottom of the valley bore evident traces of a small torrent which seems to refresh the soil occasionally; and the same was the case with several small ravines which descend from the south-eastern cliffs.

Monday, August 12th. Our route followed the windings of the valley, which, further on, exhibited more ethel- than talha-trees, besides detached specimens of the *Asclepias*. After a march of four miles and a half, we came to two wells about four feet deep, and took in a small supply of water. The granite formation at the foot of the cliffs on our left was most beautiful, looking very like syenite. While we were taking in the water, flocks of wildfowl (*Pterocles*) were flying over our heads, and expressed by repeated cries their dissatisfaction at our disturbing their solitary retreat. The ethel, the talha, and the áddwa, or abórak, enliven these secluded valleys.

Delighted by the report of Amankay, who came to meet us, that he had succeeded in detaining the caravan of the Tinýlkum at Aísala, where they were waiting for us, we cheerfully continued our march; but before we reached the place the whole character of the country changed, the cliffs being craggy and split into huge blocks heaped upon each other in a truly Cyclopean style, such as only Nature can execute, while the entire hollow was covered with granite masses, scarcely allowing a passage. Descending these, we got sight of the encampment of the caravan, in a widening of the hollow; and after paying our compliments to all the members of this motley band, we encamped a little beyond, in a recess of the western cliffs.

The Tinýlkum* as well as Bóro Serki-n-turáwa were very scantily provided. They had lost so much time on the road on our account, that it was necessary, as as well as just, to leave them part of the provisions which they were carrying for us. All our luggage we found in the best state. Very much against their will, our companions had been supplied on the road with the flesh of nine camels, which had succumbed to the fatigues of the march; and some of them, and especially our energetic friend Háj 'Omár, had obtained a tolerable supply by hunting: besides wadáns they had killed also several gazelles, though we had scarcely seen any.

They had been lingering in this place four days, and were most anxious to go on. But we had a great deal to do; for all our luggage was to be

---

* I give here a list of the stations of their route, from Eláwen:— Em-eríwuang, with water, one day; Inar-ámas, one long day; Tibállaghén, with water when there has been much rain, one day; Terhén, with water, one day; Tin-afárfa, mountain-range with sand, one day; Takíset, a valley between high mountains, three days, two of them over very sandy ground; Arikím, with water at all times; Iséti, a valley, two days; Tamiswát, valley with water, one day; Morér, high mountains, two days; Falésselez, one day, over a gravelly hammáda; Tamba- or Shamba-késa, a shallow valley rich in herbage (see p. 262.), one day; Tirárien, one day; Araer, hammáda with shallow valleys, one day; Táfak, one day; Arókam, water, one day; Tádomat, valley, one day; Kútelet, one day; Aísala, or I'sala, one day.

repacked, all the water-skins to be filled, and herbage and wood to be collected for the road. Besides Ibrahím, who was lame and useless, Overweg and myself had only two servants, one of whom (Mohammed, the liberated Tunisian slave) was at times a most insolent rascal.

Besides we were pestered by the Kél-owí and by Utaeti, and I got into a violent dispute with Fáraji, the shameless freed-slave of Lusu; stil I managed on the morning of the following day to rove about a little. Just above the well rises a confused mass of large granite blocks, the lowest range of which was covered with Tefínagh inscriptions, one of which I copied. It was written with uncommon accuracy and neatness, and if found near the coast would be $\quad \text{ᗡᐸᗧᄃ∪᙭I◆}$ generally taken for Punic.* I was obliged to be cautious, as there was a great deal of excitement and irritation in the caravan, and from what had previously taken place all the way from Múrzuk, everybody regarded us as the general purveyors, and cherished the ardent hope that at last it would be his good fortune, individually, to get possession of our property.

In the afternoon the Tinýlkum started in advance, and we followed them, the hollow gradually widening and becoming clothed with large knots of low ethel-bushes. At the point where this valley joins another, and where a large quantity of herbage bedecked the

* I read it " énfadmaschbel."

ground, we found our friends encamped, and chose our ground a little beyond them, near a low cliff of granite rocks. All the people were busily employed cutting herbage for the journey, while Mr. Richardson at length succeeded in satisfying Utaeti, who was to return. He had been begging most importunately from me; and by way of acknowledging my obligations to him I presented him, on parting, with a piece of white muslin and a red sash, together with something for Hatíta.

These parties were scarcely quieted when others took their place, urging their pretensions to our acknowledgments; and we had just started the next day when Bóro Serki-n-turáwa despatched, under-hand, my smart friend the Tawáti 'Abd el Káder, with full instructions to give me a lecture on his boundless power and influence in the country which we were fast approaching. I was aware of this before, and knew that, in our situation as unprotected travellers in a new country, we ought to have secured his friendly disposition from the beginning; but the means of the expedition being rather limited, Mr. Richardson had made it a principle never to give till compelled by the utmost necessity, when the friendly obligation connected with the present was, if not destroyed, at least greatly diminished.

The structure of the valley soon became irregular, and the character of the country more desolate,. a circumstance which seems to be expressed by its name, Ikadémmelrang. All was granite in a state of the

T 2

utmost disintegration, and partly reduced to gravel, while detached cones were rising in all directions. Marching along over this dreary and desolate country, we reached, at half past two in the afternoon, after a gradual and almost imperceptible ascent, the highest level of the desert plain, from whence the isolated rocky cones and ridges look like so many islands rising from the sea. A sketch which I made of one of these mounts will give an idea of their character.

After a march of twelve hours and a half, which I would have gladly doubled, provided our steps had been directed in a straight line towards the longed-for regions of Negroland, we encamped on hard ground, so that we had great difficulty in fixing the pegs of our tents. The sky was overcast with thick clouds; but our hopes of a refreshing rain were disappointed.

Thursday, August 15th. The character of the country continued the same, though the weather was so foggy that the heights at some distance were quite enveloped, and became entirely invisible. This was a sure indication of our approaching tropical climes. After a march of three miles and a half, the ground became more rugged for a short time, but was soon succeeded by a gravelly plain. The sky had become thickly clouded; and in the afternoon a high wind arose, succeeded, about two o'clock, by heavy rain, and by distant thunder, while the atmosphere was exceedingly heavy, and made us all feel drowsy.

It was three o'clock when we arrived at the Marárraba*, the "half-way" between Ghát and A'ír, a place regarded with a kind of religious awe by the natives, who in passing place each a stone upon the mighty granite blocks which mark the spot. To our left we had irregular rocky ground, with a few elevations rising to greater height, and ahead a very remarkable granite crest, sometimes rising, at others descending, with its slopes enveloped in sand up to the very top. This ridge, which is called Giféngwetáng, and which looks very much like an artificial wall erected between the dry desert and the more favoured region of the tropics, we crossed further on through an opening like a saddle, and among sand-hills where the slaves of our companions ran about to pick up and collect the few tufts of herbage that were scattered over the surface, in order to furnish a fresh mouthful to the poor wearied animals. At four o'clock the sand-hills ceased, and were succeeded by a wide pebbly plain, on which, after six miles travelling, we encamped.

Our encampment was by no means a quiet one;

* This is a Háusa word, from " rába " (to divide); and I shall have to notice, in the course of my proceedings, several localities so designated on various routes.

and to any one who paid due attention to the character and disposition of the people, serious indications of a storm, which was gathering over us,
became visible. Mohammed Bóro, who had so often
given vent to his feelings of revenge for the neglect
with which he had been treated, was all fire and
fury; and stirring up the whole encampment, he
summoned all the people to a council, having, as
he said, received intelligence that a large party of
Hogár was coming to Asïu. Not having paid much
attention to the report about Sídi Jáfel's expedition,
I became anxious when made aware of the man's
fury; for I knew the motives which actuated him.

Friday,
August 16th.
We started early. Gravelly and pebbly
grounds succeeded each other, the principal formation being granite; but when, after a
march of about thirteen miles, we passed the narrow
sandy spur of a considerable ridge approaching our
left, a fine species of white marble became visible.
We then passed a rugged district, of peculiar and
desolate appearance, called Ibéllakang, and crossed
a ridge of gneiss covered with gravel. Here, while a
thunder-storm was rising in the east, our caravan, to
our great regret, divided, the Tinýlkum turning off
towards the east, in order, as we were told, to look
for a little herbage among the sand-hills. Meanwhile
thick, heavy clouds, which had been discharging a
great quantity of rain towards the east, broke over us
at a quarter past four o'clock in the afternoon, when
we were just in the act of crossing another rocky

crest covered with gravel. A violent sand-storm, followed by heavy rain, which was driven along by a furious gale, soon threw the caravan into the utmost confusion, and made all observation impossible ; but fortunately it did not last long.

It was on descending from this crest, while the weather cleared up, that the Háusa slaves, with a feeling of pride and joy, pointed out in the far distance " dútsi-n-Absen " (Mount Absen). Here the granite formation had been gradually succeeded by sandstone and slate. This district, indeed, seems to be the line of demarcation between two different zones.

At twenty minutes past six o'clock we at length encamped, but were again in the saddle at eleven o'clock at night, and in pale moonlight, sleepy and worn out as we were, began a dreadful night's march. But altogether it proved to be a wise measure taken by the Kél-owí, who had reason to be afraid lest the Hogár, of whom they appeared to have trustworthy news, might overtake us before we reached the wells of Asïu, and then treat us as they pleased. Our companions, who were of course themselves not quite insensible to fatigue, as night advanced became very uncertain in their direction, and kept much too far to the south. When day dawned, our road lay over a flat, rocky, sand-stone surface, while we passed on our left a locality remarkable for nothing but its name, Efínagha.* We then descended from the rocky

* This name is evidently identical with the name given to the Berber alphabet, which is called tefínaghen ; but the coinci-

ground into the extremely shallow valley of Asíu, overgrown with scanty herbage of a kind not much liked by the camels. Here we encamped, near a group of four wells, which still belong to the Azkár, while a little further on there are others which the Kél-owí regard as their own property. How it was that we did not encamp near the latter I cannot say. But the people were glad to have got so far. The wells, or at least two of them, afforded an abundant supply of water; but it was not of a good quality, and had a peculiar taste, I think on account of the iron ore with which it was impregnated.

This, then, was Asíu*, a place important for the caravan-trade at all times, on account of the routes from Ghadámes and from Tawát joining here, and which did so even as far back as the time when the famous traveller E'bn Batúta returned from his enterprising journey to Sudán homewards by way of Tawát (in the year 1353–4). Desolate and melancholy as it appeared, it was also an important station to us, as we thought that we had now left the most

dence will cease to surprise when I remark that both words mean nothing but signs, tokens, a name which may be given as well to letters as to a district remarkable for the position of some stones or ridges. The Tawárek, as I shall have occasion to mention in another part of my narrative, call all sorts of writing not written in signs, but with letters, tefínaghen. The learned among the Tademékket and Awelímmiden were greatly surprised, when going attentively over my English books, to find that it was all tefínaghen—"tefínagh rurret."

* The form Aisou, in Mr. Richardson's Journal, is only a clerical error.

difficult part of the journey behind us. For though I myself had some forebodings of a danger threatening us, we had no idea that the difficulties which we should have to encounter were incomparably greater than those which we had passed through. Mr. Richardson supposed that because we had reached the imaginary frontier of the territories of the Azkár and Kél-owí, we were beyond the reach of any attack from the north. With the utmost obstinacy he reprobated as absurd any supposition that such a frontier might be easily crossed by nomadic roving tribes, asserting that these frontiers in the desert were respected much more scrupulously than any frontier of Austria, notwithstanding the innumerable host of its landwaiters. But he was soon to be undeceived on all the points of his desert-diplomacy, at his own expense and that of us all.

There was very little attraction for roving about in this broad gravelly plain. Now and then a group of granite blocks interrupted the monotonous level, bordered on the north by a gradually-ascending rocky ground, while the southern border rose to a somewhat higher elevation.

Desolate as the spot was, and gloomy as were our prospects, the arrival of the Tinýlkum in the course of the afternoon afforded a very cheerful sight, and inspired some confidence, as we felt that our little party had once more resumed its strength. All the people, however, displayed an outward show of tranquillity and security, with the exception of Serki-n-turáwa, who was bustling about in a state of the utmost excitement. Watering the camels and filling the waterskins employed the whole day.

Sunday, August 18th.
After a two hours' march we began to ascend, first gradually, then more steeply, all the rocks hereabouts consisting of slate, greatly split and rent, and covered with sand. In twenty-five minutes we reached the higher level, which consisted of pebbly ground with a ridge running, at a distance of about four miles, to the west.

While we were quietly pursuing our road, with the Kél-owí in the van, the Tinýlkum marching in the rear, suddenly Mohammed the Sfaksi came running behind us, swinging his musket over his head, and crying lustily, "He awelád, awelád bú, ádúna já" ("Lads, lads, our enemy has come"), and spreading the utmost alarm through the whole of the caravan. Everbody seized his arms, whether musket, spear, sword, or bow; and whosoever was riding jumped down from his camel. Some time elapsed before it was possible, amid the noise, and uproar, to learn the cause of the alarm. At length it transpired. A man named Mohammed, belonging to the caravan, having remained a little behind at the well, had observed three Tawárek mounted on mehára approaching at a rapid rate; and while he himself followed the caravan, he left his slave behind to see whether others were in the rear. The slave, after a while, overtook him with the news that several more camels had become visible in the distance; and then

Mohammed and his slave hurried on to bring us the intelligence. Even Mr. Richardson, who, being rather hard of hearing, judged of our situation only from the alarm, descended from his slender little she-camel and cocked his pistols. A warlike spirit seemed to have taken possession of the whole caravan; and I am persuaded, that had we been attacked at this moment, all would have fought valiantly. But such is not the custom of freebooting parties : they will cling artfully to a caravan, and first introduce themselves in a tranquil and peaceable way, till they have succeeded in disturbing the little unity which exists in such a troop, composed as it is of the most different elements ; they then gradually throw off the mask, and in general attain their object.

When at length a little tranquillity had been restored, and plenty of powder and shot had been distributed among those armed with firelocks, the opinion began to prevail, that, even if the whole of the report should be true, it was not probable that we should be attacked by daylight. We therefore continued our march with a greater feeling of security, while a body of archers was despatched to learn the news of a small caravan which was coming from Sudán, and marching at some distance from us, behind a low ridge of rocks. They were a few Tébu, with ten camels and between thirty and forty slaves, unconsciously going to meet a terrible fate; for we afterwards learned that the Imghád of the Hogár, or rather the Hadánara, disappointed at our having passed through their country without their getting anything from us, had attacked this little troop, murdering the Tébu, and carrying off their camels and slaves.

While the caravan was going slowly on, I was enabled to allow my méheri a little feeding on the nesí (*Panicum grossularium*, much liked by camels) in a spot called Tahasása. At noon we began to ascend on rocky ground, and, after a very gradual ascent of three miles, reached the higher level, strewn with pebbles, but exhibiting further on a rugged slaty soil, till we reached the valley Fénorang.* This valley, which is a little less than a mile in breadth and two in length, is famous for its rich supply of herbage, principally of the kind called bú-rékkeba, and the far-famed el hád (the camel's dainty), and is on this account an important halting-place for the caravans coming from the north, after having traversed that naked part of the desert, which produces scarcely any food for the camel. Notwithstanding, therefore, the danger which threatened us, it was determined to remain here not only this, but also the following day.

As soon as the loads were taken off their backs, the half-starved camels fell to devouring eagerly the fine herbage offered them. Meanwhile we encamped as close together as possible, preparing ourselves for the worst, and looking anxiously around in every direction. But nobody was to be seen till the evening, when the three men on their mehára made their

* Mr. Richardson calls it Takeesat.

appearance, and, being allowed to approach the caravan, made no secret of the fact that a greater number
was behind them.

Aware of what might happen, our small troop had
all their arms ready, in order to repulse any attack ;
but the Kél-owí and the few Azkár who were in our
caravan kept us back, and, after a little talk, allowed
the visitors to lie down for the night near our encampment, and even solicited our hospitality in their
behalf.   Nevertheless all of them well knew that the
strangers were freebooters, who could not but have
bad designs against us ; and the experienced old
Awed el Khér, the sheikh of the Káfila, came expressly
to us, warning, and begging us to be on our guard,
while Bóro Serki-n-turáwa began to play a conspicuous
part, addressing the Kél-owí and Tinýlkum in a
formal speech, and exhorting them to stand by us.
Everybody was crying for powder; and nobody could
get enough.   Our clever but occasionally very troublesome servant Mohammed conceived a strategical
plan, placing on the north side of the two tents the
four pieces of the boat, behind each of which one of
us had to take his station in case of an attack.

Having had some experience of freebooters' prac-
tices in my former wanderings, I knew that all this
was mere farce and mockery, and that the only way
of ensuring our safety would have been to prevent
these scouts from approaching us at all.   We kept
watch the whole night ; and of course the strangers,
seeing us well on our guard, and the whole caravan

still in high spirits and in unity, ventured upon nothing.

In the morning our three guests (who, as I made out, did not belong to the Azkár, but were Kél-fadé from the northern districts of A'ír) went slowly away, but only to join their companions, who had kept at some distance beyond the rocky ridge which bordered or, rather, interrupted the valley to the westward. There some individuals of the caravan, who went to cut herbage, found the fresh traces of nine camels. In spite of outward tranquillity, there was much matter for anxiety and much restlessness in the caravan, and suddenly an alarm was given that the camels had been stolen; but fortunately it proved to be unfounded.

'Abd el Káder, the Tawáti of whom I have spoken above, trying to take advantage of this state of things, came to Mr. Overweg, and urgently pressed him to deposit everything of value with Awed el Khér, the Kél-owí, and something, " of course," with him also. This was truly very disinterested advice; for if anything had happened to us, they would of course have become our heirs. In the evening we had again three guests, not, however, the same as before, but some of their companions, who belonged to the Hadá-nara, one of the divisions of the Azkár.

Tuesday, August 20th. At an early hour we started with an uneasy feeling. With the first dawn the true believers had been called together to prayer; and the bond which united the Mohammedan members

of the caravan with the Christian travellers had been
loosened in a very conspicuous manner.　Then the
encampment broke up, and we set out—not, however,
as we had been accustomed to go latterly, every little
party starting off as soon as they were ready, but
all waiting till the whole caravan had loaded their
camels, when we began our march in close order,
first along the valley, then entering upon higher
ground, sometimes gravelly, at others rocky.　The
range to our right here, a little more than a mile
distant, bears different names corresponding to the
more prominent parts into which it is separated by
hollows or saddles, the last cone towards the south
being called Timázkaren, a name most probably
connected with that of the Azkár tribe, while another
is named Tin-dúrdurang.　The Tarki or Amóshagh
is very expressive in names; and whenever the meaning of all these appellations shall be brought to light,
I am sure we shall find many interesting signifi-
cations.　Though I paid a good deal of attention to
their language, the Tarkíyeh or Temáshight, I had
not leisure enough to become master of the more
difficult and obsolete terms; and, of course, very
few even among themselves can at present tell the
exact meaning of a name derived from ancient times.

　　At length we had left behind us that remarkable
ridge, and entering another shallow valley full of
young herbage, followed its windings, the whole
presenting a very irregular structure, when suddenly
four men were seen ahead of us on an eminence, and

instantly a troop of lightly-armed people, amongst
them three archers, were despatched, as it seemed,
in order to reconnoitre, marching in regular order
straight for the eminence.

Being in the first line of our caravan, and not
feeling so sure on the camel as on foot, I dismounted,
and marched forward, leading my méheri by the nose-
cord, and with my eyes fixed upon the scene before
us. But how much was I surprised when I saw two
of the four unknown individuals executing a wild
sort of armed dance together with the Kél-owí, while
the others were sitting quietly on the ground. Much
perplexed, I continued to move slowly on, when two
of the men who had danced suddenly rushed upon
me, and grasping the rope of my camel, asked for
tribute. Quite unprepared for such a scene under
such circumstances, I grasped my pistol, when, just
at the right time, I learnt the reason and character of
this curious proceeding.

The little eminence on the top of which we had
observed the people, and at the foot of which the
armed dance was performed, is an important locality
in the modern history of the country which we had
reached. For here it was that when the Kél-owí
(at that time an unmixed and pure Berber tribe, as it
seems) took possession of the country of Old Góber
with its capital, Tin-shamán, a compromise or covenant was entered into between the red conquerors
and the black natives, that the latter should not be
destroyed, and that the principal chief of the Kél-owí

should only be allowed to marry a black woman. And as a memorial of this transaction, the custom has been preserved, that when caravans pass the spot where the covenant was entered into, near the little rock Máket-n-ikelán*, " the slaves " shall be merry and be authorized to levy upon their masters a small tribute. The black man who stopped me was the " serki-n-baï " (the principal or chief of the slaves).

These poor merry creatures, while the caravan was proceeding on its march, executed another dance; and the whole would have been an incident of the utmost interest, if our minds and those of all the well-disposed members of the caravan had not been greatly oppressed and vexed with sad forebodings of mishap. The fear was so great that the amiable and sociable Slimán (one of the Tinýlkum, who at a later period manifested his sympathy with us in our misfortunes) begged me most urgently to keep more in the middle of the caravan, as he was afraid that one of those ruffians might suddenly rush upon me, and pierce me with his spear.

The soil hereabouts consisted entirely of bare gravel;

---

* I regret that I neglected to inquire what was the original Góber name of this place; for, while there cannot be any doubt that it received its present name, Máket-n-ikelán, from this transaction, it is very probable that it was a place of ancient pagan worship, and as such had a name of its own. It is very significant that the neighbouring plain is emphatically called "the plain of A'ír,"—in the Arabic form, "shábet el Ahír."

but further on it became more uneven, and broken by granite rocks, in the cavities among which our people found some rain-water. The tract on our right was called Tisgáwade, while the heights on our left bore the name Tín-ébbeke. I here rode awhile by the side of E'meli, a Tarki of the tribe of the Azkár, a gentleman both in his dress and manners, who never descended from the back of his camel. Although he appeared not to be very hostile to the robbers on our track, and was certainly aware of their intention, I liked him on account of his distinguished manners, and, under more favourable circumstances, should have been able to obtain a great deal of information from him. But there was with him a rather disagreeable and malicious fellow named Mohammed (or, as the Tawárek pronounce it, Mokhammed), from Yánet or Jánet, who, in the course of the difficulties which befell us, did us a great deal of mischief, and was fully disposed to do us much more.

The country, which in the meantime had become more open, after a while became bordered ahead by elevations in the form of a semi-circle, while we began to ascend. The weather had been extremely sultry and close the whole day; and at last, about three o'clock in the afternoon, the storm broke out, but with less violence than on the day before our arrival at Asīu.

We encamped at length on an open gravelly plain surrounded by ridges of rocks, without pitching our tents; for our unwished-for guests had in the face of the Tinýlkum openly declared that their design was to kill us, but that they wanted first to get more assistance. Notwithstanding this, Mr. Richardson even to-night was obliged to feed these ruffians; such is the weakness of a caravan — although in our case the difference of religion, and consequent want of unity, could not but greatly contribute to paralyze its strength. I here heard that some of the party were Imghád from Tádomat.

Under such circumstances, and in such a state of feeling, it was impossible to enjoy the sport and frolics of the slaves (that is, of the domestic slaves) of the Kél-owí, who with wild gestures and cries were running about the encampment to exact from all the free individuals of the caravan their little Máket-n-ikelán tribute, receiving from one a small quantity of dates, from another a piece of muslin or a knife, from another a shirt. Everybody was obliged to give something, however small. Notwithstanding our long day's march, Overweg and I found it necessary to be on the watch the whole night.

Starting at an early hour, we ascended very rugged ground, the rocky ridges on both sides often meeting together and forming irregular defiles. After a march of five miles and a half, we reached the highest elevation, and obtained a view over the whole district, which, being sprinkled as it were with small granitic mounds, had a very desolate appearance; but in the distance to our left

Wednesday, August 21st.

an interesting mountain-group was to be seen, of
which the accompanying sketch will give some idea.

Having crossed several small valleys, we reached, a
little before ten o'clock, one of considerable breadth,
richly overgrown with herbage, and exhibiting evident traces of a violent torrent which had swept
over it the day before, while with us but little rain
had fallen.   It is called Jínninau, and improved as
we advanced, our path sometimes keeping along it,
sometimes receding to a little distance; in some
places the growth of the trees, principally the *Balanites* or abórak, was indeed splendid and luxuriant.
Unfortunately we had not sufficient leisure and
mental ease to collect all the information which,
under more favourable circumstances, would have
been within our reach.   Thus, I learnt that magnetic
ironstone was found in the mountains to our left.
After noon the valley divided into three branches,
the easternmost of which is the finest and richest
in vegetation, while the western one, called Tiyút,
has likewise a fine supply of trees and herbage;
we took the middle one, and a little further on,
where it grew narrower, encamped.

It was a very pretty and picturesque camping-ground.　At the foot of our tents was a rocky bed of a deep and winding torrent bordered by most luxuriant talha- and abórak-trees (*Balanites Ægyptiaca*), and forming a small pond where the water, rushing down from the rocks behind, had collected; the fresh green of the trees, enlivened by recent rains, formed a beautiful contrast with the dark-yellowish colour of the rocks behind.　Notwithstanding our perilous situation, I could not help straying about, and found, on the blocks over the tebki or pond, some coarse rock-sculptures representing oxen, asses, and a very tall animal which, according to the Kél-owí, was intended to represent the giraffe.

While I was enjoying the scenery of the place, Dídi stept suddenly behind me, and tried to throw me down, but not succeeding, laid his hands from behind upon the pistols which I wore in my belt, trying, by way of experiment, whether I was able to use them notwithstanding his grasp; but turning sharply round, I freed myself from his hold, and told him that no effeminate person like himself should take me.　He was a cunning and insidious fellow; and I trusted him the least of our Kél-owí friends.　A'nnur warned us that the freebooters intended to carry off the camels that we ourselves were riding, in the night; and it was fortunate that we had provided for the emergency, and were able to fasten them to strong iron rings.

While keeping the first watch during the night, I

was enabled by the splendid moonlight to address a few lines in pencil to my friends at home.

Thursday,
August 22nd. The Kél-owí having had some difficulty in finding their camels, we did not move at an early hour. To our great astonishment we crossed the rocky bed of the torrent, and entered an irregular defile where a little further on we passed another pond of rain-water. When at length we emerged from the rocks, we reached a very high level, whence we had a clear prospect over the country before us. Four considerable ranges of mountains were clearly distinguishable in the distance, forming an *ensemble* of which the accompanying sketch will give an idea. We

then entered valleys clothed with a fine fresh verdure sprinkled with flowers, and with a luxuriant vegetation such as we had not seen before. The senna-plant (*Cassia senna*) appeared in tolerable quantity. Mountains and peaks were seen all around in a great variety of forms; and at twenty minutes past nine we had a larger mountain-mass on one side, from which a dry watercourse, marked by a broad line of herbage, issued and crossed our route.

Having here allowed our camels a little feeding, we entered upon gravelly soil with projecting blocks of granite, and then went on ascending through a succession of small plains and valleys till we reached Erazar-n-Gébi, among the splendid vegetation of which we first observed the abísga, or *Capparis sodata*, called siwák or lirák by the Arabs, an important bush, the currant-like fruit of which is not only eaten fresh but also dried, and laid up in store, while the root affords that excellent remedy for the teeth which the Mohammedans, in imitation of their prophet, use to a great extent.   The root moreover, at least on the shores of the Tsád, by the process of burning, affords a substitute for salt.   It is the most characteristic bush or tree of the whole region of transition between the desert and the fertile regions of Central Africa, between the twentieth and the fifteenth degree of northern latitude ; and in the course of my travels I saw it nowhere of such size as on the northern bank of the Isa or Niger, between Timbúktu and Gágho, the whole ground which this once splendid and rich capital of the Songhay Empire occupied being at present covered and marked out by this celebrated bush. As for the camels, they like very well to feed for a short time upon its fresh leaves, if they have some other herb to mix with it ; but eaten alone it soon becomes too bitter for them.   In this valley the little berries were not yet ripe ; but further on they were ripening, and afforded a slight but refreshing addition to our food.

Leaving the pleasant valley of Gébi by a small opening bordered with large blocks of granite, while peaks of considerable elevation were seen towering over the nearer cliffs, we entered another large valley called Tághajít *, but not quite so rich in vegetation, and encamped here on an open space a little after noon. The valley is important as being the first in the frontier-region of Aïr or Asben where there is a fixed settlement — a small village of leathern tents, inhabited by people of the tribe of Fade-ang, who preserve a certain independence of the Kél-owí, while they acknowledge the supremacy of the sultan of A'gades, a state of things of which I shall have occasion to say more in another place.

* This name too is pronounced Tarhajít.

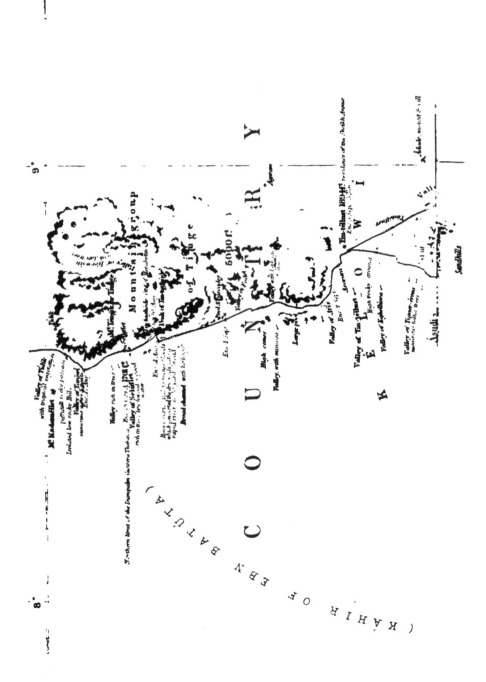

THE sensations of our guides and camel-drivers had been uneasy from the very moment of our encamping; and Mr. Richardson, at the suggestion of A'nnur, had on the preceding day sent E'meli and Mokhammed in advance, in order to bring to us the chief of Fade-ang. This person was represented to us as a man of great authority in this lawless country, and able to protect us against freebooting parties, which our guests of the other day, who had gone on in advance, were sure to collect against us. But Mokhammed, as I have observed above, was a great rascal himself, who would do all in his power to increase our difficulties, in order to profit by the confusion. The chief was accordingly reported as being absent; and a man who was said to be his brother was to take his place. This person made his appearance, accompanied by some people from the village; but it became immediately apparent that he had no authority whatever, and one of the Imghád of Tádomat, who had stuck to us for the last two days, in order to show us what respect he had for this man, struck him repeatedly with his spear upon the shoulder. Among the companions of our new protector was a Taleb of the name of Buhéda, distinguished by his talkativeness and a certain degree of arrogance, who made himself ridiculous by trying to convince us of his immense learning. What an enormous difference there was between these mean-looking and degraded half-castes and our martial pursuers, who stood close by! Though I knew the latter could and would do us much more harm than the former, I liked them much better.

Overweg and I had sat down in the shade of a talha-tree at a little distance from our tent, and had soon a whole circle of visitors around us, who in the beginning behaved with some modesty and discretion, but gradually became rather troublesome. I gave them some small presents, such as scissors, knives, mirrors, and needles, with which they expressed themselves well pleased. Presently came also several women, one with the characteristic features called in Temáshight " tebúllodén," which may be translated by the words of Leo, " le parti di dietro pienissime e grasse," and another younger one mounted upon a donkey.

The whole character of these people appeared very degraded. They were totally devoid of the noble and manly appearance which the most careless observer cannot fail to admire even in a common Tarki freebooter; and the relation between the sexes appeared in a worse light than one would expect in such a situation as this. However, we have ample testimony in ancient Arabian writers that licentious manners have always prevailed among the Berber tribes on the frontier of the desert ; and we found the same habits existing among the tribe of the Tagáma, while not only A'gades but even the little village of Tintéllust was not without its courtesans.   This is a very dis-heartening phenomenon to observe in so small a community, and in a locality where nature would seem peculiarly favourable to purity and simplicity of manners.   The names of some of these Tághajít beauties — Telíttifók, Tatináta, and Temétilé — are interesting for the character of the language.

We were anxious to buy some of the famous Aïr cheese, for which we had been longing the whole way over the dreary desert, and had kept up our spirits with the prospect of soon indulging in this luxury ; but we were not able to procure a single one, and our endeavours to buy a sheep or a goat were equally fruitless.   Instead of the plenty which we had been led to expect in this country, we found nothing but misery.   But I was rather surprised to find here a very fine and strong race of asses.

We were tolerably composed, and reclining at our ease (though our weapons were always at hand), when we were a little alarmed by a demand of six riyals for the use of the pond in Jínninau.   Our amiable but unenergetic friend A'nnur seconded the demand, by way of satisfying in some way the intruders upon our caravan.   These claims were scarcely settled when a dreadful alarm was raised, by the report that a body of from fifty to sixty Mehára were about to attack us.

Though no good authority could be named for this intelligence, the whole caravan was carried away by excitement, and all called out for powder and shot. Bóro Serki-n-turáwa once more delivered eloquent speeches, and exhorted the people to be courageous; but many of the Tinýlkum, very naturally, had a great objection to come to open hostilities with the Tawárek, which might end in their being unable to travel any longer along this route.

In this moment of extreme excitement Khweldi arrived, the chief merchant of Múrzuk, whom we had not expected to see, though we knew that he was on his way from Sudán to the north. We were in a situation wherein he was able to render us the most material service, both by his influence upon the individuals of whom our caravan was composed, and by his knowledge of the country whose frontier-territories we had just entered. But unfortunately, though a very experienced merchant, he was not a practical, sharp-sighted man; and instead of giving us clear information as to the probable amount of truth in the reports, and what sort of difficulties we might really have to encounter, and how by paying a sort of passage-money to the chiefs we might get over them, he denied in private the existence of any danger at all, while openly he went round the whole caravan extolling our importance as a mission sent by a powerful government, and encouraging the people to defend us if we should be in danger. In consequence of his exhortations the Tinýlkum took courage, but had the imprudence and absurdity to supply also the three intruders with powder and shot, who, though protesting to be now our most sincere friends, of course made no other use of the present than to supply their band with this material, which alone gave us a degree of superiority, and constituted our security.

Any one accustomed to look closely at things could not be at all satisfied with the spirit of our caravan, notwithstanding its noise and waste of powder, and with its entire want of union; but the scene which followed in the bright moonlight evening, and lasted throughout the night, was animating and interesting in the extreme. The whole caravan was drawn up in a line of battle, the left wing being formed by ourselves and the detachment of the Kél-owí. who had left their own camping-ground and posted themselves in front of our tent, while the Tinýlkum and the Sfaksi formed the centre, and the rest of the Kél-owí, with Bóro, the right wing, leaning upon the cliffs, our exposed left being defended by the four pieces of the boat. About ten o'clock a small troop of Mehára* appeared, when a heavy fusillade was kept up over their heads, and firing and shouting were continued the whole night.

* In conformity with the usage of travellers, I call Mehára people mounted upon mehára, or swift camels (in the singular form méheri). This expression has nothing whatever to do with Mehárebín, a name of which I shall speak hereafter.

Our situation remained the same the whole of the
following day; and it became very tedious, as it prevented us from making excursions, and becoming acquainted with the features of the new country which
we had entered. Another alarm having been raised in
vain, the leaders of the expedition which was collecting against us came out, with the promise that they
would not further molest the caravan if the Christians
were given up to them. This demand having been
at once rejected, we were left in tolerable tranquillity
for a while, as the freebooters now saw that in
order to obtain their object, which was plunder, they
should be obliged to bring really into the field the
whole force they had so long boasted of.

Khweldi paid us another visit in the afternoon;
and as he wanted to make us believe that there was
really no danger in this country, so he did not fail to
represent the state of things in Sudán as the most favourable we could have wished for. He also sought
to sweeten over any remnant of anxiety which we
might have, by a dish of very delicious dates which
he had received from his friend Háj Beshír in Iferwán,
and which gave us a favourable idea of what the
country before us was able to produce. Altogether
Khweldi endeavoured to be agreeable to everybody;
and on a later occasion, in 1854, when I was for
some time without means, he behaved towards me in
a very gentleman-like manner. In this company was a
brother of our quiet and faithful servant Mohammed

from Gatrón, who was now returning home with his earnings.

Not being able to refrain wholly from excursions, I undertook in the afternoon to visit the watering-place situated up a little lateral nook of the valley, adorned with very luxuriant talha-trees, and winding in a half circle by S.E. to N.E. First, at the distance of about a mile, I came to a hole where some of the Tinýlkum were scooping water; and ascending the rocky bed of the occasional torrent, I found a small pond where the camels were drinking; but our faithful friend Músa, who was not at all pleased with my having ventured so far, told me that the water obtained here did not keep long, but that higher up good water was to be found in the principal valley.

I had from the beginning attentively observed the character and proceedings of Bóro Serki-n-turáwa, and feared nothing so much as his intrigues; and at my urgent request, Mr. Richardson to-night made him a satisfactory present as an acknowledgment of the courage which he had lately shown in defending our cause. Of course the present came rather late; but it was better to give it now, in order to avert the consequences of his intrigues as much as possible, than not at all. Had it been given two months ago, it might have saved us an immense deal of difficulty, danger, and heavy loss.

We left at length our camping-ground in Tághajít, and soon passed Khweldi's en-campment, which was just about to break up. Saturday, August 24th.

Rocky ground, overtopped by higher mountain-masses or by detached peaks, and hollows overgrown with rich vegetation, and preserving for a longer or shorter time the regular form of valleys, succeed by turns, and constitute the predominant feature of the country of Asben. But instead of the fresh green pasture which had delighted and cheered us in some of the northern valleys, the herbage in some of those which we passed to-day was quite dry.

Early in the afternoon we encamped in the valley Imenán *, a little outside the line of herbage and trees, on an open spot at the southern foot of a low rocky eminence. The valley, overgrown as it was with large talha-trees and the oat-grass called bú-rékkeba, of tall, luxuriant growth, was pleasant, and invited us to repose. But before sunset our tranquillity was greatly disturbed by the appearance of five of our well-known marauding companions mounted on camels, and leading six others. They dismounted within less than a pistol-shot from our tents, and with wild ferocious laughter were discussing their projects with the Azkár in our caravan.

I could scarcely suppress a laugh when several of the Tinýlkum came and brought us the ironical assurance that there was now perfect security, and that we might indulge in sound sleep. Others came with the less agreeable, but truer warning, that we ought not to sleep that night. The greatest

* The name has probably some connexion with that of the tribe I'manang.

alarm and excitement soon spread through the caravan.   Later in the evening, while our benevolent guests were devouring their supper, Mohammed el Túnsi called me and Overweg aside, and informed us that we were threatened with great danger indeed, these Hogár, as he called them, having brought a letter from Nakhnúkhen, authorizing them to collect people in the territory of the Kél-owí, and there to despatch us in such a way that not even a trace of us should be found, but not to touch us so long as we were within the confines of the Azkár.

I was convinced that this account, so far as it regarded Nakhnúkhen, was an absurd fiction of our persecutors; and I tried to persuade our servant to this effect.   When he returned from us to the caravan, a council of war was held, and a resolution passed, that if a number of from twenty to thirty people came to attack us they would undertake to defend us, but if we should be threatened by a more numerous host they would try to make a compromise by yielding up a part of our goods.   In consequence of this resolution, all possible warlike preparations were made once more, and Bóro delivered another speech; but it seemed rather irreconcilable with such a state of things, that while we, as well as the Tinýlkum, brought all our camels close to our tents at an early hour, the Kél-owí left theirs out the whole night.   Perhaps, being natives of the country, they did not expect that the freebooters would seize their animals.

Be this as it may, great anxiety arose when early in the morning it was found that the camels were gone; and when day broke, our guests of last night, who had stolen away before midnight, were seen riding down from the rocky ridge on the south, and with a commanding air calling the principal men of the caravan to a council. Then followed the scenes which Mr. Richardson has so graphically described.

I will only mention that Bóro Serki-n-turáwa, sword in hand, led us on with great energy. He called me to keep close to him; and I think that now (when we had atoned for the neglect with which he had been treated by us, by assuring him that we were convinced of his high position and influence in the country) he had the honest intention to protect us. Of the Tinýlkum only our faithful Músa and the amiable young Slimán adhered to us, and, of the other people, the Tawáti and Mohammed e' Sfaksi, although the latter trembled with fear, and was as pale as death; Yusuf Mukni remained behind. Fáraji on this occasion behaved with great courage, and bravely challenged the enemy. What frightened the latter most were the bayonets on our guns, as they saw that, after having received our fire, they would not yet have done with us, but would still have a weapon to encounter at least as formidable as their own spears.

As soon as the enemy had protested that he was only come against us as Christians, all sympathy for us ceased in the caravan. All expected that we

would become Moslemín without great difficulty; and
our servant Mohammed, when we rejected this condition as an impossibility, immediately relapsed into
his ordinary impudence, laughing in our faces because, forsooth, we were so absurd as still to think of
some other expedient. This clever but spoiled youngster was a protégé of the British consulate in Tunis.

At length all seemed to be settled. The whole
host of the enemy, besides its rich booty, had been
treated with an enormous quantity of mohamsa;
and we had repeatedly been assured that now we
might be certain of reaching the chief A'nnur's
residence without any further disturbance, when
the little A'nnur, a man of honest but mild character, came to beg us most earnestly to be on our
guard, lest behind the rocks and ridges there might
still be some persons in ambush. At length we
left this inhospitable place; but we were far from
being at ease, for it was clear that there was still
a cloud on the horizon, which might easily gather to
another storm.

After a short march we encamped in a small valley
without pitching our tents. The Merábet who had
accompanied and sanctioned the expedition against
us was now in our company; and that was thought
to be the best means of preventing any further
molestation. This man, as I made out afterwards,
was no other than Ibrahím Aghá-batúre (the son of
Háj Beshír, a well-known and influential person settled in Ferwán, or Iferwán), who, in consequence of

these proceedings, was afterwards punished severely by the sultan of A'gades. With Aghá-batúre himself I met accidentally at a later period, in 1853, near Zinder, when he was greatly astonished to see me still alive, notwithstanding all the hardships I had gone through. Bóro, who passed the evening with him in reading the Kurán, treated him hospitably — with Mr. Richardson's mohamsa.

Monday,
August 26th. After a march of three miles and a half, having ascended a little, we obtained a clear view of the great mountain-mass which, lying between Tídik on the north and Tin-tagh-odé on the west, seems not to be marked with a collective proper name, although it is very often called by the people Mount Absen.* But I cannot say whether this name, which is the old Góber name for the whole country called by the Berbers Air, belonged originally only to these mountains, or whether it is now given to them merely on account of their being the conspicuous elevation of the country so-named, to people coming from the north ; for this, according to the unanimous statement of the Kél-owí, is the frontier of Sudán, to which neither Tághajít nor even Tídik belongs. The Tawárek, it would seem, have no indigenous proper name for Sudán (properly Beled e' sudán) or Negroland ; most of them call it Agús

* Absen and Asben are used indiscriminately, though a ba-Háushe, or Háusa man, will always say Asben, ba-Asbenchi, Asbenáwa, while the native half-castes will prefer the other form —Absen, Absenáwa.

(the south).   Nevertheless Tekrúr seems to be an ancient Libyan name for Negroland.

A remarkable peak called Téngik or Tímge towers over this mountain-mass, being, according to the intelligent old chief A'nnur (who ought to be well acquainted with his own country), the most elevated point in the whole country of Aïr.   Unfortunately our situation in the country was such that we could not think of exploring this very interesting northern barrier, which must be supposed to possess many beautiful glens and valleys.

But we were still at some distance from these picturesque mountains, and had to cross a very rugged and dreary waste, where, however, we caught sight of the first ostrich as yet seen on our journey. We encamped at length in a shallow valley devoid of any interesting features.

During the night, while I was on the first watch, walking round the encampment of the caravan, it struck me that at one end of it, beyond the Kél-owí, a small party was separately encamped.   When I went there the first time, all was quiet; but a little after eleven o'clock (for in general, on such a journey, everyone lies down at an early hour), hearing a noise on that side, and turning thither, I saw two armed Tawárek saddle their mehára, and make off in the gloom of night.   From this circumstance I concluded that something was still going on against us; but as it appeared useless to make an alarm, I

only took the precaution to put Overweg, who succeeded me on the watch, upon his guard.

Tuesday,
August 27th. We started at a very early hour; but
fortunately the moonlight was so clear and
beautiful that I was not interrupted for a moment in
marking down all the features of the country — at
least along our route, for our situation was now too
precarious to allow of our observing angles to fix
the exact position of mountains lying at some distance from us.

The road in general continued rugged for the first
six miles, and formed at times very difficult passes;
but, notwithstanding these obstacles, the whole caravan kept as close together as possible, and so frus-
trated the plans of our persecutors, who, as we concluded from the appearance of several Mehára in the
distance, intended to attack us on the road, if occasion
offered.   There are two roads, the easternmost of
which passes further on through a remarkable gorge
in the mountains, which we had for a long time
ahead of us.   Here, where we turned off with a
westerly deviation, beautiful white marble, but slightly
weather-worn on the surface, appeared between the
nodules of granite and gneiss, while on our right we
had a rocky ridge called Itsa, the crest of which was
indented in a most remarkable way.   Further on,
where for a while we entered on a gravelly soil, the
whole ground was covered with fresh footsteps of
camels and men; and there was not the least doubt
that another host was gathering against us.

Mount Kadamméllet with its tapering double peak, at a greater distance in the west, formed an interesting object, while the country was gradually

improving. While turning round the lower offshoots of the large mountain-mass which we had now approached, we entered a rather narrow but very rich valley adorned with most luxuriant talha-trees completely enwrapped and bound together by creepers, while the ground was richly clothed with herbage. This is the valley of Tídik; the village of that name, which is situated in a recess of the mountains on our left, remained invisible. It is said to consist of huts formed of a kind of long dry grass, and therefore makes some approach to the fashion of Sudán; these huts are called tághamt, or táramt, by the Southern Imóshagh. But at present the village was desolate, all the inhabitants, the Kél-tídik (people of Tídik) having gone for a while to the fine valleys in the west, which appear to be richer than those to the east.

Further on we crossed the bed of a considerable torrent, the valley terminating in a narrow passage which, though generally considered as the very en-

trance into the region of Sudán, led us once more
into a desolate rocky district, at times widening to
dry hollows. Here Mount Kadamméllet, of which
only the double peak had been previously visible, ex-

hibited to us its ample flanks. The country became
so extremely rugged that we advanced but slowly;
and having here received distinct information which
fully confirmed our apprehension of another predatory expedition against us, we marched in order
of battle. Thus we reached a pond of rain-water
in the narrow rugged hollow Tároï*, where we
filled our water-bags. We found here several donkeys of a remarkably fine breed, belonging to the
men who had brought us the news.

The country beyond this place became more interesting, and even picturesque at times, several fine
glens descending one after the other from the beauti-
fully-indented mountains on our left, which now rose
into full view, as the offshoots had gradually receded.

* Mr. Richardson calls the pond Anamghur; correctly perhaps,
though I did not hear it so called. The name of the valley, however, is Tároï; and, if I am not mistaken, Anamaghúr, or
Anemághera, means in the Southern Berber dialect, in general,
"a watering place;" for our halting-place near Tághajít was also
called by this name.

We were only about eight miles from Selúfiet, where we might expect to be tolerably safe; and we had not the least doubt that we were to sleep there, when suddenly, before noon, our old Azkár mádogu Awed el Khér turned off the road to the right, and chose the camping-ground at the border of a broad valley richly overgrown with herbage. As if moved by supernatural agency, and in ominous silence, the whole caravan followed; not a word was spoken.

It was then evident that we were to pass through another ordeal, which, according to all appearance, would be of a more serious kind than that we had already undergone. How this plot was laid is rather mysterious; and it can be explained only by supposing that a diabolical conspiracy was entered into by the various individuals of our caravan. Some certainly were in the secret; but A'nnur, not less certainly, was sincere in our interest, and wished us to get through safely. But the turbulent state of the country did not allow this weak, unenergetic man to attain his object. Blackmail had been levied upon us by the frontier-tribes; here was another strong party to be satisfied, that of the Merábetín or Aníslimen, who, enjoying great influence in the country, were in a certain degree opposed to the paramount authority of the old chief A'nnur in Tintéllust; and this man, who alone had power to check the turbulent spirit of these wild and lawless tribes, was laid up with sickness. In A'gades there was no sultan, and several parties still stood in opposition to each other, while by the great expedition against the Weléd Slimán, all the warlike passions of the people had been awakened, and their cupidity and greediness for booty and rapine excited to the utmost pitch. All these circumstances must be borne in mind, in order to form a right view of the manner in which we were sacrificed.

The whole affair had a very solemn appearance from the beginning; and it was apparent that this time there were really other motives in view besides that of robbing us. Some of our companions evidently thought that here, at such a distance from our homes and our brethren in faith, we might yield to a more serious attack upon our religion, and so far were sincerely interested in the success of the proceeding; but whether they had any accurate idea of the fate that awaited us, whether we should retain our property and be allowed to proceed, I cannot say. But it is probable that the fanatics thought little of our future destiny; and it is absurd to imagine that, if we had changed our religion as we would a suit of clothes, we should have thereby escaped absolute ruin.

Our people, who well knew what was going on, desired us to pitch only a single tent for all three of us, and not to leave it, even though a great many people should collect about us. The excitement and anxiety of our friend A'nnur had reached the highest pitch; and Bóro was writing letter after letter.

Though a great number of Merábetín had collected at
an early hour, and a host of other people arrived before sunset, the storm did not break out; but as
soon as all the people of our caravan, arranged in
a long line close to our tent, under the guidance of
the most respected of the Merábetín as Imám, had
finished their Mughreb prayers, the calm was at an
end, and the scene which followed was awful.

Our own people were so firmly convinced that, as
we stoutly refused to change our religion, though
only for a day or two, we should immediately suffer
death, that our servant Mohammed, as well as
Mukni, requested us most urgently to testify, in
writing, that they were innocent of our blood.   Mr.
Richardson himself was far from being sure that the
sheikhs did not mean exactly what they said.   Our
servants, and the chiefs of the caravan, had left us
with the plain declaration that nothing less than
certain death awaited us ; and we were sitting
silently in the tent, with the inspiring consciousness of going to our fate in a manner worthy alike
of our religion and of the nation in whose name
we were travelling among these barbarous tribes,
when Mr. Richardson interrupted the silence which
prevailed, with these words : — " Let us talk a little.
We must die; what is the use of sitting so mute ? "
For some minutes death seemed really to hover over
our heads; but the awful moment passed by.   We
had been discussing Mr. Richardson's last propositions
for an attempt to escape with our lives, when, as a

forerunner of the official messenger, the benevolent and kind-hearted Slimán rushed into our tent, and with the most sincere sympathy stammered out the few words, " You are not to die."

The amount of the spoil taken from us was regulated by the sum which we had paid to our Kél-owí escort, the party concerned presuming that they had just the same demands upon us as our companions. The principal, if not the only, actors in this affair, were the Merábetín; and A'nnur the chief of Tintéllust afterwards stated to us that it was to them we had to attribute all our losses and mishaps.   There was also just at this period a young sheríf from Medína at Tin-tagh-odé, with whom we afterwards came into intimate relations, and who confessed to us that he had contributed his part to excite the hatred of the people against the Christian intruders.   Experienced travellers have very truly remarked that this sort of sherífs are at the bottom of every intrigue.   To the honour of Bóro Serki-n-turáwa, I have to state that he was ashamed of the whole affair, and tried to protect us to the best of his power, although in the beginning he had certainly done all that he could to bring us into difficulties.

It was one of the defects of the expedition, that our merchandise, instead of comprising a few valuable things, was for the most part composed of worthless bulky objects, and that it made all the people believe that we were carrying with us enormous wealth, while the whole value of our things

scarcely amounted to two hundred pounds. We had
besides about ten large iron cases filled with dry
biscuit, but which all the ignorant people believed to
be crammed with money.   The consequence was that
the next morning, when all the claims had at length
been settled, and we wanted to move on, there was
still great danger that the rabble, which had not yet
dispersed, would fall upon the rest of our luggage;
and we were greatly obliged to the Sfaksi, who not
only passed some of our luggage as his own, but also
dashed to pieces one of the iron cases, when, to the
astonishment of the simple people, instead of heaps
of dollars, a dry and tasteless sort of bread came
forth from the strong inclosure.

Meanwhile the persecuted Christians had made off,
accompanied by some of the Kél-owí; and at length
the whole caravan collected together.   The valley
was here very beautiful, and having crossed some
smaller hollows, we reached the fine valley of Selúfiet,
rich in trees and bushes, but without herbage; while
at the distance of less than a mile on our left, the
high peak of the Tímge stood erect.   Towards the
west the valley forms a deep gap behind a projecting
mass of granite blocks; and it was here that I met
again my old acquaintance from the Saíd and Nubia,
the dúm-tree or *Cucifera Thebaïca*, here called gáriba,
after the Háusa name góreba.   From the Kél-owí I
could not learn the proper Berber name of this tree *;

* I think, however, that the more learned among them call it
tágait.   The palm tree is called táshdait.

but the Western Imóshagh call it akóf. Even the *Capparis sodata* seems to be called, by the Berber conquerors of this country, only by the Háusa name abísga, while their western brethren call it téshak. Besides the *Cucifera*, or fan-palm, there were here also a few isolated specimens of the date-palm.

The village of Selúfiet itself, consisting of sixty or seventy grass huts of peculiar shape, lies on the southern side of a broad valley running here from east to west and richly overgrown with górebas, abísgas, and talha-trees, but without any grass, for which the ground seems too elevated and stony. Our camping-ground also was of this bare character, and not at all pleasing; it was protected in the rear by large buttresses of rock.

We had not yet enjoyed much tranquillity and security; and we here felt its want the more keenly, as our camel-drivers having been hired only as far as this place, we had henceforth to take charge of all our things ourselves. A large mob of lawless people came about us in the course of the night, howling like hungry jackals; and we were obliged to assure them, by frequent firing, that we were on the watch. We had been obliged to leave our camels to the care of the Kél-owí; but the freebooters having succeeded in dispersing the camels in every direction, our friends were unable in the evening to collect either their own animals or ours, and in the night they were all driven away, as we were told, by the Merábetín themselves, who so repeatedly assured us of their protection.

In the letters which we sent to Europe during our next day's halt in this place, by a caravan of Arabs and Kél-owí, the largest part of which was already in advance, we were unable to give a perfectly satisfactory account of our progress; nevertheless we had made a great step in advance, and were justified in hoping that we should be able to overcome whatever difficulties might still await us, and the more so as we were now able to place ourselves in direct communication with the chief of Tintéllust, from whom we might soon expect to receive an escort.

Some of the stolen camels having been recovered, though fifteen were still wanting, we were enabled to move from this uncomfortable place the next day, leaving behind us, however, the boat and some other things, which were valueless to any but ourselves.

Thursday, August 29th.

Pleased as we were with our onward movement, we were still more cheered when we observed in the fine valley, which here seems to bear the name E'rasa, or rather E'razar *, some small fields with a fresh green crop of negro millet — a delicious sight to travellers from the desert, and the best assurance that we had entered cultivable regions. The fields or gardens were watered by means of a kind of khattára of very simple construction, — a simple pole with a longer cross pole, to which the bucket is fastened. A little further on, the whole valley was clothed with

---

* " E'razar," properly " éghazar," means "the valley," in general; but nevertheless here it seems to be a proper name.

fine wide-spreading bushes of the abísga or *Capparis ;*
but it soon narrowed, while we marched straight upon
the high pointed peak overtowering Tin-tagh-odé,
which forms an interesting object.   The valley of
Selúfiet seems to have no connection with that of
the latter place ; at least, the principal branch, along
which our route lay, was entirely separated from it

by rocky ground.   Here a broad gap dividing the
mountain-mass allows a peep into the glens formed
by the several ridges of which it consists, and which
seem to rise to greater elevation as they recede.   The
slope is rather precipitous; and the general elevation
of this mountain-mass seems scarcely less than 3300
feet above the bottom of the valley, or about 5000
feet above the level of the sea.
   We soon descended again from the rocky ground
into a hollow plain richly clothed with vegetation,
where, besides the abísga, the tunfáfia or *Asclepias
gigantea,* which we had entirely lost sight of since
leaving E'geri, appeared in great abundance.   Here
also was a new plant which we had not seen before—
the " állwot," with large succulent leaves and a pretty
violet flower.   The camels devoured it most eagerly,

and, in the whole district of A'ír, preferred it to any other kind of food. It has a great resemblance to the poisonous damankádda, which in Sudán is often the cause of dangerous disease, and even of death, to the camel.

After marching along this valley for two miles, we encamped on an open space encircled with the green spreading bushes of the abísga, a little beyond Tin-tagh-odé, the village of the Merábetín or Aníslimen*, which is spread in a long line over the low offshoots of the mountain-range, and contains about a hundred light huts, almost all of them being made of grass and the leaves of the dúm-palm, a few only being built of stones.

Small as this village is, it is of very great importance for the intercourse between Central Africa and the northern region beyond the desert; for under the authority of these learned and devout men, commerce is carried on with a security which is really surprising, if regard be had to the wild and predatory habits of the people around. As these Aníslimen belong to a tribe of the Kél-owí, we may infer that their settlement here was contemporaneous with the conquest of the country by the latter tribe,—a

---

* "Aníslim" is the term in the Temáshight language equivalent to the Arabic Merábet; and though it evidently has the most intimate relation to the word "selem" (Islám), meaning properly a man professing Islám, this signification has been entirely lost sight of. I was generally deemed and called by the Western Tawárek an Aníslim, because I wrote and read.

conclusion favoured by the narrative of Ebn Batúta, who does not appear to have found any settlements in this quarter.

The Aníslimen, however, though they style themselves " devout men," have not therefore relinquished all concern about the things of this world, but, on the contrary, by their ambition, intrigues, and warlike proceedings, exercise a great influence upon the whole affairs of the country, and have placed themselves, as I have already mentioned, in a sort of opposition to the powerful chief of Tintéllust. Recently, however, a great calamity had befallen them, the Awelímmiden (the " Surka" of Mungo Park, the dreaded enemies of the Kél-owí) having by a sudden inroad carried away all their camels; and it may have been partly the desire to make use of the opportunity afforded them by the arrival of some unprotected infidels, to repair their losses in some measure, which made them deal so hostilely with us.

As we encamped, the boys of the village hovered around us in great numbers; and while we kept a good look out to prevent their pilfering, we could not but admire their tall, well-formed figures and their light colour,—the best proof that this little clan does not intermarry with the black race. They wore nothing but a leathern apron; and their hair was shorn on the sides, leaving a crest in the middle.

When we had made ourselves somewhat comfortable, we were desirous of entering into some traffic with the people, in order to replace our provisions, which

were almost wholly exhausted; but we soon had reason
to be convinced how erroneous were the ideas which
we had formed from reports as to the cheapness of
provisions in this country, and that we should have
very great difficulty in procuring even the little that
was absolutely necessary. Of butter and cheese we
were unable to obtain the smallest quantity, while
only very small parcels of dukhn, or gero (millet
or *Pennisetum typhoïdeum*), were offered to us, and
greatly to our disadvantage, as the articles we had to
barter with, such as bleached and unbleached calico,
razors, and other things, were estimated at a very
low rate. A common razor brought us here ten
zekka of millet, worth, according to the estimate of
the country, one third of a mithkál, equal to 333
kurdi, or about sixpence-halfpenny. I learnt from
E'meli that the Sakomáren, a tribe of Imóshagh pos-
sessing large flocks of sheep and even much cattle,
bring almost every year a considerable supply of
butter to this country, a statement which was soon
confirmed by my own experience.

The man just mentioned, who had something extremely noble and prepossessing about him, was
about to return to Ghát; and I confided to him a
letter for Europe. In all probability this is the letter
which was afterwards found in the desert, and was
brought by Nakhnúkhen (the chief of the Azkár)
himself to Mr. Dickson, Her Majesty's agent in Ghadámes, who from its fate drew some sinister conclusions as to my own.

Several other people having left us, we remained in
tolerable quiet and repose the whole day; but it was
reported that the next day, during which we should
be obliged to stay here in order to wait for the resti-
tution of our camels, there would be a great concourse
of Mehára to celebrate a marriage in the village: but
fortunately the immense quantity of rain which fell
in the whole of the neighbourhood, and which on the
1st of September changed our valley into the broad
bed of a rapid river, placing all our property in the
utmost danger, prevented this design from being
executed, and, while it seemed to portend to us a
new misfortune, most probably saved us from a
much greater mischief.

Having just escaped from the dangers arising
from the fanaticism and the rapacity of the people,
it was a hard trial to have to contend again against
an element the power of which, in these border
regions of the desert, we had been far from appre-
ciating and acknowledging. We had no antecedents
from which to conclude the possibility that in this
region a valley, more than half a mile wide, might
be turned, in twenty-four hours, into a stream violent
enough to carry away the heaviest things, not excepting even a strong, tall animal like the camel;
and it was with almost childish satisfaction that, in
the afternoon of Saturday, we went to look at the
stream, which was just beginning to roll its floods
along. It was then a most pleasant and refreshing sight; the next day it became a grand and

awful picture of destruction, which gave us no faint idea of a deluge. To the description of the flood itself, as it is given by Mr. Richardson, I shall not add anything; but I have to mention the following circumstances, which seem not to have been placed in their true light.

Half an hour after midday, the waters began to subside, and ceased to endanger our little island, which, attacked on all sides by the destructive fury of an impetuous mountain-torrent swollen to the dimensions of a considerable river, was fast crumbling to pieces, and scarcely afforded any longer space enough to hold our party and our things. Suddenly, on the western shore, a number of Mehára were seen, while at the same time the whole population of Tin-tagh-odé, in full battle-array, came from the other side, and formed themselves in regular groups, partly round our hill, and partly opposite to the Tinýlkum. While we looked with distrust upon these preparations, most of our muskets having been wetted, the mischievous Mokhammed approached our hill and, addressing me with a very significant and malevolent look, cried out, "Lots of people!" The previous afternoon, when I had requested him, while squatting himself insolently upon my carpet, to leave this only piece of comfort for my own use, he threatened me in plain terms, and in the coolest manner, that the following night I should lie on the bottom of the wadi, and he upon my carpet. Not put out by his malice, though I was myself rather doubtful as to

the friendly intentions of all these people, I told him
that the Mehára were our friends sent by the chief
A'nnur as an escort to conduct us safely to Tintéllust.
With a threatening gesture he told me I should be
sadly disappointed, and went away.   Fortunately, it
turned out that the people mounted on camels were
really A'nnur's escort; but at the same time a large
band of robbers had collected, in order to make a last
effort to take possession of our property before we
should obtain the protection of A'nnur, and only withdrew reluctantly when they saw that they should
meet with a strong opposition.

We were then justified in hoping that we had at
length entered a harbour affording us a certain degree
of security; and with thankful and gladdened hearts
we looked forward to our further proceedings.   Our
present situation, however, was far from being comfortable: almost all our things were wet; our tents
were lying in the mud at the bottom of the stream;
and our comfortable and strong, but heavy, Tripolitan tent was so soaked with water and earth, that
a camel could scarcely carry it.   Leaving at length
our ill-chosen camping-ground, Overweg and I were
passing the principal torrent (which was still very
rapid), when the camels we rode, weakened by the
dreadful situation they had been in the whole day,
were unable to keep their feet, and, slipping on
the muddy bottom, set us down in the midst of the
stream.   Soaked and barefoot, having lost my shoes,
I was glad to reach in the dark the new encamp-

ment which had been chosen on the elevated rocky ground a little beyond the border of the valley. Our beds were in the most cheerless condition, and in an unhealthy climate would certainly have been productive of bad consequences. A'ír, however, in every respect may be called the Switzerland of the desert.

Fortunately the weather on the following morning cleared up, and, although the sun came forth only now and then, a fresh wind was very favourable for drying; and it was pleasant to see one thing after another resume a comfortable appearance. The whole encampment seemed to be one large drying-ground.

Having recovered a little from the uncomfortable state in which we had passed the night, we went to pay a visit to the principal men of our new escort, who had seated themselves in a circle, spear in hand, with their leader Hámma (a son-in-law of the chief A'nnur) in the midst of them. Entire strangers as both parties were to each other, and after the many mishaps we had gone through, and the many false reports which must have reached these men about our character, the meeting could not fail to be somewhat cool. We expressed to the leader our sincere acknowledgment of the service which the chief A'nnur had rendered us, and begged him to name us to such of his companions as were related to the chief. On this occasion Mohammed, the chief's cousin, who afterwards became a great friend of mine, made himself remarkable by his pretensions and arrogance. They were all of them tolerably good-looking; but they were not at all of the same make as the Azkár and the people living near the border of A'ír. They were blacker, and not so tall, and, instead of the austere and regular northern features, had a rounder and more cheerful, though less handsome expression of countenance. Their dress also was more gay, several of them wearing light-blue, instead of the melancholy-looking dark-blue tobes.

At about ten o'clock we at length moved on, and chose the western of the two roads, leading hence to Tintéllust, by way of Fódet; the eastern one passes through Tágo and Táni. Leaving the large green valley of Tin-tagh-odé on our left, we kept on more uneven ground, passing some smaller glens, till we reached the commencement of the fine broad valley Fódet, and encamped near the cliffs bordering its eastern side. Here the water, rushing down from the rocks in a sort of cascade, had formed a pond. which, however, was not destined to remain long.

Tuesday, September 3rd. We made a very interesting march through a country marked with bold features, and showing itself in more than one respect capable of being the abode of man. Turning away from the eastern border, we kept more along the middle of the valley, till we reached the most picturesque spot, where it divided into two branches, the eastern of which, bordered by several imposing mountain-spurs, presented a very interesting perspective, of which the

accompanying sketch, drawn as it was on the back of
my camel, will give only a faint idea.

The whole bottom of the valley, where, the day
before yesterday, a mighty torrent had been foaming
along, was now glittering with fragments of minerals.
We then passed the ruins of some houses carried
away by the floods, and met further on a little troop
of asses laden with éneli.* Our whole caravan was in
good spirits; and our escort, in order to give us a
specimen of their horsemanship, if I may so call it,

* E'neli, انلى—dukhn—is a word several times mentioned by
the learned traveller Ebn Batúta in his Travels, where it has
not been understood by the translators. See Journal Asiatique,
1843, série iv. tom i. pp. 188. 191. 200. At p. 194. he describes
the favourite beverage dakno, made of this corn.

got up a race, which, as may be readily imagined, proved a very awkward affair. Two or three of the riders were thrown off; and the sport soon came to an end. The swift camel is excellent for trotting, but it can never excel in a gallop.

In our ascent we had reached very considerable mountain-masses on our right, when some of our old companions, who had come with us from Ghát, separated from us, in order to go to their village Túngadu. Among these was A'kshi, a very modest and quiet man, who alone of all these people had never begged from me even the merest trifle, though he gave me some information, and I might have learnt much more from him if I had seen him more frequently. But I had the good fortune to meet with him again at a later period.

The country here became very mountainous, and the ascent steep, till we reached a valley called by some of the Kél-owí the upper course of the valley of Tintéllust. Having reached the crest of the elevation, we began to descend, first gradually along smaller valleys, afterwards more steeply into a deep ravine, while in the distance towards the south-west, above the lower hills, a ridge of considerable elevation became visible. Gradually the ravine widened, and became clothed with fine herbage. Here, to our great disappointment, the little A'nnur, Dídi, Fárreji, and several of the Tinýlkum (among them the intelligent and active Ibrahím) left us in order to reach their respective residences.

Of course A'nnur ought to have seen us safe to the chief's residence; but, being without energy, he allowed our new companions, with whom we had not yet been able to become acquainted, to extort from us what they could, as the Fade-ang and the Anísli-men had done before. Keeping along some smaller valleys, we reached, about noon, a considerable pond of rain-water, where I watered my thirsty camel. Almost all the smaller valleys through which we passed incline towards the west.

Much against our wish, we encamped, a little after three o'clock P.M., in a widening of the valley Afís, near the southern cliffs (which had a remarkably shattered appearance), there being a well at some little distance. We had scarcely encamped when a trouble-some scene was enacted, in the attempt to satisfy our escort, the men not being yet acquainted with us, and making importunate demands. But there was more turmoil and disturbance than real harm in it; and though half of the contents of a bale of mine were successfully carried off by the turbulent Mohammed, and a piece of scarlet cloth was cut into numberless small shreds in the most wanton manner, yet there was not much to complain of, and it was satisfac-tory to see Hámma (A'nnur's son-in-law, and the chief of the escort) display the greatest energy in his endeavours to restore what was forcibly taken.

We were glad when day dawned; but with it came very heavy rain, which had Wednesday, September 4th. been portended last night by thickly accumulated

clouds and by lightning. Rain early in the morning
seems to be rather a rare phenomenon, as well in
this country as all over Central Africa*, if it be not
in continuation of the previous night's rain; and
it was probably so on this occasion, rain having
fallen during the whole night in the country around
us.

Having waited till the rain seemed to have a little
abated, we started at seven o'clock, in order to reach
the residence of the powerful chief A'nnur, in whose
hands now lay the whole success of the expedition.
Though all that we had heard about him was calculated to inspire us with confidence in his personal character, yet we could not but feel a considerable degree
of anxiety.

Soon emerging from the valley of Afís, we ascended
rocky ground, over which we plodded, while the rain
poured down upon us with renewed violence, till we
reached the commencement of another valley, and a
little further, on its northern side, the small village
Sárara, or Asárara, divided into two groups, between
which we passed. We then crossed low rocky ground
intersected by many small beds of torrents descending from the mountains on our left, which rise to
a considerable elevation. All these channels incline towards the south, and are thickly clothed with
bushes.

It was half-past nine o'clock, the weather having now

* In many parts of India, just the contrary seems to occur.

cleared up, when we entered the valley of Tintéllust*,
forming a broad sandy channel, bare of herbage, and
only lined with bushes along its border.   On the low
rocky projections on its eastern side lay a little village, scarcely discernible from the rocks around ; it
was the long and anxiously looked-for residence of
the chief E' Núr or A'nnur.   Our servants saluted
it with a few rounds.   Leaving the village on the
eastern border of the sandy bed, we went a little
further to the south, keeping close to the low rocky
projection on our right, at the foot of which was
the little tebki or water-pond, and encamped on
a sand-hill rising in a recess of the rocky offshoots,
and adorned at its foot with the beautiful green
and widely-spreading bushes of the *Capparis sodata*,
while behind was a charming little hollow with luxuriant talha-trees.   Over the lower rocky ground rose
Mount Tunán, while towards the south the majestic mountain-group of Búnday closed the view.   As
for the prospect over the valley towards the village,

* It will be well to say a few words about this name, as the
way in which I write it has been made the subject of criticism.
Tin-téllust means " (the valley) with or of the téllust ; " " tin " is
the pronoun expressing possession, and exactly corresponds with
the Western Arabic متاع.   It is of very frequent occurrence, as
well in names of localities as of tribes, and even of men, such as
Tin-Yerátan, son of Wasembú, the celebrated King of Aúdaghost.
" Tellúst " is the feminine form of " ellus," the feminine Berber
nouns having the peculiarity of not only beginning with *t*, but
often ending with it likewise. (Newman, in Zeitschrift für Kunde
des Morgenlandes, 1845, vol. vi. p. 275.)

CHAP. XIV.

ETHNOGRAPHICAL RELATIONS OF ÁÍR.

THE name A'ír, exactly as it is written and pronounced by the natives at the present day, first
occurs in the description of Leo, which was written
in 1526.[*] The country Káher, mentioned by the
traveller Ebn Batúta [†] on his home-journey from
Tekádda by way of the wells of Asïu, is evidently
somewhere hereabouts, but seems rather to denote the
region a few days' journey west from Tintéllust, and
to be identical with the "Ghir" of Leo[‡], though this

---

[*] Leo Africanus, Descrizione dell'Africa, i. c. 6: "E *Air*, diserto
ancora esso, ma nomato dalla bontà dell' aere." This derivation of
the name is manifestly apocryphal. Comp. l. vi. cc. 55, 56.

[†] Ebn Batúta's Travels, ed. Lee, p. 45. Compare Journal
Asiatique, 1843, p. 237.

[‡] Leo, l. vi. c. 55. Ebn Batúta counts seventy days' march
from Tekádda to Tawát, or rather Búda. Now we shall see that
Tekádda is situated three days south-west from A'gades, while,
from what the traveller says about the place where the road to
Egypt separated from that to Tawát, it is evident that he went by
Asïu, or rather that the place just mentioned was identical with
Asïu. Asïu, then, forty days from Tawát, was thirty days from
Tekádda; Káher, therefore, being distant eighteen days from Asïu,
was twelve days from Tekádda, and was somewhere between the
parallels of Selúfiet and Tintéllust, but rather, as we see from the
sterile character of the country through which he travelled, and

extended more to the S.W. The name being written by the Arabs with an *h* (Ahír), most historical geographers have erroneously concluded that this is the true indigenous form of the name.*

A'ír, however, does not appear to be the original name of the country, but seems to have been introduced by the Berber conquerors, the former name being Asben or Absen, as it is still called by the black and the mixed population. Asben was formerly the country of the Góberáwa, the most considerable and noble portion of the Háusa nation, which does not seem to belong to the pure Negro races, but to have originally had some relationship with North Africa; and from this point of view the statement of Sultan Bello cannot be regarded as absurd, when in the introduction to his historical work on the conquests of the Fúlbe, " Infák él misúri fi fat hah el Tekrúri," he calls the people of Góber Copts†, though only one family is generally considered by the learned men of the country as of foreign origin.

The capital of this kingdom of Asben, at least since the 16th century, was Tin-shamán, at present a village

from the situation of Tekádda, in the more barren district to the west. About Tekádda I shall have to speak further on.

* The Tawárek, as well the Kél-owí as all the other tribes, constantly write ◊ ç· (A'ír); and the reason why the Arabs write اهير is simply to avoid the obscenity of أيـر (*veretrum*).

† Denham and Clapperton's Travels, vol. ii. p. 162.

a little to the west of the road from Aúderas to A'gades, and about twenty miles from the latter place.   The name is evidently a Berber one *; and the Berber influence is still more evident from the fact that a portion, at least, of the population of the town were Masúfa, a well known Berber tribe who in former times were the chief guides on the road from Sejilmésa to Waláta.†   Be this as it may, several learned men, inhabitants of this place, are mentioned by the native historians of Negroland, which shows that there existed in it some degree of comparative civilization.   In the middle of the 14th century not only Tekádda but even Káhír was in the hands of the Berbers, as we see from Batúta's narrative; and this eminent traveller mentions a curious custom with regard to the Berber prince, whom he styles El Gérgeri, or Tegérgeri‡, which even at the present moment is in full operation in this country, viz., that the succession went not to his own sons, but to

* I have spoken about the word "tin" before.   I have strong reason for supposing that the original name of the place was Ansamán.

† Ebn Batúta, Journal Asiatique, 1843, série iv. vol. i. p. 188.; Cooley, Negroland, p. 17.

‡ It seems to be the title of his kingdom, so that we may translate it rather "the ruler of Kerker" or Gerger.   See Cooley, p. 107., who first pointed out that Kerker was not a mere clerical error for Kaúkaú.   But what this learned gentleman says at p. 109. is based upon wrong information, there being no such town as Birni-n-Gurgar in Háusa.   The real name of the place is Góga.   It is also impossible that the name Gérgeri can have anything to do with the pagan tribe Kerékeré.

his sister's sons.* This remarkable fact is a certain proof that it was not a pure Berber state, but rather a Berber dominion ingrafted upon a Negro population, exactly as was the case in his time in Waláta. Leo, who first calls the country by its present Berber name A'ír, states also expressly that it was then occupied by Tawárek. "Targa populo;"† and we learn also from him that the ruler of A'gades (a town first mentioned by him) was likewise a Berber‡: so that it might seem as if the state of the country at that time was pretty nearly the same as it is now; but such was not the case.

The name of the Kél-owí is not mentioned either by Leo or any other writer before the time of Horneman, who, before he set out from Fezzán on his journey to Bórnu, obtained some very perspicuous information§ about these people, as well as about their country A'sben. At that time, before the rise of the Fúlbe under their reformer (el Jihádi) Othmán the son of Fódiye, it was a powerful kingdom, to which Góber was tributary. From Horneman's expression it would seem that the Kél-owí had conquered the country only at a comparatively recent date‖; and this agrees perfectly with the results of

* Ebn Batúta, p. 237.   † Leo, l. vi. c. 56.
‡ *Ibid.* i. c. 10., towards the end.
§ Horneman's Journal, 1802, p. 109. fl.
‖ That was also what Major Rennell concluded from the traveller's expression when he says, p. 181., "From recent conquest it would seem," &c. I think that the Kél-owí may have formerly

my inquiries, from which I conclude that it took place about A. D. 1740. However, we have seen that four centuries before that time the country was in the hands of the Berbers.

It appears that the Kél-owí are traceable from the north-west, and the nobler part of them belong to the once very powerful and numerous tribe of the Aurághen, whence their dialect is called Auraghíye even at the present day. Their name signifies "the people settled in (the district or valley of) Owí;" for "kél" is exactly identical with the Arabic word áhel, and seems besides to be applied with especial propriety to indicate the settled, in opposition to the nomadic tribes. For in general the characteristic mark of the Kél-owí and their kinsmen is, that they live in villages consisting of fixed and immovable huts, and not in tents made of skins, like the other tribes, or in movable huts made of mats, like the Tagáma and many of the Imghád of the Awelímmiden. With this prefix kél, may be formed the name of the inhabitants of any place or country:—Ferwán, Kél-ferwán; Bághzen, Kél-bághzen; Afélle (the north), Kél-afélle, "the people of the north," whom the Arabs in Timbúktu call A'hel e' Sáhel; and no doubt a Targi, at least of the tribe of the Awelímmiden or Kél-owí, would call the inhabitants of London

borne another name, and received this name only from a place where they were settled. I would not refer to the Cillaba mentioned by Pliny, l. v. c. 5. The name Kél-owí is properly a plural form.

Kél-london or Kél-londra, just as he says Kél-gha-
dámes,- Kél-tawát.

But there is something indeterminate in the name
Kél-owí, which has both a narrower and a wider
sense, as is frequently the case with the names of
those tribes which, having become predominant, have
grouped around them and, to a certain extent, even
incorporated with themselves many other tribes which
did not originally belong to them. In this wider
sense the name Kél-owí comprises a great many
tribes, or rather sections, generally named after their
respective settlements.

I have already observed that the Berbers, in con-
quering this country from the Negro, or I should
rather say the sub-Libyan race (the Leucæthiopes
of the ancients), did not entirely destroy the latter,
but rather mingled with them by intermarriage with
the females, thereby modifying the original type
of their race, and blending the severe and austere
manners and the fine figure of the Berber with
the cheerful and playful character and the darker
colour of the African. The way in which they
settled in this country seems to have been very
similar to that in which the ancient Greeks settled
in Lycia. For the women appear to have the superiority over the male sex in the country of A'sben,
at least to a certain extent; so that when a ba-A's-
benchi marries a woman of another village, she does
not leave her dwelling-place to follow her husband,
but he must come to her in her own village. The same

principle is shown in the regulation that the chief
of the Kél-owí must not marry a woman of the Targi
blood, but can rear children only from black women
or female slaves.

With respect to the custom that the hereditary
power does not descend from the father to the son,
but to the sister's son,— a custom well known to be
very prevalent not only in many parts of Negroland,
but also in India, at least in Malabar,—it may be
supposed to have belonged originally to the Berber
race; for the Azkár, who have preserved their original manners tolerably pure, have the same custom,
but they also might have adopted it from those tribes
(now their subjects—the Imghád) who conquered
the country from the black natives.   It may therefore seem doubtful whether, in the mixed empires
of Ghánata *, Melle †, and Waláta ‡, this custom
belonged to the black natives, or was introduced by

---

* A'bú 'Obaid Alla el Bekrí el Kórtobí, Notices et Extraits, vol.
xii. p. 644.

† With regard to Melle see what Leo says, l. i. c. 10. fin.,
"E quello (rè) che fù di Melli è dell' origine del popolo di
Zanaga."

‡ Ebn Batúta, p. 234., ed. Lee.   He says, "And the sister's son
always succeeds to property in preference to the son, a custom I
witnessed nowhere else except among the infidel Hindoos of
Malabar."   But the traveller forgot that he had soon to relate
the same of the Gérgeri dynasty (see above, p. 338.) ; or rather
the learned man who was ordered to publish his journal did not
correct the expression, which, at the time when Ebn Batúta
made his memorandum of his stay in Waláta, may have been
quite true.

the Berbers. Be this as it may, it is certain that
the noble tribe of the Awelímmiden deem the custom
in question shameful, as exhibiting only the man's
mistrust of his wife's fidelity; for such is certainly
its foundation.

As for the male portion of the ancient population
of A'sben, I suppose it to have been for the most part
exterminated, while the rest was degraded into the
state of domestic slavery, with the distinct under-
standing that neither they nor their children should
ever be sold out of the country. The consequence of
this covenant has been an entire mixture * between
the Berber conquerors and the female part of the

* This circumstance explains a curious fact in Mr. Koelle's
Polyglotta Africana, a work of the greatest merit, but in which,
on account of the immense ground over which it extends,
some errors must be expected. One of the most unfortunate
examples in this respect are his specimens of a language called
Kándín (xii. C.). Now the name Kándín is quite inadmissible in
ethnography, being a name given to the Imóshagh or Tawárek
only by the Kanúri people, to say nothing of the very odd geographical blunder involved in the expression " Absen, a town of
Egades." But the specimens of the language which Mr. Koelle
gives under this head are a curious mixture of Targíye, Háusa,
and even some Kanúri terms ; and his informant, Abárshi (a very
common name in A'sben), was most probably a slave by origin,
at least not a free man, even before he was enslaved by the
Kanúri. But these specimens are not uninteresting, giving a fair
idea of the state of things in the country, although any respectable
native would be ashamed to mix Háusa and Berber terms in this
way ; and moreover the latter as given here are mostly corrupted
from the very beginning, for " one " is not díyen, but íyen, and
the d is only added in composition, as meráw d'íyen, meráw
d'esín — " eleven," " twelve," &c.

former population, changing the original Berber character entirely, as well in manners and language as
in features and complexion.   Indeed, the Háusa language is as familiar to these people as their Auraghíye, although the men, when speaking among
themselves, generally make use of the latter.   The
consequence is, that the Kél-owí are regarded with a
sort of contempt by the purer Berber tribes, who call
them slaves (íkelán).   But there is another class of
people, not so numerous indeed in A'sben itself as
in the districts bordering upon it ; these are the
Búzawe, or Abogelíte, a mixed race, with generally
more marked Berber features than the Kél-owí,
but of darker colour and lower stature, while in
manners they are generally very debased, having
lost almost entirely that noble carriage which dis-
tinguishes even the most lawless vagabond of pure
Targi blood.   These people, who infest all the regions southwards and south-eastwards from A'sben,
are the offspring of Tawárek females with black
people, and may belong either to the Háusa or to the
Sónghay race.

What I have here said sets forth the historical view
of the state of things in this country, and is well-
known to all the enlightened natives.   The vulgar
account of the origin of the Kél-owí from the female slave of a Tinýlkum who came to A'sben, where
she gave birth to a boy who was the progenitor of
the Kél-owí, is obviously nothing but a popular tale

indicating, at the utmost, only some slight connection of this tribe with the Tinýlkum.

Having thus preliminarily discussed the name of the tribe and the way in which it settled in the country, I now proceed to give a list, as complete as possible, of all the divisions or tiúsi (*sing.* tausit) which compose the great community of the Kél-owí.

The most noble (that is to say, the most elevated, not by purity of blood, but by authority and rank) of the subdivisions of this tribe at the present time are the Irólangh, the Amanókalen or sultan family, to which belongs A'nnur, with no other title than that of Sheikh or Elder (the original meaning of the word) —" sófo " in Háusa, "ámaghár" or " ámghár " in Temáshight. The superiority of this section seems to date only from the time of the present chief's predecessor, the Kél-ferwán appearing to have had the ascendancy in earlier times. Though the head of this family has no title but that of Sheikh, he has nevertheless far greater power than the amanókal or titular sultan of the Kél-owí, who resides in A'sodi, and who is at present really nothing more than a prince in name. The next in authority to A'nnur is Háj 'Abdúwa, the son of A'nnur's eldest sister, and who resides in Táfidet.

The family or clan of the Irólangh which, in the stricter sense of the word, is called Kél-owí, is settled in ten or more villages lying to the east and the south-east of Tintéllust, the residence of A'nnur, and has formed an alliance with two other influential and

powerful families, viz. the Kél-azanéres, or people of
Azanéres, a village, as I shall have occasion to explain further on, of great importance on account of
its situation in connection with the salt lakes near
Bilma, which constitute the wealth and the vital
principle of this community.   On account of this
alliance, the section of the Kél-azanéres affected by it
is called Irólangh wuén Kél-azanéres; and to this
section belongs the powerful chief Lúsu or, properly,
el U'su, who is in reality the second man in the
country on the score of influence.

On the other side, the Irólangh have formed
alliance and relationship with the powerful and
numerous tribe of the Ikázkezan, or Ikéshkeshen,
who seem likewise to have sprung from the Aurághen;
and on this account the greater, or at least the more
influential, part of the tribe, including the powerful
chief Mghás, is sometimes called Irólangh wuén Ikázkezan, while, with regard to their dwelling-place
Támar, they bear the name Kél-támar.   But this is
only one portion of the Ikázkezan.   Another very
numerous section of them is partly scattered about
Damerghú, partly settled in a place called Elákwas
(or, as it is generally pronounced, Alákkos), a place
between Damerghú and Múnio, together with a mixed
race called Kél-elákwas. The Ikázkezan of this latter
section bear, in their beautiful manly figure and fine
complexion, much more evident traces of the pure
Berber blood than the Irólangh; but they lead a
very lawless life, and harass the districts on the

borders of Háusa and Bórnu with predatory incursions, especially those settled in Elákwas.

There are three tribes whose political relations give them greater importance, namely, the Kél-táfidet, the Kél-n-Néggaru, and the Kél-fares. The first of these three, to whom belongs the above-mentioned Háj 'Abdúwa, live in Táfidet, a group of three villages lying at the foot of a considerable mountain-chain thirty miles to the south-east of Tintéllust, and at the distance of only five good days' march from Bilma. The Kél-n-Néggaru form an important family originally settled in Néggaru, a district to the north of Selúfiet; but at present they live in A'sodi and in the village Eghellál, and some of them lead a nomadic life in the valleys of Tin-téggana and A'sada. On account of the present sultan (who belongs to them) being called Astáfidet, they are now also named Aushi-n-Astáfidet (the tribe of Astáfidet). The Kél-fares, to whom belongs the great màllem Azori, who, on account of his learning, is respected as a prince in the whole country, live in Tin-téyyat, a village about thirty-five miles E.N.E. from Tintéllust.

I now proceed to name the other sections of the Kél-owí in geographical order from north to south.

The Fadaye, or E'fadaye, dwell in the district Fáde-angh, containing several villages, the principal of which is called Zurríka, inhabited by the Kél-zurríka. The E'fadaye, although they maintain a sort of independence, are nevertheless regarded as belonging to the community of the Kél-owí, while

another tribe, likewise called from the district Fáde-angh, namely the Kél-fadaye, are viewed in a
different light, and will therefore be mentioned further on with respect to their political relation with
the sultan of A'gades. The E'fadaye are renowned
on account of their warlike propensities; and to the
wild inhabitants of these districts the Fadaye is a
model of a man—"hális."

The Kél-tédele, who were among the people who
attacked the mission, live in a place called Tédele,
a little to the north of Oinu-mákaren.

The Kél-tédek, or Kél-tídik, dwell in Tídik, the
village I noticed on our journey as lying at the
northern foot of the large mountain-chain which
forms the beginning of A'sben and Sudán.

The Im-ásrodangh.*

The Kél-ghazár, comprising the inhabitants of
Selúfiet and those of Tintágh-odé, who are more
generally named Aníslimen, or Merabetín. The
name is formed from *éghazar*, "the valley,"
meaning the large valley of Selúfiet and Tintágh-odé.

The Kél-élar, living in E'lar, three hours east from
Selúfiet in the mountain-glens.

The Kél-gharús.

The E'ndefar.

The Tanútmolet.

* *Im*, or *em*, in composition is almost identical with *kél*, meaning
"the people of," "the inhabitants of."

The Abírken.

The Tesébet.

The Kél-télak.

The Azaíken.

The Kél-úlli, meaning "the people of the goats," or goatherds. Another tribe of the same name among the Awelímmiden I shall have frequent opportunity of mentioning in the course of my travels, as my chief protectors during my stay in Timbúktu.

The Fedalála, dwelling, if I am not mistaken, in Fedékel.

The Kel-ásarar, living in Sárara, the village we passed an hour before reaching Tintéllust.

The Im-ezúkzál, a considerable family living in A'gwau.

The Kél·teget.

The Kél-enúzuk.

The Kél-tákriza.

The Kél-aghellál.

The Kél-tádenak, living in Tádenak, about half a day's journey east from Aghellál, and about eleven hours west from Tintéllust.

The Kél-wádigi, living in Wádigi, a large village about fifteen miles west from Tintéllust. This village, in consequence of erroneous native information, has been hitherto placed near the Isa, or middle course of the Niger.

The Kél-teghérmat, at present in the village

Azauraíden, E.N.E. from Tintéllust. Of their number is the active chief Háj Makhmúd.

The Kél-erárar, in Erárar, a village three hours from Tintéllust.

The Kél-zéggedan, in Zéggedan, one day and a half from Tintéllust.

The Kél-tághmart, in Tághmart, one day and a half north from the latter.

The Kél-áfarár, in A'farár, two hours east a little south from Tághmart.

The Im-ékketen, living at present round Azatár-tar, but originally settled in the neighbourhood of A'gades.

The Kél-sadáwat.

The Kél-tafíst.

The Kél-ágaten, living in A'gata, a village at the foot of Mount Belásega.

The Kél-bághzen, for the greatest part herdsmen or shepherds, living scattered over and around Mount Bághzen. These are Kél-owí; but there is another tribe, of the Kél-gerés, known by the same name, on account of their having in former times occupied those seats.

The Kél-chémia, in Chémia.

The Ikádmawen, a numerous tribe living generally in four villages which lie at the southern foot of Mount Bághzen, and are called respectively A'fasás (this being the largest of the four), Tagóra, Tamanít, and Inferéraf. But for a

great part of the year they lead rather a nomadic life.

The Kél-ajéru, in Ajéru, a village situate in the
upper part of the valley, in the lower part of
which lies A'fasás. Here resides another important personage of the name of Háj Makhmúd.

The I'tegén.

The Kél-idákka, in Idákka, the native place of the
mother of Astáfidet, the amanókal of the Kél-
owí.

The Kél-tezárenet, in Tezárenet, a district rich in
date-trees.

The Kél-tawár.

The Kél-táfasás (?). I am not quite certain with
regard to this name.

The Kél-táranet.

The Kél-átarár, living in the neighbourhood of
A'gades, and having but an indifferent reputation.

The Kél-aríl.

The Im-ersúten.

The Kél-azelálet.

The Kél-anuwísheren, in Timázgaren (?).

The Kél-táferaut.

The Kél-aghrímmat.

The Kél-awéllat.

All these tribes in a certain degree belong to the
body of the Kél-owí, whose nominal chief, if I may so
call him, is the amanókal residing in A'sodi: but there
is now another greater association or confederation,

formed by the Kél-owí, the Kél-gerés, and the Itísan and some other smaller tribes combined together ; and the head of this confederation is the great amanókal residing in A'gades.   This league, which at present hardly subsists (the Kél-gerés and Itísan having been driven by the Kél-owí from their original settlements, and being opposed to them almost constantly in open hostility), was evidently in former times very strong and close.   ⚹

But before speaking of the Kél-gerés and their intimate friends the Itísan, I shall mention those small tribes which, though not regarded as belonging to the body of the Kél-owí and placed under the special and direct supremacy or government of the sultan of A'gades, are nevertheless more intimately related to them than to the other great tribes.   These are, besides the E'm-egédesen *, or the inhabitants of A'gades or A'gadez, of whom I shall speak in the account of my journey to that interesting place, the three tribes of the Kél-fadaye, the Kél-ferwán, and the Izeráren.

As for the Kél-fadaye, they are the original and real inhabitants of the district Fáde-angh, which lies round Tághajít, while the E'fadaye, who have been called after the same district, are rather a mixture of

---

* This name clearly shows that the final consonant of the name of the great town is not distinctly a ‌ج (z) though the Arabs generally write it so.   In fact, as I shall have to state further on, it was originally *sh*.   From E'm-egédesen is formed E'm-egedesíye, " the language of the people of A'gades."

vagabonds flocking here from different quarters, and principally from that of the Azkár. But the Kél-fadaye, who, as well as their neighbours the E'fadaye, took part in the ghazzia against the expedition on the frontiers of A'ír, are a very turbulent set of people, being regarded in this light by the natives themselves, as appears from the letter of the sultan of A'gades to the chiefs A'nnur and Lúsu, of which I brought back a copy, wherein they are called Mehá-rebín*, or freebooters. Nevertheless they are of pure and noble Berber blood, and renowned for their valour; and I was greatly astonished to learn after-wards from my noble and intimate friend and pro-tector the sheikh Sídi A'hmed el Bakáy, that he had married one of their daughters, and had long resided

* Mehárebí — مَحَارِبى — though not to be found in our dic-tionaries, is a very common word with the Mohammedans all over Central Africa, and is regularly formed from "hareb," حرب, quite in the same way as meháres, the common name given in Morocco to a guard or escort, from "hares." The emír Hámedu or Hamd-Alláhi did me the honour to call me by this name, on account of the resistance I made to his attempt to seize me and my property during my stay in Timbúktu; and I do not doubt that the follow-ing passage in one of the angry and learned letters which he wrote to my protector the sheikh El Bakáy, will have some in-terest for such of my readers as understand Arabic: —

ولم ننظر بذلك معجاربتك بل الذى حاربناه النصرانى الكافر الذى

حارب الله و رسوله و هوحرب ورثناه من الاباد و اهجراد ادى هلم

جرا و حضنا عليه ربّنا و وعد نا فيه اجرا و دحزا

But his sacrilegious wishes were not fulfilled.

amongst them. Even from the letter of the sultan of
A'gades it appears that they have some relations
with the Awelímmiden. The name of their chief is
Shúrwa.

The Kél-ferwán, though they are called after the
fine and fertile place I-ferwán, in one of the valleys
to the east of Tintághodé, where a good deal of
millet is sown, and where there are plenty of date-
trees, do not all reside there at present, a numerous
portion of them having settled in the neighbourhood
of A'gades, whence they make continual marauding
expeditions, or "égehen," upon the Timbúktu road,
and against the Awelímmiden. Nevertheless the Kél-
ferwán, as the kinsmen of the Aurághen, and as
the Amanókalen (that is to say the clan to which,
before the different tribes came to the decision of
fetching their sultan from Sókotó, the family of the
sultan belonged), are of nobler and purer blood than
any of the rest. As an evidence of their former
nobility, the custom still remains, that, when the
sultan of A'gades leaves the town for any length of
time, his deputy or lieutenant in the place is the chief
of the Kél-ferwán.

The third tribe of those who are under the direct
authority of the sultan of A'gades, viz. the Izeráren,
live between A'gades and Damerghú. But I did not
come into contact with them.

The Kél-gerés and Itísan seem to have been originally situated in the fertile and partially beautiful
districts round the Bághzen, or (as these southern

tribes pronounce the name in their dialect) Mághzem, where, on our journey towards Damerghú, we found the well-built stone houses in which they had formerly dwelt.

On being driven out of their original seats by the Kél-owí, about twenty-five or thirty years ago, they settled towards the west and south-west of A'gades, in a territory which was probably given them by the Awelímmiden, with an intention hostile to the Kél-owí. From that time they have been alternately in bloody feud or on amicable terms with the Kél-owí; but a sanguinary war has recently (in 1854) broken out again between these tribes, which seems to have consumed the very sources of their strength, and cost the lives of many of my friends, and among them that of Hámma, the son-in-law of A'nnur. The principal dwelling-place of the Kél-gerés is A'rar, while their chief market-place is said to be Jóbeli, on the road from A'gades to Sókoto.

The Kél-gerés and the Itísan together are equal in effective strength to the Kél-owí, though they are not so numerous, the latter being certainly able to collect a force of at least ten thousand armed men all mounted, besides their slaves, while the former are scarcely able to furnish half as many. But the Kél-gerés and Itísan have the advantage of greater unity, while the interests of the various tribes of the Kél-owí are continually clashing, and very rarely allow the whole body to collect together, though exceptions occur, as in the expedition against the Welád Slimán, when they drove away all the camels (according to report, not less than fifty thousand), and took possession of the salt lakes near Bilma.

Moreover the Kél-gerés and Itísan, having preserved their Berber character in a purer state, are much more warlike. Their force consists for the greater part of well-mounted cavalry, while the Kél-owí, with the exception of the Ikázkezan, can muster but few horses; and of course the advantage of the horseman over the camel-driver is very great either in open or close fight. The Kél-gerés have repeatedly fought with success even against the Awelímmiden, by whom they are called Aráuwen. They have even killed their last famous chief E' Nábegha. The Kél-gerés came under the notice of Clapperton, on account of the unfortunate expedition which they undertook against the territories of the Fúlbe in the year 1823, though it seems that the expedition consisted chiefly of Tagáma, and that they were the principal sufferers in that wholesale destruction by Sultan Bello.

Their arms in general are the same as those of the Kél-owí, even the men on horseback bearing (besides the spear, the sword, and the dagger) the immense shield of antelope-hide, with which they very expertly protect themselves and their horses; but some of them use bows and arrows even on horseback, like many of the Fúlbe, in the same way as the ancient Assyrians. A few only have muskets, and those few keep them rather for show than for actual use.

The Itísan * (who seem to be the nobler tribe of the two, and as far as I was able to judge, are a very fine race of men, with expressive, sharply-cut features, and a very light complexion) have a chief or amanókal of their own, whose position seems to resemble closely that of the sultan of the Kél-owí, while the real influence and authority rests with the war-chiefs, támbelis, or támberis, the most powerful among whom were, in 1853, Wanagóda, who resides in Tswáji near Góber, on the side of the Kél-gerés, and Maiwa, or Mòáwíya, in Gulluntsúna, on the side of the Itísan. The name of the present amanókal is Ghámbelu.

I now proceed to enumerate the subdivisions of the two tribes, as far as I was able to learn them, and first those of the Itísan:—the Kél-tagáy, the Télamsé, the Máfinet or Máfidet, the Tesídderak, the Kél-mághzem, the A'laren, the Kél-innik, the Kél-dugá, the Kél-úye, and the Kél-ághelel. Probably also the Ijdánarnén†, or Jedánarnén, and the Kél-

* It has been concluded (though erroneously, as the following will show) from the circumstance of the joint salt-caravan of the Itísan and Kél-gerés, in the letter of the sultan of A'gades, being called only after the former tribe, that these two tribes were identical. The Itísan, as "Benú Itísan," are mentioned by E'bn Khaldún among the clans of the Sanhája, vol. i. p. 195., Arab. t.; vol. ii. p. 3., trad. par le baron de Slane.

† These, in the form of Ajdaranín, are mentioned by Bello, in his geographical introduction to his historical work (Clapperton's Travels, Appendix II. p. 160.), among the first Berber tribes who came from Aújila and took Ahír (Aïr) from the Sudán inhabitants of Góber.

manen belong to them. The following are the principal subdivisions of the Kél-gerés :— the Kél-téghze-ren or Tadmúkkeren, the Kél-úngwar, the Kél-garet, the Kél-n-sábtafan, or Kél-n-sáttafan*, the Kél-tadéni, the Tadáda, the Tagáyes, the Tilkátine†, the Iberúbat with the támberi Al-Hássan, the Táshil, the Tagínna, the Kél-azar, the I'ghalaf (pronounced I'ralaf), the Toiyámmawa‡, the Isóka, the Tegíbbu, the Raina, the Túji. Among the Kél-gerés is a noble family called in the Arab form A'hel e' Sheikh, which is distinguished for its learning, their chief and most learned man being at present Sídi Makhmúd.

I must here state that, in political respects, another tribe at present is closely related with the Kél-gerés, viz., that section of the Awelímmiden (the "Surka" of Mungo Park) which is called Awelímmiden wuén Bodhál; but as these belong rather to the Tawárek or Imóshagh of the west, I shall treat of them in

---

* This is the tribe of which Bello speaks (Clapperton's Travels, ii. p. 160.) when he says "they appointed a person of the family of Ansatfen." But his knowledge of the Tawárek was very insufficient; and the chapter to which that passage belongs is full of confusion.

† The tribe of the Tilkátine, appearing here among the clans of the Kél-gerés, is of the highest historical interest; for there can be no doubt of their being identical with the tribe of the Tel-káta mentioned by E'bn Khaldún (vol. i. p. 195. Arab. t., vol. ii. p. 3. trad. par le baron de Slane) as the most noble and predominant among all the sections of the Sanhája.

‡ The form of this name seems to indicate the sub-Libyan influence which this subdivision has undergone.

the narrative of my journey to Timbúktu. Other tribes settled near A'gades, and more particularly the very remarkable tribe of the I'ghdalén, will, in consequence of the influence exerted on them by the Sónghay race, be spoken of in my account of that place.

Many valleys of A'ír or A'sben* might produce much more than they do at present; but as almost the whole supply of provision is imported, as well as all the clothing-material, it is evident that the population could not be so numerous as it is, were it not sustained by the salt trade of Bilma, which furnishes the people with the means of bartering advantageously with Háusa. As far as I was able to learn from personal information, it would seem that this trade did not take the road by way of A'sben till about a century ago, consequently not before the country was occupied by the Kél-owí. It is natural to suppose that so long as the Tébu, or rather Tedá, retained political strength, they would not allow strangers

---

* The list of all the villages and towns of A'ír, given in the note at the end of the first volume of Mr. Richardson's Journal, is in general, I think, exact; there are only two mistakes of importance — with regard to the population of Talázeghrín, and that of A'fasás (p. 341.), each of which places is stated to have 1000 male inhabitants, while the whole population scarcely reaches that number. On the other hand, the estimate of the population of A'gades at 2500 (p. 343.) is too low. Besides, some places are left out there, such as Iséllef, the residence of Dídi's wife, and some others. I have to regret the loss of a paper which I sent home from A'ír, where a topographical arrangement of the villages had been attempted.

to reap the whole advantage of such natural wealth.*
At present the whole authority of A'nnur as well as
Lúsu seems to be based upon this trade, of which
they are the steady protectors, while many of their
nation deem this trade rather a degrading occupation,
and incline much more to a roving life.

I now return to our encampment near Tintéllust,
reserving a brief account of the general features of
the country till the moment when we are about to
leave it.

* In the account of the expedition of the Bórnu king Edrís
Alawóma, of which I shall have to speak in the second volume, no
mention is made of this salt-trade of the Tébu; but from this
silence no conclusion can be drawn as to the non-existence of the
salt-trade at that time.   On the contrary, we may conclude from
the interesting account of Edrísi (transl. Jaubert, vol. i. p. 117. f.),
who certainly means to speak of the salt-trade of the Tébu country,
although he uses the term " alum," that this article formed a very
important staple in remote times.

CHAP. XV.

RESIDENCE IN TINTÉLLUST.

WE saw the old chief on the day following our arrival. He received us in a straightforward and kindly manner, observing very simply that even if, as Christians, we had come to this country stained with guilt, the many dangers and difficulties we had gone through would have sufficed to wash us clean, and that we had nothing now to fear but the climate and the thieves. The presents which were spread out before him he received graciously, but without saying a single word. Of hospitality he showed no sign. All this was characteristic.

We soon received further explanations. Some days afterwards he sent us the simple and unmistakable message, that if we wished to proceed to Sudán at our own risk, we might go in company with the caravan, and he would place no obstacle in our way; but if we wanted him to go with us and to protect us, we ought to pay him a considerable sum. In stating these plain terms, he made use of a very expressive simile, saying that as the leffa (or snake) killed everything that she touched, so his word, when it had once

escaped his lips, had terminated the matter in question—there was nothing more to be said. I do not
think this such an instance of shameful extortion as
Mr. Richardson represents it, considering how much
we gave to others who did nothing for their pay,
and how much trouble we caused A'nnur. On the
contrary, having observed A'nnur's dealings to the
very last, and having arrived under his protection
safely at Kátsena, I must pronounce him a straightforward and trustworthy man, who stated his terms
plainly and dryly; but stuck to them with scrupulo-
sity; and as he did not treat us, neither did he
ask anything* from us, nor allow his people to do
so. I shall never forgive him for his niggardliness
in not offering me so much as a drink of fura or
ghussub-water when I visited him, in the heat of the
day, on his little estate near Tasáwa; but I cannot
withhold from him my esteem both as a great politi-
cian in his curious little empire, and as a man remarkable for singleness of word and purpose.

Having come into the country as hated intruders
pursued by all classes of people, we could not expect
to be received by him otherwise than coldly; but his
manner changed entirely when I was about to set out
for A'gades, in order to obtain the goodwill of the
sultan of the country. He came to our encampment
to see me off, and from that day forth did not omit to

* The little trifles which we gave him occasionally are scarcely
worth mentioning.

visit us every day, and to maintain the most familiar
intercourse with us.   So it was with all the people;
and I formed so many friendships with them, that the
turbulent Mohammed, A'nnur's cousin, used often to
point to them as a proof how impossible it was that
he could have been the instigator of the misdeeds
perpetrated on the night preceding our arrival in
Tintéllust, when we were treated with violence, and
our luggage was rifled.   Still we had, of course, many
disagreeable experiences to make before we became
naturalized in this new country.

It was the rainy season; and the rain setting in
almost daily, caused us as much interest and delight
(being a certain proof that we had reached the new
regions after which we had so long been hankering)
as served to counterbalance the trouble which it
occasioned.   Sometimes it fell very heavily, and,
coming on always with a dreadful storm, was very
difficult to be kept out from the tent, so that our
things often got wet.   The heaviest rain we had
was on the 9th of September, when an immense
torrent was formed, not only in the chief valley, but
even in the small ravine behind our encampment.
Yet we liked the rain much better than the sand-
storm.   In a few days nature all around assumed
so fresh and luxuriant a character, that so long as we
were left in repose, we felt cheered to the utmost, and
enjoyed our pleasant encampment, which was sur-
sounded by masses of granite blocks, wide-spreading
bushes of the abísga, and large luxuriant talha-trees,

in wild and most picturesque confusion. It was very pleasant and interesting to observe, every day, the rapid growth of the little fresh leaves and young offshoots, and the spreading of the shady foliage.

Monkeys now and then descended into the little hollow beyond our tents to obtain a draught of water; and numbers of jackals were heard every night roving about us, while the trees swarmed with beautiful ring-doves and hoopoes and other smaller birds. The climate of A'ír has been celebrated from the time of Leo, on account " della bontà e temperanza dell' aere." But unfortunately our little English suburb proved too distant from the protecting arm of the old chief; and after the unfortunate attack in the night of the 17th of September, which if made with vigour would inevitably have ended in our destruction, we were obliged to remove our encampment, and, crossing the broad valley, pitch it in the plain near the village.

But the circumstances connected with this attack were so curious that I must relate them, in a few words. The rain, which had wetted all our things, and made us anxious about our instruments and arms, seemed to abate; and Overweg and I decided, the very day preceding the attack in question, on cleaning our guns and pistols, which had been loaded for some time; and having cleaned them, and wishing to dry them well, we did not load them again immediately. In the afternoon we had a visit from two well-dressed men mounted on mehára; they did not beg for anything, but inspected the tents very attentively, making the remark that our tent was as strong as a house, while Mr. Richardson's was light and open at the bottom.

The moon shed a splendid light over the interesting wilderness; and our black servants being uncommonly cheerful and gay that night, music and dancing was going on in the village, and they continued playing till a very late hour, when they fell asleep. Going the round of our encampment before I went to lie down, I observed at a little distance a strange camel, or rather méheri, kneeling quietly down with its head towards our tents. I called my colleagues, and expressed my suspicion that all was not right; but our light-hearted and frivolous servant Mohammed calmed my uneasiness by pretending that he had seen the camel there before, though that was not true. Still I had some sad foreboding, and, directing my attention unluckily to the wrong point, caused our sheep to be tied close to our tent.

Being uneasy, I did not sleep soundly; and a little after two o'clock I thought I heard a very strange noise, just as if a troop of people were marching with a steady step round our tents, and muttering in a jarring voice. Listening anxiously for a moment, I felt sure that there were people near the tent, and was about to rush out; but again, on hearing the sound of music proceeding from the village, I persuaded myself that the noise came from thence, and lay down to slumber, when suddenly I heard a louder noise, as if several men were rushing up the hill, and, grasping a sword and calling aloud for our people, I jumped out of the tent; but there was nobody to be seen. Going then round the hill to Mr. Richardson's tent, I met him coming out half-dressed, and begging me to pursue the robbers, who had carried away some of his things. Some of his boxes were dragged out of the tent, but not emptied: none of his servants were to be seen except Saïd, all the rest having run away without even giving an alarm; so that all of us might have been murdered.

But immediately after this accident we received the distinct assurance of protection both from the sultan of A'gades and from the great mallem Azóri; and I began to plan my excursion to A'gades more definitely, and entered into communication with the chief on this point. Meanwhile I collected a great deal of information * about the country, partly from a Tawáti of the name of 'Abd el Káder (not the same who accompanied us on the road from Ghát), and partly from some of the Tinýlkum, who, having left us the day after our arrival in Tintéllust, had dispersed all over the country, some pasturing their camels in the most favoured localities, others engaged in little trading speculations, and paying us a visit every now and then. Small caravans came and went, and among them one from Sudán, with its goods laden

* That part of my information which regarded the topography of the country, and which I forwarded during our stay there, has unfortunately been lost.

almost entirely on pack-oxen, — a most cheerful sight, filling our hearts with the utmost delight, as we were sure that we had now passed those dreary deserts where nothing but the persevering and abstemious camel can enable man to maintain communications.

At length, then, we were enabled to write to Government, and to our friends in Europe, assuring them that we had now overcome, apparently, most of the difficulties which appeared likely to oppose our progress, and that we felt justified in believing that we had now fairly entered upon the road which would lead directly to the attainment of the objects of the expedition.

With regard to our provisions, Overweg and I were at first rather ill off, while Mr. Richardson, although he had been obliged to supply food on the road to troops both of friends and foes, had still a small remnant of the considerable stores which he had laid in at Múrzuk. We had been led to expect that we should find no difficulty in procuring all necessaries, and even a few luxuries, in A'sben (and carriage was so dear that we were obliged to rely upon these promises); but we were now sadly disappointed. After a few days, however, the inhabitants being informed that we were in want of provisions, and were ready to buy, brought us small quantities of Guinea corn, butter —the botta (or box made of rough hide, in the way common over almost the whole of Central Africa) for two or two and a half mithkáls, — and even a little fresh cheese; we were also able to buy two or three

goats, and by sending Ibrahím, who had now recovered from his guineaworm, to A'sodi, where provisions are always stored up in small quantities, we
obtained a tolerable camel-load of durra or sorghum.

But I could not relish this grain at all, and as I
was not able to introduce any variety into my diet, I
suffered much; hence it was fortunate for me that
I went to A'gades, where my food was more varied,
and my health consequently improved.   I afterwards
became accustomed to the various preparations of
sorghum and *Pennisetum*, particularly the asída or
túvo, and found that no other food is so well adapted
for a hot climate; but it requires a great deal of
labour to prepare it well, and this of course is a difficult matter for a European traveller, who has no
female slave or partner to look after his meals.   Our
food during our stay in A'sben was so ill-prepared
(being generally quite bitter, owing to the husk not
being perfectly separated from the grain) that no
native of the country would taste it.

Meanwhile my negotiation with the chief, with
regard to my going to A'gades, which I managed as
silently and secretly as possible, went on prosperously;
and on the 30th of September I took my leave of
him, having with me on the occasion a present for
himself, worth about eighty riyáls, or eleven pounds
sterling, and the presents intended for the sultan of
A'gades, in order that he might see what they were
and express his opinion upon them; and I was greatly
pleased to find that he was satisfied with both.   He

promised me perfect safety, although the undertaking
looked a little dangerous, and had a letter written to
'Abd el Káder (or, in the popular form, Kádiri—this
was the name of the new sultan), wherein he recommended me to him in the strongest terms, and
enumerated the presents I meant to offer to him.

But as soon as my intention transpired, all the
people, uninvited as well as invited, hastened to
give me their best advice, and to dissuade me from
embarking in an undertaking which would certainly
be my ruin.   Conspicuous among these motley coun-
sellors was a son of Háj 'Abdúwa, the presumptive
heir of A'nnur, who conjured me to abandon my
design.   These people, indeed, succeeded in fright-
ening Yusuf Múkní, Mr. Richardson's interpreter,
whom the latter wished to send with me; but as for
myself, I knew what I was about, and had full confidence in the old chief's promise, and was rather
glad to get rid of Múkní, whom I well knew to be
a clever, but no less malicious and intriguing person.
With difficulty I persuaded Mohammed, our Tunisian
shushán, to accompany me; and I also succeeded in
hiring Amánkay, Mr. Richardson's active black Búzu
servant, who, however, on this trip proved utterly
useless, as we had no sooner set out than he began to
suffer from his old complaint of guineaworm, and was
the whole time too lame for service.

I then arranged with Hámma, A'nnur's son-in-law,
under whose especial protection I was to undertake
my journey, but whom I had to pay separately.

I gave him the value of eleven mithkáls, or about one pound sterling, for himself, and hired from him two camels, each for six mithkáls.   After various delays, which, however, enabled me to send off two more of my journals, together with letters, to Múrzuk, by the hand of a half-caste Kél-owí of the name of Báwa Amákita, our departure was definitively fixed for the 4th of October.

CHAP. XVI.

Friday, October 4th. AT length the day arrived when I was to set out on my long-wished-for excursion to A'gades. For although at that time I was not aware of the whole extent of interest attaching to that place, it had nevertheless been to me a point of the strongest attraction. For what can be more interesting than a considerable town, said to have been once as large as Tunis, situated in the midst of lawless tribes, on the border of the desert and of the fertile tracts of an almost unknown continent, established there from ancient times, and protected as a place of rendezvous and commerce between nations of the most different character, and having the most various wants. It is by mere accident that this town has not attracted as much interest in Europe as her sister town Timbúktu.

It was a fine morning with a healthy and refreshing light breeze, invigorating both body and mind. The old chief, who had never before visited our encampment, now came out to pay us his compliments, assuring me once more, that "my safety rested upon his head." But his heart was so gladdened at witnessing our efforts to befriend the other great men of his country, that his habitual niggardliness was overcome, and with graceful hospitality he resigned one of his bullocks to our party.

The little caravan I was to accompany consisted of six camels, five and thirty asses, and two bullocks, one of which was allotted to me, till my protector Hámma should be able to hire a camel for me.   But although well accustomed to ride on horseback as well as on a camel, I had never yet in my life tried to sit astride on the broad back of a bullock; and the affair was the more difficult as there was no saddle, nor anything to sit upon, except parcels of luggage not very tightly fastened to the animal's back, and swinging from one side to the other.

After the first bullock had been rejected, as quite unfit, in its wild, intractable mood, to carry me, or indeed anything else, and when it had been allowed to return to the herd, the second was at length secured, the luggage fastened somehow on his back, and I was bid to mount.   I must truly confess that I should have been better pleased with a horse, or even an ass ; but still, hoping to manage matters, I took my seat, and, bidding my fellow-travellers farewell, followed my black companions up the broad valley by which we had come from the north.   But we soon left it and ascended the rocky ground, getting an interesting view of the broad and massive Mount Eghellál before us.

Having at first thought my seat rather too insecure for making observations, I grew by degrees a little more confident, and, taking out my compass, noted the direction of the road, when suddenly the baggage threatened to fall over to the right, whereupon I threw the whole weight of my body to the left, in order to keep the balance; but I unluckily overdid it, and so all at once down I came, with the whole baggage. The ground was rocky; and I should inevitably have been hurt not a little, if I had not fallen upon the muzzle of my musket, which I was carrying on my shoulder, and which being very strong, sustained the shock, and kept my head from the ground. Even my compass, which I had open in my left hand, most fortunately escaped uninjured; and I felt extremely glad that I had fallen so adroitly, but vowed never again to mount a bullock.

I preferred marching on foot till we reached the valley Eghellúwa, where plenty of water is found in several wells. Here we halted a moment, and I mounted behind Hámma, on the lean back of his camel, holding on by his saddle; but I could not much enjoy my seat, as I was greatly annoyed by his gun sticking out on the right, and at every moment menacing my face. I was therefore much pleased when we reached the little village of Tigger-éresa lying on the border of a broad valley well clothed with talha-trees, and a little further on encamped in a pleasant recess formed by projecting masses of granite blocks; for here I was told we should surely find camels, and in fact Hámma hired two for me, for four mithkáls each, to go to and return from A'gades. Here we also changed our companions, the very intelligent Mohammed, a son of one of A'nnur's sisters, returning to Tintéllust, while the turbulent Mohammed (I called him by no other name than Mohammed bábo hánkali), our friend from Afís, came to attend us, and with him Hámmeda, a cheerful and amiable old man, who was a fair specimen of the improvement derivable from the mixture of different blood and of different national qualities; for while he possessed all the cheerfulness and vivacity of the Góber nation, his demeanour was nevertheless moderated by the soberness and gravity peculiar to the Berber race, and though, while always busy, he was not effectively industrious, yet his character approached very closely to the European standard.

He was by trade a blacksmith, a more comprehensive profession in these countries than in Europe, although in general these famous blacksmiths have neither iron nor tools to work with. All over the Tawárek country the "énhad" (smith) is much respected, and the confraternity is most numerous. An "énhad" is generally the prime minister of every little chief. The Arabs in Timbúktu call these blacksmiths "mállem," which may give an idea of their high rank and respected character. Then there is also the "mállema," the constant female companion of the chief's wife, expert above all in beautiful leather works.

In order to avoid, as much as possible, attracting the attention of the natives, I had taken no tent with

me, and sheltered myself at night under the projecting roof of the granite blocks, my Kél-owí friends
sleeping around me.

Saturday,   Hámma was so good as to give up to me
October 5th.   his fine tall méheri, while he placed his simple
little saddle or "kíri" on the back of the young and
ill-trained camel hired here, a proceeding which in
the course of our journey almost cost him his ribs.
In truth I had no saddle; yet my seat was arranged
comfortably by placing first two leathern bags filled
with soft articles across the back of the camel, and
then fastening two others over them lengthwise, and
spreading my carpet over all.   Even for carrying
their salt, the Kél-owí very rarely employ saddles, or
if they do, only of the lightest description, made of
straw, which have nothing in common with the
heavy and hot "hawiya" of the Arabs.

The country through which we travelled was a
picturesque wilderness, with rocky ground intersected

at every moment by winding valleys and dry watercourses richly overgrown with grasses and mimosas,
while majestic mountains and detached peaks towered
over the landscape, the most interesting object during

the whole day being Mount Cheréka, with its curious double peak, as it appeared from various sides, first looking as if it were a single peak, only bifurcated at the top, then after a while showing two peaks separated almost to the very base and rising in picturesque forms nearly to the same elevation.   Unfortunately

our road did not lead us near it, although I was as anxious to explore this singular mountain as to visit the town of A'sodi, which some years ago attracted attention in Europe.   We had sent a present to Astáfidet, the chief of the Kél-owí residing here, and probably I should have been well received; but Hámma would not hear of our going there now, so we left the town at no great distance to the right, and I must content myself with here inserting the information obtained from other people who had been there repeatedly.

A'sodi*, lying at no great distance from the foot of

---

* It is an obvious mistake to derive this name, which is written أَصْطَه and أَصْوَطه, though the former is the more correct form and is evidently of sub-Libyan origin, from the Arabic word اسْوَد (black).

Mount Cheréka, which forms the most characteristic feature of the surrounding landscape, was once an important place, and a great resort for merchants, though, as it is not mentioned by any Arabic writer, not even by Leo, it would seem to be of much later origin than A'gades. Above a thousand houses built of clay and stone lie at present in ruins, while only about eighty are still inhabited; this would testify that it was once a comparatively considerable place with from eight to ten thousand inhabitants. Such an estimate of its magnitude is confirmed by the fact that there were seven tamizgídas, or mosques, in the town, the largest of which was ornamented with columns, the "mamber" alone being decorated with three, while the naves were covered in partly with a double roof made of the stems of the dúm-tree, and partly with cupolas.

The town, however, seems never to have been inclosed with a wall, and in this respect, as well as in its size, was always inferior to A'gades. At present, although the population is scattered about, the market of A'sodi is still well provided with provisions, and even with the more common merchandise. The house of the amanókal of the Kél-owí is said to stand on a little eminence in the western part of the town, surrounded by about twenty cottages. There is no well inside, all the water being fetched from a well which lies in a valley stretching from north to south.

Conversing with my companions about this place,

which we left at a short distance to our right, and
having before us the interesting picture of the mountain-range of Búnday, with its neighbouring heights,
forming one continuous group with Mount Eghellál,

we reached the fine valley Chizólen, and rested in it
during the hottest hours of the day under a beautiful
talha-tree, while the various beasts composing our
little caravan found a rich pasturage all around.

Having taken here a sufficient supply of very good
water from hollows scooped in the sand, we continued
our march over rocky ground thickly covered with
herbage, and surmounted on our right by the angular
outlines and isolated sugar-loafs of a craggy ridge,
while on our left rose the broad majestic form of
Mount Eghellál.   As evening came on I was greatly
cheered at the sight of a herd of well-fed cattle returning from their pasture-grounds to their night-
quarters near the village of Eghellál, which lies at
the foot of the mountain so named.   They were fine
sturdy bullocks of moderate size, all with the hump,
and of glossy dark-brown colour.

In the distance, as the Eghellál began to retire,
there appeared behind it in faint outlines Mount

Bághzen, which of late years has become so famous in Europe, and had filled my imagination with lofty crests and other features of romantic scenery. But how disappointed was I when, instead of all this, I saw it stretching along in one almost unbroken line! I soon turned my eyes from it to Mount Eghellál, which now disclosed to us a deep chasm or crevice (the channel of powerful floods) separating a broad cone, and apparently dividing the whole mountain-mass into two distinct groups.

At six o'clock in the evening we encamped in the shallow valley of Eghellál, at some distance from the well, and were greatly delighted at being soon joined by Háj 'Abdúwa, the son of Fátima (A'nnur's eldest sister), and the chief's presumptive heir, a man of about fifty years of age, and of intelligent and agreeable character. I treated him with a cup or two of coffee well sweetened, and conversed with him awhile about the difference between Egypt, which he had visited on his pilgrimage, and his own country. He was well aware of the immense superiority even of that state of society; but on the other hand he had not failed to observe the misery connected with great density of population, and he told me, with a certain degree of pride, that there were few people in Aïr so miserable as a large class of the inhabitants of Cairo. Being attacked by severe fever, he returned the next morning to his village Táfidet, but afterwards accompanied the chief Astáfidet on his expedition to A'gades, where I saw him again. I met him also in the course of my travels twice in Kúkawa, whither he alone of all his tribe used to go in order to maintain friendly relations with that court, which was too often disturbed by the predatory habits of roving Kél-owí.

Starting early, we soon reached a more open country, which to the eye seemed to lean towards Mount Bághzen; but this was only an _{Sunday, October 6th.}

illusion, as appeared clearly from the direction of the dry watercourses, which all ran from E. to W.S.W. On our right we had now Mount A'gata, which has given its name to the village mentioned above as lying at its foot. Here the fertility of the soil seemed greatly increased, the herbage becoming more fresh and abundant, while numerous talhas and abísgas adorned the country. Near the foot of the extensive mountain-group of Bághzen, and close to another mountain called Ajúri, there are even some very favoured spots,—especially a valley called Chímmia, ornamented with a fine date-grove, which produces fruit of excellent quality. As we entered the meandering windings of a broad watercourse, we obtained an interesting view of Mount Belásega. The plain now contracted, and, on entering a narrow defile of the ridges, we had to cross a small pass, from the top of which a most charming prospect met our eyes.

A grand and beautifully-shaped mountain rose on our right, leaving, between its base and the craggy

heights, the offshoots of which we were crossing, a broad valley running almost east and west, while at the eastern foot of the mountain a narrow but richly-adorned valley wound along through the lower rocky ground. This was Mount Abíla, or Bíla, which is at once one of the most picturesque objects in the country of Aïr, and seems to bear an interesting testimony to a connection with that great family of mankind which we call the Semitic; for the name of this mountain, or rather of the moist and " green vale" at its foot (throughout the desert, even in its most favoured parts, it is the valley which generally gives its name to the mountain), is probably the same as that of the well-known spot in Syria, from which the province of Abilene has been named.*

A little beyond the first dry watercourse, where water was to be scooped out a few feet under the surface of the ground, we rested for the heat of the day; but the vegetation around was far from being so rich here as in the valley Tíggeda, at the eastern foot of the picturesque mountain, where, after a short march in the afternoon, we encamped for the night. This was the finest valley I had yet seen in the country. The broad sandy bed of the torrent, at present dry, was bordered with the most beautiful fresh grass, forming a fine turf, shaded by the richest and densest foliage of several kinds of mimosa, the tabórak or *Balanites*, the tághmart, the abísga, and tunfáfia †, while over all this mass of verdure towered the beautiful peaks which on this side start forth from the massive mountain, the whole tinged with the varied tints of the setting sun. This delicious spectacle filled my heart with delight; and having sat down a little while quietly to enjoy it, I made

---

* See Gesenius, s. v. " abel;" and compare Porter, Five Years in Damascus, vol. i. p. 264.; Stanley, Sinai and Palestine, pp. 404. 485.

† I have noticed in my memorandum-book also, that I saw here the first túji; but what " túji " means I am at present unable to say.

a sketch of the beautiful forms of the mountain-peaks.

Just before encamping we had passed a small chapel in ruins surrounded by a cemetery. At that time I thought this valley identical with the Tekádda (as the name is generally spelt) mentioned by Ebn Khaldún and by Ebn Batúta * as an independent little Berber state between Gógo and Káhir, lying on the road of the pilgrims; but I found afterwards that there is another place which has better claims to this identification.

---

* Ebn Khaldún, texte Arabe, tom. i. p. 265.; Ebn Batúta, Journal Asiatique, 1843, p. 233.

We began a most interesting day's march, winding first along the valley Tíggeda (which now in the cool of the morning was enlivened by numerous flocks of wild pigeons), and then over a short tract of rocky ground entering the still more picturesque " érazar-n-A'sada," on the west only lined by low rocky ridges, but bordered towards the east by the steep massive forms of the Dógem. Here, indeed, a really tropical profusion of vegetation covered the whole bottom of the valley, and scarcely left a narrow low passage for the camels, the rider being obliged to stoop every moment to avoid being swept off his seat. The principal tree here is the dúm-tree, or *Cucifera Thebaïca*, which I had not seen since Selúfiet; but here it was in the wild picturesque state into which it soon relapses if left to nature. There was, besides, a great variety of the acacia tribe all growing most luxuriantly, and interwoven with creepers, which united the whole mass of vegetation into one thick canopy. I regret that there was no leisure for making a sketch, as this valley was far more picturesque even than Aúderas, of which I have been able to give the reader a slight outline.

In this interesting valley we met two droll and jovial-looking musicians, clad in a short and narrow blue shirt, well-fastened round their loins, and a small straw hat. Each of them carried a large drum, or tímbali, with which they had been cheering the spirits of a wedding-party, and were now proceeding to some other place on a similar errand. We then met a large slave-caravan, consisting of about forty camels and sixty slaves, winding along the narrow path, hemmèd in by the rank vegetation, and looking rather merry than sad, — the poor blacks gladdened doubtless by the picturesque landscape, and keeping up a lively song in their native melody. In the train of this caravan, and probably interested in its lawless merchandise, went Snúsi and Awed el Khér, two of the camel-drivers with whom we had come from Múrzuk, and who probably had laid out the money gained from the English Mission in the very article of trade which it is the desire of the English Government to prohibit. This is a sinister result of well-meant commercial impulses, which will probably subsist as long as the slave-trade itself exists on the north coast of Africa.*

On emerging from the thick forest, we obtained the first sight of the majestic cone of the Dógem, while a very narrow ravine or cleft in the steep cliffs on our left led to the village A'sada. We then began to ascend, sometimes along narrow ravines, at others on sloping rocky ground, all covered with herbage up to the summits of the lower mountains. In this way we reached the highest point of the pass, about 2500 feet, having the broad cone of the Dógem on our left, which I then thought to be the most elevated point in Air, though, as I mentioned above, the old chief A'nnur maintained that the Tímge is higher. This

* At the moment I am revising this, I am happy to state that the slave-trade is really abolished.

conspicuous mountain most probably consists of basalt; and, from what I shall observe further on, it may be inferred that the whole group of the Bághzen does so too.

From this pass we descended into the pebbly plain of Erárar-n-Déndemu, thickly overgrown with small talha-trees, and showing along the path numerous foot-prints of the lion, which is extremely common in these highland wildernesses, which, while affording sufficient vegetation and water for a variety of animals, are but thinly inhabited, and everywhere offer a safe retreat. However, from what I saw of him, he is not a very ferocious animal here.

The weather meanwhile had become sultry; and when, after having left the plain, we were winding through narrow glens, the storm, the last of the rainy season, broke out; and through the mismanagement of the slaves, not only our persons, but all our things, were soaked with the rain. Our march became rather cheerless, everything being wet, and the whole ground covered with water, which along the watercourses formed powerful torrents. At length we entered the gloomy, rugged valley of Tághist, covered with basaltic stones, mostly of the size of a child's head, and bordered by sorry-looking rocky hills.

Tághist is remarkable as the place of prayer founded by the man who introduced Islám into Central Negroland[*], and thus gave the first impulse to

[*] I trust my readers will approve of my using the expression Western Negroland to denote the countries from Fúta as

that continual struggle which, always extending further and further, seems destined to overpower the nations at the very equator, if Christianity does not presently step in to dispute the ground with it. This man was the celebrated Mohammed ben 'Abd el Kerím ben Maghíli, a native of Búda in Tawát*, and a contemporary and intimate friend of the Sheikh e' Soyúti†, that living encyclopædia and keystone, if I may be allowed the expression, of Mohammedan learning.

Living in the time when the great Sónghay empire began to decline from that pitch of power which it had reached under the energetic sway of Sónni 'Ali and Mohammed el Háj A'skia, and stung by the injustice of A'skia Ismáíl, who refused to punish the murderers of his son, he turned his eyes on the country where successful resistance had first been made against the all-absorbing power of the Asáki, and which, fresh and youthful as it was, promised a new splendour, if enlightened by the influence of a purer religion. Instigated by such motives, partly

far as Sókoto; Middle Sudán, or Central Negroland, from Sókoto to Bagírmi; and Eastern Negroland, comprising Wadäy, Darfúr Kordofán, and Sennár. However, here, when I say that Mohammed ben 'Abd el Kerím introduced Islám into Central Negroland, I exclude Bórnu, where the Mohammedan religion is much older.

* He may have been born in Telemsán; but at least from very early youth he was settled in Tawát.

† E' Soyúti's full name is Abu 'l Fadhl Jelál e' dín 'Abd e' Rahmán el Khodaíri e' Soyúti.

merely personal, partly of a more elevated character, Mohammed ben 'Abd el Kerím turned his steps towards Kátsena, where we shall find him again ; but on his way thither he founded in this spot a place of prayer, to remain a monument to the traveller of the path which the religion of the One God took from the far east to the country of the blacks.

The " msíd," or " mesálla," at present is only marked by stones laid out in a regular way, and enclosing a space from sixty to seventy feet long and fifteen broad, with a small mehhráb, which is adorned (accidentally or intentionally, I cannot say) by a young talha-tree. This is the venerated and far-famed "Makám e' Sheikh ben 'Abd el Kerím," where the traveller coming from the north never omits to say his prayers ; others call it Msíd Sídi Baghdádi, the name Baghdádi being often given by the blacks to the Sheikh, who had long resided in the east.

At length we descended from the rugged ground of Tághist into the commencement of the celebrated Valley of Aúderas, the fame of which penetrated to Europe many years ago. Here we encamped, wet as we were, on the slope of the rocky ground, in order to guard against the humidity of the valley. Opposite to us, towards the south, on the top of a hill, lay the little village Aërwen wan Tídrak. Another village, called I'farghén, is situated higher up the valley on the road from Aúderas to Damerghú. On our return I saw in this valley a barbarous mode of tillage, three slaves being yoked to a sort of plough, and driven like oxen by their master. This is probably the most southern place in Central Africa where the plough is used; for all over Sudán the hoe or fertaña is the only instrument used for preparing the ground.

While the weather was clear and fine, Tuesday, October 8th. the valley, bordered on both sides by steep precipices, and adorned with a rich grove of dúm-trees, and bush and herbage in great variety, displayed its mingled beauties, chiefly about the well, where, on our return-journey, I made the accompanying sketch. This valley, as well as those succeeding it, is able to produce not only millet, but even wheat, wine, and dates, with almost every species of vege-table; and there are said to be fifty garden fields (gó-naki) near the village of I'farghén.

But too soon we left this charming strip of cultiva-tion, and ascended the rocky ground on our right, above which again rose several detached hills, one of which had so interesting and well-marked a shape that I sketched its outlines. The road which we

followed is not the common one. The latter, after crossing very rugged ground for about fifteen miles, keeps along the fine deep valley Télwa for about ten miles, and then ascending for about an hour, reaches A'gades in three hours more. This latter road passes by Tímelén, where at times a considerable market is said to be held.

Having descended again, we found the ground in the plain covered with a thin crust of natron, and further on met people busy in collecting it; but it is not of very good quality, nor at all comparable to that of Múniyó or to that of the shores of Lake Tsád. There are several places on the border between the desert and the fertile districts of Negroland, which produce this mineral, which forms a most important article of commerce in middle Sudán. Another well-known natron-district is in Zabérma; but in Western Sudán natron is almost unknown, and it is only very rarely that a small sample of it can be got in Tim-búktu. Many of the Kél-owí have learnt (most probably from the Tedá or Tebu) the disgusting custom of chewing tobacco intermixed with natron, while only very few of them smoke.

The monotony of the country ceased when we entered the valley Búdde, which, running in the direction of our path from S.S.W. to N.N.E., is adorned with a continuous strip of dúm-trees, besides abísga and talha ; but the latter were of rather poor growth in the northern part of the valley. Having crossed at noon the broad sandy watercourse, which winds through the rich carpet of vegetation, and where there happened to be a tolerably large pond of water, we encamped in the midst of the thicket. Here the mimosas attained such an exuberance as I had scarcely observed even in the valley A'sada, and being closely interwoven with "gráffeni" or climbing plants, they formed an almost impenetrable thicket. From the midst of this thorny mass of vegetation a beautiful ripe fruit, about an inch and a half long, of the size of a date, and of dark-red colour, awakened the desire of the traveller; but having eaten a few, I found them, though sweet, rather mawkish.

Here too I first became acquainted with the troublesome nature of the "karéngia," or *Pennisetum distichum*, which, together with the ant, is to the traveller in Central Africa his greatest and most constant inconvenience. It was just ripe; and the little burr-like seeds attached themselves to every part of my dress. It is quite necessary to be always provided with small pincers, in order to draw out from the fingers the little stings, which, if left in the skin, will cause sores. None even of the wild roving natives is ever without such an instrument. But it is not a useless plant; for, besides being the most nourishing food for cattle, it furnishes even man with a rather slight, but by no means tasteless food. Many of the Tawárek, from Bórnu as far as Timbúktu, subsist more or less upon the seeds of the *Pennisetum distichum*, which they call "úzak." The drink made of it is certainly not bad, resembling in coolness the fúra or ghussub-water.

From the circumstance that our Kél-owí were here cutting grass for the camels, I concluded that the next part of our journey would lead through an entirely sterile tract; but though the herbage was here exuberant, it was not at all wanting further on. Having left the valley awhile to our right, we soon re-entered it, and crossed several beautiful branches of it very rich in vegetation. We then encamped on an open place beyond the southernmost branch, close to a cemetery of the Imghád who inhabit a small village to the east called Tawár Nwaijdúd, and further on some other villages, called Téndau, Tintabórak, and Emélloli.

While, with the rest of our companions, we tried to make ourselves comfortable on the hard ground and under the open canopy of heaven, Hámma and Mohammed took up their quarters with the Imghád, and, according to their own statement on their return the following morning, were very hospitably treated, both by the male and female part of the inhabitants. As for the Imghád who live in these fertile valleys round A'gades, they are divided into numerous sections, of which I learnt the following names: — the Ehér-heren, the Kél-chísem, the Taranaiji, the Edárreban, the Yowúswosan, the Efeléngeras, the E'heten *, the Tariwáza, the Ihíngemángh, the Egemmén, the Edellén, the Kél-tédele, and the Ikóhanén.

Our route led us over stony ground till we reached another favoured valley, called   Wednesday, October 9th.

---

* This name may be connected with the Sónghay or Sónrhay ; the Awelímmiden, at least, call the Sónghay people Ehétane.

Tefárrakad, where, owing to the watercourse being divided into several branches, vegetation is spread over a larger space. Here, while our Kél-owí hung a little behind, two Imghád, mounted on camels, attached themselves to us and became rather troublesome; but they looked so famished and thin that they awakened pity rather than any other feeling, their dress and whole attire being of the poorest description. Further on, when we had left the valley, and ascended rocky ground, we met a small caravan of the same mixed kind as our own troop, —camels, bullocks, asses, and men on foot; they were returning to their village with provision of Negro millet, which they had bought in A'gades.

We had scarcely advanced three miles when we descended again into another long, beautiful hollow in the rocky ground, the valley Bóghel, which, besides a fine grove of dúm-trees, exhibits one very large and remarkable specimen of the tree called baure* in Háusa, a large ficus with ample fleshy leaves of beautiful green. This specimen, so far to the north, measured not less than twenty-six feet in circumference at the height of eight feet from the ground, and was certainly eighty feet high, with a full, wide-spreading crown. I scarcely remember afterwards to have seen in all Sudán a larger baure than this. Here, for the first time, I heard the Guinea

---

* This tree has nothing in common with the *Adansonia*, with which it has been supposed to be identical.

fowl ("táliat" or "tailélt" in Temashight, "zabó" in
Háusa); for I did not see it, the birds keeping to
the thick and impenetrable underwood which filled
the intervals between the dúm-trees:

At noon the wood, which was rather more than
half a mile in breadth, formed one continued and
unbroken cluster of thicket in the most picturesque
state of wild luxuriance, while further on, where it
became a little clearer of underwood, the ground was
covered with a sort of wild melon; but my friend
the blacksmith, who took up one of them and applied
his teeth to it, threw it away with such a grimace,
that I rather suspect he mistook a colocynth, "jan-
gunna," for a melon, "gunna." Numbers of the
Asclepias gigantea, which never grows on a spot
incapable of cultivation, bore testimony to the fertility of the soil, which was soon more clearly demon-
strated by a small corn-field still under cultivation.
Traces of former cultivation were evident on all
sides. There can scarcely be the least doubt that
these valleys, which were expressly left to the care of
the degraded tribes or the Imghád, on condition of
their paying from the produce a certain tribute to
their masters, once presented a very different aspect;
but when the power of the ruler of A'gades dwindled
away to a shadow, and when the Imghád, who received
from him their kaid or governor, "tágaza," ceased to
fear him, preferring robbery and pillage to the cultivation of the ground, these fine valleys were left to
themselves, and relapsed into a wilderness.

We encamped at an early hour in the afternoon near the watercourse, but did not succeed in obtaining water by digging, so that we could not even cook a little supper. Further down the valley there had been a copious supply of water; and we had passed there a numerous caravan of asses near a large pool; but my companions, who were extremely negligent in this respect, would not then lay in a supply. Several Tawárek, or rather Imóshagh and Imghád, encamped around us for the night, and thus showed that we were approaching a centre of intercourse.

Owing to our want of water, we started at a very early hour, and, ascending gradually, after a little more than three miles, reached the height of the pebbly plateau on which the town of A'gades has been built. After having received several accounts of this naked "hammáda" or "ténere" stretching out to the distance of several days, I was agreeably surprised to find that it was by no means so dreary and monotonous as I had been led to expect, forming now and then shallow depressions a few feet only lower than the pebbly surface, and sometimes extending to a considerable distance, where plenty of herbage and middle-sized acacia were growing. The road was now becoming frequented; and my companions, with a certain feeling of pride, showed me in the distance the high "Mesállaje," or minaret, the glory of A'gades. Having obtained a supply of water, and quenched our thirst, to my great astonishment we proceeded to encamp at half-past seven in the morning in one of these shallow hollows; and I learnt that we were to stay here the whole day till near sunset, in order to enter the town in the dark.

We were here met by two horsemen from A'gades (the son of the kádhi, and a companion), who, I suppose, had come out on purpose to see us. They had a very *chevaleresque* look, and proved highly interesting to me, as they were the first horsemen I had seen in the country. The son of the kádhi, who was a fine, tall man, was well-dressed in a tobe and trowsers of silk and cotton ; he carried only an iron spear besides his sword and dagger, but no shield. But, for me, the most interesting part of their attire was their stirrups, which are almost European in shape, but made of copper. Of this metal were made also the ornaments on the harness of their horses; their saddles also were very unlike what I had yet seen in these countries, and nearly the same as the old Arab saddle, which differs little from the English.

While encamped here, I bought from Hámma a black Sudán tobe, which, worn over another very large white tobe or shirt, and covered with a white bernús, gave me an appearance more suited to the country, while the stains of indigo soon made my complexion a few shades darker. This exterior accommodation to the custom of the natives, my friend Hámma represented as essential for securing the success of my undertaking ; and it had, besides, the advantage that it gave rise to the rumour that the sultan of A'gades himself had presented me with this dress.

At length, when the sun was almost down, and when it was known that the Kél-gerés and Itísan (who had come to A'gades in very great numbers, in order to proceed on their journey to Bílma after the investiture of the new sultan) had retreated to their encampments at some distance from the town, we started, and were soon met by several people, who came to pay their compliments to my companions. On entering the town, we passed through a half-deserted quarter and at length reached the house of A'nnur, where we were to take up our abode. But arriving in a new place at night is never very pleasant, and must be still less so where there are no lamps; it therefore took us some time to make ourselves tolerably comfortable. But I was fortunate in receiving hospitable treatment from our travelling companion 'Abd el Káder, who being lodged in a chamber close to mine, sent me a well-prepared dish of kuskusu, made of Indian corn. I could not relish the rice sent by one of A'nnur's wives, who resides here, owing to its not being seasoned with any salt, a practice to which I became afterwards more accustomed, but which rather astonished me in a country the entire trade of which consists in salt.

Having spread my mat and carpet on the floor, I slept well, in the pleasing consciousness of having successfully reached this first object of my desires, and dreaming of the new sphere of inquiry on which I had entered.

CHAP. XVII.

A'GADES.

EARLY in the morning the whole body of people from Tawát who were residing in the place, 'Abd el Káder at their head, paid me a visit. The Tawátíye are still, at the present time (like their forefathers more than 300 years ago), the chief merchants in A'gades; and they are well adapted to the nature of this market, for, having but small means, and being more like pedlars or retail dealers, they sit quietly down with their little stock, and try to make the most of it by buying Negro millet when it is cheap, and retailing it when it becomes dear. Speculation in grain is now the principal business transacted in A'gades, since the branches of commerce of which I shall speak further on, and which once made the place rich and important, have been diverted into other channels. Here I will only remark, that it is rather curious that the inhabitants of Tawát, though enterprising travellers, never become rich. Almost all the money with which they trade belongs to the people of Ghadámes; and their profits only allow them to dress and live well, of which they are very fond. Till recently, the Kél-owí frequented the market of

Tawát, while they were excluded from those of Ghát and Múrzuk; but at present the contrary takes place, and, while they are admitted in the two latter places, Tawát has been closed against them.

Several of these Tawátíye were about to return to their native country, and were anxiously seeking information as to the time when the caravan of the Sakomáren, which had come to Tin-téllust, intended to start on their return-journey, as they wished to go in their company. Among them was a man of the name of 'Abdallah, with whom I became afterwards very intimate, and obtained from him a great deal of information. He was well acquainted with that quarter of the African continent which lies between Tawát, Timbúktu, and A'gades, having been six times to A'gades and five times to Timbúktu, and was less exacting than the mass of his countrymen. The most interesting circumstance which I learnt from them to-day was the identity of the Emgédesi language with that of Timbúktu, — a fact of which I had no previous idea, thinking that the Háusa language, as it was the vulgar tongue of the whole of A'sben, was the indigenous language of the natives of A'gades. But about this most interesting fact I shall say more afterwards.

When the Tawátíye were about to go away, A'magay, or Mággi, as he is generally called, the chief eunuch of the sultan, came; and I was ordered by my Kél-owí companions, who had put on all their finery, to make myself ready to pay a visit to the sultan. Throwing, therefore, my white heláli bernus over my black tobe, and putting on my richly-ornamented Ghadámsi shoes, which formed my greatest finery, I took up the letters and the treaty, and solicited the aid of my servant Mohammed to assist me in getting it signed; but he refused to perform any such service, regarding it as a very gracious act on his part that he went with me at all.

The streets and the market-places were still empty when we went through them, which left upon me the impression of a deserted place of by-gone times; for even in the most important and central quarters of the town, most of the dwelling-houses were in ruins. Some meat was lying ready for sale; and a bullock was tied to a stake, while numbers of large vultures, distinguished by their long naked neck, of reddish colour, and their dirty-greyish plumage, were sitting on the pinnacles of the crumbling walls ready to pounce upon any kind of offal. These natural sca-vengers I afterwards found to be the constant in-habitants of all the market-places, not only in this town, but in all the places in the interior. Directing our steps by the high watch-tower, which, although built only of clay and wood, yet, on account of its contrast to the low dwelling-houses around, forms a conspicuous object, we reached the gate which leads into the palace or fáda, a small separate quarter with a large irregular courtyard, and from twenty to twenty-five larger and smaller dwellings. Even these were partly in ruins; and one or two wretched

conical cottages built of reeds and grass, in the midst
of them, showed anything but a regard to cleanliness.
The house, however, in which the sultan himself
dwelt proved to have been recently repaired, and had
a neat and orderly appearance; the wall was nicely
polished, and the gate newly covered in with boards
made of the stem of the dúm-tree, and furnished with
a door of the same material.

We seated ourselves apart on the right side of a
vestibule, which, as is the case in all the houses
of this place, is separated from the rest of the room
by a low balustrade about ten inches high, and
in this shape [illustration]. Meanwhile Mággi had announced us to his Majesty, and, coming back, conducted us into the adjoining room, where he had
taken his seat. It was separated from the vestibule
by a very heavy wooden door, and was far more decent
than I had expected. It was about forty or fifty feet
in every direction, the rather low roof being supported
by two short and massive columns of clay, slightly

decreasing in thickness towards the top, and furnished
with a simple abacus; over which one layer of large
boards was placed in the breadth, and two in the

depth of the room, sustaining the roof formed of lighter boards. These are covered in with branches, over which mats are spread, the whole being completed with a layer of clay. At the lower end of the room, between the two columns, was a heavy door giving access into the interior of the house, while a large opening on either side admitted the light.

'Abd el Káderi, the son of the sultan el Bákiri, was seated between the column to the right and the wall, and appeared to be a tolerably stout man, with large benevolent features, as far as the white shawl wound around his face would allow us to perceive. The white colour of the lithám, and that of his shirt, which was of grey hue, together with his physiognomy, at once announced him as not belonging to the Tawárek race. Having saluted him one after the other, we took our seats at some distance opposite to him, when, after having asked Hámma some complimentary questions with regard to the old chief, he called me to come near to him, and in a very kind manner entered into conversation with me, asking me about the English nation, of which, notwithstanding all their power, he had, in his retired spot, never before heard, not suspecting that "English powder" was derived from them.

After explaining to him how the English, although placed at such an immense distance, wished to enter into friendly relations with all the chiefs and great men on the earth, in order to establish peaceable

and legitimate intercourse with them, I delivered
to him A'nnur's and Mr. Richardson's letters, and
begged him to forward another letter to 'Alíyu, the
sultan of Sókoto, wherein we apologised for our
incapability, after the heavy losses and the many extortions we had suffered, of paying him at present a
visit in his capital, expressing to 'Abd el Káder, at the
same time, how unjustly we had been treated by tribes
subject to his dominion, who had deprived us of nearly
all the presents we were bringing with us for himself
and the other princes of Sudán.   While expressing
his indignation on this account, and regretting that I
should not be able to go on directly to Sókoto, whither
he would have sent me with the greatest safety in
company with the salt-caravan of the Kél-geres, and at
the same time giving vent to his astonishment that,
although young, I had already performed journeys so
extensive, he dismissed us, after we had placed before
him the parcel containing the presents destined for
him.   The whole conversation, not only with me, but
also with my companions, was in the Háusa language.
I should have liked to have broached to him the
treaty at once; but the moment was not favourable.

On the whole, I look upon 'Abd el Káder as a man
of great worth, though devoid of energy.   All the
people assured me that he was the best of the family
to which the sultan of A'gades belongs.   He had been
already sultan before, but, a few years ago, was
deposed in order to make way for Hámed e' Rufäy,
whom he again succeeded; but in 1853, while I was

in Sókoto, he was once more compelled to resign in favour of the former.

While returning with my companions to our lodging, we met six of Bóro's sons, among whom our travelling companion Háj 'Ali was distinguished for his elegance.   They were going to the palace in order to perform their office as " fadáwa-n-serkí " (royal courtiers), and were very complaisant when they were informed that I had been graciously received by his Majesty.   Having heard from them that Bóro, since his return, had been ill with fever, I took the opportunity to induce my followers to accompany me on a visit to him.

Mohammed Bóro has a nice little house for a town like A'gades, situated on the small area called Eráramn-sákan," or " the place of the young camels."   It is shown in the accompanying sketch.   The house itself consists of two stories, and furnishes a good specimen of the better houses of the town; its interior was nicely whitewashed.   Bóro, who was greatly pleased with our visit, received us in a very friendly manner, and when we left accompanied us a long way down the street. Though he holds no office at present, he is nevertheless a very important personage, not only in A'gades, but even in Sókoto, where he is regarded as the wealthiest merchant.   He has a little republic of his own (like the venerable patriarchs) of not less than about fifty sons with their families; but he still possesses such energy and enterprise, that in 1854 he was about to undertake another pilgrimage to Mekka.

When I had returned to my quarters, Mággi brought me, as an acknowledgment of my presents, a fat large-sized ram from 'Abd el Káder, which was an excellent proof that good meat can be got here. There is a place called Aghíllad, three or four days' journey west from A'gades *, which is said to be very rich in cattle. On this occasion I gave to the influential eunuch, for himself, an aliyáfu, or subéta, — a white shawl with a red border. In the afternoon I took another walk through the town, first to the erárar-n-sákan, which, though it had been quiet in the morning, exhibited now a busy scene, about fifty camels being offered for sale, most of them very young, and the older ones rather indifferent. But while the character of the article for sale could not be estimated very high, that of the men employed in the business of the market attracted my full attention.

They were tall men with broad coarse features, very different from any I had seen before, and with long hair hanging down upon their shoulders and over their face, in a way which is an abomination to the Tawárek; but upon inquiry I learnt that they belonged to the tribe of the Ighdalén, or E'ghedel, a very curious mixed tribe of Berber and Sónghay blood, and speaking the Sónghay language. The

---

* I am not quite sure with regard to this place, as I find a note in my memorandum-book, "The name of the place in question is Ingal, on the road to Sókoto, and not Aghíllad."

mode of buying and selling, also, was very peculiar; for the price was neither fixed in dollars, nor in shells, but either in merchandise of various description, such as calico, shawls, tobes — or in Negro millet, which is the real standard of the market of A'gades at the present time, while during the period of its prime, it was apparently the gold of Gágho. This way of buying or selling is called "kárba." There was a very animated scene between two persons; and to settle the dispute it was necessary to apply to the " serki-n-káswa," who for every camel sold in the market receives three " réjel."

From this place we went to the vegetable-market, or " káswa-n-delélti *," which was but poorly supplied, only cucumbers and molukhia (or *Corchorus olitorius*) being procurable in considerable plenty. Passing thence to the butchers' market, we found it very well supplied, and giving proof that the town was not yet quite deserted, although some strangers were just gathering for the installation of the sultan, as well as for the celebration of the great holiday, the 'Aid el kebír, or Salla-léja.   I will only observe that this market (from its name, " káswa-n-rákoma," or " yóbu yoëwoëni") seems evidently to have been formerly the market, where full-grown camels were sold.   We then went to the third market, called Katánga, where, in a sort of hall supported by the stems of the dúm-tree, about six or seven women

* Delélti is not a Háusa word.

were exhibiting on a sort of frame a variety of small things, such as beads and necklaces, sandals, small oblong tin boxes such as the Kél-owí wear for carrying charms, small leather boxes of the shape here represented, but of all possible sizes, from the diameter of an inch to as much as six inches. They are very neatly made in different colours, and are used for tobacco, perfumes, and other purposes, and are called "botta." I saw here also a very nice plate of copper, which I wanted to buy the next day, but found that it was sold. A donkey-saddle, "ákomar," and a camel-saddle or "kíri," were exposed for sale. The name "Katánga" serves, I think, to explain the name by which the former (now deserted) capital of Yóruba is generally known, I mean Katúnga, which name is given to it only by the Háusa and other neighbouring tribes.

I then went, with Mohammed "the Foolish" and another Kél-owí, to a shoemaker who lived in the south-western quarter of the town, and I was greatly surprised to find here Berbers as artisans; for even if the shoemaker was an A'mghi and not a free Amóshagh (though from his frank and noble bearing I had reason to suspect the latter), at least he understood scarcely a word of Háusa, and all the conversation was carried on in Uraghíye. He and his assistants were busy in making neat sandals; and a pair of very handsome ones, which indeed could not be surpassed, either in neatness or in strength, by the best that

are made in Kanó, were just ready, and formed the
object of a long and unsuccessful bargaining.   The
following day, however, Mohammed succeeded in
obtaining them for a mithkál.   My shoes formed a
great object of curiosity for these Emgédesi shoe-
makers; and they confessed their inability to produce
anything like them.

On returning to our quarters we met several
horsemen, with whom I was obliged to enter into a
longer conversation than I liked, in the streets.   I
now observed that several of them were armed
with the bow and arrow instead of the spear.   Almost
all the horses are dressed with the " karaúrawa "
(strings of small bells attached to their heads),
which make a great noise, and sometimes create a
belief that a great host is advancing, when there are
only a few of these horsemen.   The horses in general
were in indifferent condition, though of tolerable size;
of course they are ill fed in a place where grain is
comparatively dear.   The rider places only his great
toe in the stirrup, the rest of the foot remaining
outside.

The occurrences of the day were of so varied a
nature, opening to me a glance into an entirely new
region of life, that I had ample material for my
evening's meditation, when I lay stretched out on my
mat before the door of my dark and close room.
Nor was my bodily comfort neglected, the sultan
being so kind and attentive as to send me a very
palatable dish of " finkáso," a sort of thick pancake

... after the ...
... appeared to
...

... gained a glance into the
town. ... anxious ...
... ascending, the ...wing
... house, obtained my object
... spread ... before my
... in eastern quarter. The
... was my interrupted by
... heaped up in the midst
of the people. Exce...
... first ... need not ...
... village (which forms my
... the part of the to my ... as
about it ... dwellings raised to two ...
and ... three ... and five or six inhabit...
... house also had been regularly provided with
... per store ... the ... with a single gun ...
... the ... of by one store ... and one ... case;
... ... to only serve ... ... an ...
... friend Mohammed, who
... me on the terrace, to
... the breach. ... ...
... not seem to be much
... part ... ... in the town, and kept
his ... for ... rather short allowance. By and by,
I went very ... to enjoy this panorama. I was
... like ... faithful ... the western quarter
... as seen from ... which will give a

made of wheat, and well buttered, which, after the unpalatable food I had had in Tintéllust, appeared to me the greatest luxury in the world.

Saturday, October 12th. Having thus obtained a glance into the interior of the town, I was anxious to get a view of the whole of it, and ascending, the following morning, the terrace of our house, obtained my object entirely, the whole town being spread out before my eyes, with the exception of the eastern quarter. The town is built on a level, which is only interrupted by small hills formed of rubbish heaped up in the midst of it by the negligence of the people. Excepting these, the line formed by the flat-terraced houses is interrupted only by the Mesállaje (which formed my basis for laying down the plan of the town), besides about fifty or fifty-five dwellings raised to two stories, and by three dúm-trees and five or six talha-trees. Our house also had been originally provided with an upper story, or rather with a single garret — for generally the upper story consists of nothing else; but it had yielded to time, and only served to furnish amusement to my foolish friend Mohammed, who never failed, when he found me on the terrace, to endeavour to throw me down the breach. Our old close-handed friend A'nnur did not seem to care much for the appearance of his palace in the town, and kept his wife here on rather short allowance. By and by, as I went every day to enjoy this panorama, I was able to make a faithful view of the western quarter of the town as seen from hence, which will give the

IL

he
to

e

reader a more exact idea of the place than any verbal description could do.

About noon the amanókal sent his musicians to
honour me and my companions with a performance;
they were four or five in number, and were provided
with the instruments usual in Sudán, in imitation of
the Arabs.   More interesting was the performance of
a single "maimólo," who visited us after we had
honourably rewarded the royal musicians, and accompanied his play, on a three-stringed "mólo" or
guitar, with an extemporaneous song.

My companions then took me to the house of the
kádhi, after having paid a short visit to the camel-
market.   The kádhi, or here rather alkáli, who lives
a little south-west from the mosque, in a house entirely detached on all sides, was sitting with the mufti
in the vestibule of his dwelling, where sentence is
pronounced, and after a few compliments, proceeded
to hear the case of my companions, who had a law-
suit against a native of the town, named Wá-n-seres,
and evidently of Berber origin.   Evidence was ad-
duced to the effect that he had sold a she-camel which
had been stolen from the Kél-owí, while he (the
defendant) on his part proved that he had bought it
from a man who swore that it was not a stolen camel.
The pleas of both parties having been heard, the
judge decided in favour of Wá-n-seres.   The whole
transaction was carried on in Temáshight, or rather
in Uraghíye.   Then came another party, and, while
their case was being heard, we went out and sat down

in front of the house, under the shade of a sort of verandah consisting of mats supported by long stakes, after which we took leave of the kádhi, who did not seem to relish my presence, and afterwards showed no very friendly feelings towards me.

While my lazy companions wanted to go home, I fortunately persuaded Mohammed, after much reluctance, to accompany me through the southern part of the town, where, lonely and deserted as it seemed to be, it was not prudent for me to go alone, as I might have easily got into some difficulty. My servant Amánkay was still quite lame with the guinea-worm; and Mohammed the Tunisian shushán had reached such a pitch of insolence when he saw me alone among a fanatical population, that I had given him up entirely.

First, leaving the fáda to our right, we went out through the "kófa-n-Alkáli;" for here the walls, which have been swept away entirely on the east side of the town, have still preserved some degree of elevation, though in many places one may easily climb over them. On issuing from the gate I was struck with the desolate character of the country on this side of the town, though it was enlivened by women and slaves going to fetch water from the principal well (which is distant about half a mile from the gate), all the water inside the town being of bad quality for drinking. At some distance from the gate were the ruins of an extensive suburb called Ben Gottára, half covered with sand, and presenting a very sorry spectacle. It was my design to go round the southern part of the town; but my companion either was, or pretended to be, too much afraid of the Kél-geres, whose encampment lay at no great distance from the walls. So we re-entered it, and followed the northern border of its deserted southern quarter, where only a few houses are still inhabited. Here I found three considerable pools of stagnant water, which had collected in deep hollows from whence, probably, the materials for building had been taken, though their form was a tolerably-regular oval. They have each a separate name, the westernmost being called from the Masráta, who have given their name to the whole western quarter as well as to a small gate still in existence; the next southwards from the kófa-n-Alkáli is called (in Emgedesíye) "Masráta-hogú-me," for the three languages—the Temáshight or Tarkíye, the Góber or Háusa language, and the Sónghay- or Sonrhay-kini—are very curiously mixed together in the topography of this town, the natural consequence of the mixture of these three different national elements. This mixture of languages was well calculated to make the office of interpreter in this place very important, and the class of such men a very numerous one.

In the Masráta pool, which is the largest of the three, two horses were swimming, while women were busy washing clothes. The water has a strong taste of salt, which is also the case with two of the three wells still in use within the town. Keeping from the easternmost pool (which is called, like the whole

quarter around, Terjemáne, from the interpreters
whose dwellings were chiefly hereabout) a little more
to the south-east, I was greatly pleased at finding
among the ruins in the south-eastern quarter, between
the quarters Akáfan árina and Imurdán, some very
well-built and neatly-polished houses, the walls of
which were of so excellent workmanship, that even
after having been deprived of their roofs, for many
years perhaps, they had sustained scarcely any injury.
One of them was furnished with ornamented niches,
and by the remains of pipes, and the whole arrangement, bore evident traces of warm baths.

Music and·song diverted us in the evening, while
we rested on our mats in the different corners of our
courtyard.

Sunday,
October 18th.
My Kél-owí companions regaled me with
a string of dates from Fáshi, the westernmost oasis of the Tebu or, as the Tawárek call them,
Berauni. But instead of indulging myself in this
luxury, I laid it carefully aside as a treat for my
visitors, to whom I had (so small were my means at
present) neither coffee nor sugar to offer. I then accompanied my friends once more to the Alkáli; but
the litigation which was going on being tedious, I
left them, and returned quite alone through the town,
sitting down a moment with the Tawatíye, who
generally met at the house of the Emgédesi I'dder,
a sort of Tawáti agent, and an intelligent man.

When I returned to our house I found there a very
interesting young man of the tribe of the I'ghdalén,

with a round face, very regular and agreeable features, fine lively black eyes, and an olive complexion
only a few shades darker than that of an Italian
peasant. His hair was black, and about four inches
long, standing upright, but cut away all round the
ears, which gave it a still more bristling appearance.
I hoped to see him again, but lost sight of him entirely. The Arabs call these people Arab-Tawárek,
indicating that they are a mixed race between the
Arab and Berber nation, and their complexion agrees
well with this designation; but it is remarkable that
they speak a Sónghay dialect. They possess scarcely
anything except camels, and are regarded as a kind
of Merábetín.

I afterwards went to call upon our old friend A'n-
nur Karamí from Aghwau, who had come to A'gades
a day or two before us, and had accompanied me also
on my visit to the sultan. He lived, together with
my amiable young friend the Tinýlkum Slimán, in
the upper story, or soro, of a house, and, when I
called, was very busy selling fine Egyptian sheep-
leather called kurna (which is in great request here,
particularly that of a green colour) to a number of
lively females, who are the chief artisans in leather-
work. Some of them were of tolerably good appearance, with light complexion and regular Arab
features. When the women were gone, A'nnur treated
me with fura or ghussub-water; and young Slimán,
who felt some little remorse for not having been able
to withstand the charms of the Emgédesíye coquettes,

told me that he was about to marry a Ma-A'sbenchi *
girl, and that the wedding would be celebrated in a
few days.

As to the fura, people who eat, or rather drink it
together, squat down round the bowl, where a large
spoon, the "lúdde," sometimes very neatly worked,
goes round, everybody taking a spoonful and passing
the spoon to his neighbour. Subjoined is a drawing
of this drinking-spoon as well as of the common
spoon, both of ordinary workmanship.

The houses in A'gades do not possess all the con-
venience which one would expect to find in houses
in the North of Europe; but here, as in many Italian

* It is remarkable that while *ba* in the Háusa language ex-
presses the masculine in the composition of national names, *ma*
originally served to denote the female; but the latter form seems
to be almost lost.

towns, the principle of the " da per tutto," which astonished Göthe so much at Rivoli on the Lago di Garda, is in full force, being greatly assisted by the many ruined houses which are to be found in every quarter of the town.   But the free nomadic inhabitant of the wilderness does not like this custom, and rather chooses to retreat into the open spots outside the town.   The insecurity of the country and the feuds generally raging oblige them still to congregate, even on such occasions.   When they reach some conspicuous tree, the spears are all stuck into the ground, and the party separates behind the bushes ; after which they again meet together under the tree, and return in solemn procession into the town.

By making such little excursions, I became acquainted with the shallow depressions which surround A'gades and which are not without importance for the general relations of the town, while they afford fodder for any caravan visiting the market, and also supply the inhabitants with very good water.   The name of the depression to the N. is Tagúrast; that to the S.W., Mérmeru ; towards the S.E., Amelúli, with a few kitchen-gardens; and another a little further on, S.S.E., Tésak-n-tálle, while at a greater distance, to the W. is Tára-bére * (meaning " the wide area " or plain, " babá-n-sárari "). Unfortunately, the dread my companions had of the Kél-gerés did not allow me

* I will here only observe, that "bére" is one of those words in the Sónghay language which shows its connection with Sanscrit.

to visit the valleys at a greater distance, the principal of which is that called el Hakhsás, inhabited by
Imghád, and famous for its vegetable productions,
with which the whole town is supplied.

Mahommed the Foolish succeeded in the evening in
getting me into some trouble, which gave him great
delight; for seeing that I took more than common
interest in a national dance accompanied with a song,
which was going on at some distance E.N.E. from
our house, he assured me that Hámma was there,
and had told him that I might go and join in their
amusement. Unfortunately, I was too easily induced;
and hanging only a cutlass over my shoulder, I
went thither unaccompanied, sure of finding my protector in the merry crowd. It was about ten o'clock
at night, the moon shining very brightly on the
scene. Having first viewed it from some distance,
I approached very near, in order to observe the
motions of the dancers. Four young men, placed
opposite to each other in pairs, were dancing with
warlike motions, and, stamping the ground violently
with the left foot, turned round in a circle, the motions
being accompanied by the energetic clapping of hands
of a numerous ring of spectators. It was a very
interesting sight, and I should have liked to stay
longer; but finding that Hámma was not present,
and that all the people were young, and many of
them buzawe, I followed the advice of 'Abdu, one
of A'nnur's slaves, who was among the crowd, to
withdraw as soon as possible. I had, however, re-

traced my steps but a short way, when, with the war-cry of Islam, and drawing their swords, all the young men rushed after me. Being, however, a short distance in advance, and fortunately not meeting with any one in the narrow street, I reached our house without being obliged to make use of my weapon; but my friends the Kél-owí seeing me in trouble, had thrown the chain over the door of our house, and, with a malicious laugh, left me outside with my pursuers, so that I was obliged to draw my cutlass in order to keep them at bay, though, if they had made a serious attack, I should have fared ill enough with my short blunt European weapon against their long sharp swords.

I was rather angry with my barbarous companions, particularly with Mohammed; and when after a little delay they opened the door, I loaded my pistols and threatened to shoot the first man that troubled me. However, I soon felt convinced that the chief fault was my own; and in order to obliterate the bad impression which this little adventure was likely to make in the town, particularly as the great Mohammedan feast was at hand, which of course could not but strengthen greatly the prejudice against a Christian, I resolved to stay at home the next few days. This I could do the more easily, as the terrace of our house allowed me to observe all that was going on in the place.

I therefore applied myself entirely for a few days to the study of the several routes which, with the assistance of 'Abdalla, I had been able to collect from different people, and which will be given in the Appendix, and to the language of A'gades. For though I had left all my books behind at Tintéllust, except that volume of "Prichard's Researches" which treats of Africa, I had convinced myself, from the specimens which he gives of the language of Timbúktu, that the statement of my friends from Tawát with regard to the identity of the languages of the two places was quite correct, — only with this qualification, that here this language had been greatly influenced by intercourse with the Berbers, from whom sundry words were borrowed, while the Arabic seemed to have had little influence beyond supplanting the numerals from four upwards. I was also most agreeably surprised and gratified to find this identity confirmed by the fact, that the people of A'gades give the Tawárek in general the name under which that tribe of them which lives near Timbúktu and along the Niger had become known to Mungo Park in those quarters where the language of Timbúktu is spoken. This was indeed very satisfactory, as the native name of that powerful tribe is entirely different; for the Surka, as they are called by Mungo Park, are the same as the Awelímmiden, of whom I had already heard so much in Asben (the inhabitants of which country seemed to regard them with much dread), and with whom I was afterwards to enter into the most intimate relations.

While residing in A'gades, I was not yet aware

of all the points of information which I have been able to collect in the course of my travels; and I was at a loss to account for the identity of language in places so widely separated from each other by immense tracts of desert, and by countries which seemed to have been occupied by different races. But while endeavouring, in the further course of my journey, to discover as far as possible the history of the nations with whom I had to deal, I found the clue for explaining this apparently marvellous phenomenon, and shall lay it before my readers in the following chapter.

To the Tawáti 'Abd-alla I was indebted for information on a variety of interesting matters, which I found afterwards confirmed in every respect. In a few points his statements were subject to correction, and still more to improvement; but in no single case did I find that he had deviated from the truth. I state this deliberately, in order to show that care must be taken to distinguish between information collected systematically by a native enjoying the entire confidence of his informant, and who, from his knowledge of the language and the subject about which he inquires, is able to control his informant's statements, and that which is picked up incidentally by one who scarcely knows what he asks.

But to return to my diary, the visits paid me by the other people of Tawát became less frequent, as I had no coffee to treat them with; but I was rather glad of this circumstance, as my time was too short for labouring in that wide field of new information which opened before me, and it was necessary to confine myself at present to narrower limits. In this respect I was extremely fortunate in having obeyed my impulse to visit this place, which, however desolate it may appear to the traveller who first enters it, is still the centre of a large circle of commercial intercourse, while Tintéllust is nothing but a small village, important merely from the character of the chief who resides in it, and where even those people who know a little about the country are afraid to communicate that very little. I would advise any traveller, who should hereafter visit this country, to make a long stay in this place, if he can manage to do so in comfort; for I am sure that there still remains to be collected in A'gades a store of the most valuable and interesting information.

In the afternoon of the 15th of October (the eve of the great holiday), ten chiefs of the Kél-gerés, on horseback, entered the town; and towards evening news was brought that Astáfidet, the chief of the Kél-owí residing in A'sodi, was not far off, and would make his solemn entry early in the morning. My companions therefore were extremely busy in getting ready and cleaning their holiday dress, or "yadó;" and Hámma could not procure tassels enough to adorn his high red cap, in order to give to his short figure a little more height. Poor fellow! he was really a good man, and one of the best of the Kél-owí; and the news of his being killed, in the sanguinary

battle which was fought between his tribe and the
Kél-gerés in 1854, grieved me not a little. In the
evening there was singing and dancing (" wargi" and
"wása") all over the town, and all the people were
merry except the followers of Mákita or I'mkiten,
" the Pretender;" and the sultan 'Abd el Káder was
obliged to imprison three chiefs of the Itísan, who
had come to urge Mákita's claims.

It was on this occasion that I learnt that the mighty
king of A'gades had not only a common prison,
" gida-n-damré," wherein he might confine the most
haughty chiefs, but that he even exercised over them
the power of life and death, and that he dispensed
the favours of a terrible dungeon bristling with swords
and spears standing upright, upon which he was authorized to throw any distinguished malefactor. This
latter statement, of the truth of which I had some
doubt, was afterwards confirmed to me by the old
chief A'nnur. In any case, however, such a cruel
punishment cannot but be extremely rare.

The 10th of Dhú el kadhi, 1266, was the Wednesday,
first day of the great festival 'Aid el kebír, October 16th.
or Salla-léja (the feast of the sacrifice of the sheep),
which in these regions is the greatest holiday of the
Mohammedans, and was in this instance to have a
peculiar importance and solemnity for A'gades, as the
installation of 'Abd el Káder, who had not yet pub-
licly assumed the government, was to take place the
same day. Early in the morning, before daylight,
Hámma and his companions left the house and

mounted their camels, in order to pay their compliments to Astáfidet, and join him in his procession ;
and about sunrise the young chief entered and went
directly to the "fáda," at the head of from two
hundred to three hundred Mehára, having left the
greater number of his troop, which was said to amount
to about two thousand men, outside the town.

Then, without much ceremony or delay, the installation or "sarauta" of the new sultan took place. The
ceremonial was gone through inside the fáda; but this
was the procedure. First of all, 'Abd el Káder was
conducted from his private apartments to the public
hall. Then the chiefs of the Itísan and Kél-gerés,
who went in front, begged him to sit down upon the
"gadó," a sort of couch or divan made of the leaves
of the palm-tree, or of the branches of other trees,
similar to the angaríb used in Egypt and the lands of
the Upper Nile, and covered with mats and a carpet.
Upon this the new sultan sat down, resting his feet on
the ground, not being allowed to put them upon the
gadó, and recline in the Oriental style, until the
Kél-owí desired him to do so. Such is the ceremony, symbolical of the combined participation of
these different tribes in the investiture of their
sultan.

This ceremony being concluded, the whole holiday-
procession left the palace on its way to a chapel of a
merábet called Sídi Hammáda, in Tára-bére, outside
the town, where, according to an old custom, the
prince was to say his prayers. This is a rule prevail-

ing over the whole of Mohammedan Africa, and one which I myself witnessed in some of the most important of its capitals — in A'gades, in Kúkawa, in Más-eña, in Sókoto, and in Timbúktu; everywhere the principle is the same.

Not deeming it prudent on such an occasion to mix with the people, I witnessed the whole procession from the terrace of our house, though I should have liked to have had a nearer view. The procession having taken its course through the most important quarter of the town, and through the market-places, turned round from the "káswa-n-delélti" to the oldest quarter of the town, and then returned westward, till at last it reached the above-mentioned chapel or tomb of Sídi Hammáda, where there is a small cemetery. The prayers being finished, the procession returned by the southern part of the town; and about ten o'clock the different parties which had composed the *cortége* separated.

In going as well as in returning, the order of the procession was as follows. In front of all, accompanied by the musicians, rode the sultan on a very handsome horse of Tawáti breed *, wearing, over his fine Sudán robe of coloured cotton and silk, the blue bernus I had presented to him, and wearing on his side a handsome cimetar with gold handle. Next to him rode the two sáraki-n-turáwa, — Bóro, the ex-serki on his left, and Ashu, who held the office at the time,

* The horse of Tawát is as celebrated amongst the Berber tribes of the desert as the I'manang woman or " the wealth of Tunis."

on his right, — followed by the "fádawa-n-serki,"
after whom came the chiefs of the Itísan and Kél-
gerés, all on horseback, in full dress and armour, with
their swords, daggers, long spears, and immense
shields.

Then came the longer train of the Kél-owí, mostly
on mehára, or swift camels, with Sultan Astáfidet
at their head; and last of all followed the people of
the town, a few on horseback, but most of them on
foot, and armed with swords and spears, and several
with bows and arrows. The people were all dressed
in their greatest finery; and it would have formed a
good subject for an artist. It recalled the martial
processions of the middle ages — the more so as the
high caps of the Tawárek*, surrounded by a profusion of tassels on every side, together with the black
" tesílgemist" or lithám, which covers the whole face,
leaving nothing but the eyes visible, and the shawls
wound over this and round the cap, combine to
imitate the shape of the helmet, while the black and
coloured tobes (over which on such occasions the
principal people wear a red bernus thrown across
their shoulders) represent very well the heavier dress
of the knights of yore. I will only add, that the
fact of the sultan wearing on so important and solemn
an occasion a robe which had been presented to him
by a stranger and a Christian, had a powerful influ-

* These red caps, however, are an article quite foreign to the
original dress of the Tarki, and are obnoxious to the tribes of
pure blood.

ence on the tribes collected here, and spread a beneficial report far westward over the desert.

Shortly after the procession was over, the friendly
Haj 'Abdúwa, who, after he had parted from us in
Eghellál, had attached himself to the troop of Astáfidet, came to pay me a visit. He was now tolerably
free from fever, but begged for some Epsom salts,
besides a little gunpowder. He informed me that
there was much sickness in the town, that from two
to three people died daily, and that even Astáfidet
was suffering from the prevalent disease. This was
the small-pox, a very fatal disease in Central Africa,
against which, however, several of the native pagan
tribes secured themselves by inoculation, a precaution
from which Mohammedans are withheld by religious
prejudice. I then received a visit from the sons of
Bóro in their official character as "fádawa-n-serki."
They wished to inform themselves, apparently, with
reference to my adventure the other night, whether
the townspeople behaved well towards me; and I was
prudent enough to tell them that I had nothing to
complain of, my alarm having been the consequence
of my own imprudence. In fact the people behaved
remarkably well, considering that I was the first
Christian that ever visited the town; and the little
explosions of fanaticism into which the women and
children sometimes broke out, when they saw me on
our terrace, rather amused me. During the first
days of my residence in A'gades, they most probably
took me for a pagan or a polytheist, and cried after

me the confessional words of Islam, laying all the stress upon the word Allah, "the One God;" but after a few days, when they had learnt that I likewise worshipped the Deity, they began to emphasize the name of their Prophet.

There was held about sunset a grave and well-attended divan of all the chiefs, to consult with respect to a "yáki" or "égehen," a ghazzia to be undertaken against the Mehárebín or freebooters of the Awelímmiden. While we were still in Tintéllust, the rumour had spread of an expedition undertaken by the latter tribe against A'ír, and the people were all greatly excited. For the poor Kél-owí, who have degenerated from their original vigour and warlike spirit by their intermixture with the black population, and by their peaceable pursuits, are not less afraid of the Awelímmiden than they are of the Kélgerés; and old A'nnur himself used to give me a dreadful description of that tribe, at which I afterwards often laughed heartily with the very people whom he intended to depict to me as monsters. By way of consoling us for the losses we had sustained, and the ill-treatment we had experienced, from the people of A'ír, he told us that among the Awelímmiden we should have been exposed to far greater hardships, as they would not have hesitated to cut the tent over our heads into pieces, in order to make shirts of it. The old chief's serious speeches had afterwards the more comical effect upon me, as the tent alluded to, a common English marquee, mended as it was with cotton strips of all the various fashions of Negroland, constantly formed a subject of the most lively scientific dispute among those barbarians, who, not having seen linen before, were at a loss to make out of what stuff it was originally made. But, unluckily, I had not among the Kél-owí such a steadfast protector and mediator and so sensible a friend as I had when, three years later, I went among the Awelímmiden, who would certainly have treated me in another way if I had fallen into their hands unprotected.

The old and lurking hostility amongst the Kél-owí and Kél-gerés, which was at this very moment threatening an outbreak, had been smoothed down by the influential and intelligent chief Sídi Ghalli el Háj A'nnur (properly E' Núr), one of the first men in A'gades; and those tribes had sworn to forget their private animosities, in order to defend themselves against and revenge themselves upon their common enemy the Awelímmiden. Hámma was very anxious to get from me a good supply of powder for Sídi Ghalli, who was to be the leader of the expedition; but I had scarcely any with me.

While I was reclining in the evening rather mournfully upon my mat, not having been out of the house these last few days, the old friendly blacksmith came up, and invited me to a promenade; and with the greatest pleasure I acceded to the proposal. We left the town by the eastern side, the moon shining brightly, and throwing her magic light over the ruins of this once-wealthy abode of commerce. Turning then a little south, we wandered over the pebbly plain till the voices heard from the encampment of the Kél-gerés frightened my companion, and we turned more northwards to the wells in Amelúli; having rested here awhile, we returned to our quarters.

Thursday, October 17th. A'nnur karamí, our amiable and indolent attendant, left this place for Tintéllust with a note which I wrote to my colleagues, informing them of my safe arrival, my gracious reception, and the general character of the place. To-day the whole town was in agitation in consequence of one of those characteristic events which, in a place like A'gades, serve to mark the different periods of the year; for here a man can do nothing singly, but all must act together. The salt-caravan of the Itísan and Kél-gerés had collected, mustering, I was told, not less than ten thousand camels, and had encamped in Mérmeru and Tésak-n-tállem ready to start for the salt-mines of Bilma, along a road which will be indicated further on. However exaggerated the number of the camels might be, it was certainly a very large caravan; and a great many of the inhabitants went out to settle their little business with the men, and take leave of their friends. Ghámbelu, the chief of the Itísan, very often himself accompanies this expedition, in which also many of the Tagáma take a part.

In the course of the day I had a rather curious conversation with a man from Táfidet, the native

place of Háj 'Abdúwa. After exchanging compliments
with me, he asked me, abruptly, whether I always
knew where water was to be found; and when I told
him that, though I could not exactly say in every case
at what depth water was to be found, yet that, from
the configuration of the ground, I should be able to
tell the spot where it was most likely to be met with,
he asked whether I had seen rock-inscriptions on the
road from Ghát; and I answered him that I had, and
generally near watering-places. He then told me
that I was quite right, but that in Táfidet there were
many inscriptions upon the rocks at a distance from
water. I told him that perhaps at an earlier period
water might have been found there, or that the inscriptions might have been made by shepherds; but
this he thought very improbable, and persisted in
his opinion, that these inscriptions indicated ancient
sepulchres, in which, probably, treasures were concealed. I was rather surprised at the philosophical
conclusions at which this barbarian had arrived, and
conjectured, as was really the case, that he had accompanied Háj 'Abdúwa on his pilgrimage and on
his passage through Egypt, and had there learned to
make some archæological observations. He affected
to believe that I was able to read the inscriptions,
and tell all about the treasures; but I assured
him that, while he was partially right with regard
to the inscriptions, he was quite wrong so far
as regarded the treasures, as these rock-inscriptions, so far as I was able to decipher them, indi-

cated only names. But I was rather sorry that I did not myself see the inscriptions of which this man spoke, as I had heard many reports about them, which had excited my curiosity, and I had even sent the little Fezzáni Fáki Makhlúk expressly to copy them, who, however, brought me back only an illegible scrawl.

Friday, October 18th. The last day of the Salla-léja was a merry day for the lower class of the inhabitants, but a serious one for the men of influence and authority; and many councils were held, one of them in my room. I then received a visit from a sister's son of the sultan, whose name was Alkáli, a tall gentlemanlike man, who asked me why I did not yet leave A'gades and return to Tintéllust. It seemed that he suspected me of waiting till the sultan had made me a present in return for that received by him; but I told him that, though I wished 'Abd el Káder to write me a letter for my sultan, which would guarantee the safety of some future traveller belonging to our tribe, I had no further business here, but was only waiting for Hámma, who had not yet finished his bartering for provisions. He had seen me sketching on the terrace, and was somewhat inquisitive about what I had been doing there; but I succeeded in directing his attention to the wonderful powers of the pencil, with which he became so delighted, that when I gave him one, he begged another from me, in order that they might suffice for his lifetime.

Interesting also was the visit of Háj Beshír, the wealthy man of Iferwán whom I have already mentioned repeatedly, and who is an important personage in the country of A'ír. Unfortunately, instead of using his influence to facilitate our entrance into the country, his son had been among the chief leaders of the expedition against us. Though not young, he was lively and social, and asked me whether I should not like to marry some nice Emgedesíye girl. When he was gone, I took a long walk through the town with Hámma, who was somewhat more communicative to-day than usual; but his intelligence was not equal to his energy and personal courage, which had been proved in many a battle. He had been often wounded; and having in the last skirmish received a deep cut on his head, he had made an enormous charm, which was generally believed to guarantee him from any further wound; and in fact, if the charm were to receive the blow, it would not be altogether useless, for it was a thick book. But his destiny was written.

There was a rather amusing episode in the incidents of the day. The ex-sultan Hámed e' Rufáy, who had left many debts behind him, sent ten camel-loads of provisions and merchandise to be divided among his creditors; but a few Tawárek to whom he owed something seized the whole, so that the other poor people never obtained a farthing. To-day the great salt-caravan of the Kél-gerés and Itísan really started.

Saturday,
October 19. Hámma and his companions were summoned to a council which was to decide definitely in what quarter the arm of justice, now raised in wrath, was to strike the first blow; and it was resolved that the expedition should first punish the Imghád, the Ikázkezan, and Fádëangh. The officer who made the proclamation through the town was provided with a very rude sort of drum, which was, in fact, nothing but an old barrel covered with a skin.

Sunday,
October 20th. The most important event in the course of the day was a visit which I received from Mohammed Bóro, our travelling companion from Múrzuk, with his sons. It was the best proof of his noble character, that before we separated, perhaps never to meet again, he came to speak with me, and to explain our mutual relations fairly. He certainly could not deny that he had been extremely angry with us; and I could not condemn him on this account, for he had been treated ignominiously. While Mr. Gagliuffi told him that we were persuaded that the whole success of our proceedings lay in his hands, he had been plainly given to understand that we set very little value on his services. Besides, he had sustained some heavy losses on the journey, and by waiting for us had consumed the provisions which he had got ready for the march.

Although an old man, he was first going with the expedition, after which he intended accompanying the caravan of the Kél-gerés to Sókoto with his whole

family; for Sókoto is his real home.   The salt-caravan and the company of this man offered a splendid
opportunity for reaching that place in safety and
by the most direct road; but our means did not
allow of such a journey, and after all it was better, at
least for myself, that it was not undertaken, since, as
matters went, it was reserved for me, before I traced
my steps towards the western regions, to discover the
upper navigable course of the eastern branch of the
so-called Niger, and make sundry other important
discoveries.   Nevertheless Bóro expressed his hope of
seeing me again in Sókoto; and his wish might easily
have been accomplished.   He certainly must have
been, when in the vigour of life, a man — in the full
sense of the word, and well deserved the praise of
the Emgedesíye, who have a popular song beginning
with the words " A'gades has no men but Bóro and
Dahámmi."   I now also became aware why he had
many enemies in Múrzuk, who unfortunately succeeded in making Gagliuffi believe that he had no
authority whatever in his own country; for as serkí-
n-turáwa, he had to levy the tax of ten mithkáls on
every camel-load of merchandise, and this he is said
to have done with some degree of severity.   After a
long conversation on the steps of the terráce, we
parted, the best possible friends.

Not so pleasant to me, though not without interest,
was the visit of another great man — Belróji, the
támberi or war-chieftain of the Ighólar Im-esághlar.
He was still in his prime, but my Kél-owí (who were

always wrangling like children) got up a desperate
fight with him in my very room, which was soon
filled with clouds of dust; and the young Slimán
entering during the row, and joining in it, it became
really frightful. The Kél-owí were just like children;
when they went out they never failed to put on all
their finery, which they threw off as soon as they
came within doors, resuming their old dirty clothes.

It was my custom in the afternoon, when the sun
had set behind the opposite buildings, to walk up and
down in front of our house; and while so doing to-
day I had a long conversation with two chiefs of
the Itísan on horseback, who came to see me, and
avowed their sincere friendship and regard. They
were fine, tall men, but rather slim, with a noble
expression of countenance, and of light colour. Their
dress was simple, but handsome, and arranged with
great care. All the Tawárek, from Ghát as far
as Háusa, and from Alákkos to Timbúktu, are pas-
sionately fond of the tobes and trowsers called
" tailelt" (the Guinea-fowl), or "fílfil" (the pepper),
on account of their speckled colour. They are made
of silk and cotton interwoven *, and look very neat.
The lowest part of the trowsers, which forms a narrow
band about two inches broad, closing rather tightly,
is embroidered in different colours. None of the

---

* I have brought home a specimen of these tobes, among various
others. The tailelt was my common dress during all the latter
part of my journey. A representation of its distinguishing ornaments will be given in the next volume.

Tawárek of pure blood would, I think, degrade themselves by wearing on their head the red cap.

Early in the morning I went with Hámma to take leave of the sultan, who Monday, October 21st. had been too busy, for some days, to favour me with an audience; and I urged my friend to speak of the treaty, though I was myself fully aware of the great difficulty which so complicated a paper, written in a form entirely unknown to the natives, and which must naturally be expected to awaken their suspicion, would create, and of the great improbability of its being signed while the sultan was pressed with a variety of business.   On the way to the fáda we met A'shu, the present serkí-n-turáwa, a large-sized man, clad in an entirely-white dress, which may not improbably be a sign of his authority over the white men (Turáwa*). He is said to be a very wealthy man.   He replied to my compliments with much kindness, and entered into conversation with me about the difference of our country and theirs, and ordered one of his companions to take me to a small garden which he had planted near his house in the midst of the town, in order to see what plants we had in common with them.   Of course there was nothing like our plants; and my cicerone conceived rather a poor idea of our country when he heard that all the things which they had, we had not — neither senna, nor bamia, nor indigo, nor cotton, nor Guinea corn, nor, in short, the most beautiful of all trees of the creation, as he thought — the

* Who these Turáwa are I shall explain further on.

talha, or *Mimosa ferruginea*; and he seemed rather incredulous when told that we had much finer plants than they.

We then went to the fáda. The sultan seemed quite ready for starting. He was sitting in the courtyard of his palace, surrounded by a multitude of people and camels, while the loud murmuring noise of a number of schoolboys who were learning the Kurán proceeded from the opposite corner, and prevented my hearing the conversation of the people. The crowd and the open locality were, of course, not very favourable to my last audience; and it was necessarily a cold one. Supported by Hamma, I informed the sultan that I expected still to receive a letter from him to the government under whose auspices I was travelling, expressive of the pleasure and satisfaction he had felt in being honoured with a visit from one of the mission, and that he would gladly grant protection to any future traveller who should happen to visit his country. The sultan promised that such a letter should be written; however, the result proved that either he had not quite understood what I meant, or, what is more probable, that in his precarious situation he felt himself not justified in writing to a Christian government, especially as he had received no letter from it.

When I had returned to my quarters, Hamma brought me three letters, in which 'Abd el Káder recommended my person and my luggage to the care of the governors of Kanó, Kátsena, and Dáura, and which were written in rather incorrect Arabic, and in nearly the same terms.   They were as follows:—

"In the name of God, &c.

"From the Emír of Ahir*, 'Abd el Káder, son of the Sultan Mohammed el Bákeri, to the Emír of Dáura, son of the late Emír of Dáura, Is-hhák.   The mercy of God upon the eldest companions of the Prophet, and his blessing upon the Khalífa; Amín. The most lasting blessing and the highest well-being to you without end. I send this message to you with regard to a stranger, my guest, of the name of 'Abd el Kerím†, who came to me, and is going to the Emír el Mumenín [the Sultan of Sókoto], in order that, when he proceeds to you, you may protect him and treat him well, so that none of the freebooters and evildoers‡ may hurt him or his property, but that he may reach the Emír el Mumenín. Indeed we wrote this on account of the freebooters, in order that you may protect him against them in the most efficacious manner. Farewell." .

These letters were all sealed with the seal of the sultan.

Hámma showed me also another letter which he had received from the sultan, and which I think interesting enough to be here inserted, as it is a faithful image of the turbulent state of the country at that time, and as it contains the simple expression of the sincere and just proceedings of the new sultan. Its purport was as follows, though the language in

---

* Here also the name of the country is written with an *h*— اهير —as is always done by the Arabs (see what I have said above).

† 'Abd el Kerím was the name I adopted from the beginning as my travelling name.

‡ ‏من المحاربين و الظالمين.‏

which it is written is so incorrect that several passages admit of different interpretations.[*]

"In the name of God, &c.

"From the Commander, the faithful Minister of Justice[†], the Sultan 'Abd el Káder, son of the Sultan Mohammed el Bákeri, to the chiefs of all the tribe of E' Núr, and Hámed, and Sëis, and all those among you who have large possessions, perfect peace to you.

"Your eloquence, compliments, and information are deserving of praise. We have seen the auxiliaries sent to us by your tribe; and we have taken energetic measures with them against the marauders, who obstruct the way of the caravans of devout people[‡], and the intercourse of those who travel as well as those who remain at home. On this account we desire to receive aid from you against their incursions. The people of the Kél-fadaye, they are the marauders. We should not have prohibited their chiefs to exercise rule over them, except for three things:—first, because I am afraid they will betake themselves from the Aníkel [the community of the people of A'ír] to the Awelímmiden; secondly, in order that they may not make an alliance with them against us, for they are all marauders; and thirdly, in order that you may approve of their paying us the tribute. Come, then, to us quickly. You know that what the hand holds it holds only with the aid of the fingers; for without the fingers the hand can seize nothing.

"We therefore will expect your determination, that is to say your coming, after the departure of the salt-caravan of the Itísan, fixed among you for the fifteenth of the month. God! God is

---

[*] I follow the translation of the learned Rev. G. C. Renouard.

[†] The Rev. G. C. Renouard, in interpreting this passage, has evidently made a mistake in translating "the Minister *of the* Sultan," and adding in a note that Emír "is here a title given to the Emír el Núr," while it is to be referred to the sultan himself.

[‡] By the expression "el fókarah" the sultan certainly meant us, who were not travelling for trading purposes, but rather like dervishes.

merciful and answereth prayer! Come therefore to us; and we will tuck up our sleeves*, and drive away the marauders, and fight valiantly against them as God (be He glorified!) hath commanded.

"Lo, corruption hath multiplied on the face of the earth. May the Lord not question us on account of the poor and needy, orphans and widows, according to His word:— 'You are all herdsmen, and ye shall all be questioned respecting your herds, whether ye have indeed taken good care of them or dried them up.'

"Delay not, therefore, but hasten to our residence where we are all assembled; for 'zeal in the cause of religion is the duty of all;' or send thy messenger to us quickly with a positive answer; send thy messenger as soon as possible. Farewell."

The whole population was in alarm; and everybody who was able to bear arms prepared for the expedition. About sunset the "égehen" left the town, numbering about four hundred men, partly on camels, partly on horseback, besides the people on foot. Bóro as well as A'shu accompanied the sultan, who this time was himself mounted on a camel. They went to take their encampment near that of Astáfidet, in Tagúrast, 'Abd el Káder pitching a tent of grey colour, and in size like that of a Turkish aghá, in the midst of the Kél-geres, the Kél-ferwán, and the Emgedesíye, while Astáfidet, who had no tent, was surrounded by the Kél-owí. The sultan was kind and attentive enough not to forget me even now; and having heard that I had not yet departed, Hámma not having finished his business in the town, he sent me some wheat,

---

* All the tribes in Central Africa, who wear the large tobes or shirts, tuck their sleeves up when about to undertake any work, or going to fight.

a large botta with butter and vegetables (chiefly melons and cucumbers), and the promise of another sheep.

In the evening the drummer again went his rounds through the town, proclaiming the strict order of the sultan that everybody should lay in a large supply of provisions. Although the town in general had become very silent when deserted by so many people, our house was kept in constant bustle; and in the course of the night three mehára came from the camp, with people who could get no supper there and sought it with us. Bóro sent a messenger to me early the next morning, urgently begging for a little powder, as the " Mehárebín" of the Imghád had sent off their camels and other property, and were determined to resist the army of the sultan. However, I could send him but very little. My amusing friend Mohammed spent the whole day with us, when he went to join the ghazzia. I afterwards learnt that he obtained four head of cattle as his share. There must be considerable herds of cattle in the more favoured valleys of Asben; for the expedition had nothing else to live upon, as Mohammed afterwards informed me, and slaughtered an immense quantity of them. Altogether the expedition was successful; and the Fádëang and many tribes of the Imghád lost almost all their property. Even the influential Háj Beshír was punished, on account of his son's having taken part in the expedition against us. I received also the satisfactory information that 'Abd el Káder had taken

nine camels from the man who retained my méheri;
but I gained nothing thereby, neither my own camel
being returned nor another given me in its stead.
The case was the same with all our things; but nevertheless the proceeding had a good effect, seeing that
people were punished expressly for having robbed
Christians, and thus the principle was established
that it was not less illegal to rob Christians than it
was to rob Mohammedans, both creeds being placed,
as far as regards the obligations of peace and honesty,
on equally favourable terms.

I spent the whole of Tuesday in my house, principally in taking down information which I received
from the intelligent Ghadámsi merchant Mohammed,
who, having left his native town from fear of the
Turks, had resided six years in A'gades, and was a
well-informed man.

My old friend the blacksmith Hámmeda, Wednesday,
and the tall Elíyas, went off this morning October 23rd.
with several camels laden with provision, while
Hámma still staid behind to finish the purchases;
for on account of the expedition, and the insecure
state of the road to Damerghú, it had been difficult
to procure provisions in sufficient quantity. Our
house therefore became almost as silent and desolate as the rest of the town; but I found a great
advantage in remaining a few days longer, for my
chivalrous friend and protector, who, as long as the
sultan and the great men were present, had been
very reserved and cautious, had now no further

scruple about taking me everywhere, and showing me the town " within and without."

We first visited the house of I'dder, a broker, who lived at a short distance to the south from our house, and had also lodged Háj 'Abdúwa during his stay here.

It was a large spacious dwelling, well arranged with a view to comfort and privacy, according to the conceptions and customs of the inhabitants, while our house (being a mere temporary re-sidence for A'nnur's people occasionally visiting the town) was a dirty, comfortless abode. We entered first a vestibule, about twenty-five feet long and nine broad, having on each side a separate space marked off by that low kind of balustrade mentioned in my description of the sultan's house. This vestibule or ante-room was followed by a second room of larger size and irregular arrangement ; opposite the entrance it opened into another apartment which, with two doors, led into a spacious inner courtyard, which was very irregularly circumscribed by several rooms projecting into it, while to the left it was occupied by an enor-mous bedstead (1). These bedsteads are a most cha-racteristic article of furniture in all the dwellings of the Sónghay. In A'gades they are generally very so-lidly built of thick boards, and furnished with a strong canopy resting upon four posts, covered with mats on the top and on three sides, the remaining side being shut in with boards. Such a canopied bed looks like a little house by itself. On the wall of the first

chamber, which on the right projected into the courtyard, several lines of large pots had been arranged,
one above the other (2), forming so many warm nests
for a number of turtle-doves which were playing all
about the courtyard, while on the left, in the half-
decayed walls of two other rooms (3), about a dozen
goats were fastened each to a separate pole. The
background of the courtyard contained several rooms;
and in front of it a large shade (4) had been built of
mats, forming a rather pleasant and cool resting-
place. Numbers of children were gambolling about,
and gave to the whole a very cheerful appearance.
There is something very peculiar in these houses,
which are constructed evidently with a view to comfort and quiet enjoyment.

We then went to visit a female friend of Hámma,
who lived in the south quarter of the town, in a house
which likewise bespoke much comfort; but here, on
account of the number of inmates, the arrangement
was different, the second vestibule being furnished
on each side with a large bedstead instead of mats,
though here also there was in the courtyard an
immense bedstead. The courtyard was comparatively
small, and a long corridor on the left of it led to an
inner courtyard or "tsakangída," which I was not
allowed to see. The mistress of the house was still a
very comely person, although she had born several
children. She had a fine figure, though rather under
the middle size, and a fair complexion. I may here
remark that many of the women of A'gades are not

a shade darker than Arab women in general. She
wore a great quantity of silver ornaments, and was
well dressed in a gown of coloured cotton and silk.
Hámma was very intimate with her, and introduced
me to her as his friend and protégé, whom she ought
to value as highly as himself. She was married ; but
her husband was residing in Kátsena, and she did not
seem to await his return in the Penelopean style.
The house had as many as twenty inmates, there
being no less than six children, I think, under five
years of age, and among them a very handsome little
girl, the mother's favourite ; besides, there were six
or seven full-grown slaves.* The children were all
naked, but wore ornaments of beads and silver.

After we had taken leave of this Emgedesíye lady,
we followed the street towards the south, where there
were some very good houses, although the quarter in
general was in ruins ; and here I saw the very best
and most comfortable-looking dwelling in the town.
All the pinnacles were ornamented with ostrich-eggs.
One will often find in an eastern town, after the first
impression of its desolate appearance is gone by, many
proofs that the period of its utter prostration is not
yet come, but that even in the midst of the ruins there

* Leo, in the interesting description which he gives of this
town, l. vii. c. 9., expressly praises the size and architecture of the
houses : "Le case sono benissimo edificate a modo delle case di
Barberia." He also speaks here of the great number of male slaves
whom the merchants were obliged to keep, in order to protect
themselves on the roads to Negroland.

is still a good deal of ease and comfort.   Among the
ruins of the southern quarter are to be seen the pinnacled walls of a building of immense circumference
and considerable elevation ; but unfortunately I could
not learn from Hámma for what purpose it had been
used : however, it was certainly a public building, and
probably a large khán rather than the residence of the
chief.*   With its high, towering walls, it still forms a
sort of outwork on the south side of the town, where
in general the wall is entirely destroyed, and the way
is everywhere open.   Hámma had a great prejudice
against this desolate quarter.   Even the more intelligent Mohammedans are often afraid to enter former
dwelling-places of men, believing them to be haunted
by spirits; but he took me to some inhabited houses,
which were all built on the same principle as that described, but varying greatly in depth, and in the size
of the courtyard ; the staircases (abi-n-háwa) leading
to the upper story are in the courtyard, and are
rather irregularly built of stones and clay.   In some
of them young ostriches were running about.   The
inhabitants of all the houses seemed to have the same
cheerful disposition ; and I was glad to find scarcely a
single instance of misery.   I give here the ground-
plan of another house.

* From Leo's description, l. vii. c. 9., it would appear that the
palace of the sultan in former times was in the middle of the town
— "un bel palazzo in mezzo della città."   He kept a numerous
host of soldiers.

The artisans who work in leather (an occupation left entirely to females) seem to
live in a quarter by themselves, which originally was quite separated from the rest of
the town by a sort of gate; but I did not
make a sufficient survey of this quarter to mark it
distinctly in the ground-plan of the town. We also
visited some of the mat makers.

Our maimólo of the other day, who had discovered
that we had slaughtered our sheep, paid us a visit in
the evening, and for a piece of meat entertained me
with a clever performance on his instrument, accompanied with a song. Hámma spent his evening with
our friend the Emgedesíye lady, and was kind enough
to beg me to accompany him. This I declined, but
gave him a small present to take to her.

I had a fair sample of the state of morals in A'gades
the following day, when five or six girls and women
came to pay me a visit in our house, and with much
simplicity invited me to make merry with them, there
being now, as they said, no longer reason for reserve,
" as the sultan was gone." It was indeed rather
amusing to see what conclusions they drew from the
motto, " serkí yátafi." Two of them were tolerably.
pretty and well-formed, with fine black hair hanging
down in plaits or tresses, lively eyes, and very fair
complexion. Their dress was decent, and that of one
of them even elegant, consisting of an under gown
reaching from the neck to the ankles, and an upper
one drawn over the head, both of white colour ; but

their demeanour was very free, and I too clearly understood the caution requisite in a European who would pass through these countries unharmed and respected by the natives, to allow myself to be tempted by these wantons. It would be better for a traveller in these regions, both for his own comfort, and for the respect felt for him by the natives, if he could take his wife with him ; for these simple people do not understand how a man can live without a partner. The Western Tawárek, who in general are very rigorous in their manners, and quite unlike the Kél-owí, had nothing to object against me except my being a bachelor. But as it is difficult to find a female companion for such journeys, and as by marrying a native he would expose himself to much trouble and inconvenience on the score of religion, he will do best to maintain the greatest austerity of manners with regard to the other sex, though he may thereby expose himself to a good deal of derision from some of the lighter-hearted natives. The ladies, however, became so troublesome that I thought it best to remain at home for a few days, and was thus enabled at the same time to note down the information which I had been able to pick up. During these occupations I was always greatly pleased with the companionship of a diminutive species of finches which frequent all the rooms in A'gades, and, as I may add from later experience, in Timbúktu also ; the male, with its red neck, in particular looks extremely pretty. The poults were just about to fledge.

There was one very characteristic building in the town, which though a most
conspicuous object from the terrace of our house, I had
never yet investigated with sufficient accuracy.   This
was the mesállaje, or high tower rising over the roof
of the mosque.   The reason why this building in particular (the most famous and remarkable one in the
town) had been hitherto observed by me only from a
distance, and in passing by, must be obvious.   Difference of religious creed repelled me from it; and so long
as the town was full of strangers, some of them very
fanatical, it was dangerous for me to approach it too
closely.   I had often inquired whether it would not
be possible to ascend the tower without entering the
mosque; but I had always received for answer, that
the entrance was locked up.   As soon, however, as the
sultan was gone, and when the town became rather
quiet, I urged Hámma to do his best that I might
ascend to the top of this curious building, which I
represented to him as a matter of the utmost
importance to me, since it would enable me not
only to control my route by taking a few angles
of the principal elevations round the valley Aúderas,
but also to obtain a distant view over the country
towards the west and south, which it was not my
good luck to visit myself.   To-day Hámma promised
me that he would try what could be done.

Having once more visited the lively house of
I'dder, we took our way over the market-places, which
were now rather dull.   The vultures looked out with

visible greediness and eagerness from the pinnacles of the ruined walls around for their wonted food— their share of offal during these days, when so many people were absent, being of course much reduced, though some of them probably had followed their fellow-citizens on the expedition. So few people being in the streets, the town had a more ruined look than ever; and the large heap of rubbish accumulated on the south side of the butchers' market seemed to me more disgusting than before. We kept along the principal street between Dígi and Arrafíya, passing the deep well Shedwánka on our right, and on the other side a school, which resounded with the shrill voices of about fifty little boys repeating with energy and enthusiasm the verses of the Kurán, which their master had written for them upon their little wooden tablets.

Having reached the open space in front of the mosque ("súrari-n-mesállaje"), and there being no-body to disturb me, I could view at my leisure this simple but curious building, which in the subsequent course of my journey became still more interesting to me, as I saw plainly that it was built on exactly the same principle as the tower which rises over the sepulchre of the famed conqueror Háj Mohammed A'skiá (the "Ischia" of Leo).

The Mesállaje starts up from the platform or terrace formed by the roof of the mosque, which is extremely low, resting apparently, as we shall see, in its interior, upon four massive pillars. It is square, and measures at its base about thirty feet, having a small lean-to, on its east side, on the terrace of the mosque, where most probably there was formerly the entrance. From this the tower rises (decreasing in width, and with a sort of swelling or entasis in the middle of its eleva-

tion, something like the beautiful model adopted by nature in the deléb palm, and imitated by architects in the columns of the Ionic and Corinthian orders) to a height of from ninety to ninety-five feet. It measures at its summit not more than about eight feet in width. The interior is lighted by seven openings on each side. Like most of the houses in A'gades, it is built entirely of clay ; and in order to strengthen a building so lofty and of so soft a material, its four walls are united by thirteen layers of boards of the dúm-tree crossing the whole tower in its entire breadth and width, and coming out on each side from three to four feet, while at the same time they afford

the only means of getting to the top. Its purpose is
to serve as a watch-tower, or at least was so at a
former time, when the town, surrounded by a strong
wall and supplied with water, was well capable of
making resistance, if warned in due time of an
approaching danger. But at present it seems rather
to be kept in repair only as a decoration of the town.

The Mesállaje in its present state was only six years
old at the time of my visit (in 1850), and perhaps
was not even quite finished in the interior, as I was
told that the layers of boards were originally intended
to support a staircase of clay. About fifty paces
from the south-western corner of the mosque, the
ruins of an older tower are seen still rising to a considerable height, though leaning much to one side,
more so than the celebrated tower of Pisa, and
most probably in a few years it will give way to an
attack of storm and rain. This more ancient tower
seems to have stood quite detached from the mosque.

Having sufficiently surveyed the exterior of the
tower, and made a sketch of it, I accompanied my
impatient companion into the interior of the mosque,
into which he felt no scruple in conducting me. The
lowness of the structure had already surprised me
from without; but I was still more astonished when I
entered the interior, and saw that it consisted of low,
narrow naves divided by pillars of immense thickness,
the reason of which it is not possible at present to
understand, as they have nothing to support but a
roof of dúm-tree boards, mats, and a layer of clay;

but I think it scarcely doubtful that originally these naves were but the vaults or cellars of a grander superstructure, designed but not executed; and this conjecture seems to be confirmed by all that at present remains of the mosque. The gloomy halls were buried in a mournful silence, interrupted only by the voice of a solitary man, seated on a dirty mat at the western wall of the tower, and reading diligently the torn leaves of a manuscript. Seeing that it was the kádhi, we went up to him and saluted him most respectfully; but it was not in the most cheerful and amiable way that he received our compliments — mine in particular — continuing to read, and scarcely raising his eyes from the sheets before him.* Hámma then asked for permission to ascend the tower, but received a plain and unmistakeable refusal, the thing being impossible, there being no entrance to the tower at present. It was shut up, he said, on account of the Kél-gerés, who used to ascend the tower in great numbers. Displeased with his uncourteous behaviour, and seeing that he was determined not to permit me to climb the tower, were it ever so feasible, we withdrew and called upon the imám, who lives in a house attached to these vaults, and which looked a little neater from having been white-

---

* The hostile disposition of the kádhi towards me was most unfortunate, as he would have been the very man to give me the information I wanted; for I did not meet any other native of the place well versed in Arabic literature, and but a few were able to speak Arabic at all.

washed; however, he had no power to aid us in our purpose, but rather confirmed the statement of the kádhi.

This is the principal mosque of the town, and seems to have always been so, although there are said to have been formerly as many as seventy mosques, of which ten are still in use. They deserve no mention, however, with the exception of three, the Msíd Míli*, Msíd E'heni, and Msíd el Mékki. I will only add here that the Emgedesíye, so far as their very slender stock of theological learning and doctrine entitles them to rank with any sect, are Malekíye, as well as the Kél-owí.

Resigning myself to the disappointment of not being able to ascend the tower, I persuaded my friend to take a longer walk with me round the northern quarter of the town. But I forgot to mention that besides Hámma I had another companion of a very different character. This was Zúmmuzuk, a reprobate of the worst description, and whose features bore distinct impress of the vile and brutal passions which actuated him; yet being a clever fellow, and (as the illegitimate son, or " dan néma," of an Emgédesi woman) fully master of the peculiar idiom of A'gades, he was tolerated not only by the old chief A'nnur, who employed him as interpreter, but even by me.

---

* Whether this name be a corruption of Mghíli, meaning the fanatical Mohammedan apostle Mohammed ben 'Abd el Kerím el Maghíli, of whom I have spoken above, I cannot say.

How insolent the knave could be, I shall soon have occasion to mention.

With this fellow, therefore, and with Hámma, I continued my walk, passing the kófa-n-alkáli, and then, from the ruins of the quarter Ben-Gottára, turning to the north. Here the wall of the town is in a tolerable state of preservation, but very weak and insufficient, though it is kept in repair, even to the pinnacles, on account of its surrounding the palace of the sultan. Not far from this is an open space called Azarmádarangh, " the place of execution," where occasionally the head of a rebellious chieftain or a murderer is cut off by the " dóka; " but as far as I could learn, such things happen very seldom. Even on the north side, two gates are in a tolerable state of preservation.

Having entered the town from this side, we went to visit the quarter of the leather-workers, which, as I stated before, seems to have formed originally a regular ward; all this handicraft, with the exception of saddlework, is carried on by women, who work with great neatness. Very beautiful provision-bags are made here, although those which I brought back from Timbúktu are much handsomer. We saw also some fine specimens of mats, woven of a very soft kind of grass, and dyed of various colours. Unfortunately, I had but little with me wherewith to buy; and even if I had been able to make purchases, the destination of our journey being so distant, there was not much hope of carrying the things safe to Europe. The blacksmiths' work of A'gades is also interesting, although showy and barbarous, and not unlike the work with which the Spaniards used to adorn their long daggers.

During all this time I prosecuted in- Monday,
quiries with regard to several subjects October 28th.
connected with the geography and ethnography of this quarter of the world. I received several visits from Emgédesi tradesmen, many of whom are established in the northern provinces of Háusa, chiefly in Kátsena and Tasáwa, where living is infinitely cheaper than in A'gades. All these I found to be intelligent men, having been brought up in the centre of intercourse between a variety of tribes and nations of the most different organization, and, through the web of routes which join here, receiving information of distant regions. Several of them had even made the Pilgrimage, and thus come in contact with the relatively high state of civilization in Egypt and near the coast; and I shall not easily forget the enlightened view which the màllem Háj Mohammed 'Omár, who visited me several times, took of Islámism and Christianity. The last day of my stay in A'gades, he reverted to the subject of religion, and asked me, in a manner fully expressive of his astonishment, how it came to pass that the Christians and Moslemín were so fiercely opposed to one another, although their creeds, in essential principles, approximated so closely. To this I replied by saying that I thought the reason was that the great majority

both of Christians and Moslemín paid less regard to
the dogmas of their creeds than to external matters,
which have very little or no reference to religion
itself. I also tried to explain to him, that in the
time of Mohammed Christianity had entirely lost that
purity which was its original character, and that it
had been mixed up with many idolatrous elements,
from which it was not entirely disengaged till a few
centuries ago, while the Mohammedans had scarcely
any acquaintance with Christians except those of the
old sects of the Jacobites and Nestorians. Mutually
pleased with our conversation, we parted from each
other with regret.

In the afternoon I was agreeably surprised by the
arrival of the Tinýlkum Ibrahim, for the purpose of
supplying his brother's house with what was wanted;
and being determined to make only one day's stay
in the town, he had learned with pleasure that we
were about to return by way of A'fasás, the village
whither he himself was going. I myself had cherished this hope, as all the people had represented
that place as one of the largest in the country, and
as pleasantly situated. Hámma had promised to take
me this way on our return to Tintéllust; but having
stayed so much longer in the town than he had intended, and being afraid of arriving too late for the
salt-caravan of the Kél-owí on their way to Bilma,
which he was to supply with provisions, he changed
his plan, and determined to return by the shortest
road. Meanwhile he informed me that the old chief

would certainly not go with us to Zínder till the salt-caravan had returned from Bilma.

Fortunately, in the course of the 29th a small caravan with corn arrived from Damerghú; and Hámma completed his purchases.   He had, however, first to settle a disagreeable affair; for our friend Zúmmuzuk had bought in Hámma's name several things, for which payment was now demanded. Hámma flew into a terrible rage, and nearly finished the rogue.   My Arab and Tawáti friends, who heard that we were to start the following day, though they were rather busy buying corn, came to take leave of me; and I was glad to part from all of them in friendship.   But before bidding farewell to this interesting place, I shall make a few general observations on its history.

CHAP. XVIII.

HISTORY OF A'GADES.

IF we had before us the historical work upon the authority of which Mohammed el Bágeri assured Sultan Bello that the people of Góber, who formerly possessed the country of A'ír, were Copts*, we should most probably find in it the history of A'gades. As it is, however, until that book shall come to light, of which I do not at all despair, provided future travel-lers inquire diligently for it, we must be content with endeavouring to concentrate the faint and few rays of light which dimly reveal to us, in its principal features, the history of this remarkable town.

Previously to Mr. Cooley's perspicuous inquiries into the Negroland of the Arabs, this place was identified with Aúdaghost, merely on account of a supposed similarity of name. But A'gades, or rather E'gedesh, is itself a pure Berber word, in no way connected with Aúdaghost. It is of very frequent occurrence, particularly among the Awelímmiden, and means " family ;" and the name was well chosen for a town consisting of mixed elements. Moreover,

* Sultan Bello's " Enfák el Misúri fi taríkh belád el Tekrúri," in Denham and Clapperton's Travels, Appendix, vol. ii. p. 162.   I myself have a copy of the same extracts from this work of Bello.

while we find Aúdaghost in the far west in the 12th
century, we have the distinct statement of Marmol *,
that A'gades was founded a hundred and sixty years
before the time when he wrote (that is to say, in 1460),
the truth of which statement, harmonizing as it does
with Leo's more general account, that it was a modern
town †, we have no reason to doubt. Neither of these
authors tells us who built it; but as we know that
the great Sónghay conqueror Háj Mohammed A'skiá,
who conquered the town of A'gades in the year of the
Hejra 921, or 1515 of our era ‡, expelled from it the
five Berber tribes who, according to the information
collected by me during my stay in A'gades, and which
I shall soon lay before my readers, must have been
long resident in the town, it appears highly probable
that these Berbers were its founders. And if this be
assumed, there will be no difficulty in explaining why
the language of the natives of the place at present is
a dialect of the Sónghay language, as it is most probable that that great and enlightened conqueror, after
he had driven out the old inhabitants, established in

* Marmol, Descripcion dell' Africa, vol. iii. fl. xxiv. b. : " Agadez es una provincia . . . ay en ella una ciudad del proprio
nombre, que a sido edificada de ciento y sesenta años a este parte."

† Leo Africanus, l. vii. c. 9. : "Edificata dai moderni re (?) ne'
confini di Libia." The word " re " is very suspicious.

‡ See the extracts of Bábá Ahmed's " Taríkh e' Sudán," sent
by me to Europe, and published in the Journal of the German
Oriental Society, 1855. This statement agrees exactly with an
interesting passage in Sultan Bello's "Enfák el Misúri," which
has been unaccountably omitted by Saláme in the translation ap-
pended to Denham and Clapperton's Travels.

this important place a new colony of his own people. In a similar way we find the Sónghay nation, which seems not to have originally extended to a great distance eastward of Gágho or Gógo, now extending into the very heart of Kébbi, although we shall find other people speaking the same language in the neighbourhood of A'gades, and perhaps may be able in the course of our researches to trace some connection between the Sónghay and ancient Egypt.

It is therefore highly probable that those five Berber tribes formed the settlement in question as an entrepôt for their commerce with Negroland, though the foundation of such a grand settlement on the border of the desert presumes that they had at that time a preponderating influence in all these regions; and the whole affair is so peculiar, that its history could not fail to gratify curiosity if more could be known of it. From Bello's account, it would appear that they, or at least one of these tribes (the Aújila*), conquered the whole of A'ír.

It is certainly remarkable to see people from five places separated from each other by immense tracts, and united only by the bond of commerce and in-

---

* Bello took an erroneous view of the subject in supposing all the five tribes to have come from Aújila. Only one of them was originally from that place; and the names of the five tribes as mentioned by him are evidently erroneous. (See the following note.) The error in deriving all these five tribes from Aújila originated, probably, in the general tradition that the whole nation of the Berbers had spread over North Africa from Syria by way of the oasis of Aújila.

terest, founding a large colony far away from their homes, and on the very border of the desert. For, according to all that I could learn by the most sedulous inquiries in A'gades, those tribes belonged to the Gurára of Tawát, to the Tafimáta, to the Beni Wazít, and the Tésko of Ghadámes, to the once powerful and numerous tribe of the Masráta, and finally to the Aújila; and as the names of almost all these different tribes, and of their divisions, are still attached to localities of the town, we can scarcely doubt the correctness of this information, and must suppose that Sultan Bello was mistaken in referring the five tribes (settled in A'gades) to Aújila alone.*

Though nothing is related about the manner in which Háj Mohammed A'skiá took possession of the town †, except that it is stated distinctly that he

* Bello, in Appendix to Denham and Clapperton's Travels, vol. ii. p. 160. Indeed in this passage he does not mention distinctly A'gades, but speaks in general of the province of Ahír (A'ír); it is clear, however, that the five tribes mentioned here as having wrested the whole country from the hands of the Goberáwa are identical with those settled in A'gades. Bello, in this case, was evidently ill-informed, for Amákitan seems not to be the name of a tribe, but of a man; Ajdaranin is the name of a section of the Kél-gerés; the Agdálar seem to be identical with the I'ghdalén. Certainly the Aújila were a most celebrated tribe ; and it appears from Edrísi's report (Jaubert, vol. i. p. 238.), that even at so early an age as the middle of the 12th century of our era they carried on intercourse with Kawár and Gógo by way of Ghadámes.

† A'hmed Bábá, in relating this most interesting expedition of the greatest hero of his historical work, is most provokingly brief ; but the reason is, that he was well acquainted only with the countries near Timbúktu.

drove out the five tribes, it seems, from the traditions current in A'gades, that a considerable number of the Berbers, with five hundred " jákhfa " (cages mounted on camels, such as only wealthy people can afford to keep for carrying their wives), left the town, but were all massacred. But no one who regards with the least attention the character of the present population of the town, can doubt for a moment that a considerable number of the Berber population remained behind, and in course of time mixed with the Sónghay colonists ; for, even if we set aside the consideration of the language (which is greatly intermixed with Berber words), there is evidently much Berber blood in the population even at the present day,—a fact which is more evident in the females than in the males.

It is a pity that Leo says nothing about the language spoken in A'gades * ; for he lived just at the very period during which the town, from a Berber settlement, became a Negro town. His expression † certainly implies that he regarded it as a Negro town. But, while well-informed in general respecting the great conquests of Mohammed A'skiá

---

* In the Report which I sent to Government from my journey, and which has been printed in the Journal of the Royal Geographical Society, I stated, that according to Leo's account the Háusa language was spoken at that time in A'gades; but it was a mere lapse of memory. From no passage of his can any conclusion be drawn with regard to this subject.

† " E questa città è quasi vicina alla città dei Bianchi piú che alcun' altra de' Negri."

(or, as he calls him, Ischia, whom he erroneously
styles king of Timbúktu), he does not once mention
his expedition against A'gades, of which he might
have heard as easily as of those against Kátsena and
Kanó, which preceded the former only by two years.
From his account it would seem that the town was
then in a very flourishing state, full of foreign merchants and slaves, and that the king, though he paid
a tribute of 150,000 ducats to the king of Timbúktu
(Gágho), enjoyed a great degree of independence, at
least from that quarter, and had even a military force
of his own.   Besides, it is stated expressly that he belonged to the Berber race.* But it would almost seem
as if Leo in this passage represented the state of things
as it was when he visited the town, before A'skiá's time,
and not at the date when he wrote, though the circumstance of the tribute payable to that king may have been
learnt from later information.   In general, the great
defect in Leo's description is, that the reader has no
exact dates to which to refer the several statements,
and that he cannot be sure how far the author speaks
as an eye-witness, and how far from information.†

* Leo, l. vii. c. 9., et l. i. c. 10. near the end.

† What Leo says, l. vii. c. 1., of Abubakr Ischia (that is to
say, Mohammed ben Abú Bakr el Háj A'skiá)— " Acquistando in
anni quindici appresso molti regni, e poichè ebbe reso pacifico e
quieto il suo, gli venne disio di andar come pellegrino a Mecca "—
is very confused; for Mohammed A'skiá, having ascended the
throne on the 14th of Jumád II. 898, began the pilgrimage in
Safer, 902, consequently in the fifth year of his reign; yet Leo
received information of his expedition against Kátsena and the
adjoining provinces, which was made in 919.

Of course it is possible that the Berbers found a Sónghay population, if not in the place itself, which most probably did not exist before the time of their arrival, yet in the district around it; and it would seem that there existed in ancient times, in the celebrated valley of I'r-n-allem, a small town, of which* some vestiges are said to remain at the present day, as well as two or three date-trees—the solitary remains of a large plantation. From this town, tradition says, the present inhabitants of A'gades were transplanted. But be this as it may, it is certain that the same dialect of the Sónghay language which is spoken in A'gades, is also still spoken in a few places in the neighbourhood, by the tribe of the I'ghdalén, or Ighedálen, whose whole appearance, especially their long hair, shows them to be a mixed race of Sónghay and Berbers; and there is some reason to suppose that they belonged originally to the Zenága or Senhája. These people live in and around I'ngal, a small town four days' journey from A'gades, on the road to Sókoto †, and in and around Tegídda, a place three days' journey from I'ngal, and about five from A'gades W.S.W. This latter place is of considerable interest, being evidently identical with the town of the same name mentioned by E'bn Khaldún‡ and by E'bn Batúta§ as

---

* See itinerary in the Appendix.　　† See Appendix.

‡ E'bn Khaldún, ed. Slane, Alger. 1847, tom. i. p. 267.　E'bn Khaldún evidently says that the chief of Tegídda had friendly intercourse with Wárgela and Mzáb, although Mr. Cooley (Negroland, p. 65.) has referred these expressions to Músa, the king of Sónghay.

§ E'bn Batúta in the passage referred to above.　It is curious

a wealthy place, lying eastward from Gógo, on the
road to Egypt, and in intimate connection and friendly
intercourse with the Mzáb and Wárgela. It was governed by a Berber chief, with the title of sultan.
This place, too, was for some time subject to Gógo, or
rather to the empire of Mélle or Máli, which then comprised Sónghay, in the latter part of the 14th century;
and the circumstance that here too the Sónghay
language is still spoken may be best explained by
referring it to colonization, since it is evident that
A'skiá, when he took possession of A'gades, must
have occupied Tegídda also, which lay on the road
from Gógo to that place. However, I will not indulge in conjectures, and will merely enter into historical questions so far as they contribute to furnish
a vivid and coherent picture of the tribes and countries with which my journey brought me into contact.
I will therefore only add, that this place, Tegídda or
Tekádda, was famous, in the time of Ebn Batúta, for
its copper-mines, the ores of which were exported as
far as Bórnu and Góber, while at present nothing is
known of the existence of copper hereabouts; but a
very good species of salt of red colour (já-n-gísherí),
which is far superior to that of Bílma, is obtained
here, as well as in I'ngal. But I recommend this
point to the inquiry of future travellers. I have

that both these writers give the exact distance of Tegídda from
Búda, in Tawát, and from Wárgela, both distances as of seventy
marches, while they omit to mention its distance from Gógo.

mentioned above the presence of loadstone on the border of A'ír.

Having thus attempted to elucidate and illustrate the remarkable fact, that the language of A'gades is derived from and akin to the Sónghay,—a fact which of course appeared to me more surprising before I discovered, in the course of 1853, that this language extends eastward far beyond the so-called Niger,—I return once more to the settlement of the Berbers in A'gades. It is evident that this settlement, if it was of the nature described above, was made for the purpose of serving as a great commercial entrepôt for the commerce with another country; and if we duly consider the statements made by El Bekri *, Ebn Batúta †, Leo ‡, Ca da Mosto §, and by the author of the "History of Sónghay," with regard to the importance of the market of Gógo, and if we pay due attention to that circuitous route which led from Gógo by way of Tegídda not only to Egypt, but even to Tawát ‖, there cannot be the least doubt that

* El Bekri, "Notices et Extraits," tom. xii. p. 649.

† Ebn Batúta repeatedly calls it the largest, handsomest, and strongest of all the cities in Negroland.

‡ Leo, l. vii. c. 7.

§ Navigazioni di Aloise Ca da Mosto, c. 13.: "La prima parte di loro va con la carovana che tiene il cammino di Melli ad un luogo che si chiama Cochia."

‖ We shall see, in the further course of our proceedings, that there is another direct road from Gógo to Tawát; but this, in ancient times, seems not to have been frequented, on account either of the difficulties of the road itself, or the dangerous character of the tribes in its vicinity.

A'gades was founded by those Berber tribes, with the distinct purpose that it might serve them as a secure abode and fortified magazine in their commercial intercourse with that splendid capital of the Sónghay empire, the principal article of which was gold, which formed also the chief article in the former commerce of A'gades. For A'gades had its own standard weight of this precious metal,—the mithkál, which even at the present day regulates the circulating medium. And this mithkál of A'gades is totally different from the standard of the same name which is in use in Timbúktu, the latter being, in regard to the value of the Spanish dollar, as 1½ to 1, and the former only as ⅔ to 1. But for wholesale business a greater weight was in use, called "kárruwe," the smaller kárruwe containing thirty-three mithákel or mithkals and a third, equal to two rottls and a sixth, while the larger kárruwe contained a hundred mithkals, and was equal to six rottls and a half.

The importance of the trade of A'gades, and the wealth of the place in general, appear very clearly from the large tribute, of a hundred and fifty thousand ducats, which the king of A'gades was able to pay to that of Sónghay, especially if we bear in mind that Leo, in order to give an idea of the great expense which this same king of Sónghay had incurred on his prilgrimage to Mekka, states in another passage* that having spent all he took with him, he contracted a debt amounting

* Leo, l. vii. c. 1.: "E rimase debitore di centocinquanta mila ducati."

to that very sum. As for the king of A'gades, his situation was at that time just what it is now; and we cannot better describe his precarious position, entirely dependent on the caprice and intrigues of the influential chiefs of the Tawárek, than by using the very words of Leo, " Alle volte scacciano il re e pongono qualche suo parente in luogo di lui, nè usano ammazzar alcuno; e quel che più contenta gli abitatori del diserto è fatto re in Agadez."

Unfortunately, we are not able to fix a date for that very peculiar covenant between the different tribes with regard to the installation of the sultan of A'gades, and the establishing of the principle that he must belong to a certain family, which is regarded as of sheríf nobility *, and lives not in A'gades, nor even in the country of A'ír, but in a town of Góber. I was once inclined to think that this was an arrangement made in consequence of the power and influence which the Emír of Sókoto had arrogated to himself; but I have now reason to doubt this, for even the grandfather of 'Abd el Káder was sultan. Certainly even now, when the power of the Fulfúlde or Féllani empire is fast crumbling to pieces, the Emír of Sókoto has a certain influence upon the choice of the sultan of A'gades. Of this fact I myself became witness during my stay in Sókoto in April 1853, when Hámed e' Rufäy was once more sent out to succeed 'Abd el Káder.

---

* Whether the story which circulates among the people, that this family originally came from Stambúl or Constantinople has any reasonable foundation, I am unable to decide.

Indeed Ittegáma, 'Abd el Káder's brother, who thought that I enjoyed the favour and confidence of the Emír, called upon me (as I shall relate in due time) expressly in order to entreat me most urgently to exert my influence in order to restore my former host to his authority.

I have described already in what way the union of the tribes of the Itísan, the Kél-gerés, and the Kél-owí is expressed in installing the sultan ; but though without the presence and assent of the former the new prince could never arrive at his place of residence, the final decision seems to rest with the chief A'nnur, the inhabitants of the town having no voice in the matter. The sultan is rather a chief of the Tawárek tribes residing in A'gades than the ruler of A'gades. How difficult and precarious his position must be, may be easily conceived if it be considered that these tribes are generally at war with one another ; the father of Hámed e' Rufäy was even killed by the Kél-gerés. Nevertheless, if he be an intelligent and energetic man, his influence in the midst of this wild conflict and struggle of clashing interests and inclinations must be very beneficial.

What the revenue of the sultan may at present amount to, it is difficult to say. His means and income consist chiefly in the presents which he receives on his accession to authority, in a contribution of one bullock's hide or kulábu (being about the value of half a Spanish dollar) from each family, in a more considerable but rather uncertain tribute levied upon the Imghád, in the tax of ten mithkáls or four Spanish dollars which he levies on each camel-load of foreign merchandise which enters the town of A'gades * (articles of food being exempt from charge), in a small tribute derived from the salt brought from Bílma, and in the fines levied on lawless people and marauders, and often on whole tribes. Thus it is very probable that the expedition which 'Abd el Káder undertook immediately after his accession, against the tribes who had plundered us, enriched him considerably. As for the inhabitants of A'gades themselves, I was assured that they do not pay him any tribute at all, but are obliged only to accompany him on his expeditions. Of course in earlier times, when the commerce of the town was infinitely greater than at present, and when the Imghád (who had to provide him with cattle, corn, fruit, and vegetables) were strictly obedient, his income far exceeded that of the present day. When taken altogether it is certainly considerably under twenty thousand dollars. His title is Amanókal, or Amanókal Imakóren, in Temáshight, Kókoy† bére in

* This seems also to have been the most important income in the time of Leo: "Riceve il re gran rendita delle gabelle che pagano le robe de' forestieri."

† In the Sónghay language " koy" means master, and is not only employed in other compositions, such as kút-koy (the shepherd), bír-koy (the marksman), but even as title for a governor, such as Túmbutu-koy (the governor of Timbúktu), Jínni-koy (the governor of Jínni). I therefore conclude that kó-koy means the master of the masters, or greatest master — the king of kings, like the Háusa " serkí sárakay."

the Emgédesi, and Babá-n-Serkí, in the Háusa language.

The person second in authority in the town, and in certain respects the vizier, is now, and apparently was also in ancient times, the "kókoy gerégeré"* (i. e. master of the courtyard or the interior of the palace). This is his real indigenous character, while the foreigners, who regarded him only in his relation to themselves, called him sheikh el 'Arab, or, in the Háusa language, serkí-n-turáwa† (the chief of the Whites); and this is the title by which he is generally known. For it was he who had to levy the tax on the merchandise imported into the town,—an office which in former times, when a considerable trade was carried on, was of great importance. But the chief duty of the "serkí-n-turáwa," at the present time, is to accompany annually the salt-caravan of the Kél-gerés, which supplies the western part of Middle Sudán with the salt of Bílma, from A'gades to Sókoto,

---

* Perhaps some might conjecture that this word geré-geré has some connection with the Gér-geri of Ebn Batúta (see above); but I think there is none.

† "Turáwa" is the plural of "ba-túre." "Túre," or "túri," is an old word, already mentioned by Ebn Batúta (Journal Asiatique, 1843, tom. i. p. 201.); "Les hommes blancs, qui professent les doctrines sonnites et suivent le rite de Malik, sont designés ici (dans le royaume de Melle) par le nom de توري " The word, therefore, seems to have been introduced into the Háusa language at a later period as designating the white people, and I think has connection with the word "túra" (to pray) in Fulfúlde, the language of the Fúlbe. I have only to mention that it never refers to any but Arabs or Europeans.

and to protect it on the road as well as to secure it against exorbitant exactions on the part of the Fúlbe of Sókoto. For this trouble he receives one "kántu," that is to say the eighth part (eight kántu weighing three Turkish kantars or quintals) of a middle-sized camel-load, a contribution which forms a considerable income in this country, probably of from eight to ten thousand Spanish dollars, the caravan consisting generally of some thousand camels, not all equally laden, and the kántu of salt fetching in Sudán from five thousand to seven and eight thousand kurdi or shells, which are worth from two to three dollars. Under such circumstances those officers, who at the same time trade on their own account, cannot but amass considerable wealth. Mohammed Bóro as well as A'shu are very rich, considering the circumstances of the country.

After having escorted the salt-caravan to Sókoto, and settled the business with the Emir of this place, the serkí-n-turáwa in former times had to go to Kanó, where he received a small portion of the six hundred kurdí, the duty levied on each slave brought to the slave-market, after which he returned to A'gades with the Kél-gerés that had frequented the market of Kanó. I had full opportunity, in the further course of my journey, to convince myself that such is not now the case; but I cannot say what is the reason of this custom having been discontinued, though it may be the dangerous state of the road between Sókoto and Kanó. Mohammed Bóro, the former serkí-n-turáwa, has still residences as well in Kanó and Zínder as in Sókoto and A'gades.

From what I have said it is clear that at present the serkí-n-turáwa has much more to do with the Tawárek and Fúlbe than with the Arabs, and at the same time is a sort of mediator between A'gades and Sókoto.

Of the other persons in connection with the sultan, the "kókoy kaina" or "bába-n-serkí" * (the chief eunuch), at present A'magay, the fadawa-n-serkí (the aides-de-camp of the sultan), as well as the kádhi or alkáli, and the war-chief Sidi Ghalli, I have spoken in the diary of my residence in the place.

I have already stated above, that the southern part of the town, which at present is almost entirely deserted, formed the oldest quarter, while Katánga, or " báki-n-bírni," seems to have been its northern limit. Within these limits the town was about two miles in circuit, and when thickly peopled, may have contained about thirty thousand inhabitants; but after the northern quarter was added, the whole town had a circuit of about three miles and a half, and may easily have mustered as many as fifty thousand inhabitants, or even more. The highest degree of power seems to have been attained before the conquest of the town by Mohammed A'skiá in the year 1515, though it is

---

* "Kókoy kaina" properly means the little master, a very appropriate term for a eunuch in an Oriental court. The homonymy of bába-n-serkí, the chief eunuch, and babá-n-serkí, the great lord or king, in the Háusa language, is really provoking.

said to have been a considerable and wealthy place till about sixty years ago (reckoned from 1850), when the greatest part of the inhabitants emigrated to the neighbouring towns of Háusa, chiefly Kátsena, Tasáwa, Marádi, and Kanó. The exact circumstances which brought about this deplorable desertion and desolation of the place I was not able to learn; and the date of the event cannot be made to coincide with the period of the great revolution effected in Middle Sudán by the rising of the Jihádi, "the reformer," 'Othmán da-n-Fódiye, which it preceded by more than fifteen years; but it coincides with or closely follows upon an event which I shall have to dwell upon in the further course of my proceedings. This is the conquest of Gáo or Gógo (the former capital of the Sónghay empire, and which since 1591 had become a province of the empire of Morocco) by the Tawárek. As we have seen above that A'gades had evidently been founded as an entrepôt for the great trade with this most flourishing commercial place on the I'sa or Niger, at that time the centre of the gold-trade, of course the ransacking and wholesale destruction of this town could not but affect in the most serious manner the well-being of A'gades, cutting away the very roots through which it received life.

At present I still think that I was not far wrong in estimating the number of the inhabited houses at from six hundred to seven hundred, and the population at about seven thousand, though it must be borne in mind that, as the inhabitants have still preserved

their trading character, a great many of the male
inhabitants are always absent from home, a circumstance which reduces the armed force of the place to
about six hundred.   A numerical element capable of
controlling the estimated amount of the population, is offered by the number of from two hundred
and fifty to three hundred well-bred boys, who at the
time of my visit were learning a little reading and
writing, in five or six schools scattered over the
town; for it is not every boy who is sent to school,
but only those belonging to families in easy circumstances, and they are all about the same age, from
eight to ten years old.

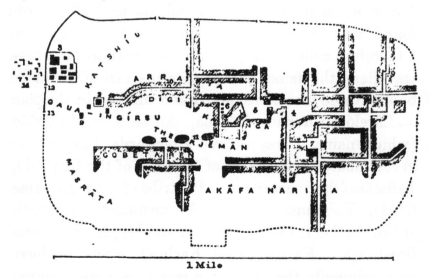

1 Mile

1. House where I lodged.
2. Great mosque or Mesállaje.
3. Palace or Fáda.
4. Káswa-n-delélti or Táma-n-lókoy.
5. Káswa-n-rákoma.
6. Katánga.
7. Erárar-n-zákan.

8. Mohammed Boró's house.
9. House of the Kádhi.
10. Well Shedwánka.
11. Pools of stagnant water.
12. Kófa-n-Alkáli.
13. Masráta hogúme.
14. Suburb of Ben Gottára.

With regard to the names of the quarters of the town, which are interesting in an historical point of view, I was not able to learn exactly the application of each of the names ; and I am sure very few even of the inhabitants themselves can now tell the limits of the quarters, on account of the desolate state of many of them. The principal names which can be laid down with certainty in the plan, are Masráta, Gobetáren, Gáwa-Ngírsu, Dígi or Dégi, Katánga, Terjemán, and Arrafía, which comprise the south-western quarter of the town. The names of the other quarters, which I attempted to lay down on the plan sent to Government together with my report, I now deem it prudent to withdraw, as I afterwards found that there was some uncertainty about them. I therefore collect here, for the information of future travellers, the names of the other quarters of the place besides those mentioned above and marked in the plan — Lárelóg, Churúd, Hásena, Amaréwuël, Imurdán (which name, I was assured afterwards, has nothing in common with the name of the tribe of the Imghád), Tafimáta (the quarter where the tribe of the same name lived), Yobímme ("yobu-mé" meaning the mouth of the market), Dégi-n-béne, or the Upper Dégi, and Bosenrára. Kachíyu (not Kachín) seems to have been originally the name of a pool ; as I was assured that, besides the three ponds still visible, there were formerly seven others, namely Kudúru, Kachíyu, Chikinéwan, Lángusú-gázará, Kurungúsu, and Raba-fáda, — this latter in the square of the palace.

The whole ground upon which the town is built (being the edge of a table-land, which coincides with the transition from granite to sandstone*), seems to be greatly impregnated with salt at a certain depth, of which not only the ponds, but even the wells bear evidence,—two of the three wells still in use having saltish water, and only that of Shedwánka being, as to taste, free from salt, though it is still regarded as unwholesome, and all the water used for drinking is brought from the wells outside the walls.   Formerly, it is said, there were nine wells inside the town.

From what I have said above, it may be concluded that the commerce of A'gades is now inconsiderable. Its characteristic feature is, that no kind of money whatever is current in the market, neither gold, nor silver, nor kurdí, nor shells ; while strips of cotton or gábagá (the Kanúri, and not the Háusa term being employed in this case, because the small quantity of this stuff which is current is imported from the north-western province of Bórnu) are very rare, and indeed form almost as merely nominal a standard as the mithkál.   Nevertheless the value of the mithkál is divided into ten rijáls or érjel, which measure means eight drá or cubits of gábagá.   The real standard of the market, I must repeat, is millet or dukhn ("gero"

---

* Unfortunately I was unable to ascertain the elevation of the locality by observation, as I could only take a common thermometer with me on this trip ; but, considering the whole ground along the road from Tintéllust, I think it can scarcely be less than 2500 feet.

in Háusa, " éneli" in Temáshight, *Pennisetum ty-phoïdeum*), durra or *Holcus sorghum* being scarcely ever brought to market. And it is very remarkable, that with this article a man may buy everything at a much cheaper rate than with merchandise, which in general fetches a low price in the place; at least it did so during my stay, when the market had been well-stocked with everything in demand, by the people who had come along with us. English calico of very good quality was sold by me at twenty per cent. less than it had been bought for at Múrzuk. Senna in former times formed an article of export of some importance; but the price which it fetches on the coast has so decreased that it scarcely pays the carriage, the distance from the coast being so very great; and it scarcely formed at all an article in request here, nor did we meet on our whole journey a single camel laden with it, though it grows in considerable quantities in the valleys hereabouts.

A'gades is in no respect a place of resort for wealthy merchants, not even Arabs, while with regard to Europe its importance at present consists in its lying on the most direct road to Sókoto and that part of Sudán. In my opinion it would form for a European agent a very good and comparatively healthy place from which to open relations with Central Africa. The native merchants seem only to visit the markets of Kátsena, Tasáwa, Marádi, Kanó and Sókoto, and, as far as I was able to learn, never go to the northern markets of Ghát or Múrzuk, unless on a journey to Mekka, which several of them have

made. Neither does there seem to exist any intercourse at present with Gágho or Gógo, or with Timbúktu; but the Arabs of Azawád and those parts,
when undertaking a pilgrimage, generally go by way
of A'gades.

I here add the prices of different articles, as they
were sold in the market during my residence in the
place: —

	Mithkál.*	Béjel.
Dukhn "géro" (*Pennisetum*), or durra "dáwa" (*sorghum*), twenty zekka, being equal to forty of the measure used in Tin-téllust - -	1	0
Rice, ten zekka - - - -	1	0
Camel, a young one, two years old, not yet fit for carrying loads - - - -	18	0
Ditto, full grown - - - -	25	0
Horse, a good strong one - - -	100	0
Ditto, a fine one, of Tawát breed - -	1000	0
Ass - - - - - -	6 to 8	0
Ox - - - - - -	8	0
Calf - - - - - -	4	0
Ram - - - - - -	1	5
Sandals, a pair of common ones - -	0	1
Ditto, a pair of fine ones - - -	0	5
Camel-saddle (or "rákhla" in Arabic, "kígi" in Temáshight) - - - -	10	0
Ditto, a common one - - -	5	0
Leather bag, of common leather, for containing clothes - - - - -	1	0
Mat, a fine coloured one - - -	0	6
English calico, ten dra or cubits - -	1	0
Subéta, or white Egyptian shawl with red border - - - - -	1	0
Kórnu, or the fine Egyptian coloured sheep-leather, a piece - - - -	1	0

* The mithkál of A'gades is equal to 1000 kurdí, 2500 of which
make a Spanish or Austrian dollar.

	Míthkál.	Réjel.
Túrkedi, or the dark-coloured cotton cloth for female dress of Kanó manufacture, common -	2	0
Ditto, of finer texture - - - - 3 to 5		3

I must here add, that I did not observe that the people of A'gades use manna in their food, nor that it is collected in the neighbourhood of the town; but I did not inquire about it on the spot, not having taken notice of the passage of Leo relating to it.

My stay in A'gades was too short to justify my entering into detail about the private life of the people, but all that I saw convinced me that, although open to most serious censure on the part of the moralist, it presented many striking features of cheerfulness and happiness, and nothing like the misery which is often met with in towns which have declined from their former glory. It still contains many active germs of national life, which are most gratifying to the philosophic traveller. The situation, on an elevated plateau, cannot but be healthy, as the few waterpools, of small dimensions, are incapable of infecting the air. The disease which I have mentioned in my diary as prevalent at the time of my sojourn was epidemic. Besides, it must be borne in mind that the end of the rainy season everywhere in the tropical regions is the most unhealthy period of the year.[*]

[*] In an Appendix will be given some routes which connect A'gades with other places, and, radiating from it in various directions, serve as rays of light to discover to us districts not yet visited by any European.

CHAP. XIX.

DEPARTURE FROM ÁGADES. — STAY IN TIN-TÉGGANA.

WE at length left A'gades. I felt as if I Wednesday, October 30th. had enjoyed a glimpse of a totally different world, a new region of life, many relations of which were as yet obscure to me. Timbúktu, which was in the background of this novel and living picture, seemed an almost unattainable object. An acquaintance with it would not fail to throw light upon this advanced post of Sónghay nationality, and its state of civilization; but at that time I little expected that it would be my destiny to dwell a year in that mysterious place, and I had even reason to doubt the possibility of reaching it from this quarter. All my thoughts were bent on the south; and although at present retracing my steps towards the north, yet, as it carried me back to our head-quarters, whence I might soon expect to start for the southern regions, I regarded it as a step in advance.

But the commencement of the journey was most abortive, and made me rather regret that I had not spent the day in the town. Hámma was unable to find some of the asses belonging to the caravan, for the simple reason that our friend Zúmmuzuk had sold them; and the whole day was lost, so that we encamped after a march of scarcely two miles and a

half.   Here we were joined by Ibrahím and by a very amiable, intelligent Kél-owí of the name of Rábbot, who informed me that to the east of the valley Te-
ʻfárrakad there were several other valleys not at all inferior to it in exuberance and variety of vegetation. As the most important among them, he named to me A'mdegra, E'dob, Téwarni, Tíndawén, and Asá-gatay.

When at length, on Thursday morning, we fairly began our journey, we followed entirely our old road, Hámma being anxious to get home; but nevertheless, as the mountains and ridges which characterize this region now met the eyes from the other side, the scenery was a good deal varied, and I had frequent opportunities of completing my map of this part of the country.   Besides, we chose our encampments in new localities; and many little incidents varied our journey, the most interesting of which was the approach of a party of five lions in the valley Búdde, when Hámma called us to arms.   He, Rábbot, Mohammed, and I advanced to meet them, but they soon turned their backs, leaping over the rocky ground towards their mountain-retreat.   The lion of Aïr does not seem to be a very ferocious animal, and, like those of all this border-region of the desert, has no mane — that is to say, as compared with other lions.   The mane-less lion of Guzerat is well known, but a similar species seems also to occur in Sind and Persia.   The lion of Central Africa, at least of Bórnu and Logón, has a beautiful mane; and the skin of a lion of that region, which I took with me on my journey to western Sudán, excited the admiration of all who saw it.

The valley Tíggeda had now a very different aspect from that which it wore when we were going to A'gades; for while at that time, beautiful as it was, it was not enlivened by a single human being, now at its very head we met a considerable caravan of Kélowí laden with salt, and accompanied by a herd of young camels to be bartered in the market of A'gades for corn, and further on we found a herd of from sixty to seventy head of cattle, and numerous flocks of goats, indulging in the rich herbage which had previously excited my astonishment. Our minds likewise were here excited by the important news that the old chief of Tintéllust had started for Sudán, not only with my fellow-travellers, but with the whole caravan; but while my fiery and frivolous Mohammed heaped conjecture upon conjecture, meditating how we should be able to reach them, Hámma, who knew his father-in-law better, and who was conscious of his own importance and dignity, remained incredulous. We had some very pretty mountain-views from this side, especially when we approached Mount Eghellál, behind which the Búnday and other mountains rose into view.

On the morning of the 5th of November, which was to be the day of our arrival in Tintéllust, it was so cold that we started rather late, Hámma simply declaring that the cold did not allow him to go on —

" Dári yahánna fataúchi." Having started at length,
we made a long day's march; and after eleven hours
and a half travelling reached the well-known sand-
hill opposite Tintéllust, where our encampment had
stayed so long, not by the great road along the valley,
but by " The Thief's Passage," in order to observe
before we were observed.

But the residence of the great chief A'nnur was
buried in the deepest silence; the courtiers, the blacksmiths, all the great men and ladies, had gone away.
Hámma went to see if anybody remained behind, while
we cooked our rice, and prepared to make ourselves
comfortable for the night. That, however, was out of
the question, for when he returned, he ordered us to
decamp at once; and though nothing is more dreadful
than a night's march, particularly when it succeeds to
a long day's journey, yet in the enthusiasm awakened
by the thought of going southwards, I with all my
heart joined in the exclamation " sé fataúchi sé Kanó"
(" no rest before Kanó" — properly, " nothing but
travelling, nothing but Kanó") !

It was ten o'clock in the evening when we started
again along the broad valley, taking leave for ever
of " the English Hill;" but I soon began to suffer
from the consequences of fatigue. In order to
avoid falling from my camel in my drowsy state,
I was obliged to drag myself along, great part of
the night, on foot, which was not at all agreeable, as
the round was at times very rugged, and covered
with long grass. Having crossed a rocky flat, we

entered, about four o'clock in the morning, the wide
plain of Tin-téggana, stumbling along through the
thick cover of bú-rékkeba and other sorts of herbage,
till dawn, coming on with rather chilly air, revealed
to our benumbed senses the encampment of the
caravan. Having therefore made repeated halts, to
give the people time to recognize us, in order not to
occasion any alarm, as our leader Hámma was not with
us, but had lain down at the roadside to get a few
hours' rest, we made straight for the two European
tents which showed us precisely the residence of my
fellow-travellers. The old chief A'nnur was up, and
received me with great kindness—more kindly, I must
say, than my colleagues, who apparently felt some
jealousy on account of the success which had attended
my proceedings.

Having once more taken possession of the well-
known home of our little tent, I preferred looking
about the encampment to lying down; for sleeping
after sunrise is not agreeable to me.

The valley Tin-téggana, wherein A'nnur, with his
people, was encamped, is in this place about three
miles broad, being bordered towards the east by a low
range of hills with the small cone of A'dode rising to
a greater elevation; towards the west by the Búnday
and some smaller mountains; towards the south, where
the ground rises, it is lined by more detached peaks,
while on the north side an open view extends down
the valley as far as the large mountain-mass which
borders the valley of Tintéllust on the north. Al-

together it was a fine open landscape, embracing the country which forms the nucleus, if I may say so, of the domain of the old chief, whose camels pasture here the whole year round, while he himself usually takes up his residence in this place about this season, when nature is in its prime, and the weather becomes cool, in order to enjoy the country air.

We ourselves had as yet no idea of making a long stay here, but indulged in the hope of starting the next day, when all of a sudden about noon our old friend declared solemnly that he was unable to go with us at present, that he himself was obliged to wait for the salt-caravan, while his confidential slave Zinghína was now to go southwards. He said that, if we chose, we might go on with the latter. He supposed, perhaps, that none of us would dare to do so; but when I insisted upon it afterwards, he as well as Zinghína declared that the attempt was too dangerous; and it would have been absurd to insist on accompanying the slave. For the moment such a disappointment was very trying. However, I afterwards perceived that, though we had lost more than a month of the finest season for travelling, we had thereby acquired all possible security for safely attaining the object of our journey; for now we were obliged to send off all our luggage with Zinghína in advance, and might fully expect to travel with infinitely more ease and less trouble, when no longer encumbered with things which, though of little value, nevertheless attracted the cupidity of the people. At the time, however, even this was not at all agreeable, as Overweg and I had to part with almost all our things and to send them on to Kanó, to the care of a man of whose character we knew nothing.

Nearly all the Arabs and many of the Kél-owí started; and it awakened some feeling of regret to see them go and to be ourselves obliged to stay behind. Our friend Músa, who had been the most faithful of our Tinýlkum camel-drivers, who had visited us almost daily in our tent, and from whom we had obtained so much valuable information*, was the last to take leave of us. But as soon as the caravan was out of sight, I determined to make the best possible use of this involuntary leisure, by sifting elaborately the varied information which I had been able to collect in A'gades, and by sending a full report to Europe, in order to engage the interest of the scientific public in our expedition, and to justify Her Majesty's Government in granting us new supplies, without which, after our heavy losses, we should be obliged to return directly, leaving the chief objects of the expedition unattained. Owing to this resolution, our quiet life in A'sben was not, I hope, without its fruits.

Our encampment, too, became more cheerful and

Friday, November 8th.

---

* I am sorry that a long letter on the topography of the country (written chiefly from Músa's information), which I sent to Europe, appears never to have arrived. It is for this reason that I am unable to lay down with some degree of accuracy that part of the country of A'sben which I did not visit myself.

agreeable when, on the following day, we transferred
it to the korámma Ofáyet, a beautiful little branch-
wadi of the spacious valley Tin-téggana, issuing from
a defile (a "kógo-n-dútsi") formed by the Búnday
and a lower mount to the south, along which led the
path to A'sodi. It was most densely wooded with
talha-trees, and overgrown with tall bu-rékkeba and
allwot, and was thinned only very gradually, as immense branches and whole trees were cut down daily
to feed the fires during the night; for it was at
times extremely cold, and we felt most comfortable
when in the evening we stretched ourselves in front of

our tents, round an enormous fire. The tall herbage
also was by degrees consumed, not only by the camels,
but by the construction of small conical huts; so that

gradually a varied and pleasant little village sprang up in this wild spot, which is represented in the accompanying wood-cut. The time which we were obliged to stay here would indeed have passed by most pleasantly but for the trouble occasioned to Overweg and myself by our impudent and dissolute Tunisian half-caste servant, who had become quite insupportable. Unfortunately we did not find an opportunity of sending him back; and I thought it best to take him with me to Kanó, where I was sure to get rid of him. Our other servant Ibrahím, also, though much more prudent, was not at all trustworthy, which was the more to be regretted as he had travelled all over Háusa, and even as far as Gónja, and might have proved of immense service. But fortunately I had another servant — a thin youth of most unattractive appearance, but who nevertheless was the most useful attendant I ever had; and though young he had roamed about a great deal over the whole eastern half of the desert, and shared in many adventures of the most serious kind. He possessed, too, a strong sense of honour, and was perfectly to berelied upon. This was Mohammed el Gatróni, a native of Gatrón, in the southern part of Fezzán, who, with a short interruption (when I sent him to Múrzuk with the late Mr. Richardson's papers and effects), remained in my service till I returned to Fezzán in 1855.

The zeal with which I had commenced finishing my report was well rewarded; for on the 14th the Ghadámsi merchant Abu Bakr el Wákhshi (an old

man whom I shall have occasion to mention repeatedly in the course of my journey) came to A'nnur to
complain of a robbery committed upon part of his merchandise at Tasáwa. But for this circumstance he
would not have touched at this place, and his people,
whom he was sending to Ghadámes, would have travelled along the great road by A'sodi without our
knowing anything about them. Being assured by
the trustworthy old man that the parcel would reach
Ghadámes in two months, I sent off the first part of
my report; but unfortunately it arrived at that place
when Her Majesty's Agent, Mr. Charles Dickson, to
whom I had addressed it, was absent in Tripoli, —
the consequence being that it lay there for several
months.

In the course of the 15th, while sitting quietly in
my tent, I suddenly heard my name, "'Abd el
Kerím," pronounced by a well-known voice, and
looking out, to my great astonishment saw the little
sturdy figure of my friend Hámma trotting along at
a steady pace, his iron spear in his hand. I thought
he was gone to Bílma, as we had been told; but it
appeared that, having come up with the salt-caravan at the commencement of the Hammáda, he only
supplied them with more corn, and having conferred
with them, had come back to assist his old father-in-
law in the arduous task of keeping the turbulent
tribes in some state of quiet. The degree of secrecy
with which everything is done in this wild country
is indeed remarkable, and no doubt contributes in a

great measure to the influence and power of the sagacious chief of Tintéllust.

Four days later came my other friend, the foolish Mohammed, who had accompanied the expedition of the sultan of A'gades, and who was full of interesting details of this little campaign. Neither Astáfidet, the prince of the Kél-owí, nor 'Abd el Káder, the sultan residing in A'gades, actually took part in the attack or "súkkùa," but kept at a distance. On asking my merry friend what was the result of the whole, and whether the state of the country to the north was now settled, and the road secure, he exclaimed, with a significant grimace, " Bábu dádi ". (not very pleasant); and to what extent strength was sacrificed to euphony in this expression we were soon to learn; for the next day the " makéria," the wife of the "mákeri" Elíyas, came to tell us that a ghazzia of the E'fadaye had suddenly fallen upon Tin-taghóde, and had carried off two large droves (gérki) of camels and all the moveable property. Such is the state of this country, where the chiefs, instead of punishing systematically the rebels and marauders, regard such instances of crime only as opportunities for enriching themselves with plunder. The E'fadaye do not muster more than from two hundred to three hundred spears; but they are generally assisted by the I'gammén and E'delén, two of the tribes of the Imghád whom I mentioned above.

The next day the old chief, accompanied by Hámma and seven other trusty companions, set out for Tin-

téyyat, in order to consult with the old màllem Azóri,
" the wise man of Aïr," about the means of preventing
the bad consequences likely to arise from the turbulent
state into which the country had fallen just when he
was about to set out for Sudán.

The old chief, on his return from his important
consultation, gave us some interesting information
about " the Lion of Tintéyyat" (Azóri). Azóri, he
said, had attained the highest degree of wisdom and
learning, comprehending all divine and human things,
without ever leaving the country of Aïr. He was
now nearly blind, though younger in years than himself. His father had likewise been a very wise man.
Formerly, according to our friend, there was another
great màllem in the country, named Hámi, a native of
Tìntághódé; and as long as he lived, the Aníslimen, his
fellow-citizens, had been good people and followed the
way of justice, while at present their name " Anislim"
was become a mere mockery, for they were the worst
of the lawless, and had lost all fear of God; indeed
almost all the troubles into which the country had
been plunged might be ascribed to their agency and
intrigues. Here the old chief had touched on his favourite theme; and he gave vent to all his anger and
wrath against those holy men, who were evidently
opposed to his authority.

The old man was, in fact, on the most friendly terms
with us, and instead of being suspicious of our "writing down his country," was anxious to correct any
erroneous idea which we might entertain respecting

it.   I shall never forget with what pleasure he looked over my sketch of the route from Tintéllust to A'gades, while I explained to him the principal features of it; and he felt a proud satisfaction in seeing a stranger from a far distant country appreciate the peculiar charms of the glens and mountains of his own native land.   He was, in short, so pleased with our manners and our whole demeanour, that one day, after he had been reposing in my tent and chatting with me, he sent for Yusuf, and told him plainly that he apprehended that our religion was better than theirs; whereupon the Arab explained to him that our manners indeed were excellent, but that our religious creed had some great defects, in violating the unity of the Almighty God, and elevating one of His prophets from his real rank of servant of God to that of His Son.   A'nnur, rising a little from his couch, looked steadily into Yusuf's face, and said, " hákkanánne " (is it so)?   As for me, in order not to provoke a disputation with Yusuf, who united in himself some of the most amiable with some of the most hateful qualities, I kept silence as long as he was present; but when he retired I explained to the chief that, as there was a great variety of sects among the Mohammedans, so there was also among the Christians, many of whom laid greater stress upon the unimpaired unity of the Creator than even the Mohammedans.   So much sufficed for the justification of our religion; for the old man did not like to talk much upon the subject, though he was strict in his prayers, as far as we were able to observe.

He was a man of business, who desired to maintain some sort of order in a country where everything naturally inclines to turbulence and disorder. In other respects, he allowed every man to do as he liked; and notwithstanding his practical severity, he was rather of a mild disposition, for he thought Europeans dreadful barbarians for slaughtering without pity such numbers of people in their battles, using big guns instead of spears and swords, which were, as he thought, the only manly and becoming weapons.

The 25th of November was a great market-day for our little settlement, for on the preceding day the long-expected caravan with provisions arrived from Damerghú, and all the people were buying their necessary supply; but we had much difficulty in obtaining what we wanted, as all our things — even the few dollars we had still left — were depreciated, and estimated at more than thirty per cent. less than their real value. After having recovered in A'gades a little from the weakness of my stomach, by the aid of the princely dishes sent me by 'Abd el Káder, I had, notwithstanding the fine cool weather, once more to suffer from the effects of our almost raw and bitter dishes of Guinea corn, and the more so as I had no tea left to wash down this unpalatable and indigestible paste; and I felt more than common delight when we were regaled on the 27th by a fine strong soup made from the meat of the bullock which we had bought from A'nnur for twelve thousand kurdí. It was a day of great rejoicing, and a new

epoch in our peaceful and dull existence, in consequence of which I found my health greatly restored.

Our patience, indeed, was tried to the utmost; and
I looked for some moments with a sort of despair
into Hámma's face, when, on his return from a mission
to the E'fadaye, which seemed not to have been quite
successful, he told me on the 28th of November that
we should still make a stay here of twenty-five days.
Fortunately he always chose to view things on the
worst side; and I was happy to be assured by the old
chief himself, that our stay here would certainly not
exceed fifteen days.   Nevertheless, as the first short
days of our sham travelling afterwards convinced me,
the veracious Hámma, who had never deceived me,
was in reality quite right in his statement.   My
friend came to take leave of me, as he was to absent
himself for a few days, in order to visit an elder sister
of his, who lived in Telíshiet, further up the valley of
Tin-téggana; and of course I had to supply him
with some handsome little production of European
manufacture.

We had full reason to admire the energy of the old
chief, who on the 30th of November went to a " privy
council" with Màllem Azóri and Sultan Astáfidet,
which was appointed to be held in some solitary glen,
halfway between Tin-téggana and A'sodi, and, after he
had returned late in the evening of the 1st of December,
was galloping along our encampment in the morning
of the 2nd, in order to visit the new watering-place
lower down in the principal valley, — the former well

beginning to dry up, or rather requiring to be dug to a greater depth, as the moisture collected during the rainy season was gradually receding. This was the first time we saw our friend on horseback; and though he was seventy-six years of age, he sat very well and upright in his saddle. Overweg went on one of the following days to see the well (which was about four miles distant from our encampment, in a W.N.W. direction, beyond a little village of the name of O'brasen), but found it rather a basin formed between the rocky cliffs, and fed, according to report, by a spring.

Meanwhile I was surprised to learn from Mohammed Byrji, A'nnur's grandson, and next claimant to the succession after Háj 'Abdúwa, that the last-named, together with El U'su or Lúsu, the influential chief of Azanéres, and El Hossén, had started for the south six days previously in order to purchase provisions for the salt-caravan. In this little country something is always going on, and the people all appear to lead a very restless life; what wonder, then, if most of them are the progeny of wayfarers, begotten from fortuitous and short-lived matches? Perhaps in no country is domestic life wanting to such a degree as among the Kél-owí properly so called; but it would be wrong to include in this category the tribes of purer blood living at some distance from this centre of the salt-trade.

At length, on the 5th of December, the first body of the salt-caravan arrived from Bílma, opening the prospect of a speedy departure from this our African home; but although we were very eager to obtain a glance at them, they did not become visible, but kept further to the west.   The following evening, however, several friends and partisans of the old chief arrived, mounted on mehára, and were received by the women with loud shrill cries of welcome ("tirlelák" in Temáshight) very similar to the "tehlíl" of the Arabs.

Preparations were now gradually made for our setting out; but previously it was necessary to provide a supply of water, not only for the immediate use of the numerous salt-caravan, but for the constant one of those people who were to remain behind during the absence of their chief and master.   Accordingly on the 7th of December the old chief left our encampment, with all his people, in solemn procession, in order to dig a new well; and after having long searched with a spear for the most favourable spot, they set to work close to the entrance of a small branch-wádi, joining the main valley from the east side, not far from A'dode; and having obtained a sufficient supply of water, they walled the well in with branches and stones, so that it was capable of retaining water at least till the beginning of the next rainy season, when, most probably, the floods would destroy it.   There are, indeed, in these countries very few undertakings of this kind the existence of which is calculated upon for more than a year.

Meanwhile, during our long lazy stay in this tranquil alpine retreat of the wilderness, after I had

finished my report on A'gades, I began to study in a
more comprehensive way the interesting language of
that place, and in order to effect that purpose had been
obliged to make a sort of treaty with that shameless
profligate Zúmmuzuk, who, for his exploits in A'gades,
had received severe punishment from his master. The
chief conditions of our covenant were, that he was
to receive every day a certain allowance, but that
during his presence in my tent he was not to move
from the place assigned him, the limits of which were
very accurately defined — of course at a respectable
distance from my luggage; and if he touched anything
I was officially permitted by A'nnur to shoot him on
the spot. Notwithstanding the coolness and reserve
which I was obliged to adopt in my intercourse
with this man, I was fully capable of estimating his
veracity; and in the course of my journey and my
researches I convinced myself that in no one instance
did he deviate from the truth.

Going on in this way, I had completed, by the 8th
of the month, an exact and full vocabulary of the Emgédesi language, and could with more leisure indulge
in a conversation with my friend A'magay, the chief
eunuch and confidential servant of the sultan of
A'gades, who paid me a visit, and brought me the
most recent news from the capital. Affairs were all in
the best state, his business now being merely to ar-
range a few matters with A'nnur before the latter set
out for Sudán. He informed me that the salt-caravan of the Kél-gerés and Itísan had long ago returned

from Bílma, taking with them our letter to the sultan of Sókoto, and accompanied by Mohammed Bóro, who had taken all his children with him except those who were still attending school. A'magay had also brought with him the curious letter from Mustapha the governor of Fezzán, which is spoken of by Mr. Richardson. I treated him with some coffee (which was now with me a very precious article, as I had but little left), and made him a small present.

CHAP. XX.

Thursday,
December 12th,
1850. Safer
7th, 1266.

AT length the day broke when we were to move on and get nearer the longed-for object of our journey, though we were aware that our first progress would be slow. But before we departed from this region, which had become so familiar to us, I wished to take a last glimpse down the valley towards Tintéllust, and wandered towards the offshoots of Mount Búnday, which afforded me a fine prospect over the whole valley up to that beautiful mountain-mass which forms so characteristic a feature in the configuration of the whole country. The hills which I ascended consisted of basalt, and formed a low ridge, which was separated from the principal mountain-mass by a hollow of sandstone formation. Having bade farewell to the blue mountains of Tintéllust, I took leave of the charming little valley Ofáyet, which, having been a few moments previously a busy scene of life, was now left to silence and solitude.

Late in the morning we began to move, but very slowly, halting every now and then. At length the old chief himself came up, walking like a young man before his méheri, which he led by the nose-cord; and the varied groups composing the caravan began to march more steadily. It was a whole nation in motion, the men on camels or on foot, the women on bullocks or on asses, with all the necessaries of the little household, as well as the houses themselves,—a herd of cattle, another of milk-goats, and numbers of young camels running playfully along-side, and sometimes getting between the regular lines of the laden animals. The ground was very rocky and rugged, and looked bare and desolate in the extreme, the plain being strewn for a while with loose basaltic stones, like the plain of Tághist.

Several high peaks characterize this volcanic region; and after having left to our right the peak called Ebárrasa, we encamped, a little before noon, at the north-eastern foot of a very conspicuous peak called Teléshera, which had long attracted my attention. We had scarcely chosen our ground when I set out on foot in order to ascend this high mountain, from which I expected to obtain a view over the eastern side of the picturesque mass of the Eghellál; but its ascent proved very difficult, chiefly because I had not exerted my strength much during our long stay in this country. The flanks of the peak, after I had ascended the offshoots, which consisted of sandstone, were most precipitous and abrupt, and covered with loose stones, which gave way under my feet, and often carried me a long way down. The summit consisted of perpendicular trachytic pillars, of quadrangular and almost regular form, $2\frac{1}{2}$ feet in thickness, as if cut by the hand of man, some of them about one hundred feet high, while others had been broken off at greater or less height. It is at least 1500 feet above the bottom of the valley. The view was interesting, although the sky was not clear; I was able to take several angles; but the western flank of the Eghellál, which I was particularly anxious to obtain a sight of, was covered by other heights.

Beyond the branch-wádi which surrounds this mountain on the south side, there is a ridge ranging to a greater length, and rising from the ground with a very precipitous wall; this was examined by Mr. Overweg, and found to consist likewise of trachyte interspersed with black basaltic stone, and crystals of glassy felspar. Having attained my purpose, I began my retreat, but found the descent more troublesome than the ascent, particularly as my boots were torn to pieces by the sharp stones; and the fragments giving way under my feet, I fell repeatedly. I was quite exhausted when I reached the tent; but a cup of strong coffee soon restored me. However, I never afterwards on my whole journey felt strong enough to ascend a mountain of moderate elevation.

Friday, December 18th. Starting rather late, we continued through the mountainous region, generally ascending, while a cold wind made our old friend the chief shiver and regard with feelings of envy my thick black bernús, although he had got bernúses enough from us not only to protect him against cold, but us too against any envious feeling for the little

which was left us. Further on, in several places the
granite (which at the bottom of the valley alternates
with sandstone) was perfectly disintegrated, and had
become like meal. Here the passage narrowed for
about an hour, when we obtained a view of a long
range stretching out before us with a considerable
cone lying in front of it. Keeping now over rocky
ground, then along the bottom of a valley called
Tánegat, about half a mile broad, where we passed a
well on our right, we at length reached a mountain-
spur starting off from the ridge on our right, and
entered a beautiful broad plain stretching out to the
foot of a considerable mountain-group, which was
capped by a remarkable picturesquely-indented cone
called Mári. Here we saw the numerous camels of
the salt-caravan grazing in the distance to our left;
and after having crossed a small rocky flat, we encamped in the very channel of the torrent, being
certain that at this season no such danger as overwhelmed us in the valley E'ghazar was to be feared.
A'magay, who was still with us, paid me a visit in the
afternoon, and had a cup of coffee; he also came
the next morning. Near our encampment were some
fine acacia-trees of the species called gáwo, which I
shall have to mention repeatedly in my travels.

We started early, but encamped, after   Saturday,
a short march of about six miles, on un-   December 14th.
even ground intersected by numbers of small ridges.
The reason of the halt was, that the whole of the
caravan was to come up and to join together; and

our old chief here put on his official dress (a yellow bernús of good quality), to show his dignity as leader of such a host of people.

Salt forms the only article conveyed by this caravan. The form of the largest cake is very remarkable; but it must be borne in mind that the salt in Bílma is in a fluid state, and is formed into this shape by pouring it into a wooden mould. This pedestal or loaf of salt (kántu) is equal to five of the smaller cakes, which are called áserím; and each áserím equals four of the smallest cakes, which are called " fótu." The bags, made of the leaves of the dúm-palm (or the " kábba"), in which these loaves are packed up, are called " tákrufa." But the finest salt is generally in loose grains; and this is the only palatable salt, while the ordinary salt of Bílma is very bitter to the European palate, and spoils everything: but the former is more than three times the value of the latter. The price paid in Bílma is but two zékkas for three kántus.

In the evening there was " urgí," or " éddil" (play-ing), and " ráwa" or " adéllul" (dancing), all over the large camp of the salt-caravan, and the drummers or " masugánga" were all vying with each other, when I observed that our drummer, Hassan, who was proud of his talent, and used to call for a little present, was quite outdone by the drummer of that portion of the caravan which was nearest to us, who performed his work with great skill, and caused general enthusiasm among the dancing people. The many lively and merry scenes, ranging over a wide district, itself picturesque, and illuminated by large fires in the dusk of evening, presented a cheerful picture of animated native life, looking at which a traveller might easily forget the weak points discoverable in other phases of life in the desert.

The general start of the united "aīri," or caravan, took place with great spirit; Sunday, December 15th. and a wild enthusiastic cry, raised over the whole extent of the encampment, answered to the beating of the drums. For, though the Kél-owí are greatly civilized by the influence of the black population, nevertheless they are still "half demons," while the thoroughbred and freeborn Amóshagh (whatever name he may bear, whether Tárki, ba-A'sbenchi, Kindín, or Chapáto) is regarded by all the neighbouring tribes, Arabs as well as Africans, as a real demon ("jin"). Notwithstanding all this uproar we were rather astonished at the small number of camels laden with salt, which formed A'nnur's caravan; for they did not exceed two hundred, and their loads in the aggregate would realize in Kanó at the very utmost three thousand dollars, which, if taken as the principal revenue of the chief, seems very little. The whole number of the caravan did not exceed two thousand camels.

However enthusiastically the people had answered to the call of the drums, the loading of the camels took a long time; and the old chief himself had remarkably few people to get ready his train: but the

reason probably was, that he was obliged to leave as
many people behind as possible for the security of
the country.   When at length we set out, the view
which presented itself was really highly exciting;
for here a whole nation was in motion, going on
its great errand of supplying the wants of other
tribes, and bartering for what they stood in need of
themselves.   All the drums were beating; and one
string of camels after the other marched up in martial order, led on by the " mádogu," the most experienced and steadfast among the servants or followers
of each chief.   It was clear that our last night's
encampment had been chosen only on account of its
being well protected all around by ridges of rock;
for on setting out to-day we had to follow up, in
the beginning, a course due west, in order to return
into our main direction along the valley.   We then
gradually began to turn round the very remarkable

Mount Mári, which here assumed the figure shown
in the sketch.   Further on I saw the people busy in
digging up a species of edible bulbous roots called

"adíllewan" by the Kél-owí. This, I think, besides the "bába," or "níle" (the *Indigofera endecaphylla*), the first specimens of which we had observed two days ago shooting up unostentatiously among the herbage, was the most evident proof that we had left the region of the true desert, though we had still to cross a very sterile tract.

Having changed our direction from south to south-west, about noon we entered the highroad coming directly from A'sodi, but which was, in fact, nothing better than a narrow pathway. Here we were winding through a labyrinth of large detached projecting blocks, while Mount Mári presented itself in an entirely different shape. Gradually the bottom of

the valley became free from blocks, and we were crossing and recrossing the bed of the watercourse, when we met a small caravan belonging to my friend the Emgédesi I'dder, who had been to Damerghú to buy corn. Shortly afterwards, we encamped at the side of the watercourse, which is called Adóral, and which joins, further downwards, another channel called Wéllek, which runs close along the western range.   Here we saw the first specimens of the pendent nests of the weaver bird (*Ploceus Abyssiniacus*).

While I was filling up my journal in the afternoon, I received a visit from Mohammed Býrji, who had this morning left Tin-téggana; he informed me that the women and the old men whom we had left there had not returned to Tintéllust, but had gone to Tintághalén.   All the population of the other villages in the northern districts of A'ír were likewise retreating southwards during the absence of the salt-caravan.

On starting this morning we were glad to find some variety in the vegetation; for instead of the monotonous talha-trees, which with some justice have been called "vegetable mummies,"* the whole valley-plain was adorned with beautiful spreading addwa- or tabórak-trees (the *Balanites Ægyptiaca*), the foliage of which often reached down to the very ground, forming a dense canopy of the freshest green.   After winding along, and crossing and recrossing the small channel, the path ascended the rocky ground, and we soon got sight of the mountains of Bághzen, looking out from behind the first mountain-range, from whose southern end a

Monday, December 16th.

---

* It is remarkable and significant, that the Tawárek employ one and the same name for talha and firewood in general, namely the word "ésarér;" but it is still more significant that the Kanúri or Bórnu seem to employ the same name, "kindín," for the Tárki and the talha.

point called A'nfisék rises to a considerable elevation.
This higher level, however, was not bare and naked,
but overgrown with the "knotted" grass bú-rékkeba
and with the addwa- and gawo-tree, while on our left
the broad but nevertheless sharply-marked peak of
Mount Mári towered over the whole, and gave to
the landscape a peculiar character. At an early hour
we encamped between buttresses of scattered blocks
shooting out of the plain, which seems to stretch to
the very foot of the Bághzen, and to be noted pre-
eminently as the Plain, "erárar."

In the afternoon I walked to a considerable distance, first to a hill S.W. from our camp, from which
I was able to take several angles, and then to the
well. The latter was at the distance of a mile and a
half from our tent in a westerly direction, and was
carefully walled up with stones ; it measured three
fathoms and a half to the surface of the water, while
the depth of the water itself was at present little less
than three fathoms, so that it is evident that there is
water here at all seasons. Its name is A'lbes. As,
on account of our slow travelling, we had been four
days without water, the meeting with a well was
rather agreeable to us. Between the well and the
foot of the mountain there was a temporary encampment of shepherds, who sent a sheep and a good deal
of cheese to the old chief.

Here we remained the two following days, in order
to repose from the fatigue of our sham travelling!
I went once more all over my Emgédesi collection,

and made a present to the servants of the mission, of
twenty-two zékkas of Bílma dates, which I bought
from the people of the caravan; they were all
thankful for this little present.　I was extremely glad
to find that even the Tunisian shushán, when he had
to receive orders only from me, behaved much better;
and I wrote from his recital a Góber story which, as
being characteristic of the imagination of the natives
and illustrating their ancient pagan worship of the
dodó, might perhaps prove of interest even to the
general reader.　The several divisions of the "aïri"
came slowly up; among them we observed the Kél-
azanéres, the people of Lúsu, the chief himself having
gone on in advance, as I observed above.

Thursday,
December 19th.　Our heavy caravan at length set out
again, the camels having now recovered a
little from the trying march over the naked desert
which divides the mountainous district of A'sben
from the "hénderi-Tedá," the fertile hollow of the
Tébu country.　It attracted my attention, that the
shrubby and thick-leaved "allwot" (the blue Crucifera mentioned before) had ceased altogether; even
the eternal bú-rékkeba began to be scarce, while only
a few solitary trees were scattered about.

While marching over this dreary plain, we noticed some Tébu merchants, natives of Dírki, with
only three camels, who had come with the salt-caravan from Bílma, and were going to Kanó; from
them we learnt that a Tébu caravan had started from
Kawár for Bórnu at the time of the 'Aïd el kebír.　The

example of these solitary travellers, indeed, might perhaps be followed with advantage by Europeans also, in order to avoid the country of the Azkár and the insecure border-districts of the Kél-owí, especially if they chose to stay in the Tébu oasis till they had obtained the protection of one of the great men of this country.

For a little while the plain was adorned with talha-trees; but then it became very rugged, like a rough floor of black basalt, through which wound a narrow path, pressing the whole caravan into one long string. At length, at half-past two o'clock in the afternoon, after having traversed extremely rugged ground, we began to descend from this broad basaltic level, and having crossed the dry watercourse of a winter torrent, entered the valley Télliya, which has a good supply of trees, but very little herbage. A cemetery here gave indication of the occasional or temporary residence of nomadic settlers.

On ascending again from the bottom of the valley to a higher level, and looking backwards, we obtained a fine view of Mount Ajúri, at the foot of which lies Chémia, a valley and village celebrated for its date-trees. It was not our fate to see any of those places in A'sben which are distinguished by the presence of this tree — neither the valley just mentioned, nor Iferwán, nor I'r-n-Allem; and a visit to them will form one of the interesting objects of some future traveller in this country. Having kept along the plain for an hour, we encamped at a little distance west from the dry bed of a watercourse running from north to south along the eastern foot of a low basaltic

ridge, with a fine display of trees, but a scanty one

of herbage. I went to ascend the ridge, supposing it to be connected with the Bághzen, but found that it was completely separated from the latter by a depression or hollow quite bare and naked.

This was the best point from whence to obtain a view over the eastern flank of Mount Bághzen, with its deep crevices or ravines, which seemed to separate the mountain-mass into several distinct groups; and in the evening I made the sketch of it given above.

However, we had full leisure to contemplate this mountain, which is not distinguished by great elevation, the highest peaks being little more than 2000 feet above the plain*; but it is interesting, as consisting probably of basaltic formation. We staid here longer than we desired, as we did not find an opportunity to penetrate into the glens in its interior, which, from this place, seem excessively barren, but are said to contain some favoured and inhabited spots, where even corn is reared. But our companions spoke with timorous exclamations of the numbers of lions which infest these retired mountain-passes; and not one of them would offer himself as a companion. The reason of our longer stay in this place was, that our camels had strayed to a very great distance southwards, so that they could not be found in the forenoon of the following day. The blame of letting them stray was thrown upon

---

* It is scarcely necessary to say that the village Bághzen, reported to be situated on the very highest peak of these mountains, does not exist. There is no village of this name.

Hassan, whose inferiority as a drummer I had occasion to notice above. How he was punished Mr. Richardson has described; and I will only add that the handkerchief which he paid, was to be given to the "serkí-n-kárfi"* ("the task-master," properly "the master of the iron" or "of the force"); but the whole affair was rather a piece of pleasantry.

In the morning Mghás, the chief of Téllwa, a fine, sturdy man mounted upon a strong grey horse, passed by, going southward, followed by a long string of camels; and shortly afterwards a small caravan of people of Selúfiet, who had bought corn in Damerghú, passed in the opposite direction.

Saturday, December 21st. The weather was clear and cheerful; and the sun was warmer than hitherto. We went on, and approached a district more favoured by nature, when, having passed an irregular formation in a state of great decomposition, we reached about ten o'clock the valley Unán, or rather a branch-wádi of the chief valley of that name, where dúm-palms began to appear, at first solitary and scattered about, but gradually forming a handsome grove, particularly after the junction with the chief valley, where a thick cluster of verdure, formed by a variety of trees, greeted the eye. There is also a village of the name of Unán, lying on the border of the principal valley a little higher up; and wells occur in different spots. But the valley was not merely rich in vegetation—it

---

* Kárfi has both meanings, by a metaphor easily to be understood; da-kárfi is "by force."

was the richest indeed as yet seen on this road—it was also enlivened by man; and after we had met two I'ghdalén whom I had known in A'gades, we passed a large troop of Ikádmawen, who were busy watering their camels, cattle, and goats at one of the wells. We also saw here the first specimens of stone houses, which characterize the district to which the valley Unán forms the entrance-hall, if I may use the expression. On its western side is an irregular plain, where a division of the salt-caravan lay encamped.

Proceeding then, after midday we passed by a low white cone on our left, after which the valley, with its variety of vegetation, and animated as it was by numerous herds of goats, made a cheerful impression. Here the remains of stone dwellings became numerous; and further on we passed an entire village consisting of such houses, which, as I was distinctly informed, constituted in former times one of the principal settlements of the Kél-gerés, who were then masters of all the territory as far as the road to A'gades. The whole valley here formed a thick grove of dúm-palms; and stone houses, entire or in ruins, were scattered all about. About three o'clock in the afternoon we left it for an hour, traversing a rocky flat with a low ridge of basalt ranging on our right, when we descended again into the dúm-valley, which had been winding round on the same side, and encamped, at half-past four o'clock in the afternoon, in the midst of very wild and rank vegetation nourished by an immense torrent which occasionally rolls its floods along the channel, and which had left, on the stems of the baggarúwa-trees with which it was lined, evident traces of the depth which it may sometimes attain.   The bed of the torrent was thickly overgrown with wild melons.

Although there is no well in the neighbourhood, we were to stay here the two following days, in order to give the camels a good feed.   A well, called Tánis-n-tánode, lies lower down the valley, but at a considerable distance.   The valley itself runs south-westward: by some it is said to join the Erázar-n-Bargót; but this seems scarcely possible.   Numerous flocks of wild pigeons passed over our heads the following morning, looking for water.   The monotony of the halt was interrupted, in the course of the day, by the arrival of Hámma, who had been to A'fasás, and by that of Astáfidet, the young titular Kél-owí chief residing in A'sodi, among whose companions or followers was a very intelligent and communicative man of the name of El Hasár, who gave me a great deal of interesting information.   All the eminences in the neighbourhood consist of basaltic formation.

Tuesday, December 24th. We again moved on a little, following the rich valley, which in some places reminded me of the scenery of the Upper Nile, the only difference being that here the broad sandy bottom of the watercourse takes the place of the fine river in the scenery of Nubia.   We made a short halt on the road, in order to supply ourselves with water from the well which I mentioned before.   About noon the fresh fleshy allwot, which had not been observed by us for several days, again appeared, to the great delight of the camels, which like it more than anything else, and, having been deprived of it for some time, attacked it with the utmost greediness. Two miles and a half further on, where the valley widened to a sort of irregular plain with several little channels, we encamped; there was a profusion of herbage all around.

It was Christmas eve; but we had nothing to celebrate it with, and we were cast down by the sad news of the appearance of the cholera in Tripoli. This we had learned during our march, from a small caravan which had left that place three months previously without bringing us a single line, or even as much as a greeting. The eternal bitter "túwo" was to be devoured to-day also, as we had no means of adding a little festivity to our repast.

We remained here the two following days, and were entertained on the morning of Christmas day by a performance of Astáfidet's musicians. This was a somewhat cheerful holiday entertainment, although our visitors had not that object in view, but merely plied their talents to obtain a present. There were only two of them, a drummer and a flutist; and though they did not much excel the other virtuosi of the country, whose abilities we had already tested, nevertheless, having regard to the occasion, we were greatly pleased with them. Here I took leave of my best Kél-owí friend, Hámma, a trustworthy man in

every respect — except, perhaps, as regards the softer
sex — and a cheerful companion, to whom the whole
mission, and I in particular, were under great
obligations.   He, as well as Mohammed Býrji, the
youthful grandson of A'nnur, who accompanied him
on this occasion, were to return hence with Astáfidet,
in order to assist this young titular prince in his arduous task of maintaining order in the country during
the absence of the old chief and the greater part
of the male population of the north-eastern districts.
They were both cheerful, though they felt some
sorrow at parting; but they consoled themselves
with the hope of seeing me again one day.   But,
poor fellows, they were both doomed to fall in the
sanguinary struggle which broke out between the
Kél-gerés and the Kél-owí in 1854.

CHAP. XXI.

THE BORDER-REGION OF THE DESERT. — THE TAGÁMA.

AT length we were to exchange our too easy wandering for the rate of real travelling. Early in the morning a consultation was held with the elder men of the Kél-táfidet, who had come from their villages. We then set out, taking leave of the regions behind us, and looking forward with confidence and hope to the unknown or half-known regions before us.

The valley continued to be well clothed with a profusion of herbage, but it was closely hemmed in on both sides; after a march, however, of four miles and a half, it widened again to more than a mile, and began gradually to lose its character of a valley altogether; but even here the allwot was still seen, although of a stunted and dry appearance. We then left the green hollow, which is the valley Bargót, and I thought we should now enter upon the Hammáda or "ténere;" but after a while the valley again approached close on our left. To my disappointment, we encamped even before noon, at the easy northern slope of the rocky ground, where there is a watering-

place called Aghálle.   The afternoon, however, passed
away very pleasantly, as I had a conversation with
the old chief, who honoured me with a visit, and
touched on many points of the highest interest.

Saturday,   Starting at a tolerably early hour, we
December 28th. ascended the slope; but no sooner had we
reached the level of the plain than we halted, beating
the drum until all the different strings of camels had
come up; we then proceeded.   At first the plain consisted almost exclusively of gravel overgrown with
herbage and allwot, with only now and then a rock
seen projecting; but gradually it became more pebbly, and was then intersected by a great many low
crests of rock consisting chiefly of gneiss.   We gradually ascended towards a low ridge called Abadárjen,
remarkable as forming in this district the northern
border of the elevated sandy plain, which seems to
stretch across a great part of the continent, and
forms the real transition-land between the rocky
wilderness of the desert and the fertile arable zone
of Central Africa.   This sandy ledge is the real home
of the giraffe and of the *Antilope leucoryx*.

Just about noon we entered upon this district,
leaving the rocky range at less than a mile on our
left, and seeing before us a sandy level broken only
now and then by blocks of granite thickly overgrown with the " knotted " grass called bú-rékkeba,
and dotted with scattered talha-trees.   Two miles
further on we encamped.   A very long ear of géro
(*Pennisetum typhoïdeum*), which was broken from a

plant growing wild near the border of the path, was the most interesting object met with to-day, while an ostrich-egg, though accidentally the very first which we had yet seen on this journey, afforded us more material interest, as it enabled us to indulge our palates with a little tasteful *hors d'œuvre*, which caused us more delight, perhaps, than scientific travellers are strictly justified in deriving from such causes.   Our caravan to-day had been joined by Gajére, a faithful servant of A'nnur, who was coming from A'gades, and who, though a stranger at the time, very shortly became closely attached to me, and at present figures among the most agreeable reminiscences of my journey.

When we started we were surprised at the quantity of hád with which the plain Sunday, December 29th. began to be covered.   This excellent plant is regarded by the Arab as the most nutritious of all the herbs of the desert, for the camel; and in the western part of that arid zone it seems to constitute its chief food. Numerous footprints of giraffes were seen, besides those of gazelles and ostriches, and towards the end of the march those of the welwaiji, the large and beautiful antelope called *leucoryx*, from the skin of which the Tawárek make their large bucklers.   Further on, the plain presented some ups and downs, being at times naked, at others well wooded and overgrown with grass.   At length, after a good day's march we encamped.

To-day we made the acquaintance of another

native of Middle Sudán, the name of which plays a very important part in the nomenclature of articles of the daily market in all the towns and villages. This was the magariá (called by the Kanúri "kúsulu"), a middle-sized tree with small leaves of olive-green colour, and producing a fruit nearly equal in size to a small cherry, but in other respects more resembling the fruit of the cornel (*Cornus*), and of light-brown colour. This fruit, when dried, is pounded and formed into little cakes, which are sold all over Háusa as "túwo-n-magariá," and may be safely eaten in small quantities even by a European, to allay his hunger for a while, till he can obtain something more substantial; for it certainly is not a very solid food, and if eaten in great quantities, has a very mawkish taste.

While the cattle and the asses went on already in the dark, the camels were left out during the night to pick up what food they could; but early in the morning, when they were to be brought back, a great many of A'nnur's camels could not be found. Hereupon the old chief himself set his people an example; and galloping to the spot where their traces had been lost, he recovered the camels, which were brought in at an early hour. Meanwhile, however, being informed how difficult it would be to obtain water at the well before us, in the scramble of people which was sure to take place, I arranged with Overweg that while I remained behind with Mohammed and the things, he should go on in advance with the Gatróni

and Ibrahím to fill the waterskins; and we afterwards had reason to congratulate ourselves on this
arrangement, for the well, though spacious and built
up with wood, contained at the time but a very moderate supply of muddy water for so large a number
of men and beasts.   Its name is Terguláwen.

This locality, desolate and bare in the extreme, is
considered most dangerous, on account of the continual ghazzias of the Awelímmiden and Kél-gerés,
who are sure to surprise and carry off the straggling
travellers who, if they would not perish by thirst,
must resort to this well.   Our whole road from our
encampment, for more than seven hours and a half,
led over bare, barren sand-hills.   The camping-ground
was chosen at no great distance beyond the well, in
a shallow valley or depression ranging east and west,
and bordered by sand-hills on its south side, with
a little sprinkling of herbage.   The wind, which came
down with a cold blast from N.N.E. was so strong,
that we had great difficulty in pitching the tent.

Last day of 1850.   A cold day, and a
mountainous country.   After we had   December 31st.
crossed the sand-hills, there was nothing before us
but one flat expanse of sand, mostly bare, and clothed
with trees only in favoured spots.   The most remarkable phenomenon was the appearance of the feathery
bristle, the *Pennisetum distichum*, which on the road
to A'gades begins much further northwards.   Indeed, when we encamped, we had some difficulty in
finding a spot free from this nuisance, though of

course the strong wind carried the seeds to a great
distance. All our enjoyment of the last evening of the
old year centred in an extra dish of two ostrich-eggs.

January 1st, 1851. This morning the condition in which
the people composing the caravan
crawled out of their berths was most miserable and
piteous; and moreover nobody thought of starting
early, as several camels had been lost. At length,
when the intense cold began to abate, and when the
animals had been found, everybody endeavoured to
free himself and his clothing from the bristles, which
joined each part of his dress to the others like so many
needles; but what one succeeded in getting rid of was
immediately carried by the strong wind to another,
so that all were in every respect peevish when they
set out at half-past nine o'clock. Nevertheless the
day was to be a very important one to me, and one
on which princely favour was to be shown to me in
a most marked manner.

I have remarked above that on the day I started
for A'gades the old chief made a present of a bullock
to the other members of the mission; but in this
present I myself did not participate, and I had not
yet received anything from him. Perhaps he was
sensible of this, and wanted to give me likewise a
proof of his royal generosity; but I am afraid he
was at the same time actuated by feelings of a very
different nature. He had several times praised my
Turkish jacket, and I had consoled him with a razor
or some other trifle; he had avowedly coveted my

warm black bernús, and had effected, by his frank intimations, nothing more than to make me draw my warm clothing closer round my body. In order to bear the fatigue of the journey more easily, he had long ago exchanged the little narrow kígi or méheri-saddle for the broad pack-saddle, with a load of salt, as a secure seat.

He was one of the foremost in his string, while I, mounted upon my Bú-Séfi (who, since the loss of my méheri, had once more become my favourite saddle-horse), was riding outside the caravan, separated from him by several strings of camels. He called me by name; and on my answering his call, he invited me to come to him :. to do this I had to ride round all the strings. At length I reached him. He began to complain of the intense cold, from which he was suffering so acutely, while I seemed to be so comfortable in my warm clothes ; then he asked if the ostrich-eggs of yesterday evening had pleased us, whereupon I told him that his people had cheered us greatly by contributing, with their gift, to enable us to celebrate our chief festival. He then put his hand into his knapsack, and drawing forth a little cheese, and lifting it high up, so that all his people might see it, he presented the princely gift to me, with a gracious and condescending air, as a "mágani-n-dári" (a remedy against the cold), words which I, indeed, was not sure whether they were not meant ironically, as an intimation that I had withheld from him the real mágani-n-dári, my black bernús.

We were gladdened when, about noon, the plain became clothed with brushwood, and after a while also with bú-rékkeba. Large troops of ostriches were seen,—once a whole family, the parents with several young ones of various ages, all running in single file one after the other. We encamped at half-past three in the afternoon, on a spot tolerably free from ka-réngia, where we observed a great many holes of the fox, the fének, or ñauñáwa (*Megalotis famelicus*), particularly in the neighbourhood of ant-hills. There were also the larger holes of the earth-hog (*Ory-cteropus Æthiopicus*), an animal which never leaves its hole in the daytime, and is rarely seen even by the natives. The holes, which are from fourteen to sixteen inches in diameter, and descend gradually, are generally made with great accuracy.

The following day, the country during the first part of our march continued rather bare; but after half-past two in the afternoon it became richer in trees and bushes, forming the southern zone of this sandy inland plateau, which admits of pastoral settlements. The elevation of this plain or transition-zone seems to be in general about two thousand feet above the level of the sea. We encamped at length in the midst of prickly underwood, and had a good deal of trouble before we could clear a spot for pitching the tent.

Thursday, January 2nd. Soon after setting out on our march, we met a caravan consisting of twenty oxen laden with corn, and further on passed a herd of cattle

belonging to the Tagáma,—a most cheerful sight to us.
We then encamped before ten o'clock a little beyond a
village of the same tribe, which, from a neighbouring
well, bears the name In-asámet.   The village consisted
of huts exactly of the kind described by Leo ; for
they were built of mats (*stuore*) erected upon stalks
(*frasche*), and covered with hides over a layer of
branches, and were very low.   Numbers of children
and cattle gave to the encampment a lively aspect.
The well is rather deep, not less than seventeen
fathoms.

We had scarcely encamped, when we were visited
by the male inhabitants of the village, mounted upon
a small ill-looking breed of horses.   They proved to
be somewhat troublesome, instigated as they were by
curiosity, as well as by their begging propensities;
but in order to learn as much as possible, I thought
it better to sacrifice the comfort of my tent, and con-
verse with them.   They were generally tall men, and
much fairer than the Kél-owí ; but in their customs
they showed that they had fallen off much from
ancient usages, through intercourse with strangers.
The women not only made the first advances, but,
what is worse, they were offered even by the men,
—their brethren, or husbands.   Even those among
the men whose behaviour was least vile and revolting,
did not cease urging us to engage with the women,
who failed not to present themselves soon afterwards.
I could scarcely be taken as a joke.   Some of the
women were immensely fat, particularly in the hinder

regions, for which the Tawárek have a peculiar and
expressive name—tebúlloden. Their features were
very regular and their skin fair. The two most distinguished amongst them gave me their names as
Shabó and Támatu, which latter word, though signi-
fying "woman" in general, may nevertheless be also
used as a proper name. The wealthier among them
were dressed 'in black túrkedí and the zénne; the
poorer in white cotton. The dress of most of the
men was also white; but the chief peculiarity of the
latter was, that several of them wore their hair hanging down in long tresses. This is a token of their
being Aníslimen or Merábetín (holy men), which
character they assume notwithstanding their dissolute manners. They have no school, but pride themselves on having a mállem appointed at their mesállaje, which must be miserable enough. Having once
allowed the people to come into my tent, I could
not clear it again the whole day. The names of
the more respectable among the men ·were Kílle,
El Khassén, Efárret, Cháy, Ríssa, Khándel, and
Amaghár (properly "the Elder"). All these people,
men and women, brought with them a variety of
objects for sale; and I bought from them some dried
meat of the welwaiji (*Antilope leucoryx*), which proved
to be very fine, as good as beef; others, however,
asserted that it was the flesh of the "rákomi-n-dáwa"
or giraffe.

Hunting, together with cattle-breeding, is the chief
occupation of the Tagáma; and they are expert

enough with their little swift horses, to catch the
large antelope as well as the giraffe. Others engage
in the salt-trade, and accompany the Kél-gerés on
their way to Bílma, without however following them
to Sókoto, where, for the reason which I shall presently explain, they are not now allowed to enter;
but they bring their salt to Kanó. In this respect
the Tagáma acknowledge also, in a certain degree,
the supremacy of the sultan of A'gades.

Their slaves were busy in collecting and pounding
the seeds of the karéngia, or úzak (*Pennisetum distichum*), which constitutes a great part of their food.
Whatever may be got here is procurable only with
money,—even the water is sold — the water-skin for
a zekka of millet; but of course grain is here- very
much cheaper than in A'ír, and even than in A'gades.
Altogether the Tagáma * form at present a very
small tribe, able to muster, at the utmost, three hundred spears; but most of them are mounted on
horseback. Formerly, however, they were far more
numerous, till I'bram, the father of the present chief,
undertook, with the assistance of the Kél-gerés, the
unfortunate expedition against Sókoto (then governed
by Bello), of which Clapperton has given a somewhat

---

* The Tagáma were said by some of our informants to have
come from Jánet; but I was not able to confirm this piece of information. However, I am sure that they belong to a stock settled
in these regions long before the Kél-owí. We find them settled
on the borders of Negroland in very ancient times. Horneman,
from what he heard about them, believed them to be Christians.

exaggerated account.* The country around is said
to be greatly infested by lions, which often carry off
camels.

Friday,   Our setting out this morning, after the
January 4th. camels were all laden and the men mounted,
was retarded by the arrival of a queen of the desert,
a beauty of the first rank, at least as regarded her
dimensions. The lady, with really handsome features,
was mounted upon a white bullock, which snorted
violently under his immense burden. Nevertheless
this luxurious specimen of womankind was sickly, and
required the assistance of the tabíb, or " ne-meglán †,"
a title which Overweg had earned for himself by his
doctoring, though his practice was rather of a remarkable kind; for he used generally to treat his patients,
not according to the character of their sickness, but
according to the days of the week on which they
came. Thus he had one day of calomel, another of
Dover's powder, one of Epsom salts, one of magnesia,
one of tartar emetic: the two remaining days being
devoted to some other medicines; and it of course
sometimes happened that the man who suffered from
diarrhœa got Epsom salts, and he who required opening medicine was blessed with a dose of Dover's powder. Of course my friend made numerous exceptions
to this calendary method of treating disease, whenever time and circumstances allowed him to study

* Clapperton and Denham's Travels, vol. ii. p. 107.
† The Western Tawárek call the doctor "anéssafar."

more fully the state of a patient. However, in the hurry in which we just then were, he could scarcely make out what the imaginary or real infirmity of this lady was; and I cannot say what she got. She was certainly a woman of great authority, as the old chief himself was full of kind regards and deference to her. We were rather astonished that he exchanged here his brown mare for a lean white horse, the owners of which seemed, with good reason, excessively delighted with their bargain.

At length we got off, proceeding towards the land of promise in an almost direct southerly course. After three miles' march the thick bush " dílu " made its appearance in the denser underwood, and the country became more hilly and full of ant-holes, while in the distance ahead of us, a little to our left, a low range became visible, stretching east and west. Suddenly the ground became a rocky flat, and the whole caravan was thrown into disorder. We did not at first perceive its cause, till we saw, to our great astonishment, that a steep descent by a regular terrace was here formed, at least a hundred feet high, which conducted to a lower level, — the first distinct proof that we had passed the Hammáda. The vegetation here was different, and a new plant made its appearance called " ágwau," a middle-sized bush consisting of a dense cluster of thick branches of very white wood, at present without leaves, the young shoots just coming out ; melons also were plentiful here, but they had no taste. The rocky descent only extends to a short distance towards the west, when it breaks off, while on our left it stretched far to the south-east. When we had kept along this plain for a little more than two miles, we passed, a short distance on our right, a large pond or "tébki" of water, called "Fárak," spreading out in a hollow. I had here a long conversation with my frolicsome friend Mohammed A'nnur's cousin, who was also going to Sudán; I told him that his uncle seemed to know his people well, and showed his wisdom in not leaving such a wanton youngster as himself behind him. He was, as usual, full of good humour, and informed me that A'nnur's troop was almost the first, being preceded only by the caravan of Sálah, the chief of Egéllat. He prided himself again on his exploits in the late ghazzia, when they had overtaken the E'fadaye marauders in Tálak and Búgarén. Further on we passed the well called Fárak, which was now dry, and encamped two miles beyond it in a district thickly overgrown with karéngias.

Saturday, January 5th. We had scarcely started, when I observed an entirely new species of plant, which is rather rare in Central Negroland, and which I afterwards met in considerable quantities along the north shore of the so-called Niger, between Timbúktu and Tosáye. It is here, in Háusa, called "kumkúmmia," a euphorbia growing from one and a half to two feet in height, and is very poisonous; indeed hereabouts, as in other districts of Central Africa, it furnishes the chief material with which arrows are poisoned. The principal

vegetation consisted of "árza" (a species of laurel) and
dílu ; and further on parasitical plants were seen, but
not in a very vigorous state. Altogether the country
announced its fertility by its appearance ; and a little
before noon, when low ranges of hills encompassed the
view on both sides, and gave it a more pleasant character, we passed, close on our left, another pastoral
settlement of half mat and half leather tents *, enlivened by numerous cattle and flocks, and leaning
against a beautiful cluster of most luxuriant trees.
But more cheerful still was the aspect of a little lake
or tank of considerable extent, and bordered all around
with the thickest grove of luxuriant acacias of the
kind called "baggarúwa," which formed overhead a
dense and most beautiful canopy. This little lake is
called "Gúmrek," and was full of cattle, which came
hither to cool themselves in the shade during the hot
hours of the day. In this pleasant scenery we
marched along, while a good number of horsemen
collected around us, and gave us a little trouble; but
I liked them far better, with their rough and warlike
appearance, than their more civilized and degraded
brethren of the day before. At about half-past two
we encamped on the border of a dry watercourse with
a white sandy bed, such as we had not seen for a long
time. But here we made the acquaintance of a new
plant and a new nuisance ; this is the "aidó," a grass

---

* I shall describe this sort of tent in the narrative of my stay
amongst the Western Tawárek.

with a prickly involucrum of black colour, and of larger size and stronger prickles than the karéngia (or *Pennisetum distichum*), and more dangerous for naked feet than for the clothes. A new string of camels joined us here, led on by Mohammed A'nnur.

Sunday, January 6th. We were greatly surprised at the appearance of the weather this morning; the sky was covered with thick clouds, and even a light rain fell while the caravan was loading. We felt some fear on account of the salt; but the rain soon ceased. In the course of my travels, principally during my stay in Timbúktu, I had more opportunities of observing these little incidental rain-falls of the cold season, or "the black nights," during January and February; and further on, as occasion offers, I shall state the result of my observations.

At a little more than a mile from our camping-ground, the aspect of the country became greatly changed, and we ascended a hilly country of a very remarkable character, the tops of the hills looking bare, and partly of a deep, partly of a greyish black, like so many mounds of volcanic *débris*, while the openings or hollows were clothed with underwood. Here our companions began already to collect wood as a provision for the woodless corn-fields of Damerghú; but we were as yet some distance off. Ascending gradually, we reached the highest point at nine o'clock, while close on our right we had a hill rising to greater elevation; and here we obtained an interesting view — just as the sun burst through the clouds — over the hilly country before us, through which a bushy depression ran in a very winding course.   Along this tortuous thread of underwood lay our path.   As we were proceeding, Ibrahím, our Furáwi freeman, who was a very good marksman for a black, brought down a large lizard (Draconina) " demmó," or, as the Arabs call it, " wárel," which was sunning itself on a tree ; it is regarded by the people as a great delicacy.   A little before noon the country seemed to become more open, but only to be covered with rank reeds ten feet high — quite a new sight for us, and a great inconvenience to the camels, which stumbled along over the little hillocks from which the bunches of reeds shot forth.   Further on, the ground (being evidently very marshy during the rainy season) was so greatly torn and rent by deep fissures, that the caravan was obliged to separate into two distinct parties.   The very pleasant and truly park-like hilly country continued nearly unchanged till one o'clock in the afternoon, when, at a considerable distance on our left, we got sight of the first corn-fields of Damerghú, belonging to the villages of Kulakérki and Banuwélki.

This was certainly an important stage in our journey.   For although we had before seen a few small patches of garden-fields, where corn was produced (as in Selúfiet, A'uderas, and other favoured places), yet they were on so small a scale as to be incapable of sustaining even a small fraction of the population ; but here we had at length reached those fertile regions of Central Africa, which are not only able to sustain their own population, but even to export to foreign countries. My heart gladdened at this sight, and I felt thankful to Providence that our endeavours had been so far crowned with success; for here a more promising field for our labours was opened, which might become of the utmost importance in the future history of mankind.

We soon after saw another village, which several of our companions named Olalówa, and which may indeed be so called, although I thought at the time they applied to it the name of the more famous place further on, with which they were acquainted; and I afterwards convinced myself that such was really the case. The country became open and level, the whole ground being split and rent by fissures. While I was indulging in pleasing reveries of new discoveries and successful return, I was suddenly startled by three horsemen riding up to me and saluting me with a "Lá ílah ilá Allah." It was Dan l'bra (or l'braın, the " son of Ibrahím "), the famous and dreaded chief of the Tamizgída*, whom the ruler of Tintéllust himself in former times had not been able to subdue, but had been obliged to pay him a sort of small tribute or transit-money, in order to secure the unmolested passage of his caravans on their way to Sudán. The warlike chief had put on all his finery, wearing a

* This name means " the mosque; " and the tribe, apparently, has formerly been settled somewhere in a town. By the Arabs it is regarded as greatly Arabicized, and is even called 'A'raba. We shall meet another tribe of the same name in the West.

handsome blue bernús, with gold embroidery, over a rich Sudán tobe, and was tolerably well mounted. I answered his salute, swearing by Allah that I knew Allah better than he himself, when he became more friendly, and exchanged with me a few phrases, asking me what we wanted to see in this country. He then went to take his turn with Mr. Richardson. I plainly saw that if we had not been accompanied by A'nnur himself, and almost all our luggage sent on in advance, we should have had here much more serious colloquies.

After having ascended a little from the lower ground, where evidently, during the rains, a large sheet of water collects, and having left on our right a little village surrounded by stubble-fields, we passed along the western foot of the gently sloping ground on whose summit lies the village ("úngwa") Sámmit. It was past four o'clock in the afternoon when we encamped upon an open stubble-field, and we were greatly cheered at observing here the first specimen of industry in a good sense,—for of industry in a bad sense the Tagáma had already given us some proof. As soon as we were dismounted, two muscular blacks, girded with leather aprons round their loins, came bounding forward, and in an instant cleared the whole open space around us, while in a few minutes several people, male and female, followed, offering a variety of things for sale, such as millet, beans (of two sorts), and those cakes called dodówa, which were duly appreciated by the late Captain Clapperton for

the excellent soup made of them. Of their prepara-
tion I shall speak when we meet the first tree of that
species, the doròwa—the name of the cake and that
of the tree being distinguished by the change of
a consonant. The cakes obtained here, however,
as I afterwards learned, were of a most inferior
and spurious character—of that kind called "dodówa-
n-bòsso" in Háusa, and in some districts "yákwa."
We felt here the benefit of civilization in a most pal-
pable way, by getting most excellent chicken-broth
for our supper. Our servants, indeed, were cooking
the whole night.

Monday,
January 7th. There were again a few drops of rain
in the morning. Soon after starting, we
were greeted by the aspect of a few green kitchen-
gardens, while we were still gradually ascending. On
reaching the highest level, we obtained a sight of the
mountains of Damerghú ("dúwatsu n Damerghú," as
they are called), a low range stretching parallel with
the road towards the east, while ahead of us and
westward, the country was entirely open, resembling
one unbroken stubble-field. Having crossed a hollow
with a dry pond and some trees, we had at about
eight o'clock a village close on our right, where, for
the first time, I saw that peculiar style of architecture
which, with some more or less important varieties,
extends through the whole of Central Africa.

These huts, in as far as they are generally erected
entirely with the stalks of the Indian corn, almost
without any other support except that derived from

the feeble branches of the *Asclepias gigantea*, certainly
do not possess the solidity of the huts of the villages
of A'sben, which are supported by a strong framework
of branches and young trees; but they greatly surpass
them in cleanliness, on account of the large available supply of the light material of which they are
built.   It is, however, to be remarked that the inhabitants of this district depend in a great measure for
their fuel too upon the stalks of the Indian corn.
The huts in general are lower than those in A'sben,
and are distinguished from them entirely by the
curved top of the thatched roof, which sustains the
whole.   In examining these structures, one cannot
but feel surprised at the great similarity which they
bear to the huts of the aboriginal inhabitants of
Latium, such as they are described by Vitruvius
and other authors, and represented occasionally on
terra-cotta utensils, while the name in the Bórnu or
Kanúri language, "kósi," bears a remarkable resemblance to the Latin name "casa," however accidental
it may be.   It is still more remarkable that a similar
name, "kúde," is given to a cottage in the Tamil
and other Asiatic languages.

More remarkable and peculiar than the huts, and
equally new and interesting to us, as the most evident symptom of the great productiveness of this
country, were the little stacks of corn scattered among
the huts, and in reality consisting of nothing but an
enormous basket made of reeds, and placed upon a
scaffold of thick pieces of wood about two feet high,

in order to protect the corn against the "kúsu" and the "gará" (the mouse and the ant), and covered over on the top with a thatched roof, like that of the huts.* Of these little corn-stacks we shall find some most interesting architectural varieties in the course of our travels. The "gará," or white ant (*Termes fatalis*), is here the greatest nuisance, being most destructive to the corn as well as to all softer kinds of house-furniture, or rather to the houses them-selves. Every possible precaution must be taken against it. The "kúsu," or mouse, abounds here in great numbers, and of several species : particularly frequent is the jerbóa (*dipus*), which for the traveller certainly forms a very pleasant object to look at as it jumps about on the fields, but not so to the native, who is anxious about his corn.

While reflecting on the feeble resistance which this kind of architecture must necessarily offer in case of conflagration, particularly as water is at so great a distance, I perceived almost opposite to this little hamlet a larger one called Mája, on the other side of the road, and shaded by some thorn-trees. From both villages the people came forth to offer cheese and Indian corn for sale. They differed widely from the fanatical people among whom we had been travelling ; most of them were pagans and slaves. Their dress was mean and scanty ; this of course is an expensive article in a country where no cotton is produced, and

* A representation of such a stack of corn is given in the next volume.

where articles of dress can only be obtained in exchange for the produce of the country. On a field near the path the Guinea corn was still lying unthreshed, though the harvest had been collected two months before. The threshing is done with long poles. The whole of Damerghú produces no durra or sorghum, but only millet or *Pennisetum typhoïdeum*, and all, as far as I know, of the white species.

Further on, the stubble-fields were pleasantly interrupted by a little pasture-ground, where we saw a tolerably large herd of cattle. Then followed a tract of country entirely covered with the monotonous *Asclepias gigantea*, which at present is useful only as affording materials for the framework of the thatched roofs, or for fences. It is worthless for fuel, although the pith is employed as tinder. The milky juice (which at present is used by the pagan natives, as far as I know, only to ferment their gíya, and which greatly annoys the traveller in crossing the fields, as it produces spots on the clothes, and even injures the hair of the horses) might become an important article of trade. The cattle, at least in districts where they have not good pasturage, feed on the leaves of the asclepias.

We were gradually ascending, and reached at about a quarter-past ten o'clock the summit of a rising ground, the soil of which consisted of red clay. Altogether it was an undulating country, appearing rather monotonous, from its almost total want of trees, but nevertheless of the highest interest to one just arrived from the arid regions of the north.

Having passed several detached farms, which left a very agreeable impression of security and peaceful ness, we came upon a group of wells, some dry, but others well filled, where besides cattle a good many horses were led to water—a cheerful and to us quite a novel sight; many more were seen grazing around on the small patches of pasture-ground which interrupted the stubble-fields, and some of them were in splendid condition—strong and well-fed, and with fine sleek coats; all of them were of brown colour. But there was another object which attracted our attention: the trough at the well was formed of a tortoiseshell of more than two feet in length; and on inquiry we learnt that this animal, of a large size, is not at all rare in this district. It was already mentioned, as common in these regions, by the famous Andalusian geographer El Bekri.

Villages, stubble-fields, tracts covered with turfáfia (the *Asclepias*), detached farms, herds of cattle and troops of horses tranquilly grazing, succeeded each other, while the country continued undulating, and was now and then intersected by the dry bed of a watercourse. Having passed two divisions of the áír, or áíri, which had preceded us, and had encamped near some villages, we obtained quite a new sight— a large quadrangular place called Dam-mágaj i(properly Dan Mágaji, "the son of the lieutenant," after whom it is called), surrounded with a clay wall,

spreading out at a short distance on our left, while
in the distance before us in the direction of Zinder,
a high cone called Zozáwa became visible.   Leaving
a village of considerable size on our right, at a
quarter to three o'clock we reached a small hamlet,
from which numbers of people were hurrying forward, saluting us in a friendly and cheerful manner,
and informing us that this was Tágelel, the old
chief's property.   We now saw that the village consisted of two distinct groups separated from each
other by a cluster of four or five tsámias or tamarind-
trees—the first poor specimens of this magnificent
tree, which is the greatest ornament of Negroland.

Our camping-ground was at first somewhat uncomfortable and troublesome, it being absolutely necessary to take all possible precautions against the
dreadful little foe that infests the ground wherever
there is arable land in Sudán—the white ant; but
we gradually succeeded in making ourselves at home
and comfortable for the next day's halt.

The greatest part of the following day was spent
in receiving visits.   The first of these was interesting,
although its interest was diminished by the length
to which it was protracted.   The visitor was a gallant
freeborn Ikázkezan, of a fine though not tall figure,
regular, well-marked features, and fair complexion,
which at once bespoke his noble birth; he was clad
in a very good red bernús, of the value of 70,000
kurdí in Kanó, and altogether was extremely neatly
and well dressed.   He came first on horseback with

two companions on camels, but soon sent his horse
and companions away, and squatted down in my
tent, apparently for a somewhat long talk with me;
and he remained with me for full three hours. But
he was personally interesting, and a very fine specimen of his tribe; and the interest attaching to his
person was greatly enhanced by his having accompanied the expedition against the Welád Slimán,
which none of our other friends the Kél-owí had done.
On this account I was greatly pleased to find that his
statements confirmed and corroborated the general
reports which we had heard before. He was all admiration at the large fortification which, as soon as
they heard that the Tawárek intended an expedition
against them, the Arabs had constructed at Késkáwa,
on the shore of lake Tsád (carrying trees of immense
size from a great distance), and where they had remained for two months awaiting the arrival of their
enraged foe. He expressed his opinion that nothing
but the Great God himself could have induced them
to leave at length such a secure retreat and impreg-
nable stronghold, by crazing their wits, and con-
founding their understandings. I also learnt that
these daring vagabonds had not contented themselves
with taking away all the camels of the Kél-owí that
came to Bílma for salt, but, crossing that most desolate tract which separates Kawár or Hénderi Tedá
(the Tébu country) from A'ír, pursued the former as
far as Agwáu.

At the time I conversed with my Ikázkezan friend

about this subject I was not yet aware how soon I was to try my fortune with the shattered remains of that Arab horde, although its fate had formed an object of the highest interest to the expedition from the beginning. As for ourselves, my visitor was perfectly well acquainted with the whole history of our proceedings; and he was persuaded that, out of any material, we were able to make what we liked, but especially fine bernúses, — an opinion which gave rise to some amusing conversation between us.

This interesting visitor was succeeded by a great many tiresome people, so that I was heartily glad when Overweg, who had made a little excursion to a great pond of stagnant water, at the foot of the hill of Farára, the residence of Mákita, returned, and, lying outside the little shed of tanned skins, which was spread over his luggage, drew the crowd away from my tent. Overweg, as well as Ibrahím, who had accompanied him, had shot several ducks, which afforded us a good supper, and made us support with some degree of patience the trying spectacle of a long procession of men and women laden with eatables, passing by us in the evening towards the camping-ground of the chief, while not a single dish found its way to us; and though we informed them that they were missing their way, they would not understand the hint, and answered us with a smile. Many severe remarks on the niggardliness of the old chief were that evening made round our fire. While music, dancing, and merriment were going

on in the village, a solitary " maimólo" found his way
to us, to console the three forsaken travellers from a
foreign land, by extolling them to the skies, and
representing them as special ministers of the Almighty.

Wednesday,
January 8th. To-day I began a list of the principal
towns and villages of Dam-erghú, which I
shall now give as it was corrected and completed by
my subsequent inquiries; but first I shall make a few
general observations.

A'ír, or rather A'sben, as we have seen above, was
originally inhabited by the Góber race,—that is to say,
the most noble and original stock of what is now, by
the natives themselves, called the Háusa nation; but
the boundaries of A'sben appear not to have originally
included the district of Dam-erghú, as not even those
of A'ír do at the present day, Dam-erghú being considered as an outlying province, and the granary of
A'ír.   On the contrary, the name of Dam-erghú
(which is formed of the same root as the names Daw-
erghú, Gam-erghú, and others, all lying round Bórnu
Proper) seems to show that the country to which it
applied belonged to the Kanúri race, who are in
truth its chief occupants even at the present day, the
Bórnu population being far more numerous than the
Háusa; and though a great many of them are at present reduced to a servile condition, they are not imported slaves, as Mr. Richardson thought, but most
of them are serfs or prædial slaves, the original inhabitants of the country.   It is true that a great

many of the names of the villages in Dam-erghú belong to the Háusa language; but these I conceive to
be of a former date. The district extends for about
sixty miles in length, and forty in breadth. It is
altogether an undulating country of very fertile soil,
capable of maintaining the densest population, and
was in former times certainly far more thickly inhabited than at present. The bloody wars carried on
between the Bórnu king 'Alí 'Omármi on the one
side, and the sultan of A'gades and the Tawárek
of A'ír on the other, must have greatly depopulated
these border districts.

In giving a list of the principal villages of this
region, I shall first mention five places which owe
their celebrity and importance, not to their size or
the number of their inhabitants, but rather to their
political rank, being the temporary residences of the
chiefs.

I name first Kúla-n-kérki — not the village mentioned above as being seen in the distance, but another
place half-a-day's journey ("wúëni," as the Háusa
people say) east from Tágelel — of considerable size,
and the residence of the chief Músa, who may with
some truth be called master of the soil of Dam-erghú,
and is entitled serkí-n-Dam-erghú in the same sense
in which Mazáwaji was formerly called serkí-n-A'sben;
and to him all the inhabitants of the district, with the
sole exception of the people of the three other chiefs,
have to do homage and present offerings.

Olalówa, about three miles or three miles and a half S.W. of Tágelel, is rather smaller than Kúla-n-kérki. It is the residence of Mazáwaji, a man of the same family as A'nnur, who, till a short time before our arrival in A'ír, was " amanókal-n-Kél-owí," residing in A'sodi, in the place of Astáfidet. Though he has left A'ír voluntarily, he still retains the title " serki-n-Kél-owí," and is a friendly and benevolent old man. Olalówa has a market-place provided with rúnfona, or rúnfas (sheds), where a market is held every Sunday; but it is not well attended by the inhabitants of the other places, owing to the fear entertained of Mazáwaji's slaves, who seem (mild as their master is) to be disposed to violence.

Farára, the residence of Mákita or I'mkiten, the man who played the chief part during the interregnum, or rather the reign of anarchy, in A'sben, before the installation of 'Abd el Káder It is situated about two miles from Tágelel, on the west side of the road which we were to take, on the top of a hill, at the foot of which is a very extensive lagoon of water, from which the inhabitants of Tágelel also, and of many surrounding villages, draw their supply.

Tágelel, the residence of A'nnur, although of small size (the two groups together containing scarcely more than a hundred and twenty cottages), is nevertheless of great political importance in all the relations of this distracted country.

Here also I will mention Dankámsa, the residence of an influential man of the name of U'mma, which in a certain respect enjoys ·the same rank as the four above-named villages.[*]

I will also add in this place the little which I was able to learn about the mixed settlements of Tawárek and black natives between Dam-erghú and Múniyo. As these places are the chief centres whence proceed the predatory excursions which are carried on continually against the northern districts of Bọ́rnu, information with regard to them is not easily obtained. The chief among them is the principality of Alákkos

[*] Besides these I learnt the names of the following places of Dam-erghú :—Nimináka, Gómtu, Sabón-garí, Dágabi, Dagábitáng, Bíri-n-bága ; Kúfkúf (called Kobkob by Mr. Richardson in the itinerary which, on his first journey to Ghát, he forwarded to Government[a]), in the W., with a lake of very great dimensions ; Babá-n-bírni, a place which I think in former times has been the chief town of the district; Kuyáwa, Da-n-kúmbu, Da-n-gérki, Marké (a very common name in Central Sudán) ; Zozáwa, at the foot of the high cone of the same name mentioned above ; Lekári, also S. ; Dammágaji, the place mentioned above; Ngól-mata, N.; Ngól-ganó, Ngól-kalé, Banwélki, Gagáwa, Karíkau, Keshír-keshír, Dammó-kochi, Nakéfadáng, Damméle, Guyé-guyé, Kabíwa, Fókeni, Gáma-kay, Burúru, Gángará, Tágelel-ta-Dágabi (different from A'nnur's residence) ; Maryámatángh, Kusúmmetángh (both these places are Tawárek settlements); Maizáki, Málemrí, Malenkáderi (prop. Mallem Káderi), Chírrim, Esúwi, Músherí, Músajá, Aikáuri, Addankólle, Jémagu-Gomaigéne, Lamá, Hámedan, Karáza, Al-kúre, Dantánka, Agwá, Makárarí, Kasallíya, Fárag, Gámaran, Ungwa Sámmit, Yesíyu-Négdar, Chílim-pótuk (N. of Kulankérki), Ginnári, Golmaija, Kúnkuré (the tortoise), Báya-n-Dúchi (a village so called on account of its being situated behind a hillock or rocky eminence, and the birthplace of the chief Músa), Dakári, Majá, Gílmirám, Maibánkuba.

[a] b, p, and f (or rather ph, p̄) are frequently interchanged in all the dialects of the Central African languages.

or Elákwas*, about three (long) days N.E. from Zínder, and two from Gúre, the present residence of Muniyóma. The ruling class in this sequestered haunt of robbers and freebooters seems to belong to the tribe of the Tagáma; and the name of the present chief is A'bú-Bakr, who can lead into the field perhaps two hundred horsemen. The chief place bears the same name as the whole principality; and besides it there are but a few small places, among which I learnt the name of Dáucha. Alákkos is celebrated among the hungry inhabitants of the desert, on account of its grain; and in the desert-song, the verse which celebrates the horse of Tawát, is followed by another one celebrating the grain of Alákkos, "tádak Elákwas."

Quite apart seems to be a place called Gáyim, which is governed by a chief called Kámmedán; and I know not whether another place called Kárbo be comprised in the same principality or not. These are the great haunts of the freebooters, who infest the border districts, from Dam-erghú to the very heart of Kánem.

Thursday, January 9th. This was the great market-day in Tágelel, on which account our departure was put off till the following day; but the market did not become thronged until a late hour. I went there in the afternoon. The market-place, which was about 800 yards distant from our encampment, towards the west, upon a small hilly eminence, was provided

* There can scarcely be any doubt that this place has some connection with the tribe of Ilasgwas mentioned by Corippus.

with several sheds or rúnfas.   The articles laid out
for sale consisted of cotton (which was imported),
tobacco, ostrich-eggs, cheese, mats, ropes, nets, earthen-
ware, pots, gúras (or drinking-vessels made of the
Cucurbita ovifera and *C. lagenaria*) and kórios (or
vessels made of a fine sort of reed, for containing
fluids, especially milk) ; besides these there were a
tolerable supply of vegetables, and two oxẹn, for sale.
The buyers numbered about a hundred.

In the afternoon two magozáwa, or pagans, in a
wild and fanciful attire (the dry leaves of Indian corn
or sorghum hanging down from their barbarous head-
dress, and from the leather apron which was girt
round their loins and richly ornamented with shells and
bits of coloured cloth), danced in front of our tents
the " devil's dance " — a performance of great interest
in regard to the ancient pagan customs of these countries, and to which I may have occasion to revert
when I speak about Dodó, or the evil spirit, and the
representation of the souls of the dead.

Tágelel was a very important point for the proceedings of the mission on several accounts. For here we
had reached the lands where travellers are able to
proceed singly on their way ; and here Overweg and
I were to part from Mr. Richardson, on account of the
low state of our finances, in order to try what each of
us might be able to accomplish single-handed and
without ostentation, till new supplies should arrive
from home.   Here, therefore, the first section of my
narrative will most appropriately terminate.

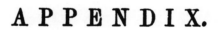

APPENDIX.

APPENDIX.

I.—ROUTE FROM A'GADES TO SÓKOTO.

Day.

1st. Leaving A'gades in the afternoon, you encamp in the valley called U'leye, where there is a well.

2nd. Kerbúb, a valley with water in the sand; start at daybreak, arrive after sunset.

3rd. A'azeru; arrive at sunset, having started before daylight. The whole ground travelled over is covered with pebbles, and now and then with a little sand.

4th. Tebérkurt; arrive after sunset, having passed a watering-place called Arúthes. All pebbles and stones.

5th. I'ngal, a small town; salt of very good quality, and of red colour, is obtained, but only in small quantities. The inhabitants, mostly belonging to the tribe of the I'ghdalén, speak a dialect of the Sónghay, and possess much cattle, with which they supply the market of A'gades. Formerly the S.W. gate of that town was therefore called " Kófa-n-I'ngal." Arrive at sunset; ground pebbly, very few large stones.

6th. ————, a well, the name of which my informant did not remember; arrive about 4 o'clock in the afternoon.

7th. Afáyen, a valley, where you arrive about the same time; pebbles and sand.

8th. Encamp on the pebbly plain a little before sunset.

9th. The same; the plain here is overgrown with a little herbage.

10th. A spot called Semye-táyen; arrive at sunset.

Day.

11th. Jóbeli, a considerable place belonging to the province of A'dar, the territory of which begins here.* It is the market of the Kél-gerés. The language of the inhabitants is said to be a dialect of the Sónghay; you arrive at about three o'clock P.M., after having passed on your road " Tésaki," a locality probably so called from the *Capparis sodata.*

12th. Awelímmiden, an encampment of the section of this great Tawárek tribe which is called " Awelímmiden wuén Bodhál;" at sunset.

13th. Ir-zaghúr, a village; arrive about one o'clock P.M.; road very rugged.

14th. Tinfáf, a village (N.B. I forgot to ask my informant to what tribe belong the inhabitants of these two places); road rocky.

15th. Dúk-rausu, a village; about one o'clock P.M.

16th. Múzki, a village; at sunset; stony.

17th. Kónni, a considerable place, residence of A'dam, a chief who commands a large body of cavalry; arrive a little after mid-day; road very rocky.

18th. Jáni, a village; at sunset.

19th. Wúrno, a considerable place, the present residence of Emír el Mumenín Alíyu, son of Bello; arrive at one o'clock P.M., after having passed Saláme and other villages.

20th. Sókoto, after a march of about eight or nine hours.

II.—ROUTE FROM A'GADES TO MARÁDI, ACCORDING TO THE IN-FORMATION OF THE KÉL-GERÉS GOJÉRI AND HIS COMPANION GHÁSER.

1st. E'razar, a valley, where you arrive about three o'clock P.M., having started from A'gades in the morning.

* I shall say more about A'dar in the fourth volume of my journal.

Day.

2nd. E'm-réndel, a valley; arrive about the same hour.

3rd. Urzédem, a valley; arrive at sunset, your march having led over a sandy region.

4th. A valley, with water, which (according to Gojéri) is called Témiye, but according to Gháser, Afénkúk; at about four o'clock. Probably these are different valleys at a short distance from each other.

5th. A valley, Tewuílu, or another called Bégem; at sunset.

6th. Akúku; at áser (about four o'clock), after having passed a valley called Zeríten, where you fill your water-skins. The whole road consists of pebbles.

7th. Tígger-áderez, a valley; at four o'clock.

8th. Etíddul, high sand-hills, where you arrive about noon.

9th. Jénkeb, a valley; about two o'clock P.M.

10th. Yamímma, a valley with water; arrive at áser.

11th. Zermenétta, a village; about áser.

12th. Awelímmid, a considerable place called after a settlement of the Awelímmiden; arrive about one o'clock P.M.

13th. Ladémmau, or Eladémmau, the northernmost village of the province of Góber, and the residence of Ittegáma, the brother of 'Abd el Káder, the sultan of A'gades.

14th. Gudunnézna, a village; arrive about one o'clock P.M.

15th. A'kerúf, a village; at the áser.

16th, and the two following days, travel over the Hammáda or sárari.

19th. Arrive at Marádi, Mariyádi, or, as the Emgédesi people frequently call it (apparently adopting the Berber idiom), Amrádi. I shall have to say more about this country in the course of my narrative, and therefore omit a list of the places in Góber, which I collected in A'gades.

III.—ITINERARY FROM A'GADES TO DAM-ERGHÚ, ACCORDING TO
VARIOUS INFORMANTS.

Day.
1st. Leave the town in the afternoon, and sleep in Tésak-
n-tállemt.
2nd. Valley E'riyán, with water; about 'aser.
3rd. Sofó-n-bírni, a place now deserted, and a well filled
up, but evidently once a seat of government, being
called "the old capital;" the whole country is flat;
arrive about three o'clock in the afternoon.
4th. Faífaí, a place with plenty of herbage; no water on
the roadside except in holes in the rocks.
5th. Lágato, a basin or pool of water, "tébki," of very
remarkable extent, and surrounded with abundant
herbage.
6th. Riyán, or "Eriyán-embísge," with plenty of herbage;
about sunset. Another road from Lágato to Téténi seems to touch at the village Takóko.
7th. Téténi, with much herbage, no water; between four
and five o'clock P.M.
8th. Gagáwa, a village belonging to the district of Dam-erghú, with a basin of water which is said to be
connected in the rainy season with that of Lágato;
arrive about 'aser.
9th. Tágelel, the village belonging to the chief A'nnur;
about noon.

IV.—ROUTE FROM A'GADES TO BÍLMA, ACCORDING TO THE
EMGÉDESI E'DERI.

1st. Leaving A'gades in the evening, sleep the first night
at about half an hour's distance from the town, in
the depression called Efígi-n-tághalamt.

Day.
2nd. Tin-tabórak, a valley with water, where you arrive at the áser, after having passed early in the morning the valley called Amelúli.

3rd. Binébbu, a valley ornamented with dúm-palms, where you arrive a little before sunset. In the morning you keep for a while along the valley of Tin-tabórak, after which your way lies over the rocks, crossing three different valleys, viz. Eméller, Aráta, and the valley of Amdégeru, before you arrive at that called Binébbu.

4th. Tín-dawén, a valley with water; arrive about one o'clock P.M.

5th. Atezérket, after the áser; all rocky ground.

6th. Encamp on the Hammáda, or ténere, consisting of pebbles; about the áser.

7th. Tázel, a spot among the rocks; about the same hour.

8th. Efígagén, a locality of similar character; about sunset.*

9th. Débradu Ezákker, a hollow between the rocks; halt two hours after sunset and rest awhile, then start again.

10th, and the four following days, you travel night and day over the Hammáda, making only a short halt from ashá to about midnight. On the Hammáda there are neither trees nor stones, and scarcely any herbage.

15th. Fáshi, the westernmost oasis of the " Hénderi Tedá," or, as it is called by the Arabs, Wádí Kawár, with plenty of date-trees, and two castles, one of which is in ruins, while the other is in good condition.

16th. About two hours after sunset, encamp on the Hammáda,

---

* About the name Efígagén, which is probably only a dialectic variety of Efínagen, I have spoken in a former passage.

Day.

when, after about three or four hours' repose, you
start again, and continue the whole of the night.

17th. Encamp late in the evening and start again, as the day
before.

18th. Bílma, the well-known town in Kawár, with the salt-
pits. The Tawárek call all the Tedá or Tébu
Beraúni, a name which in the following volume I
shall endeavour to explain, from the original connection between this people and the Kanúri or Bórnu
race.

V.—Route from A'gades to Tawát, according to 'Abd-Alla.

N. B. Although the first part of this route, as far as
Neswa, coincides in many places with my own route, I shall
nevertheless not omit it, as the coincidence in question proves
the accuracy and intelligence of the informant.

1st. Leaving the town in the afternoon, you encamp the
first night near the village called El Khasás, or El
Hakhsás, in the fertile valley of the same name, distant from A'gades about eight miles.

2nd. Télwa, a valley, where you arrive about the áser, after
having passed on your road several valleys separated from each other by rocky ground, more or less
elevated. Early in the morning you cross the valley
called A'zal, then that called Tufátekín; after
which, about noon, you pass the celebrated valley of
I'r-n-allem, with ruins of old houses, and two fruit-
bearing date-trees; after which, before you arrive
at Télwa, there is still another valley to be crossed,
which is called Isérserén.

3rd. U'klef, a valley with water, like Télwa; arrive at the
time of the 'aser, after having crossed the Wádi
A'sa, and afterwards gone over a pebbly level called
Tínin.

Day.

4th. Makám e' Sheikh ben 'Abd el Kerím, a sort of mosque known to some under the name of Msíd Sídi Baghdádi, where you arrive about an hour before sunset, after having rested, during the greatest heat, near Aúderas. In the morning, your road passes for some time along the valley U'klef.

5th. Tíggeda; about áser.

6th. Encamp about sunset on rocky ground. Pass in the morning the valley called Tefárrowet; then cross for some hours gravelly ground, with a few large white projecting stones; after which you descend into the valley called A'gaten, where, near a well, you pass the hours of the greatest heat.

7th. Ténsif; arrive before the áser.

8th. Iferwán, one of the finest valleys of A'ír, with a village of the same name, and plenty of date-trees bearing excellent fruit. Arrive at sunset, after having passed a number of small valleys called Aghítam.

9th. Tídik, a valley, with a village of the same name, where you arrive before the áser, after having passed the well called Néggaru.

10th. Súf méllel, "the white sand," a place in the gravelly ground, over which your route lies the whole day; arrive about áser.

11th. Zelíl, an inhabited spot, where you arrive about one o'clock P. M., after having passed valleys called respectively Ageléndi, Fadé, and Merátha. (N. B. The valley can be called by this last name only by the Arabs.)

12th. Ifígi or Ifíne-makkéder, called by others Ifíne-bákka, where you arrive at sunset, after having marched the whole day over a pebbly plain called by the Arabs "Shábet el Ahír." The reason why this plain received such a remarkable name was evidently because it was here, in the neighbourhood of the hill Máket-n-ikelán *, that the ancient Góber country of Asben was changed into the Berber country of A'ír, or, as the Arabs call it, Ahír.

13th. You encamp on the hammáda, where there is a little herbage, after having crossed a rocky ground full of pebbles, and having passed a valley called Tiyúten.

14th. You encamp at one o'clock P. M. on a spot with a little herbage of the species called "el hád," after having crossed a stony tract called by the people Tim-ázgaren.

15th. Néswa, a well, not far west of the well Asïu, where you arrive after the áser, after having crossed a valley called Tafsástan.

16th. Teráf, a place on the hammáda, where you encamp at the áser.

17th. Tin-terámbe, a valley, with a famous cavern called A'agídet e' Níb, where you arrive at the áser, proceeding always on the hammáda.

18th. Encamp at sunset between sand-hills called by the Arabs "el Ark," or "Irk" (the Hills).

19th. Tageréra, a valley, where you arrive about one o'clock P. M., after having entered a mountainous tract called "Aghíl."

20th. El A'ghsul, a valley with water, where you arrive a little after noon, after having passed over rugged ground called Esfaméllesa.

21st. Tékderen, a valley, where you arrive after the áser.

22nd. Egháraghén, a valley, where you arrive at the time of the áser, after having crossed a flat plain covered with pebbles.

23rd. Zérzer, a valley with water; arrival at the áser. The ground of the same character.

* See my narrative, p 289.

Day.

24th. Ifék, a valley; arrival at the áser. Country the same.

25th. *El Imkám**, a valley, where you arrive at one o'clock P. M., pebbly ground.

26th. A'gnar, a plain inclosed by ridges; arrive at the áser, after having kept first along the valley which is called by the Arabs el Imkám, and leads into another valley called Temághaset, from which you enter upon the plain.

27th. Turaghén, a valley, where you encamp about the áser, after having crossed another valley called Utúl, into which you descend from the gravelly level.

28th. Tílak, a valley, where you arrive after the áser, having crossed another valley called E'heri.

29th. Tema-sanéggeti, a valley; arrive at the áser, having crossed another valley called Tín-agh-ákeli.

30th. E'n-émmegel, a valley rich in trees, where you encamp at sunset. To-day you have to pass two other valleys called Erésnughén and Tin-táheli, all these valleys being separated from each other by a hammáda of an even surface, without stones.

31st. Tehárraket, a valley commanded by a mountain called Turéret, where you arrive about the áser; pebbles and stones.

N.B. Tehárraket is a very important point on this route, as, having now turned the high mountainous region of the desert of the Hogár or Hágara, which you leave on your right, you change your direction, and turn northwards.

---

* The name Imkám is remarkable. It seems to denote a religious "station;" and it is interesting, as it exactly corresponds with the station Dekhár, mentioned by the famous traveller Ebn Batúta as ten days distant from the well where the road to Tawát separated from that to Egypt, which, there cannot be the least doubt, is identical with Asíu or with Néswa.

Day.

32nd. Hágara, a valley with a well called Tehelehóhet, where you arrive after the áser.

33rd. Súf méllel, another locality of the same name as that above mentioned, where you arrive about the áser, after having passed two valleys, the first of which is called Akdhau, and the other E'm-njáj.

34th. Sheikh Sálah with the surname Melá el ákhsen, "the best of men," * near to whose chapel, situate in the mountainous tract Tésennu, there is water; you arrive a little before sunset, having passed over a pebbly level.

35th. Terazart, "the little valley" or "glen;" shortly before sunset; hammáda.

36th. Emmesír, a valley, where you arrive after the áser. In the morning you keep along a valley called Méniyet, with a well, beyond which you cross another valley called Afísfes, while the last part of your road leads over the hammáda, consisting of gravel.

37th. Etgúlgulet, where you arrive at the time of the áser. In the morning you keep for a while along the valley Emmesír, till you reach the valley called Arák; and following it up, you pass two watering-places, one of which is called (by the Arabs) Sekíyah, and the other "el Hájar."

38th. Tajemút, a valley, where you encamp before the áser.

39th. Koikewát, a cluster of small valleys, where you encamp at one o'clock, P. M.

40th. Gurdí, a valley, where you arrive a little before sunset, after having crossed another valley called Teráttimín, with water.

41st. The well in the long valley A'ghmemár.

42nd. Encamp about the same hour, still in the same valley A'ghmemár.

* Whether this Sheikh Sálah be the same as the famous sheikh of the same name, who has given his name to the celebrated Wadi el Sheikh, in the peninsula of Sinai, I cannot tell.

Day.

43rd. E'n-semméd, where you arrive after the áser. In the morning you still keep along the broad valley of A'ghmemár until you ascend a mountain, from which you descend into another valley called by the Arabs "el Botta," probably on account of its hollow shape; here is a well called "Tin-Slimán." Proceeding along the valley, you reach the place of your encampment for the night.

44th. El Ghábah (the Forest), of great extent and full of brushwood; arrive at the áser, after having crossed on your road a depression or hollow called e' Shaáb, from which you enter upon rising ground and come to the forest.

45th. I'n-sálah, the great market-place of the southernmost district of Tawát, where you arrive about the áser, first keeping in the forest, then ascending a little.

N.B.—Along this route, as I learned on a later occasion, there are several places where *salt* is found, which, as the fact is one of the greatest interest, I shall here name together, although I am unfortunately not able to connect the first places which I have to mention with the corresponding points of the itinerary. These are E'm-éddarór, said to be six days' march from Asīu; further on, Ahóren, and, one day S. from the well Tin-slimán, E'n-méllel.

I here also add what information I could collect about the tribes dwelling on or near this road. As far as Néswa, we know them from what I have said above; but the first part also of the road from this place is inhabited by sections of the Imghád, as the Kél-áhenet, while the Ijrán have their settlements even as far west as the valley 'Tájemút.

a. *The Sakomáren.*

Next to the Imghád, on the north side of the road, are the Sakomáren, a tribe who in the middle age of the Arabs lived N.E. from the middle course of the so-called Niger, and of whom some remains are still to be found in the neighbourhood of that river, near Timbúktu; for there can be no doubt about the identity of these tribes.* By what revolution this tribe was driven from their ancient seats we are not yet able to say; however it may be, Ebn Batúta found the Berdáma where the Sakomáren had formerly resided.

Their present settlements seem not to be so very dreary, and are said to be rich in pasture-grounds, so that they are enabled to breed plenty of cattle, and make a good deal of butter, with which they supply the less favoured districts of A'sben. They appear to possess, however, little strength, and are greatly influenced apparently by their intimate friendship with the Tawátíye; part of them live even in the territory of the latter oasis, principally belonging to the section called Welád-wúen-Tawát, a name manifesting a curious mixture of Arabic and Temáshight, though the main body of them is said to dwell in the district of Amgíd. Besides the name of this tribe, I learnt the names of the following: viz.,

The Kél-tegéttuft, who inhabit the district called Ahó-boghén;

The Kél-úhet, whose tents are generally pitched in Ahél-legen;

The Welád Témenít, living in Fazólet;

The tribe of the Háj 'Ali, living in a valley called Gháris: and,

The Ihiyáwen-háda, a tribe living in Imáhir, and probably related to the tribe called simply Ihiyáwen.

b. The Hogár or Hágara.

Formerly I thought that the Hogár were more numerous than their eastern kinsmen the Azkár, and that they were

---

* The Arab authors always write صغماره; but with regard to African names there is the greatest uncertainty in the use of the غ, the ة, and the ك. Thus some write غرمه others قرمه; Gober is written غوبر, by others كوبر; Tagant تكانت and تغانت.

able to bring into the field as many as three thousand men; but I have discovered in the course of my proceedings, that the free men, the real " hharár " or Imóshagh among them scarcely exceed five hundred, while of course their Imghád and slaves muster a greater number. But notwithstanding their small number, the Hogár are much feared by the other tribes, on account of their great bodily size and strength, and because they are armed with a variety of weapons, and are thickly clothed. They live entirely upon meat and milk, and have few resources but their herds, as they do not levy tribute on the caravans, but receive only small sums from the Kúnta, the Berabísh, and even a light tax from Arawán. They are not capable of turning to account the salt-mines of Taodénni, which are rather distant from their seats, though they levy a small tribute from the chief of that place. But their relations to the western part of the desert will be more clearly understood from what I shall say in another place.

The Hogár are divided into six branches: —

The Kél-ghálla, inhabiting the valley of Erárar (a general appellation for a large valley plain);

The Bu-ghelán, living in the valley of Téfedist;

The Tai-túk, inhabiting the fine valley Arák;

The Tégehin-usídi, who have their abode in the valley of Téghazart;

The Inémba, who pitch their tents in the valley Tífi-n-ákeli;

The I'kdeyén, who inhabit Anímmegel.

I will now add a few remarks on the centre of the district occupied by this tribe, which seems to present traits of peculiar interest. It is generally called by the Arabs "jébel Hagár," but this is not the original appellation, its true or indigenous name being "Atakór." This mountain-mass (which evidently lies in the angle formed by the route from Asíu to Tawát) stretches from three to four days' march in length, and one in breadth, from S. to N., at the distance of seven days' march S.E. from Tawát. My intelligent friend the sheikh

Sídi Ahmed el Bakáy, in Timbúktu, who had lived some time among the Hogár, as well as among the tribes of A'ír, especially the Kél-fadaye, assured me, in the most positive way, that this mountain-group, and one long range of it in particular, is far higher than the mountains of A'ír; the rocks being very steep and of red colour. He represented to me, as very remarkable and probably the highest of the group, the isolated, detached, and steep peak I'limán or E'limán. Very fine valleys and glens are formed between these mountains, some of them watered by lively perennial streams, and producing figs and grapes.

In this place may be fitly mentioned those Tawárek tribes that live within the boundaries of Tawát. These are the Kél-eméllel or Welád Fákki, as they are called by the people of Tawát, and their kinsmen the Tígge-n-sákkel, and also the Tígge-n-gáli. These tribes are regarded as belonging to the Tawárek, while the Gurára are considered as Zenáta; and it is very erroneous to regard Tawát as almost a Tawárek country.

VI.—Route from A'gades to the Hillet f' Sheikh Sídi el Mukhtár in Azawád, according to the Kél-ferwán Baina.

N.B. This route is a path taken at present every year by the Kél-ferwán when they sally forth to plunder the caravans on the road from Tawát to Timbúktu; it is not altogether a direct road, as I learnt afterwards. But unfortunately none of the people of Azawád (who, as I mentioned above, when they do not go by way of Timbúktu, generally take the road to Mekka by way of A'gades) was able to give me the exact details of the direct road. This road passes through the seats of the Awelímmiden.

Day.
1st. E'nwágged, a valley, where you arrive at the áser, having started from A'gades in the morning.
2nd. Imintédent (perhaps E'm-n-tédent), where you arrive

Day.

> about the same hour, having crossed many depressions or hollows in the rocky ground.

3rd. Sakéret, a valley; arrive at sunset.

4th. Etmet Tadérret, a valley; arrive two hours after sunset.

5th. Agrédem; about aser. The whole day's journey lies over a hammáda of red soil (recalling to mind the sameness of all these elevated levels in Central Africa), the red colour being produced by the iron oxide.

6th. Etsá-n-élimán; at aser. Hammáda.

7th. Tímmia; at aser. Hammáda.

8th. Ebelághlaghén; about the same hour. Hammáda.

9th. Isakeríyen; about the same hour. The hammáda is here covered with a little herbage. The road thus far seems to be about N.N.W.; hence it turns north-westward.

10th. Etsá-n-Hébbi; about the aser.

11th. Igédian; about one o'clock P. M.

12th. Akár; about the aser.

13th. Kélijít; a little after noon.

14th. A'kalú, a considerable valley with water, which you reach at one o'clock.

15th. A'kerír, an inhabited valley, where you arrive about the aser, having travelled the morning till after mid-day along the valley A'kalú.

16th. Kídal; after the aser.

> This name, as I learnt afterwards, is not applied to a single locality, but comprises a district with fertile valleys, inhabited by the Debákal, who breed an excellent race of horses.

17th. Tim-áklali; about aser.

18th. Asalágh; at sunset, after having crossed several hollows in the rocky ground. Here you find inhabitants,

Day.

partly Arabs, of the tribe of the Kúnta, partly Ta-wárek, of the widely dispersed tribe of the I'fógas.

19th. Aghasher (Eghazar), a fine valley with date-trees, corn, and tobacco. At some distance from it is another fertile valley called Tesillíte, likewise abounding in dates.

20th. Tigháughawen; about the áser.

21st. Hillet e' Sheikh Sídi el Mukhtár, a celebrated place of worship, where you arrive about one o'clock P. M. This place ought to have considerable interest for all those who take an interest in the circumstances attending the frequent sacrifice of life made in the arduous endeavour to open the African continent to European science and intercourse; for this is the very spot where the unfortunate Major Laing, under the protection of Sídi Mohammed, the father of my noble friend the sheikh el Bakáy, recovered from those fearful wounds which he had received in the nocturnal attack by the Tawárek in Wadi Ahénnet. Hence, in the few letters which he sent home, so full of resignation and heroic courage, he called the place "belád Sídi Mohammed." In the further course of our narrative this spot will be connected with Timbúktu.

FRAGMENTS OF METEOROLOGICAL REGISTER.

Date.	Hour of Day.	Degrees in scale of Fahrenheit.	Remarks.	Date.	Hour of Day.	Degrees in scale of Fahrenheit.	Remarks.
1850. April				1850. April			
1	5.15 a.m.	48·6	Rain the whole day.	21	No observation.		
2	6.0 a.m.	50		22	5.0 a.m.	48·2	
3	6.15 a.m.	55·4		23	6.0 a.m.	50	El Hási.
4	No observation.				12.30	86	
5	5.15 a.m.	51·8		24	5.30 a.m.	40·1	
6	5.0 a.m.	50			12.0	82·4	
	7.30 p.m.	55·4			9.0 p.m.	60·8	
7	5.10 a.m.	45		25	5.0 a.m.	46·4	
8	9.30 p.m.	72·5			12.0	86	
9	10.0 p.m.	72·5			2.0 p.m.	109·4	
10	5.30 a.m.	66·6			7.0 p.m.	78·8	
	12.0	84·2		26	5.0 a.m.	59	
	6.30 p.m.	77			12.0	84·4	
11	5.30 a.m.	53·6			7.0 p.m.	75·6	
	6.0 p.m.	68	Easterly wind for some days.	27	5.30 a.m.	51·8	
12	5.30 a.m.	50			7.30 p.m.	80·6	
13	5.15 a.m.	50		28	12.0	106·7	
	2.0 p.m.	91·8		29	5.0 a.m.	85	
14	5.0 a.m.	43·2			12.15	104	Most of these days a southerly hot wind towards noon.
	12.0	86			7.30 p.m.	89·6	
	9.30 p.m.	59		30	5.15 a.m.	73·4	
15	5.0 a.m.	42			7.30 p.m.	93·2	
	12.0	78·3		May			
	9.0 p.m.	57·2		1	5.0 a.m.	77	
16	5.0 a.m.	43·7			12.0	102·2	
	1.30 p.m.	80·6			7.0 p.m.	95	
	9.0 p.m.	66·6		2	5.15 a.m.	73·4	
17	5.0 a.m.	50·4			7.0 p.m.	98·6	
	12.0	89·6		3	5.0 a.m.	73·4	
	9.0 p.m.	66·2			12.25	96·8	
18	5.0 a.m.	45·5			8.45 p.m.	82·4	
	12.0	78·8		4	6.30 a.m.	62·6	
	8.45 p.m.	63·5			12.0	89·6	
19	5.0 a.m.	50·5			7.20 p.m.	73·4	
20	5.30 a.m.	45·5		5	1.30 p.m.	89·6	
	12.15	68			7.0 p.m.	82·4	

Date.	Hour of Day.	Degrees in scale of Fahrenheit.	Remarks.	Date.	Degrees in scale of Fahrenheit.	R
1850. May				1850. May		
6	No observation.			21	6.15 a.m. 72	
7	6.30 a.m.	80·6	(Múrzuk.)		1.0 p.m. 90	
	2.0 p.m.	98·6			7·0 p.m. 85	
8	12.30	97·7	A heavy gibleh; the first time to-day we had a covered sky, and found it in the course of our residence characteristic of Múrzuk in this season. Towards evening the sky became generally clouded.	22	6.0 a.m. 71·6	
					12.0 86	
					2.30 p.m. 90	
					7.0 p.m. 84·6	
				23	6.30 a.m. 73·8	
					12.0 89·6	
					1.30 p.m. 91·4	
					3.30 p.m. 94	
					7.0 p.m. 91·4	
					11.30 p.m. 82·4	
				24	5.45 a.m. 78·8	
					12.15 95	
9	12.0	96			1.45 p.m. 96·8	
	7.0 p.m.	93·2			10.30 p.m. 89·6	
10	6.30 a.m.	75·2		25	6.15 a.m. 82·4	In the
11	6.0 a.m.	73·4				cool N
12	6.30 a.m.	77				which
	1.30 p.m.	93·2				blowing
13	6.0 a.m.	77				night.
	12.0	87·8			12.30 87	
	7.0 p.m.	86			10.30 p.m. 82·4	
14	6.45 a.m.	75·2		26	6.0 a.m. 76	At 8 a.m. i
	12.0	90·5				to rain ;
	7.0 p.m.	88·7				N.E. wind
15	7.0 a.m.	78				heavy, onl
	12.0	95				rain fell
	7.0 p.m.	94				the town ;
16	6.15 a.m.	75·2				however,
	12.0	95				desert.
	2.45 p.m.	98·6			1.0 p.m. 82·4	
	7.0 p.m.	91·4			10.30 p.m. 77	
17	6.0 a.m.	80·6		27	6.30 a.m. 72	
	12.45	96			3.0 p.m. 90	
	2.40 p.m.	98·6			7.0 p.m. 85	
18	7.0 a.m.	75·2			10.30 p.m. 78	
	12.30	94		28	6.0 a.m. 71·6	
	7.0 p.m.	91·4			12.0 84·2	
19	6.0 a.m.	77·3			3.15 p.m. 89·6	
	12.0	89·6			11.0 p.m. 78	
	3.0 p.m.	96		29	6.0 a.m. 72	
	7.0 p.m.	91·4			12.0 87	
20	6.0 a.m.	77			3.0 p.m. 86	The sky in the
	12.45	86				noon thickl
	3.0 p.m.	89·6			10.15 p.m. 80·6	cast.

METEOROLOGICAL REGISTER.

Date.	Hour of Day.	Degrees in scale of Fahrenheit.	Remarks.	Date.	Hour of Day.	Degrees in scale of Fahrenheit.	Remarks.
1850. May				1850. June			
30	6.30 a.m.	75·2	11.30 a.m. it began to rain, the rain becoming gradually heavier, and lasting an hour; but at half-past 8 o'clock in the evening the storm broke forth in its full force, with much lightning but little rain.	8	6.0 a.m.	71·6	
					12.0	84·2	
					4.15 p.m.	90	
					7.0 p.m.	86	
				9	6.0 a.m.	76	
					12.0	86	
					11.0 p.m.	82·4	
				10	6.0 a.m.	76	
					2.30 p.m.	94	
					11.0 p.m.	85	
				11	5.0 a.m.	69·8	
					6.30 a.m.	78	
	12.0	78·8			12.30	94	
	10.0 p.m.	80·6		12	6.0 a.m.	78·8	
31	5.45 a.m.	76			12.0	96·8	
	12.0	90			7.0 p.m.	95	
	2.45 p.m.	93·2		13	5.30 a.m.	80·6	
					1.30 p.m.	105	
June 1				14	5.0 a.m.	70·7	A strong gal
	6.0 a.m.	80·6			1.30 p.m.	107·6	
	12.0	95		15	5.15 a.m.	75·2	
	2.0 p.m.	98·6			12.0	111·2	
	3.0 p.m.	100·4			7.0 p.m.	93·2	
	10.30 p.m.	91·4		16	5.45 a.m.	71·6	
2	7.0 a.m.	85			12.0	102·2	
	12.0	89·6			1.30 p.m.	105·8	
	3.0 p.m.	103	At 5 p.m. a heavy storm arose from the westward.		7.0 p.m.	94	
	11.45 p.m.	93·2		17	12.0	111·2	(Encampmen Tiggérodé.)
3	5.15 a.m.	84·2			1.45 p.m.	114·8	Sky covered.
	12.0	99			9.0 p.m.	89·6	
	3.0 p.m.	100·4		18	5.30 a.m.	77	
	7.0 p.m.	98·6			12.45	111·2	
	10.45 p.m.	89·6			9.0 p.m.	95	
4	6.0 a.m.	82·8		19	5.0 a.m.	77	
	12.0	96·8			2.0 p.m.	108·5	
	3.0 p.m.	102·2		20	5.0 a.m.	77	
	10.15 p.m.	91·4		21	1.0 p.m.	99·5	
5	7.0 a.m.	86		22	5.30 a.m.	87	
	1.0 p.m.	100·4			12.0	99·5	
	4.0 p.m.	105		23	5.30 a.m.	86	
	10.30 p.m.	93·2			12.30	102·2	
6	12.0	95			11.30 p.m.	86	
	2.30 p.m.	100·4		24	5.15 a.m.	87·8	
7	6.0 a.m	80·6			12.0	101·3	A fresh gale.
	12.0	86		25	6.0 a.m.	78	
	10.15 p.m.	82·4			1.30 p.m.	108·5	
					7.30 p.m.	98·6	

Date.	Hour of Day.	Degrees in scale of Fahrenheit.	Remarks.	Date.	Hour of Day.	Degrees in scale of Fahrenheit.
1850. June				1850. July		
26	5.0 a.m.	78	The sky towards the east covered. Twice in the morning a few drops of rain.	10	12.0	104
	10.30 a.m.	102·2			8.0 p.m.	86
				11	5.0 a.m.	68
					1.0 p.m.	105·8
27	5.0 a.m.	69			8.30 p.m.	87·8
	12.0	93·2		12	5.15 a.m.	65·3
	7.0 p.m.	90·5			1.0 p.m.	106·7
28	5.0 a.m.	66·2			8.15 p.m.	89·6
	12.0	93·2		13	4.45 a.m.	75·2
29	5.30 a.m.	69			12.30	107·6
	12.30	98·6			7.30 p.m.	95
	7.45 p.m.	85		14	4.30 a.m.	84·2
30	4.50 a.m.	63·5			12.30	105
	1.30 p.m.	103			7.30 p.m.	93·2
	7.15 p.m.	87·8		15	4.30 a.m.	75·2
July 1	4.50 a.m.	66·2		18	4.45 a.m.	64·4
	12.0	99·5			2.15 p.m.	105·8
	7.30 p.m.	86		19	5.30 a.m.	76
2	5.0 a.m.	68		20-24		
	12.30	100·4		25	12.30	104
	7.45 p.m.	83·3	In the afternoon and the following day very heavy N.E. gales.		7.45 p.m.	95
				26	4.45 a.m.	82·4
					1.15 p.m.	107·6
					7.0 p.m.	97·7
3	5.0 a.m.	69		27	5.0 a.m.	75·2
	12.0	102·2			12.45	103
	7.30 p.m.	91·4			7.30 p.m.	93·2
4	5.0 a.m.	69·8		28	4.15 a.m.	69·8
	12.15	107·6			12.45	104
	7.30 p.m.	88·7			7.30 p.m.	93·2
5	4.45 a.m.	70·7		29	4.45 a.m.	85
	12.15	91·4			12.30	99·5
	7.30 p.m.	84·2			8.0 p.m.	89·6
6	4.45 a.m.	70·7		30	4.30 a.m.	77
	1.0 p.m.	89·6			1.0 p.m.	96·8
	7.30 p.m.	83·3			8.30 p.m.	89·6
7	4.45 a.m.	6·5		31	5.0 a.m.	71·6
	12.0	85	In the very cool shade of a rock.		1.0 p.m.	93·2
8	4.45 a.m.	85		Aug. 1	4.45 a.m.	66·2
	12.45	102·2			12.25	98·6
	9.0 p.m.	87·8			8.0 p.m.	85
9	4.30 a.m.	75·2		2	5.0 a.m.	68
	12.30	105·8			8.0 p.m.	86
	9.0 p.m.	89·6		3	4.30 a.m.	67
10	4.30 a.m.	70·7			12.40	105·8
					8.15 p.m.	85

On these warm wind. (Bárakat (Ghát) no tions.

(E'geri.)

In the afte light breeze.

Hour of Day.	Degrees in scale of Fahrenheit.	Remarks.	Date.	Hour of Day.	Degrees in scale of Fahrenheit.	Remarks.
			1850. Aug.			
5.0 a.m.	74·3	(Falésselez.)	16	5.0 a.m.	78.8	The whole day the southern sky was covered with small clouds. The sun was piercing. At 2.30 p.m. a violent storm arose in the east, but did not break forth till 4.30 p.m., when it was followed by a heavy shower.
12.30	111·2	In the afternoon clouded sky, foreboding rain.				
8.0 p.m.	91					
5.15 a.m.	75·2					
1.0 p.m.	102·2					
8.0 p.m.	89·6					
5.0 a.m.	68					
1.0 p.m.	100·4					
8.0 p.m.	86					
4.45 a.m.	69					
1.0 p.m.	95			12.45	98·6	
8.30 p.m.	84·2			9.0 p.m.	78·8	
4.45 a.m.	74·3		17	2.0 p.m.	87	
1.0 p.m.	95		18 to 30	No observation.		
No observation.			31	- -		At 3 p.m. a storm, accompanied by a little rain, lasting about an hour; further southwards more rain; during the night another fall of rain.
5.0 a.m.	68					
2.0 p.m.	94					
8.0 p.m.	85					
5.30 a.m.	73·4					
1.0 p.m.	93·2					
8.0 p.m.	85					
5.10 a.m.	67	A cool breeze.				
1.20 p.m.	93·2					
5.30 a.m.	77					
1.45 p.m. {	96·8	{ In the cool shade of a rock.	Sept.			
	107·6	In aired tent.	1	- -		Rain the whole of the morning.
1.0 p.m.	98·6	Generally a light breeze arose at 10 a.m.	2	- -		A fresh wind.
			4	- -		A heavy shower in the morning, lasting about two hours.
9.30 p.m.	87·8					
5.0 a.m.	78	The wind to-day got up at an early hour, the sky becoming more and more clouded, till at 1 p.m. a heavy storm broke forth, followed by a heavy shower at 2 o'clock, accompanied by distant thunder.	5	- -		(Tintéllust.) After mid-day a heavy tornado, followed at 2 p.m. by a shower, lasting till 4 p.m.
			6	- -		In the afternoon a tornado, and rain till the evening.
1.0 p.m.	98·6		7	- -		Sky the whole day clear; no rain.
9.15 p.m.	88·7					

No thermometrical observations.

Date.	Hour of Day.	Degrees in scale of Fahrenheit.	Remarks.
1850. Sept.			
8	- -		A very heavy tornado in the afternoon from S.S.W., followed by much rain, lasting from 4 p.m. till 10 p.m
9	- -	No thermometrical observations.	In the afternoon a storm gathering from N.E., but reaching us from S.S.W. at 3 p.m., with heavy rain lasting till 7 p.m.
10	- -		A storm all around us; no rain near us.
11	12.30	96·8	No rain.
12	5.45 a.m.	71·6	
	12.45	96·8	In the afternoon a tornado, with rain.
13	1.0 p.m.	100·4	In the afternoon a storm, without rain.
14	5.30 a.m.	68	
	1.0 p.m.	81·5	
15	6.0 a.m.	69·8	No storm.
	12.30	99·5	
16	5.30 a.m.	69	
	1.0 p.m.	99	
17	- -	-	Fine weather.
18	- -	-	
19	- -	-	At 2 p.m. a storm gathering from S. S. W. and N.N.E., but only a little rain at 3 p.m.
20	- -	-	At 1 p.m. a storm, followed by heavy rain at 2 p.m.
21	- -	-	No storm.
22	- -	-	
23	6.0 a.m.	71·6	
	12.0	96·8	At 2 p.m. a heavy storm, but without rain.

Date.	Hour of Day.	Degrees in scale of Fahrenheit.	
1850. Sept.			
24	6.15 a.m.	73·4	
	1.0 p.m.	98·6	At 2 p.m. a storm, w set our te was accon by heavy
25	6.0 a.m.	64·4	
	1.30 p.m.	95	
	6.45 p.m.	86	
26	6.45 a.m.	64·2	No storm.
	12.30	96	
	6.0 p.m.	91·4	
27	6.15 a.m.	69·8	
	12.30	95	
	6.30 p.m.	91·4	
28	6.15 a.m.	75·2	
	12.10	95	At 2 p.m. a tornado, wi a few rain.
	6.20 p.m.	86	
29	5.40 a.m.	67	
	12.15	99·5	Sultry w no storm.
	6.15 p.m.	91·4	
30	5.30 a.m.	68	
	6.15 p.m.	93·2	
Oct.			
1	5.40 a.m.	69·8	
	1.30 p.m.	101·3	
	6.20 p.m.	95	
2	5.45 a.m.	73·4	
	12.30	97·7	
	6.45 p.m.	92·3	
3	12.30	91·4	
4	5.45 a.m.	68	
5	12.0	95·7	
	6.30 p.m.	87·8	
6	12.0	100·4	
	6.15 p.m.	88·7	
7	No observation.		The last the rainy 1850, sett shortly noon, and half an ho

Date.	Hour of Day.	Degrees in scale of Fahrenheit.	Remarks.	Hour of Day.	Remarks.
1850. Oct.					
8	6.10 p.m.	87	At 8.30 p.m., while encamped in the valley Bóghel, a meteor fell in our neighbourhood with a very great noise.		Sky covered; windy. Sky very cloud Theweathercl up.

From October 9. till November 8. no observations ; weather generally clear ; cool in the morning ; on October 20. sky a little overcast.

Date.	Hour of Day.	Degrees in scale of Fahrenheit.	Remarks.	Hour of Day.	Remarks.
Nov.*					
9	r.	43·7			
	s.	69			Sky covered.
10	r.	47·3			At 9.30 a.m. the s
	s.	69·8			broke forth.
11	r.	47·3			
	s.	66·2			
12	r.	43·7			
	1.15 p.m.	86			
	s.	67·1			
13	r.	45·5			
	12·0	77			
	5.30 p.m.	66·2			
14	r.	43·7			
	6.0 p.m.	59·9			
15	½ h. bef. r.	50			
	real r.	41·9			
	s.	66·2			Sky very cloudy.
16	r.	46·4			
	s.	67·1			
17	r.	47·3			
	s.	69·8			
18	r.	48·2			
	s.	69·8			
19	r.	50			Very cold easter
	s.	68			wind.
20	r.	50			
	s.	68		s.	
21	r.	48·2		r.	
	s.	68		s.	
22	r.	50		r.	Sky not clear.
	s.	68		s.	

* From this date forwards the observations were made a quarter of an hour before r.) and half an hour past sunset (s.).

Hour of Day.	Remarks.	Hour of Day.	Remarks
	(Telésbera.)		
r.			The cold
r.			tinuing.
s.			
r.			
s.			
r.			The same cold
s.			it fell
r.			hour after
s.			rise.
r.			
s.		r.	Again the
r.		s.	cold N.E.
s.			it abated
r.			7 p.m.
s.		r.	
r.		s.	
s.		r.	
r.		r.	The sun
r.			overcast a
s.			rise.
r.		r.	The sky
s.		s.	clouded ;
r.			rain.
s.		r.	The sky
r.		s.	clouded ;
s.			drops of
No observ		r.	
r.	The sky at sunrise now in general overcast.	s.	
s.		r.	
r.		r.	
s.		s.	
r.	Very cold N.E. wind.		

The few thermometrical observations made by Mr. Overweg differ partially owing to the different situations we gave to our thermometers. I have always e1 to raise the thermometer five or six feet from the ground, and to prevent its being by any object. I have always looked for the best shade. Overweg marks, under I a quarter of an hour before sunrise, 46·4, and at sunset 66·2 ; under December 9, have made no observation, he gives 48·2 at sunrise, and 59 at sunset. December gives 38·3 half an hour before sunrise, and December 12, about the same time, 37·

END OF THE FIRST VOLUME.

RECENT VOYAGES AND TRAVELS, &c.

CLASSIFIED INDEX.

PUBLISHED BY

Messrs. LONGMAN, BROWN, GREEN, LONGMANS, and ROBERT

PATERNOSTER ROW, LONDON.

Miss Acton's Modern Cookery, for Private Families, reduced to a System of Easy Practice in a Series of carefully-tested Receipts, in which the Principles of Baron Liebig and other eminent Writers have been as much as possible applied and explained. Newly revised and enlarged Edition; with 8 Plates, comprising 27 Figures, and 150 Woodcuts. Fcp. 8vo. 7s. 6d.

Acton.—The English Bread-Book, for Domestic Use, adapted to Families of every grade: Containing plain Instructions and Practical Receipts for making numerous varieties of Bread; with Notices of the present System of Adulteration and its Consequences, and of the Improved Baking Processes and Institutions established Abroad. By ELIZA ACTON. [In the press.

Arago (F.)—Meteorological Essays. By FRANCIS ARAGO. With an Introduction by BARON HUMBOLDT. Translated under the superintendence of Lieut.-Colonel E. SABINE, R.A., Treasurer and V.P.R.S. 8vo. 18s.

Arago's Popular Astronomy. Translated and Edited by Admiral W. H. SMYTH, For. Sec. R.S.; and ROBERT GRANT, M.A., F.R.A.S. In Two Volumes. Vol. I. 8vo. with Plates and Woodcuts, 21s.

Arago's Lives of Distinguished Scientific Men. Translated by the Rev. BADEN POWELL, M.A.; Rear-Admiral W. H. SMYTH; and R. GRANT, M.A. 8vo. [Nearly ready.

Aikin.—Select Works of the British Poets, from Ben Jonson to Beattie. With Biographical and Critical Prefaces by DR. AIKIN. New Edition, with Supplement by LUCY AIKIN; consisting of additional Selections from more recent Poets. 8vo. price 18s.

Arnold.—Oakfield; or, Fellowship in the East. By W. D. ARNOLD, Lieutenant 58th Regiment, Bengal Native Infantry. Second Edition. 2 vols. post 8vo. price 21s.

Arnold.—Poems. By Matthew Arno Second Edition of the First Series. F 8vo. price 5s. 6d.

Arnold.—Poems. By Matthew Arn Second Series, about one-third new; the finally selected from the Volumes of 1849 1852, now withdrawn. Fcp. 8vo. price 5

Arnott.—On the Smokeless Fire-p Chimney-valves, and other means, old new, of obtaining Healthful Warmth Ventilation. By NEIL ARNOTT, M.D., F F.G.S. 8vo. 6s.

Arrowsmith. — A Geographical tionary of the Holy Scriptures: Inclu also Notices of the chief Places and Peo mentioned in the APOCRYPHA. By Rev. A. ARROWSMITH, M.A. 8vo. 15s.

Joanna Baillie's Dramatic and Poeti Works: Comprising the Plays of the P sions, Miscellaneous Dramas, Metrical gends, Fugitive Pieces, and Ahalya B Second Edition, with a Life of J Baillie, Portrait, and Vignette. crown 8vo. 21s. cloth; or 42s. bound morocco by Hayday.

Baker.—Eight Years' Wanderings Ceylon. By S. W. BAKER, Esq. W 6 coloured Plates. 8vo. price 15s.

Baker.—The Rifle and the Hound in Cey By S. W. BAKER, Esq. With colo Plates and Woodcuts. 8vo. price 14s.

Dr. Barth's Travels and Discoveries Africa. With Maps and Illustrations. Co prising Journeys from Tripoli to Kouk from Kouka to Yola, the Capital of A mawa, and back; to Kanem, accompany a Slave-Hunting Expedition to Musgo; his Journey to and Residence in Bag Also, a Journey from Kouka to Timbuct Residence in Timbuctoo; and Journey ba to Kouka. Vols. I., II., and III. 8vo. [Nearly ready.

B 2

Bayldon's Art of Valuing Rents and Tillages, and Claims of Tenants upon Quitting Farms, both at Michaelmas and Lady-Day; as revised by Mr. DONALDSON. *Seventh Edition*, enlarged and adapted to the Present Time: With the Principles and Mode of Valuing Land and other Property for Parochial Assessment and Enfranchisement of Copyholds, under the recent Acts of Parliament. By ROBERT BAKER, Land-Agent and Valuer. 8vo. 10s. 6d.

Black's Practical Treatise on Brewing, based on Chemical and Economical Principles: With Formulæ for Public Brewers, and Instructions for Private Families. New Edition, with Additions. 8vo. 10s. 6d.

Blaine's Encyclopædia of Rural Sports; or, a complete Account, Historical, Practical, and Descriptive, of Hunting, Shooting, Fishing, Racing, and other Field Sports and Athletic Amusements of the present day. New Edition, revised by HARRY HIEOVER, EPHEMERA, and Mr. A. GRAHAM. With upwards of 600 Woodcuts. 8vo. price 50s. half-bound.

Blair's Chronological and Historical Tables, from the Creation to the Present Time: With Additions and Corrections from the most authentic Writers; including the Computation of St. Paul, as connecting the Period from the Exode to the Temple. Under the revision of SIR HENRY ELLIS, K.H. Imperial 8vo. 31s. 6d. half-morocco.

Bloomfield. — The Greek Testament, with copious English Notes, Critical, Philological, and Explanatory. Especially adapted to the use of Theological Students and Ministers. By the Rev. S. T. BLOOMFIELD, D.D., F.S.A. Ninth Edition, revised throughout; with Dr. Bloomfield's *Supplementary Annotations* incorporated. 2 vols. 8vo. with Map, price £2. 8s.

Dr. Bloomfield's College and School Greek Testament: With brief English Notes, chiefly Philological and Explanatory, especially formed for use in Colleges and the Public Schools. Seventh Edition, improved; with Map and Index. Fcp. 8vo. 7s. 6d.

Dr. Bloomfield's College and School Lexi-con to the Greek Testament. Fcp. 8vo. price 10s. 6d.

Bourne.—A Treatise on the gine, in its Application to Steam-Navigation, and Railways Artisan Club. Edited by JOHN BO New Edition; with 33 Steel Plat Wood Engravings. 4to. price 27

Bourne's Catechism of the its various Applications to Steam-Navigation, Railways, and ture: With Practical Instruction Manufacture and Management of of every class. Fourth Edition, with 89 Woodcuts. Fcp. 8vo. 6s.

Bourne.—A Treatise on the peller: With various Suggest provement. By JOHN BOURNE Edition, thoroughly revised an With 20 large Plates and n cuts. 4to. price 38s.

Brande.—A Dictionary of Scie ture, and Art: Comprising Description, and Scientific every Branch of Human Know the Derivation and Definition Terms in general use. Edited by BRANDE, F.R.S.L. and E.; assisted J. CAUVIN. Third Edition, revised rected; with numerous Woodcuts.

Professor Brande's Lectures on Chemistry, as applied to Man including Dyeing, Bleaching. ing, Sugar-Manufacture, the of Wood, Tanning, &c.; delivered Members of the Royal Institution. by permission from the Lecturer's J. SCOFFERN, M.B. Fcp. 8vo. with outs, price 7s. 6d.

Brewer.—An Atlas of History an graphy, from the Commencement Christian Era to the Present Time prising a Series of Sixteen coloured arranged in Chronological Order, wi trative Memoirs. By the Rev. J. S. B M.A., Professor of English Literature in King's College, Lond Maps engraved by E. Weller, Royal 8vo. 12s. 6d. half-bound.

Brodie. — Psychological Inquiri Series of Essays intended to illu Influence of the Physical Org the Mental Faculties. By SIR BEN BRODIE, Bart. Third Edition. Fc

Brougham and Routh.—Analyti of Sir Isaac Newton's Princi

Buckingham.—Autobiography o James
Silk Buckingham: Including his Voyages, Travels, Adventures, Speculations, Successes and Failures, frankly and faithfully narrated; with Characteristic Sketches of Public Men. Vols. I. and II. post 8vo. 21s.

*** Vols. III. and IV., edited by the Author's Son, and completing the work, are preparing for publication.

Bull. — The Maternal Management of
Children in Health and Disease. By T. BULL, M.D., Member of the Royal College of Physicians; formerly Physician-Accoucheur to the Finsbury Midwifery Institution. New Edition. Fcp. 8vo. 5s.

Dr. T. Bull's Hints to Mothers on the Management of their Health during the Period of Pregnancy and in the Lying-in Room: With an Exposure of Popular Errors in connexion with those subjects, &c.; and Hints upon Nursing. New Edition. Fcp. 8vo. 5s.

Bunsen. — Christianity and Mankind,
their Beginnings and Prospects. By CHRISTIAN CHARLES JOSIAS BUNSEN, D.D., D.C.L., D.Ph. Being a New Edition, corrected, remodelled, and extended, of *Hippolytus and his Age.* 7 vols. 8vo. £5. 5s.

*** This Second Edition of the *Hippolytus* is composed of three distinct works, which may be had separately, as follows:—

1. Hippolytus and his Age: or, the Beginnings and Prospects of Christianity. 2 vols. 8vo. price £1. 10s.
2. Outline of the Philosophy of Universal History applied to Language and Religion: Containing an Account of the Alphabetical Conferences. 2 vols. 8vo. price £1. 13s.
3. Analecta Ante-Nicæna. 3 vols. 8vo. price £2. 2s.

Bunsen.—Lyra Germanica: Hymns for
the Sundays and chief Festivals of the Christian Year. Translated from the German by CATHERINE WINKWORTH. Second Edition. Fcp. 8vo. 5s.

*** This selection of German Hymns has been made from a collection published in Germany by the Chevalier BUNSEN; and forms a companion volume to

Theologia Germanica: Which setteth forth many fair lineaments of Divine Truth, and saith very lofty and lovely things touching a Perfect Life. Translated by SUSANNA WINKWORTH. With a Preface by the Rev. CHARLES KINGSLEY; and a Letter by Chevalier BUNSEN. Second Edition. Fcp. 8vo. 5s.

Bunsen. — Egypt's Place in Universal
History: An Historical Investigation, in Five Books. By C. C. J. BUNSEN, D.D., D.C.L., D.Ph. Translated from the German by C. H. COTTRELL, Esq., M.A. With many Illustrations. Vol. I. 8vo. 28s.; Vol. II. 8vo. 30s.

Burton.—
or, an Exploration of Harar. By RIC F. BURTON, Bombay Army; Author *Pilgrimage to Medina and Mecca.* With and coloured Plates. 8vo. 18s.

Burton. — Personal Narrative of a
grimage to El-Medinah and Meccah. RICHARD F. BURTON, Bombay Army. Map, Plates, and Woodcuts. 3 vols price £2. 3s.

Burton (J. H.)—The History of Sco
from the Revolution to the Extinction Last Jacobite Insurrection (1689–1748 JOHN HILL BURTON. 2 vols. 8vo. 26s

Bishop S. Butler's General A
Modern and Ancient Geography; co ing Fifty-two full-coloured Maps; complete Indices. New Edition, nea re-engraved, enlarged, and greatly imp Edited by the Author's Son. Royal 24s. half-bound.

| Separately | { | The Modern Atlas of 28 full-coloured Royal 8vo. price 12s. The Ancient Atlas of 24 full-coloured Royal 8vo. price 12s. |

Bishop S. Butler's Sketch of Modern
- Ancient Geography. New Edition, roughly revised, with such Alterations duced as continually progressive Disco and the latest Information have ren necessary. Post 8vo. price 7s. 6d.

Bishop J. Butler's Fifteen Se
preached at the Rolls Chapel. With N Analytical, Explanatory, and Illustr and Observations in reply to Mackin Wardlaw, and Maurice, by Rev. Ro CARMICHAEL, M.A., Fellow of Trinity lege, Dublin. 8vo. 9s.

The Cabinet Lawyer: A Popular Di
of the Laws of England, Civil and Cri with a Dictionary of Law Terms, Statutes, and Judicial Antiquities; C Tables of Assessed Taxes, Stamp I Excise Licenses, and Post-Horse D Post-Office Regulations; and Prison pline. 17th Edition, comprising the l Acts of the Session 1856. Fcp. 8vo. 10

The Cabinet Gazetteer: A Popular
sition of All the Countries of the W their Government, Population, Rev Commerce, and Industries; Agricult Manufactured, and Mineral Products; ligion, Laws, Manners, and Social S With brief Notices of their History and tiquities. By the Author of *The Ca Lawyer.* Fcp. 8vo. 10s. 6d. cloth; or bound in calf.

Commissioner of *The Times*. The Second Edition. 8vo. price 14s.

Calvert.—Pneuma; or, the Wandering Soul: A Parable, in Rhyme and Outline. By the Rev. WILLIAM CALVERT, M.A., Minor Canon of St. Paul's Cathedral. With 20 Etchings by the Author. Square crown 8vo. 10s. 6d.

Calvert. — The Wife's Manual; or, Prayers, Thoughts, and Songs on Several Occasions of a Matron's Life. By the Rev. W. CALVERT, M.A. Ornamented from Designs by the Author in the style of *Queen Elizabeth's Prayer-Book*. Second Edition. Crown 8vo. 10s. 6d.

Carlisle (Lord).—A Diary in Turkish and Greek Waters. By the Right Hon. the EARL of CARLISLE. Fifth Edition. Post 8vo. price 10s. 6d.

Catlow.—Popular Conchology; or, the Shell Cabinet arranged according to the Modern System : With a detailed Account of the Animals, and a complete Descriptive List of the Families and Genera of Recent and Fossil Shells. By AGNES CATLOW. Second Edition, much improved; with 405 Woodcut Illustrations. Post 8vo. price 14s.

Cecil. — The Stud Farm; or, Hints on Breeding Horses for the Turf, the Chase, and the Road. Addressed to Breeders of Race-Horses and Hunters, Landed Proprietors, and especially to Tenant Farmers. By CECIL. Fcp. 8vo. with Frontispiece, 5s.

Cecil's Stable Practice; or, Hints on Training for the Turf, the Chase, and the Road; with Observations on Racing and Hunting, Wasting, Race-Riding, and Handicapping: Addressed to Owners of Racers, Hunters, and other Horses, and to all who are concerned in Racing, Steeple-Chasing, and Fox-Hunting. Fcp. 8vo. with Plate, price 5s. half-bound.

Chevreul On the Harmony and Contrast of Colours, and their Applications to the Arts : Including Painting, Interior Decoration, Tapestries, Carpets, Mosaics, Coloured Glazing, Paper-Staining, Calico-Printing, Letterpress-Printing, Map-Colouring, Dress, Landscape and Flower-Gardening, &c. &c. Translated by CHARLES MARTEL. Second Edition; with 4 Plates. Crown 8vo. price 10s. 6d.

usion by the Peace of W 1648. By B. CHAPMAN, M.A., Letherhead. 8vo. with Plans, 12s.

Clinton.—Literary Remains of Fynes Clinton, M.A., Author of *Hellenici*, the *Fasti Romani*, &c. : an Autobiography and Literary and brief Essays on Theological Edited by the Rev. C. J. FYNES M.A. Post 8vo. 9s. 6d.

Conybeare.—Essays, Eccl Social : Reprinted, with Additions, *Edinburgh Review*. By the Rev. CONYBEARE, M.A., late Fellow of College, Cambridge. 8vo. 12s.

Conybeare and Howson.—The Epistles of Saint Paul : Com complete Biography of the a Translation of his Epistles Chronological Order. By the Rev CONYBEARE, M.A.; and the Re HOWSON, M.A. *Second Edition*, revised and corrected, and printed in convenient form; with several M Woodcuts, and 4 Plates. 2 vols crown 8vo. 31s. 6d. cloth.

*** The Original Edition, with more n tions, in 2 vols. 4to. price 48s.—may also be ha

Dr. Copland's Dictionary of Medicine : Comprising General the Nature and Treatment of Morbid Structures, and the Di pecially incidental to Climates, to the different Epochs of Life; rous approved Formulæ of the recommended. Vols. I. and II. £3; and Parts X. to XVII. 4s. (

*** Part XVIII., completing the work, is publication.

Cresy's Encyclopædia of Civi neering, Historical, Theoretical, a tical. Illustrated by upwards Woodcuts. *Second Edition*, brought down to the Present Supplement, comprising Metropolit Supply, Drainage of Towns, Cubical Proportion, Brick and struction, Iron Screw Piles, Tubula &c. 8vo. 63s. cloth. — The Su separately, price 10s. 6d. cloth.

Cotton.—Instructions in the and Practice of Christianity. chiefly as an Introduction to Co By G. E. L. COTTON, M.A., late F Trinity College, Cambridge. 18mo

ket-Field; or, the Science and
of the Game of Cricket. By the
r of *Principles of Scientific Batting*.
d Edition, greatly improved; with
and Woodcuts. Fcp. 8vo. price 5s.
ound.

Cust's Invalid's Book. — The In-
s Own Book: A Collection of Recipes
various Books and various Countries.
he Honourable LADY CUST. *Second*
. Fcp. 8vo. price 2s. 6d.

he Domestic Liturgy and Family
, in Two Parts: PART I. Church
adapted for Domestic Use, with
s for Every Day of the Week, selected
he Book of Common Prayer; PART
appropriate Sermon for Every Sunday
Year. By the Rev. THOMAS DALE,
Canon Residentiary of St. Paul's.
Edition. Post 4to. 21s. cloth;
. calf; or £2. 10s. morocco.
ly { THE FAMILY CHAPLAIN, 12s.
{ THE DOMESTIC LITURGY, 10s. 6d.

(Dr. J.) — The Angler and his
d; or, Piscatory Colloquies and Fish-
xcursions. By JOHN DAVY, M.D.,
., &c. Fcp. 8vo. price 6s.

he. — Report on the Geology of
all, Devon, and West Somerset. By
ENRY T. DELABECHE, F.R.S., late
or-General of the Geological Survey.
Maps, Plates, and Woodcuts. 8vo.
4s.

ve. — A Treatise on Electricity,
ry and Practice. By A. DE LA RIVE,
or in the Academy of Geneva. Trans-
or the Author by C. V. WALKER,
In Three Volumes; with numerous
ats. Vol. I. 8vo. price 18s.; Vol. II.

un. — Memoirs of Sir Robert
, Knight, Engraver, Member of
Foreign Academies of Design; and
Brother-in-law, Andrew Lumisden.
MES DENNISTOUN, of Dennistoun.
post 8vo. with Illustrations, 21s.

The Lover's Seat: Kathemerina;
mon Things in relation to Beauty,
and Truth. By KENELM HENRY
Author of *Mores Catholici*, &c. 2 vols.
. 12s.

ne. By the Author of "Letters

Dodd. — The Food of London: A Sketch
of the chief Varieties, Sources of Supply,
probable Quantities, Modes of Arrival, Processes of Manufacture, suspected Adulteration, and Machinery of Distribution of the
Food for a Community of Two Millions and
a Half. By GEORGE DODD, Author of
British Manufactures, &c. Post 8vo. 10s. 6d.

The Eclipse of Faith; or, a Visit to a
Religious Sceptic. *7th Edition*. Fcp. 8vo. 5s.

Defence of The Eclipse of Faith, by its
Author: Being a Rejoinder to Professor
Newman's *Reply:* Including a full Exami-
nation of that Writer's Criticism on the
Character of Christ; and a Chapter on the
Aspects and Pretensions of Modern Deism.
Second Edition, revised. Post 8vo. 5s. 6d.

The Englishman's Greek Concordance of
the New Testament: Being an Attempt at a
Verbal Connexion between the Greek and
the English Texts; including a Concordance
to the Proper Names, with Indexes, Greek-
English and English-Greek. New Edition,
with a new Index. Royal 8vo. price 42s.

The Englishman's Hebrew and Chaldee Concordance of the Old Testament: Being an
Attempt at a Verbal Connexion between
the Original and the English Translations;
with Indexes, a List of the Proper Names
and their Occurrences, &c. 2 vols. royal
8vo. £3. 13s. 6d.; large paper, £4. 14s. 6d.

Ephemera's Handbook of Angling;
teaching Fly-Fishing, Trolling, Bottom-
Fishing, Salmon-Fishing; with the Natural
History of River-Fish, and the best Modes
of Catching them. Third Edition, corrected
and improved; with Woodcuts. Fcp. 8vo 5s.

Ephemera. — The Book of the Salmon: Comprising the Theory, Principles, and Practice of Fly-Fishing for Salmon; Lists of
good Salmon Flies for every good River in
the Empire; the Natural History of the
Salmon, its Habits described, and the best
way of artificially Breeding it. By EPHE-
MERA; assisted by ANDREW YOUNG. Fcp.
8vo. with coloured Plates, price 14s.

W. Erskine, Esq. — History of India
under Báber and Humáyun, the First Two
Sovereigns of the House of Taimur. By
WILLIAM ERSKINE, Esq. 2 vols. 8vo. 32s.

Etheridge. — Jerusalem and Tiberias;
Sora and Cordova: A View of the Religious
and Scholastic Learning of the Jews. Designed as an Introduction to Hebrew Lite-

Fairbairn.—Useful Information for Engineers: Being a Series of Lectures delivered to the Working Engineers of Yorkshire and Lancashire. With a Series of Appendices, containing the Results of Experimental Inquiries into the Strength of Materials, the Causes of Boiler Explosions, &c. By WILLIAM FAIRBAIRN, F.R.S., F.G.S. With Plates and Woodcuts. Royal 8vo. price 15s.

Faraday (Professor). — The Subject-Matter of Six Lectures on the Non-Metallic Elements, delivered before the Members of the Royal Institution, by PROFESSOR FARADAY, D.C.L., F.R.S., &c. Arranged by permission from the Lecturer's Notes by J. SCOFFERN, M.B. Fcp. 8vo. price 5s. 6d.

Flemish Interiors. By the Writer of *A Glance behind the Grilles of Religious Houses in France.* Fcp. 8vo. 7s. 6d.

Forester.—Travels in the Islands of Corsica and Sardinia. By THOMAS FORESTER, Author of *Rambles in Norway.* With numerous coloured Illustrations and Woodcuts, from Sketches made during the Tour by Lieutenant-Colonel M. A. BIDDULPH, R.A. Imperial 8vo. [*In the press.*]

Fulcher.—Life of Thomas Gainsborough, R.A. By the late GEORGE WILLIAMS FULCHER. Edited by his SON. With 4 Illustrations. *New Edition.* Fcp. 8vo. [*Nearly ready.*]

Gilbart.—A Practical Treatise on Banking. By JAMES WILLIAM GILBART, F.R.S., General Manager of the London and Westminster Bank. *Sixth Edition,* revised and enlarged. 2 vols. 12mo. Portrait, 16s.

Gilbart. — Logic for the Million: a Familiar Exposition of the Art of Reasoning. By J. W. GILBART, F.R.S. 4th Edition; with Portrait of the Author. 12mo. 3s. 6d.

Gilbart.—Logic for the Young: Consisting of Twenty-five Lessons in the Art of Reasoning. Selected from the *Logic* of Dr. Isaac Watts. By J. W. GILBART, F.R.S. 12mo. 1s.

The Poetical Works of Oliver Goldsmith. Edited by BOLTON CORNEY, Esq. Illustrated by Wood Engravings, from Designs by Members of the Etching Club. Square crown 8vo. cloth, 21s.; morocco, £1. 16s.

Gosse. — A Naturalist's Sojourn in Jamaica. By P. H. GOSSE, Esq. With Plates. Post 8vo. price 14s.

Mr. W. R. Greg's Contribution Edinburgh Review.—Essays on P Social Science. Contributed chie *Edinburgh Review.* By WILLIAM 2 vols. 8vo. price 24s.

Grove. — The Correlation of Forces. By W. R. GROVE, Q.C F.R.S., &c. *Third Edition;* with N References. 8vo. price 7s.

Gurney.—St. Louis and Henri IV. a Second Series of Historical By the Rev. J. HAMPDEN G Fcp. 8vo. 6s.

Evening Recreations; or, the Lecture-Room. Edite JOHN HAMPDEN GURNEY,] St. Mary's, Marylebone. C

Gwilt.—An Encyclopædia o Historical, Theoretical, and JOSEPH GWILT. With more Wood Engravings, from Desig GWILT. Third Edition. 8vo.

Halloran.—Eight Months' Jo Visit to Japan, Loochoo, and F ALFRED LAURENCE HALLOR R.N., F.R.G.S., Polperro, Corn Etchings and Woodcuts from the Author. Post 8vo. [*New*

Hare (Archdeacon).—The Life in Forty-eight Historical Engra GUSTAV KÖNIG. With Explana ARCHDEACON HARE and SUSANNA WORTH. Fcp. 4to. price 28s.

Harford.—Life of Michael Angel narrotti; comprising Memoirs of and Vittoria Colonna, and mucl poraneous History. By JOHN S. D.C.L., F.R.S., Member of the demy of Painting of St. Luke, an Archæological Society of Rome. 8vo. with Portrait of Michael An numerous Illustrations. [*In th*

Also, to be sold separately, in fo

Engravings illustrative of the Works Angelo, both in Painting and Architecture planatory Descriptions of the latter, by C. RRELL, Esq., R.A.

Harrison.—The Light of the Fo Counsels drawn from the Sick-Bed By the Rev. W. HARRISON, M.A., Chaplain to H.R.H. the Duchess o rice 5s.

By HARRY IEOVER. New E tion, 2 vols. 8vo. with Portrait, price 24s.

Harry Hieover.—The Hunting-Field. By Harry HIEOVER. With Two Plates. Fcp. 8vo. 5s. half-bound.

Harry Hieover.—Practical Horseman-ship. By HARRY HIEOVER. *Second Edition*; with 2 Plates. Fcp. 8vo. 5s. half-bound.

Harry Hieover.—The Stud, for Practical Purposes and Practical Men: Being a Guide to the Choice of a Horse for use more than for show. By HARRY HIEOVER. With 2 Plates. Fcp. 8vo. price 5s. half-bound.

Harry Hieover.—The Pocket and the Stud; or, Practical Hints on the Management of the Stable. By HARRY HIEOVER. Second Edition; with Portrait of the Author. Fcp. 8vo. price 5s. half-bound.

Hassall (Dr.)—Food and its Adultera-tions: Comprising the Reports of the Analytical Sanitary Commission of *The Lancet* for the Years 1851 to 1854 inclusive, revised and extended. By ARTHUR HILL HASSALL, M.D., &c., Chief Analyst of the Commission. 8vo. with 159 Woodcuts, 28s.

Col. Hawker's Instructions to Young Sportsmen in all that relates to Guns and Shooting. 10th Edition, revised and brought down to the Present Time, by the Author's Son, Major P. W. L. HAWKER. With a New Portrait of the Author, and numerous Plates and Woodcuts. 8vo. 21s.

Haydon.—The Life of Benjamin Robert Haydon, Historical Painter, from his Autobiography and Journals. Edited and compiled by TOM TAYLOR, M.A., of the Inner Temple, Esq. 3 vols. post 8vo. 31s. 6d.

Haydn's Book of Dignities: Containing Rolls of the Official Personages of the British Empire, Civil, Ecclesiastical, Judicial, Military, Naval, and Municipal, from the Earliest Periods to the Present Time. Together with the Sovereigns of Europe, from the Foundation of their respective States; the Peerage and Nobility of Great Britain; &c. Being a New Edition, improved and continued, of Beatson's Political Index. 8vo. 25s. half-bound.

Herring. — Paper and Paper-Making, Ancient and Modern. By RICHARD HERRING. With an Introduction by the Rev. GEORGE CROLY, LL.D. *Second Edition*, with Plates and Specimens. 8vo. 7s. 6d.

Bart., &c. New Edition; with P' Wood Engravings. 8vo. price 18s.

Hill.—Travels in Siberia. By S. Esq., Author of *Travels on the S the Baltic.* With a large Map of E and Asiatic Russia. 2 vols. post 8v

Hints on Etiquette and the Us Society: With a Glance at Bad New Edition, revised (with Additio Lady of Rank. Fcp. 8vo. price Half-

Holland.—Medical Notes and tions. By SIR HENRY HOLLAN M.D., F.R.S., &c., Physician in to the Queen and Prince Albert. Edition, with Alterations and Ad 8vo. 18s.

Holland.—Chapters on Mental Physiol SIR HENRY HOLLAND, Bart., F.F Founded chiefly on Chapters con the First and Second Editions of *Notes and Reflections* by the same 8vo. price 10s. 6d.

Hook.—The Last Days of Our Ministry: A Course of Lectures principal Events of Passion Wee the Rev. W. F. HOOK, D.D. New Fcp. 8vo. price 6s.

Hooker.—Kew Gardens; or, a 1 Guide to the Royal Botanic Kew. By SIR WILLIAM JACKSON K.H., &c., Director. New Editic many Woodcuts. 16mo. price Six

Hooker.—Museum of Economic 1 or, a Popular Guide to the Useful markable Vegetable Products of the in the Royal Gardens of Kew. By S HOOKER, K.H., &c., Director. Woodcuts. 16mo. price 1s.

Hooker and Arnott.—The British comprising the Phænogamous or Fl Plants, and the Ferns. Seventh E with Additions and Corrections; merous Figures illustrative of the T ferous Plants, the Composite Plar Grasses, and the Ferns. By SIR HOOKER, F.R.A. and L.S., &c.; an WALKER-ARNOTT, LL.D., F.L.S. with 12 Plates, price 14s.; with the coloured, price 21s.

Horne's Introduction to the Critical Study and Knowledge of the Holy Scriptures. *Tenth Edition*, revised, corrected, and brought down to the present time. Edited by the Rev. T. HARTWELL HORNE, B.D. (the Author); the Rev. SAMUEL DAVIDSON, D.D. of the University of Halle, and LL.D.; and S. PRIDEAUX TREGELLES, LL.D. With 4 Maps and 22 Vignettes and Facsimiles. 4 vols. 8vo. £3. 13s. 6d.

* The Four Volumes may also be had *separately* as follows:—
VOL. I.—A Summary of the Evidence for the Genuineness, Authenticity, Uncorrupted Preservation, and Inspiration of the Holy Scriptures. By the Rev. T. H. Horne, B.D..8vo.15s.
VOL. II.—The Text of the *Old Testament* considered: With a Treatise on Sacred Interpretation; and a brief Introduction to the *Old Testament* Books and the *Apocrypha*. By S. Davidson, D.D. (Halle) and LL.D. ....8vo. 25s.
VOL. III.—A Summary of Biblical Geography and Antiquities. By the Rev. T. H. Horne, B.D. .... 8vo.18s.
VOL. IV.—An Introduction to the Textual Criticism of the *New Testament*. By the Rev. T. H. Horne, B.D. The Critical Part re-written, and the remainder revised and edited by S. P. Tregelles, LL.D. ....8vo. 18s.

Horne.—A Compendious Introduction to the Study of the Bible. By the Rev. T. HARTWELL HORNE, B.D. New Edition, with Maps and Illustrations. 12mo. 9s.

How to Nurse Sick Children: Intended especially as a Help to the Nurses in the Hospital for Sick Children; but containing Directions of service to all who have the charge of the Young. Fcp. 8vo. 1s. 6d.

Howitt (A. M.)—An Art-Student in Munich. By ANNA MARY HOWITT. 2 vols. post 8vo. price 14s.

Howitt.—The Children's Year. By Mary HOWITT. With Four Illustrations, from Designs by A. M. HOWITT. Square 16mo. 5s.

Howitt. — Land, Labour, and Gold; or, Two Years in Victoria: With Visit to Sydney and Van Diemen's Land. By WILLIAM HOWITT. 2 vols. post 8vo. 21s.

?witt.—Visits to Remarkable Places: Old Halls, Battle-Fields, and Scenes illustrative of Striking Passages in English History and Poetry. By WILLIAM HOWITT. With about 80 Wood Engravings. *New Edition.* 2 vols. square crown 8vo. 25s. cloth, gilt top.

William Howitt's Boy's Country Book: Being the Real Life of a Country Boy, written by himself; exhibiting all the Amusements, Pleasures, and Pursuits of Children in the Country. New Edition; with 40 Woodcuts. Fcp. 8vo. price 6s.

Huc.—The Chinese Empire to Huc and Gabet's *Journey and Thibet*. By the Abbé Missionary Apostolic in *Edition*; with Map. 2 vols. 8v

Hudson's Plain Directions Wills in conformity with the clear Exposition of the Law distribution of Personal Esta of Intestacy, two Forms of W useful information. New and tion; including the Provisions o Act Amendment Act. Fcp. 8vo.

Hudson's Executor's Guide. enlarged Edition; with the Directions for paying Succession Real Property under Wills and and a Table for finding the V ties and the Amount of Lege sion Duty thereon. Fcp. 8v

Hudson and Kennedy.— a Will there's a Way: An Ascen Blanc by a New Route and Witho By the Rev. C. HUDSON, M.A., College, Cambridge; and E. S. B.A., Caius College, Cambridge *Edition*, with Two Ascents of Mon Plate, and a coloured Map. Post

Humboldt's Cosmos. Transla the Author's authority, by M Vols. I. and II. 16mo. Half-a sewed; 3s. 6d. each, cloth: or 12s. each, cloth. Vol. III. 12s. 6d. cloth: or in 16mo. Part sewed, 3s. 6d. cloth; and Part II. 4s. cloth.

Humboldt's Aspects of Nature. with the Author's authority, by 16mo. price 6s.: or in 2 vols. 3s cloth; 2s. 6d. each, sewed.

Humphreys. — Parables of illuminated and ornamented in the Missals of the Renaissance b NOEL HUMPHREYS. Square fcp. in massive carved covers; or 30s. morocco by Hayday.

Hunt. — Researches on Light Chemical Relations; emb sideration of all the Photographic By ROBERT HUNT, F.R.S. Secon with Plate and Woodcuts. 8vo.

us Woodcuts, and 16 Etchings by the or. Square crown 8vo. 28s.

ameson's Legends of the Monastic ers, as represented in the Fine Arts: nd Series of *Sacred and Legendary Art*. nd Edition, enlarged; with 11 Etchings he Author, and 88 Woodcuts. Square 8vo. price 28s.

ameson's Legends of the Madonna, presented in the Fine Arts: Third es of *Sacred and Legendary Art*. With rawings by the Author, and 152 Woodc. Square crown 8vo. 28s.

Jameson's Commonplace-Book of ughts, Memories, and Fancies, Original Selected. Part I. Ethics and Character; II. Literature and Art. *Second Edit.* and corrected; with Etchings and cuts. Crown 8vo. 18s.

ameson's Two Lectures on the Employt of Women.

isters of Charity. Catholic and Protestant, Abroad and at Home. *Second Edition*, with new Preface. Fcp. 8vo. 4s.

he Communion of Labour: A Second Lecture on the Social Employments of Women. Fcp. 8vo. 3s.

met's Compendium of Chronology: taining the most important Dates of eral History, Political, Ecclesiastical, Literary, from the Creation of the rld to the end of the Year 1854. Edited the Rev. J. Alcorn, M.A. Post 8vo. e 7s. 6d.

gs.—Social Delusions concerning th and Want. By Richard Jennings, ., Trinity College, Cambridge; Author *Natural Elements of Political Economy.* 8vo. 4s.

Jeffrey's Contributions to The burgh Review. A New Edition, com. in One Volume, with a Portrait en- by Henry Robinson, and a Vignette. are crown 8vo. 21s. cloth; or 30s. calf. r in 3 vols. 8vo. price 42s.

p Jeremy Taylor's Entire Works: th Life by Bishop Heber. Revised and ted by the Rev. Charles Page Eden, w of Oriel College, Oxford. Now lete in 10 vols. 8vo. 10s. 6d. each.

quest y on very in the Year, from the Earliest Period to the Battle of Inkermann. Fcp. 8vo. 12s. 6d.

Johnston.—A Dictionary of Geography, Descriptive, Physical, Statistical, and Historical: Forming a complete General Gazetteer of the World. By A. Keith Johnston, F.R.S.E., F.R.G.S., F.G.S., Geographer at Edinburgh in Ordinary to Her Majesty. Second Edition, thoroughly revised. In 1 vol. of 1,360 pages, comprising about 50,000 Names of Places. 8vo. 36s. cloth; or half-bound in russia, 41s.

Jones (Owen).—Flowers and their Kin- dred Thoughts: A Series of Stanzas. By Mary Anne Bacon. With beautiful Illustrations of Flowers, designed and executed in illuminated printing by Owen Jones. Reprinted. Imperial 8vo. price 31s. 6d. calf.

Kalisch.—Historical and Critical Com- mentary on the Old Testament. By Dr. M. Kalisch, M.A. First Portion—Exodus: in Hebrew and English, with copious Notes, Critical, Philological, and Explanatory. 8vo. 15s.

*** An edition of the *Exodus*, as above (for the use of English readers), comprising the English Translation, and an abridged Commentary. 8vo. price 12s.

Kemble.—The Saxons in England: A History of the English Commonwealth till the Norman Conquest. By John M. Kemble, M.A., &c. 2 vols. 8vo. 28s.

Kemp.—The Phasis of Matter: Being an Outline of the Discoveries and Applications of Modern Chemistry. By T. Lindley Kemp, M.D. With 148 Woodcuts. 2 vols. crown 8vo. 21s.

Kennard. — **Eastern Experiences** collected during a Winter's Tour in Egypt and the Holy Land. By Adam Steinmetz Kennard. Post 8vo. 10s. 6d.

Kesteven.—A Manual of the Domestic Practice of Medicine. By W. B. Kesteven, Fellow of the Royal College of Surgeons of England, &c. Square post 8vo. 7s. 6d.

Kirby and Spence's Introduction to Entomology; or, Elements of the Natural History of Insects: Comprising an Account of Noxious and Useful Insects, of their Metamorphoses, Food, Stratagems, Habitations, Societies, Motions, Noises, Hybernation, Instinct, &c. *Seventh Edition*, with an Appendix relative to the Origin and Progress of the work. Crown 8vo. 5s.

B 6

LARDNER'S CABINET CYCLOPÆDIA

Of History, Biography, Literature, the Arts and Sciences, Natural History, and
A Series of Original Works by

SIR JOHN HERSCHEL,	THOMAS KEIGHTLEY,	BISHOP THIRLWALL,
SIR JAMES MACKINTOSH,	JOHN FORSTER,	THE REV. G. R. GLE
ROBERT SOUTHEY,	SIR WALTER SCOTT,	J. C. L. DE SISMOND
SIR DAVID BREWSTER,	THOMAS MOORE,	JOHN PHILLIPS, F.R.

AND OTHER EMINENT WRITERS.

Complete in 132 vols. fcp. 8vo. with Vignette Titles, price, in cloth, Nineteen Guin
The Works *separately*, in Sets or Series, price Three Shillings and Sixpence each Vol

A List of the WORKS *composing the* CABINET CYCLOPÆDIA:—

Mrs. R. Lee's Elements of Natural History; or, First Principles of Zoology: Comprising the Principles of Classification, interspersed with amusing and instructive Accounts of the most remarkable Animals. New Edition; Woodcuts. Fcp. 8vo. 7s. 6d.

Letters to my Unknown Friends. By a LADY, Author of *Letters on Happiness*. Fourth Edition. Fcp. 8vo. 5s.

Letters on , addressed to a Friend.

L. E. L.—The Poetical Works of Elizabeth Landon; comprising *visatrice*, the *Venetian Bracelet*, th *Violet*, the *Troubadour*, and Poetical New Edition; with 2 Vignettes by 2 vols. 16mo. 10s. cloth; morocco,

Dr. John Lindley's Theory and of Horticulture; or, an Attempt the principal Operations of Gard Physiological Grounds: Being t

r. John Lindley's Introduction to Botany. New Edition, with Corrections and copious Additions. 2 vols. 8vo. with Six Plates and numerous Woodcuts, price 24s.

nwood.—Anthologia Oxoniensis, sive Florilegium e Lusibus poeticis diversorum Oxoniensium Græcis et Latinis decerptum. Curante GULIELMO LINWOOD, M.A., Ædis Christi Alumno. 8vo. price 14s.

rimer's (C.) Letters to a Young Master Mariner on some Subjects connected with his Calling. New Edition. Fcp. 8vo. 5s. 6d.

udon's Encyclopædia of Gardening: Comprising the Theory and Practice of Horticulture, Floriculture, Arboriculture, and Landscape-Gardening. With many hundred Woodcuts. New Edition, corrected and improved by MRS. LOUDON. 8vo. 50s.

udon's Encyclopædia of Trees and Shrubs, or Arboretum et Fruticetum Britanicum abridged: Containing the Hardy Trees and Shrubs of Great Britain, Native and Foreign, Scientifically and Popularly Described. With about 2,000 Woodcuts. 8vo. 50s.

udon's Encyclopædia of Agriculture: Comprising the Theory and Practice of the Valuation, Transfer, Laying-out, Improvement, and Management of Landed Property, and of the Cultivation and Economy of the Animal and Vegetable Productions of Agriculture. New Edition; with 1,100 Woodcuts. 8vo. 50s.

udon's Encyclopædia of Plants: Comprising the Specific Character, Description, Culture, History, Application in the Arts, and every other desirable Particular respecting all the Plants found in Great Britain. New Edition, corrected by MRS. LOUDON. With upwards of 12,000 Woodcuts. 8vo. £3. 13s. 6d.—Second Supplement, 21s.

udon's Encyclopædia of Cottage, Farm, and Villa Architecture and Furniture. New Edition, edited by MRS. LOUDON; with more than 2,000 Woodcuts. 8vo. 63s.

udon's Self-Instruction for Young Gardeners, Foresters, Bailiffs, Land Stewards, and Farmers; in Arithmetic, Book-, Mensuration, Practical

Loudon's Hortus Britannicus; or, logue of all the Plants found in Britain. New Edition, corrected b LOUDON. 8vo. 31s. 6d.

Mrs. Loudon's Lady's Country C nion; or, How to Enjoy a Count Rationally. Fourth Edition, with and Woodcuts. Fcp. 8vo. 5s.

Mrs. Loudon's Amateur Calendar, or Monthly Guide to what be avoided and done in a Garden. with Woodcuts, 7s. 6d.

Low's Elements of Practical Agric comprehending the Cultivation of Pl Husbandry of the Domestic Anim the Economy of the Farm. New E with 200 Woodcuts. 8vo. 21s.

Lynch.—The Rivulet: A Contri to Sacred Song. By THOMAS T. Author of Memorials of Theophilus Tri Second Edition, printed in a more con form. Royal 32mo. 2s. 6d.

Macaulay.—Speeches of the Righ T. B. Macaulay, M.P. Corrected b SELF. 8vo. price 12s.

Macaulay. — The History of E from the Accession of James I THOMAS BABINGTON MACAULAY. Edition. Vols. I. and II. 8vo. pri Vols III. and IV. price 36s.

Mr. Macaulay's Critical and His Essays contributed to The Ed Review. Four Editions, as follows:

1. A LIBRARY EDITION (the Eighth), in 3 price 36s.
2. Complete in ONE VOLUME, with Portrait nette. Square crown 8vo. price 21s. 30s. calf.
3. Another NEW EDITION, in 3 vols. fcp. 8 21s. cloth.
4. The PEOPLE'S EDITION, in 2 vols. crown 8s. cloth.

Macaulay.—Lays of Ancient Rome Ivry and the Armada. By T BABINGTON MACAULAY. New 16mo. price 4s. 6d. cloth; or 1 bound in morocco.

Mr. Macaulay's Lays of Ancient With numerous Illustrations. O

Dramatic Poem. By GEORGE MACDONALD. Crown 8vo. 7s. 6d.

Macdonald. — Villa Verocchio; or, the Youth of Leonardo da Vinci: A Tale. By the late MISS D. L. MACDONALD. Fcp. 8vo. price 6s.

MacDougall. — The Theory of War illustrated by numerous Examples from Military History. By Lieutenant-Colonel MACDOUGALL, Superintendent of Studies in the Royal Military College, Sandhurst. Post 8vo. with Plans. [*Just ready.*

Sir James Mackintosh's Miscellaneous Works: Including his Contributions to The Edinburgh Review. Complete in One Volume; with Portrait and Vignette. Square crown 8vo. 21s. cloth; or 30s. bound in calf: or in 3 vols. fcp. 8vo. 21s.

Sir James Mackintosh's History of England from the Earliest Times to the final Establishment of the Reformation. Library Edition, revised. 2 vols. 8vo. 21s.

Macleod. — The Theory and Practice of Banking: With the Elementary Principles of Currency, Prices, Credit, and Exchanges. By HENRY DUNNING MACLEOD, of the Inner Temple, Esq., Barrister-at-Law. 2 vols. royal 8vo. price 30s.

M'Clure. — A Narrative of the Discovery of the North-West Passage by H.M.S. *Investigator*, Capt. SIR ROBERT M'CLURE, R.N. Edited by Capt. SHERARD OSBORN, C.B., from the Logs, Journals, and Private Letters of Sir R. M'Clure: With Chart and 4 Views. 8vo. 15s.

Macnaught. — The Doctrine of Inspiration: Being an Inquiry concerning the Infallibility, Inspiration, and Authority of Holy Writ. By the Rev. JOHN MACNAUGHT, M.A. *Second Edition*, revised. [*Just ready.*

M'Culloch's Dictionary, Practical, Theoretical, and Historical, of Commerce and Commercial Navigation. Illustrated with Maps and Plans. New Edition, corrected to the Present Time; with a Supplement. 8vo. price 50s. cloth; half-russia, 55s.

M'Culloch's Dictionary, Geographical, Statistical, and Historical, of the various Countries, Places, and principal Natural Objects in the World. Illustrated with Six large Maps. New Edition, revised; with a Supplement. 2 vols. 8vo. price 63s.

combs: A Description of the Church of Rome. Illustrated chral Remains. By the Rev MAITLAND. New Edition; Woodcuts. 8vo. price 14s.

Out-of-Doors Drawing. — Apho Drawing. By the Rev. S. C. of Balliol College, Oxford; V windsor, Dorset. Post 8vo. 3s

Mann. — The Philosophy of Re By ROBERT JAMES MANN, M.D Fcp. 8vo. with Woodcuts, price

Mrs. Marcet's Conversations o try, in which the Elements of are familiarly explained and il Experiments. New Edition, improved. 2 vols. fcp. 8vo. price

Mrs. Marcet's Conversations on losophy, in which the Science are familiarly explain tion, enlarged and corrected; Fcp. 8vo. price 10s. 6d.

Mrs. Marcet's Conversations table Physiology; comprehen ments of Botany, with their to Agriculture. New Edition Plates. Fcp. 8vo. price 9s.

Martineau. — Endeavours after tian Life: Discourses. By J TINEAU. 2 vols. post 8vo. 7s. 6d

Martineau. — Hymns for the and Home. Collected and edited MARTINEAU. *Eleventh Edition*, 3 cloth, or 5s. calf; *Fifth Edition*, 3 cloth, or 1s. 8d. roan.

Martineau. — Miscellanies. Com on Dr. Priestley, Arnold's *Life spondence*, Church and State, Parker's *Discourse of Religion*, Faith," the Church of England, Battle of the Churches. By J TINEAU. Post 8vo. 9s.

Maunder's Biographical Tre sisting of Memoirs, Sketches, Notices of above 12,000 Eminer All Ages and Nations, from Period of History: Forming a n plete Dictionary of Universal Ninth Edition, revised through 10s. cloth; bound in roan, 12s.;

der's **Geographical Treasury.** — e Treasury of Geography, Physical, Historical, Descriptive, and Political; containing a succinct Account of Every Country in the World: Preceded by an Introductory utline of the History of Geography; a Inquiry into the Varieties of Race anguage exhibited by different Nations; View of the Relations of Geography tronomy and the Physical Sciences. enced by the late SAMUEL MAUNDER; ipleted by WILLIAM HUGHES, F.R.G.S., Professor of Geography in the College Civil Engineers. With 7 Maps and 16 el. Plates. Fcp. 8vo. 10s. cloth; roan, .; calf, 12s. 6d.

der's **Historical Treasury**; coming a General Introductory Outline of rersal History, Ancient and Modern, a Series of separate Histories of Every cipal Nation that exists; their Rise, and Present Condition, the Moral l Social Character of their respective Inhabitants, their Religion, Manners and Customs, &c. New Edition; revised throughout, with a new GENERAL INDEX. Fcp. 8vo. . cloth; roan, 12s.; calf, 12s. 6d.

der's **Scientific and Literary Trea**-sury: A new and popular Encyclopædia of mce and the Belles-Lettres; including Branches of Science, and every subject nected with Literature and Art. New tion. Fcp. 8vo. price 10s. cloth; bound oan, 12s.; calf, 12s. 6d.

der's **Treasury of Natural History**; a Popular Dictionary of Animated are: In which the Zoological Characters that distinguish the different Classes, ra, and Species, are combined with a of interesting Information illustrative the Habits, Instincts, and General Economy of the Animal Kingdom. With 900 oodcuts. New Edition. Fcp. 8vo. price . cloth; roan, 12s.; calf, 12s. 6d.

der's **Treasury of Knowledge, and** ry of Reference. Comprising an English Dictionary and Grammar, an Universal :teer, a Classical Dictionary, a Chronoa Law Dictionary, a Synopsis of the , numerous useful Tables, &c. New tion, carefully revised and corrected ughout: With Additions. Fcp. 8vo. . cloth; bound in roan, 12s.; calf, 12s. 6d.

vale. — **A History of the Romans** ler the Empire. By the Rev. CHARLES RIVALE, B.D., late Fellow of St. John's

Merivale.—The Fall of the Roman Repub-lic: A Short History of the Last Century of the Commonwealth. By the Rev. C. MERIVALE, B.D, late Fellow of St. John's College, Cambridge. New Edition. 12mo. 7s. 6d.

Merivale.—An Account of the Life and Letters of Cicero. Translated from the German of ABEKEN; and Edited by the Rev. CHARLES MERIVALE, B.D. 12mo. 9s. 6d.

Miles.—The Horse's Foot, and How to Keep it Sound. *Eighth Edition;* with an Appendix on Shoeing in general, and Hunters in particular, 12 Plates and 12 Woodcuts. By W. MILES, Esq. Imperial 8vo. 12s. 6d.

*** Two Casts or Models of Off Fore Feet, No. 1, *Shod for All Purposes*, No. 2, *Shod with Leather*, on Mr. Miles's plan, may be had, price 3s. each.

Miles.—A Plain Treatise on Horse-Shoeing. By WILLIAM MILES, Esq. With Plates and Woodcuts. Small 4to. price 5s.

Milner.—Russia, its Rise and Progress, Tragedies and Revolutions. By the Rev T. MILNER, M.A., F.R.G.S. Post 8vo with Plate, price 10s. 6d.

Milner.—The Crimea, its Ancient and Modern History: The Khans, the Sultans, and the Czars: With Sketches of its Scenery and Population. By the Rev. T. MILNER, M.A. Post 8vo. with 3 Maps, price 10s. 6d.

Milner.—The Baltic; its Gates, Shores, and Cities: With a Notice of the White Sea. By the Rev. T. MILNER, M.A., F.R.G.S. Post 8vo. with Map, price 10s. 6d.

Milner's History of the Church of Christ. With Additions by the late Rev. ISAAC MILNER, D.D., F.R.S. A New Edition, revised, with additional Notes by the Rev. T. GRANTHAM, B.D. 4 vols. 8vo. price 52s.

Montgomery.—Memoirs of the Life and Writings of James Montgomery: Including Selections from his Correspondence, Remains in Prose and Verse, and Conversations. By JOHN HOLLAND and JAMES EVERETT. With Portraits and Vignettes. 7 vols. post 8vo. price £3. 13s. 6d.

James Montgomery's Poetical Works: Collective Edition; with the Author's Autobiographical Prefaces, complete in One Volume; with Portrait and Vignette. Square crown 8vo. price 10s. 6d. cloth; morocco, 21s.—Or, in 4 vols. fcp. 8vo. with Portrait, and 7 other Plates, price 14s.

Morals. By GEORGE MOORE, M.D. *Fifth Edition*. Fcp. 8vo. 6s.

Moore.—Man and his Motives. By George MOORE, M.D. *Third Edition*. Fcp. 8vo. 6s.

Moore.—The Use of the Body in relation to the Mind. By GEORGE MOORE, M.D. *Third Edition*. Fcp. 8vo. 6s.

Moore's Epicurean. New Edition, with the Notes from the Collective Edition of *Moore's Poetical Works*; and a Vignette engraved on Wood: Uniform with Moore's *Irish Melodies* and *Lalla Rookh*, and with the first collected edition of Moore's *Songs, Ballads, and Sacred Songs*. 16mo. [*In the press.*

Moore's Irish Melodies. A New Edition, with 13 highly-finished Steel Plates, from Original Designs by

C. W. COPE, R.A.;	D. MACLISE, R.A.;
T. CRESWICK, R.A.;	J. E. MILLAIS, A.R.A.;
A. L. EGG, A.R.A.;	W. MULREADY, R.A.;
W. P. FRITH, R.A.;	J. SANT;
W. E. FROST, A.R.A.;	F. STONE, A.R.A.; and
J. C. HORSLEY;	E. M. WARD, R.A.

Square crown 8vo. price 21s. cloth; or 31s. 6d. handsomely bound in morocco.

Moore's Irish Melodies. Illustrated by D. Maclise, R.A. New Edition; with 161 Designs, and the whole of the Letterpress engraved on Steel, by F. P. Becker. Super-royal 8vo. 31s. 6d. boards; £2. 12s. 6d. morocco by Hayday.

Moore's Irish Melodies. New Edition, printed in Diamond Type; with the Preface and Notes from the collective edition of *Moore's Poetical Works*, the Advertisements originally prefixed to the *Melodies*, and a Portrait of the Author. 32mo. 2s. 6d.—An Edition in 16mo. with Vignette, 5s.; or 12s. 6d. morocco by Hayday.

Moore's Lalla Rookh: An Oriental Romance. With 13 highly-finished Steel Plates from Original Designs by Corbould, Meadows, and Stephanoff, engraved under the superintendence of the late Charles Heath. New Edition. Square crown 8vo. price 15s. cloth; morocco, 28s.

Moore's Lalla Rookh. New Edition, printed in Diamond Type; with the Preface and Notes from the collective edition of *Moore's Poetical Works*, and a Frontispiece from a Design by Kenny Meadows. 32mo. 2s. 6d. —An Edition in 16mo. with Vignette, 5s.; or 12s. 6d. morocco by Hayday.

Type; with the Notes from edition of *Moore's Poetical* Vignette from a Design by T. 32mo. 2s. 6d.—An Edition in 1 Vignette by R. Doyle, price 5s.; morocco by Hayday.

Thomas Moore's Poetical Wor prising the Author's recent In and Notes. Complete in printed in Ruby Type; with Crown 8vo. 12s. 6d. cloth; Hayday, 21s.—Also an Edition 1 vol. medium 8vo. with Portrait nette, 21s. cloth; morocco by Ha —Another, in 10 vols. fcp. 8vo. and 19 Plates, price 35s.

Moore.—Memoirs, Journal, an spondence of Thomas Moore. the Right Hon. LORD JOHN R With Portraits and Vignette 8 vols. post 8vo. price 10s. 6d.

Morell.—Elements of Psycho I., containing the Analysis of th Powers. By J. D. MORELL, Her Majesty's Inspectors of Sch 8vo. 7s. 6d.

Moseley.—The Mechanical Engineering and Architecture. MOSELEY, M.A., F.R.S., Canon &c. Second Edition, enlarged; merous Corrections and Woodcuts

Mure.—A Critical History of guage and Literature of Ancien By WILLIAM MURE, M.P. of Second Edition. Vols. I. to III. 36s.; Vol. IV. price 15s.

Murray's Encyclopædia of Geo comprising a complete Descri Earth: Exhibiting its Rela Heavenly Bodies, its Physical Natural History of each Countr Industry, Commerce, Political I and Civil and Social State of A Second Edition; with 82 Maps, an of 1,000 other Woodcuts. 8vo.

Neale.—The Closing Scene; o tianity and Infidelity contrasted Hours of Remarkable Persons. Rev. ERSKINE NEALE, M.A. New 2 vols. fcp. 8vo. price 6s. each.

Newman. — The Office and Universities. By JOHN HENRY D.D., of the Oratory. Fcp. 8vo.

NEWMAN, D.D. Second E tion. 8vo. 12s.

Nomos: An Attempt to Demonstrate a Central Physical Law in Nature. Post 8vo. price 7s. 6d.

Lord Normanby.—A Year of Revolution. From a Journal kept in Paris in the Year 1848. By the MARQUIS of NORMANBY, K.G. 2 vols. 8vo.   [*Just ready.*]

Oldacre.—The Last of the Old Squires. A Sketch. By CEDRIC OLDACRE, Esq., of Sax - Normanbury, sometime of Christ Church, Oxon. Crown 8vo. price 9s. 6d.

Owen. — Lectures on the Comparative Anatomy and Physiology of the Invertebrate Animals, delivered at the Royal College of Surgeons. By RICHARD OWEN, F.R.S., Hunterian Professor to the College. Second Edition, with 235 Woodcuts. 8vo. 21s.

Professor Owen's Lectures on the Comparative Anatomy and Physiology of the Vertebrate Animals, delivered at the Royal College of Surgeons in 1844 and 1846. With numerous Woodcuts. Vol. I. 8vo. price 14s.

The Complete Works of Blaise Pascal. Translated from the French, with Memoir, Introductions to the various Works, Editorial Notes, and Appendices, by GEORGE PEARCE, Esq. 3 vols. post 8vo. with Portrait, 25s. 6d.

VOL. 1. PASCAL'S PROVINCIAL LETters: with M. Villemain's Essay on Pascal prefixed, and a new Memoir. Post 8vo. Portrait, 8s. 6d.

VOL. 2. PASCAL'S THOUGHTS ON RELigion and Evidences of Christianity, with Additions from original MSS.: from M. Faugère's Edition. Post 8vo. price 8s. 6d.

VOL. 3. PASCAL'S MISCELLANEOUS Writings, Correspondence, Detached Thoughts, &c.: from M. Faugère's Edition. Post 8vo. 8s. 6d.

Dr. Pereira's Elements of Materia Medica and Therapeutics. *Third Edition,* enlarged and improved from the Author's Materials, by A. S. TAYLOR, M.D., and G. O. REES, M.D.: With numerous Woodcuts. Vol. I. 8vo. 28s.; Vol. II. Part I. 21s.; Vol. II. Part II. 24s.

Dr. Pereira's Lectures on Polarised Light, together with a Lecture on the Microscope. 2d Edition, enlarged from Materials left by the Author, by the Rev. B. POWELL, M.A., &c. Fcp. 8vo. with Woodcuts, 7s.

E. WEST. With Diagrams and W 3 vols. fcp. 8vo. 21s.

Ida Pfeiffer's Lady's Second Jo round the World: From London Cape of Good Hope, Borneo, Java, S Celebes, Ceram, the Moluccas &c., C Panama, Peru, Ecuador, and the States. 2 vols. post 8vo. 21s.

Phillips's Elementary Introducti Mineralogy. A New Edition, with ex Alterations and Additions, by H. J. B F.R.S., F.G.S.; and W. H. MIL F.G.S. With numerous Wood En Post 8vo. 18s.

Phillips.—A Guide to Geology. B PHILLIPS, M.A., F.R.S., F.G.S., &c. Edition, corrected to the Present with 4 Plates. Fcp. 8vo. 5s.

Phillips. — Figures and Descriptions Palæozoic Fossils of Cornwall, Dev West Somerset; observed in the of the Ordnance Geological Survey District. By JOHN PHILLIPS, F.R.S., &c. 8vo. with 60 Plates, price 9s.

Piesse's Art of Perfumery, and M of Obtaining the Odours of Plants Instructions for the Manufacture of P for the Handkerchief, Scented P Odorous Vinegars, Dentifrices, Po Cosmétiques, Perfumed Soap, &c.; Appendix on the Colours of Flowe ficial Fruit Essences, &c. *Second* revised and improved; with 46 W Crown 8vo. 8s. 6d.

Pillans.—Contributions to the C Education. By J. PILLANS, Esq., of Humanity in the University of E 8vo. 12s.

Pinney.—The Duration of Hum and its Three Eras: When Men at be more than 900 Years of Age; Wh attained to only 450; and When they to only 70. Showing the probable and material Agents that have Shorte Lives of the Human Race; and th riers that prevent a return to the Lo of the Early Patriarchs. By JOEL P Esq. 8vo. 7s. 6d.

Piscator.—The Choice and Cook Fish: A Practical Treatise. By PIS Fcp. 8vo. price 5s. 6d.

of the County of Londonderry, and of Parts of Tyrone and Fermanagh, examined and described under the Authority of the Master-General and Board of Ordnance. 8vo. with 48 Plates, price 24s.

Powell.—Essays on the Spirit of the Inductive Philosophy, the Unity of Worlds, and the Philosophy of Creation. By the Rev. BADEN POWELL, M.A., F.R.S., F.R.A.S., F.G.S., Savilian Professor of Geometry in the University of Oxford. Second Edition, revised. Crown 8vo. with Woodcuts, 12s. 6d.

Pycroft's Course of English Reading, adapted to every taste and capacity: With Literary Anecdotes. New and cheaper Edition. Fcp. 8vo. price 5s.

Raikes.—A Portion of the Journal kept by THOMAS RAIKES, Esq., from 1831 to 1847: Comprising Reminiscences of Social and Political Life in London and Paris during that period. *Second Edition.* Vols. I. and II. post 8vo. with Portrait, price 21s.

. Vols. III. and IV., with Portraits of Count Montrond and Prince Talleyrand, after Sketches by Count D'Orsay, and completing the work, are in the press.

Reade.—Man in Paradise: A Poem in Six Books. With Lyrical Poems. By JOHN EDMUND READE, Author of "Italy," "Revelations of Life," &c. *Second Edition.* Fcp. 8vo. 5s.

Dr. Reece's Medical Guide: Comprising a complete Modern Dispensatory, and a Practical Treatise on the distinguishing Symptoms, Causes, Prevention, Cure, and Palliation of the Diseases incident to the Human Frame. Seventeenth Edition, corrected and enlarged by the Author's Son, DR. H. REECE, M.R.C.S., &c. 8vo. 12s.

Rich's Illustrated Companion to the Latin Dictionary and Greek Lexicon: Forming a Glossary of all the Words representing Visible Objects connected with the Arts, Manufactures, and Every-Day Life of the Ancients. With about 2,000 Woodcuts from the Antique. Post 8vo. 21s.

Horsemanship; or, the Art of Riding and Managing a Horse, adapted to the Guidance of Ladies and Gentlemen on the Road and in the Field: With Instructions for Breaking-in Colts and Young Horses. By CAPTAIN RICHARDSON, late of the 4th Light Dragoons. With 5 Plates. Square crown 8vo. 14s.

English-Latin Dictionary, for Colleges and Schools. *New* and *Edition,* revised and corrected. 8v

Separately { The English-Latin Dictionary { The Latin-English Dictionary

Riddle's Diamond Latin-English Dict A Guide to the Meaning, right Accentuation of Latin Classical Royal 32mo. price 4s.

Riddle's Copious and Critical English Lexicon, founded on the Latin Dictionaries of Dr. William New *and cheaper* Edition. Post 4to.

Rivers's Rose-Amateur's Guide; ing ample Descriptions of all the fine varieties of Roses, regularly classed respective Families; their Mode of Culture. Fifth Edition, and improved. Fcp. 8vo. 3s. 6d.

Roberts. — The Social History People of the Southern Counties of in Past Centuries, illustrated in their Habits, Municipal B La Progress, &c., from the GEORGE ROBERTS, Author of *Life Duke of Monmouth*, &c. 8vo. with W price 18s.

Dr. E. Robinson's Greek and Lexicon to the Greek Testament. Edition, revised and in great part re 8vo. price 18s.

Mr. Henry Rogers's Essays selec Contributions to the *Edinburgh* Second *and cheaper* Edition, with A 3 vols. fcp. 8vo. 21s.

Dr. Roget's Thesaurus of English and Phrases classified and arranged facilitate the Expression of Ideas in Literary Composition. Third revised and improved. Crown 8vc

Ronalds's Fly-Fisher's Ento With coloured Representations Natural and Artificial Insect, and a servations and Instructions on Grayling Fishing. *Fifth Edition,* thor revised by an Experienced Fly-Fisher 20 Plates coloured after improved 8vo. 14s.

Rowton's Debater: A Series of c Debates, Outlines of Debates, and for Discussion; with ample to the best Sources of Information Edition. Fcp. 8vo. 6s.

tters of Rachel Lady Russell. A New Edition, including several unpublished Letters, together with those edited by MISS BERRY. With Portraits, Vignettes, and Facsimile. 2 vols. post 8vo. price 15s.

ie Life of William Lord Russell. By the Right Hon. LORD JOHN RUSSELL, M.P. Fourth Edition; with a Portrait after Sir Peter Lely. Post 8vo. 10s. 6d.

John (Mrs.)—Audubon the Naturalist in the New World: His Adventures and Discoveries. By MRS. HORACE ST. JOHN. Fcp. 8vo. price 2s. 6d.

ie Saints our Example. By the Author of *Letters to my Unknown Friends*, &c. Fcp. 8vo. price 7s.

. L. Schmitz's History of Greece, from the Earliest Times to the Taking of Corinth by the Romans, B.C. 146, mainly based upon Bishop Thirlwall's History. *Fourth Edition*, with Supplementary Chapters on the Literature and Arts of Ancient Greece; and illustrated with a Map of Athens, and 137 Woodcuts, designed from the Antique by G. Scharf, jun., F.S.A. 12mo. 7s. 6d.

'The fourth edition of Dr. Schmitz's *History of* ece has been improved by the addition of chapters on ek art and literature,—a want which we had occasion ly to notice in our review of a rival manual. Dr. mitz's book must now be considered the most complete glish history of Greece in a single volume, and well :ulated to form either an introduction or a companion he great works of Bishop Thirlwall and Mr. Grote. Its ie is enhanced by numerous woodcuts by Mr. G. Scharf, , of much higher quality than we usually meet with in nentary books." GUARDIAN, *Oct.* 22, 1856.

ott.—The Danes and the Swedes: Being an Account of a Visit to Denmark, ncluding Schleswig-Holstein and the Danish Islands; with a Peep into Jutland, and a Tourney across the Peninsula of Sweden. Embracing a Sketch of the most interesting points in the History of those Countries. By CHARLES HENRY SCOTT. Post 8vo. price 10s. 6d.

rivenor's History of the Iron Trade, from the Earliest Records to the Present Period. New Edition, corrected. 8vo. price 10s. 6d.

Edward Seaward's Narrative of his Shipwreck, and consequent Discovery of certain Islands in the Caribbean Sea. Third Edition. 2 vols. post 8vo. 21s.—An ABRIDGMENT, in 16mo. price 2s. 6d.

Sewell.—Amy Herbert.] Edited by the Rev. WILLIAM Fellow and Tutor of Exeter College, New Edition. Fcp. 8vo. price 6s.

Sewell.—The Earl's Daughter. Author of *Amy Herbert*. Edited by W. SEWELL, B.D. 2 vols. fcp. 8vo.

Sewell. — Gertrude : A Tale.] Author of *Amy Herbert*. Edited by W. SEWELL, B.D. New Edition. 8vo. price 6s.

Sewell.—Laneton Parsonage: A T Children, on the Practical Use of a of the Church Catechism. By the of *Amy Herbert*. Edited by the SEWELL, B.D. New Edition. 3 v 8vo. price 16s.

Sewell. — Margaret Percival. E Author of *Amy Herbert*. Edited by W. SEWELL, B.D. New Edition. fcp. 8vo. price 12s.

By the same Author,

Ivors. 2 vols. fcp. 8vo. price 12s.

Cleve Hall. 2 vols. fcp. 8vo. price 12s.

The Experience of Life. New Edition. 8vo. price 7s. 6d.

Katharine Ashton. New Edition. fcp. 8vo. price 12s.

Readings for Every Day in Lent: Co from the Writings of BISHOP J TAYLOR. Fcp. 8vo. price 5s.

Readings for a Month preparatory to tion : Compiled from the Works of of the Early and of the English New *and cheaper* Edition. Fcp. 8vo

Bowdler's Family Shakspeare: In nothing is *added* to the Original Tea those words and expressions are which cannot with propriety be read New Edition, in Pocket Volumes ; Woodcuts, from Designs by Smirke, and other Artists. 6 vols. fcp. 8vo.

* A LIBRARY EDITION, with the same 1 vol. medium 8vo. price 21s.

Sharp's New British Gazettee graphical Dictionary of the Bri

Short Whist; its Rise, Progress, and
Laws : With Observations to make any one a
Whist-Player. Containing also the Laws of
Piquet, Cassino, Ecarté, Cribbage, Back-
gammon. By Major A. New Edition ; to
which are added, Precepts for Tyros, by
Mrs. B. Fcp. 8vo. 3s.

Sinclair. — The Journey of Life. By
CATHERINE SINCLAIR, Author of *The Business of Life.* New Edition, corrected and
enlarged. Fcp. 8vo. 5s.

Sir Roger De Coverley. From The Spec-
tator. With Notes and Illustrations, by
W. HENRY WILLS; and 12 Wood Engravings from Designs by F. TAYLER. Second
and cheaper Edition. Crown 8vo. 10s. 6d. ;
or 21s. in morocco by Hayday.—An Edition
without Woodcuts, in 16mo. price 1s.

Smee's Elements of Electro-Metallurgy.
Third Edition, revised, corrected, and considerably enlarged ; with Electrotypes and
numerous Woodcuts. Post 8vo. 10s. 6d.

Smith (G.) — Harmony of the Divine
Dispensations : A Series of Discourses on
Select Portions of Holy Scripture, designed
to show the Spirituality, Efficacy, and Har-
mony of the Divine Revelations made to
Mankind from the Beginning. By GEORGE
SMITH, F.A.S., &c. Crown 8vo. 7s. 6d.

Smith (G.)—Sacred Annals; or, Researches
into the History and Religion of Mankind.
By GEORGE SMITH, F.A.S., &c. 3 vols.
crown 8vo. price £1. 14s.

> VOL. I. — THE PATRIARCHAL AGE, from the Cre-
> ation to the Death of Isaac. Crown 8vo. price 10s.
>
> VOL. II.—THE HEBREW PEOPLE, from the Origin
> of the Israelite Nation to the Time of Christ. Crown
> 8vo. in 2 Parts, price 12s.
>
> VOL. III. — THE GENTILE NATIONS — Egyptians,
> Assyrians, Babylonians, Medes, Persians, Greeks,
> and Romans. Crown 8vo. in 2 Parts, price 12s.

Smith (J.) — The Voyage and Shipwreck
of St. Paul : With Dissertations on the Life
and Writings of St. Luke, and the Ships and
Navigation of the Ancients. By JAMES
SMITH, of Jordanhill, Esq., F.R.S. *Second
Edition,* with additional Proofs and Illus-
trations ; Charts, Views, and Woodcuts.
Crown 8vo. 8s. 6d.

The Rev. Sydney Smith's
Works : Including his Contri
Edinburgh Review. Three

> 1. A LIBRARY EDITION (the *Fourth*
> with Portrait, 36s.
>
> 2. Complete in ONE VOLUME, with
> nette. Square crown 8vo. price 2
> bound in calf.
>
> 3. Another NEW EDITION, in 3 vols. 2

The Rev. Sydney Smith's
Sketches of Moral Philosophy,
the Royal Institution in the Y
1805, and 1806. Third *and cheaper*
Fcp. 8vo. 7s.

Robert Southey's Complete P
Works ; containing all the Author's
troductions and Notes. Complete
Volume, with Portrait and Vignette.
8vo. price 21s. cloth ; 42s. bound in
Or in 10 vols. fcp. 8vo. with P
19 Plates, price 35s.

Select Works of the British Poets
Chaucer to Lovelace inclusive.
Biographical Sketches by the late
SOUTHEY. Medium 8vo. price 30s.

Southey's Correspondence.—
from the Letters of Robert Sou
Edited by his Son-in-Law, the R
WOOD WARTER, B.D., Vicar
Tarring, Sussex. 4 vols. post 8vo.

The Life and Correspondence of the la
Southey. Edited by his Son,
C. C. SOUTHEY, M.A., Vicar of
With Portraits and Landscape
tions. 6 vols. post 8vo. price 63s.

Southey's The Doctor &c. compl
One Volume. Edited by the Rev
WARTER, B.D. With Portrait, V
Bust, and coloured Plate. New
Square crown 8vo. price 21s.

Southey's Commonplace-Books,
Four Volumes. Edited by the
WARTER, B.D. 4 vols. square
price £3. 18s.

> Each *Commonplace-Book,* complete in itself
> had separately, as follows :—
>
> FIRST SERIES — CHOICE PASSAGES, &c. 18s.
> SECOND SERIES — SPECIAL COLLECTIONS.
> THIRD SERIES — ANALYTICAL READINGS.
> FOURTH SERIES — ORIGINAL MEMORANDA.

s Life of Wesley ; and

cer.—The Principles of Psychology. HERBERT SPENCER, Author of *Social tics*. 8vo. 16s.

ton.—June: A Book for the Country Summer Time. By H. T. STAINTON, hor of *The Entomologist's Manual*, and various other popular Works on Natural History. Fcp. 8vo. 3s.

1en.—Lectures on the History of nce. By the Right Hon. SIR JAMES PHEN, K.C.B., LL.D., Professor of Modern tory in the University of Cambridge. nd Edition. 2 vols. 8vo. price 24s.

hen.—Essays in Ecclesiastical Biophy; from The Edinburgh Review. By Right Hon. SIR JAMES STEPHEN, K.C.B., .D., Professor of Modern History in University of Cambridge. Third Edin. 2 vols. 8vo. 24s.

ehenge.—The Greyhound: Being a tise on the Art of Breeding, Rearing, Training Greyhounds for Public Run-; their Diseases and Treatment: Cong also Rules for the Management of ursing Meetings, and for the Decision of urses. By STONEHENGE. With Frontisce and many Woodcuts. Square crown o. 21s.

.— The Training System, Moral School, and Normal Seminary for paring Schoolmasters and Governesses. y DAVID STOW, Esq., Honorary Secretary the Glasgow Normal Free Seminary. nth Edition; with Plates and Woodcuts. st 8vo. price 6s.

chey.—Hebrew Politics in the Times Sargon and Sennacherib: An Inquiry into Historical Meaning and Purpose of the rophecies of Isaiah, with some Notice of eir Bearings on the Social and Political ife of England. By EDWARD STRACHEY, sq. *Cheaper Issue.* 8vo. price 8s. 6d.

By the same Author,

es and Science. Post 8vo. price 1s.

ler.—Christian Aspects of Faith and uty: Twenty Discourses. By JOHN IMES TAYLER, B.A. Second Edition. st 8vo. price 7s. 6d.

lor.—Loyola: And Jesuitism in its ndiments. By ISAAC TAYLOR. Post 8vo.

Tegoborski.—Commentaries on the Productive Forces of Russia. By L. DE TEGOBORSKI, Privy-Councillor and Member of the Imperial Council of Russia. Vols. I. and II. 8vo. price 14s. each.

Thacker's Courser's Annual Remembrancer and Stud-Book: Being an Alphabetical Return of the Running at all the Public Coursing Clubs in England, Ireland, and Scotland, for the Season 1855-56; with the *Pedigrees* (as far as received) of the DOGS. By ROBERT ABRAM WELSH, Liverpool. 8vo. 21s.

⁎ Published annually in *October*.

Thirlwall.— The History of Greece. By the Right Rev. the LORD BISHOP of ST. DAVID's (the Rev. Connop Thirlwall). An improved Library Edition; with Maps. 8 vols. 8vo. price £3.

⁎ Also, an Edition in 8 vols. fcp. 8vo. with Vignette Titles, price 28s.

Thomson's Seasons. Edited by Bolton CORNEY, Esq. Illustrated with 77 fine Wood Engravings from Designs by Members of the Etching Club. Square crown 8vo. 21s. cloth; or 36s. bound in morocco.

Thomson (the Rev. W.)—The Atoning Work of Christ reviewed in relation to some current Theories; in Eight Bampton Lectures, with numerous Notes. By the Rev. W. THOMSON, M.A., Provost of Queen's College, Oxford. 8vo. 8s.

Thomson.—An Outline of the Laws of Thought: Being a Treatise on Pure and Applied Logic. By the Rev. W. THOMSON, M.A. Third Edition, enlarged. Fcp. 8vo. price 7s. 6d.

Thomson's Tables of Interest, at Three, Four, Four-and-a-Half, and Five per Cent., from One Pound to Ten Thousand, and from 1 to 365 Days; with Interest at all the above Rates, from One to Twelve Months, and from One to Ten Years. Also, numerous other Tables of Exchanges, Time, and Discounts. New Edition. 12mo. price 8s.

Thornbury.—Shakspeare's England; or, Sketches of Social History during the Reign of Elizabeth. By G. W. THORNBURY, Author of *History of the Buccaneers*, &c. 2 vols. crown 8vo. 21s.

The Thumb Bible; or, Verbum Sempi-

Bishop Tomline's Introduction to the Study of the Bible: Containing Proofs of the Authenticity and Inspiration of the Scriptures; a Summary of the History of the Jews; an Account of the Jewish Sects; and a brief Statement of Contents of several Books of the *Old Testament*. New Edition. Fcp. 8vo. 5s. 6d.

Tooke.—History of Prices, and of the State of the Circulation, from 1847 to the close of 1855. By THOMAS TOOKE, F.R.S. With Contributions by WILLIAM NEWMARCH. Being the Fifth and concluding Volume of Tooke's *History of Prices*, with an Index to the whole work. 8vo.

Townsend.—Modern State Trials revised and illustrated with Essays and Notes. By W. C. TOWNSEND, Esq., M.A., Q.C. 2 vols. 8vo. price 30s.

Trollope.—The Warden. By Anthony TROLLOPE. Post 8vo. 10s. 6d.

Sharon Turner's Sacred History of the World, attempted to be Philosophically considered, in a Series of Letters to a Son. New Edition, edited by the Rev. S. TURNER. 3 vols. post 8vo. price 31s. 6d.

Sharon Turner's History of England during the Middle Ages: Comprising the Reigns from the Norman Conquest to the Accession of Henry VIII. Fifth Edition, revised by the Rev. S. TURNER. 4 vols. 8vo. price 50s.

Sharon Turner's History of the Anglo-Saxons, from the Earliest Period to the Norman Conquest. Seventh Edition, revised by the Rev. S. TURNER. 3 vols. 8vo. 36s.

Dr. Turton's Manual of the Land and Fresh-Water Shells of the British Islands. A New Edition, with considerable Additions by JOHN EDWARD GRAY: With Woodcuts, and 12 coloured Plates. Post 8vo. price 15s.

Tuson.—The British Consul's Manual: Being a Practical Guide for Consuls, as well as for the Merchant, Shipowner, and Master Mariner, in all their Consular Transactions; and containing the Commercial Treaties between Great Britain and Foreign Countries, brought down to the present date. By E. W. A. TUSON, of the Inner Temple; Chancellor of the Imperial Austrian Consulate-General in London. 8vo. price 15s.

Twining.—Types and Figures of the

Dr. Ure's Dictionary of Arts, tures, and Mines: Containing a sition of their Principles an Fourth Edition, much enlarge the Articles being entirely remany new Articles added. 1,600 Woodcuts. 2 vols. 8vo.

Van Der Hoeven's Handbook Translated from the Second Du by the Rev. WILLIAM CLARK, &c., late Fellow of Trinity fessor of Anatomy in the Cambridge; with additional nished by the Author. In T Vol. I. *Invertebrate Animals*; wi comprising very numerous F price 30s.

Vehse.—Memoirs of the cracy, and Diplomacy of Austria. VEHSE. Translated from the FRANZ DEMMLER. 2 vols. post

Wade. — England's Greatness and Progress in Government, and Social Life; Agricultu and Manufactures; Science, the Arts, from the Earliest Peace of Paris. By JOHN W Institut d'Afrique (Historical Paris; Author of *History and P losophy of the Productive Cla Cabinet Lawyer*, &c. Fcp. 8vo.

Waterton.—Essays on N chiefly Ornithology. By C. WA With an Autobiography of the Views of Walton Hall. New Edition. 2 vols. fcp. 8vo. price

Webster and Parkes's Ency Domestic Economy; comprisi jects as are most immediately Housekeeping: As, The Domestic Edifices, with the ing, Ventilating, and Light scription of the various articles with the nature of their Ma Servants—&c. New Edition 1,000 Woodcuts. 8vo. price

Weld.—A Vacation Tour in States and Canada. By C. R. W ter-at-Law. Post 8vo. with

West. —Lectures on the Infancy and Childhood. By

PUBLISHED BY LONGMAN, BROWN, AND CO.

COMPLETION

OF

THE TRAVELLER'S LIBRARY.

Summary of the Contents of the TRAVELLER'S LIBRARY, *now complete in* 1
*Parts, price One Shilling each, or in 50 Volumes, price 2s. 6d. each in cloth.
To be had also, in complete Sets only, at Five Guineas per Set, bound in clot
lettered, in 25 Volumes, classified as follows:—*

VOYAGES AND TRAVELS.

IN EUROPE.

A CONTINENTAL TOUR .... BY J. BARROW.
ARCTIC VOYAGES AND } ...... BY F. MAYNE.
   DISCOVERIES ....
BRITTANY AND THE BIBLE ...... BY I. HOPE.
BRITTANY AND THE CHASE .... BY I. HOPE.
CORSICA .... BY F. GREGOROVIUS.
GERMANY, ETC.: NOTES OF } .... BY S. LAING.
   A TRAVELLER ....
ICELAND .... BY P. MILES.
NORWAY, A RESIDENCE IN ...... BY S. LAING.
NORWAY, RAMBLES IN ...... BY T. FORESTER.
RUSSIA .... BY THE MARQUIS DE CUSTINE.
RUSSIA AND TURKEY .. BY J. R. M'CULLOCH.
ST. PETERSBURG.......... BY M. JERRMANN.
THE RUSSIANS OF THE SOUTH, BY S. BROOKS.
SWISS MEN AND SWISS } BY R. FERGUSON.
   MOUNTAINS
MONT BLANC, ASCENT OF ...... BY J. AULDJO.
SKETCHES OF NATURE } BY F. VON TSCHUDI.
   IN THE ALPS..........

VISIT TO THE VAUDOIS } ...... BY E. BAINE
   OF PIEDMONT ....

IN ASIA.

CHINA AND THIBET........ BY THE ABBÉ HU
SYRIA AND PALESTINE............ "EOTHEN
THE PHILIPPINE ISLANDS, BY P. GIRONIÈ

IN AFRICA.

AFRICAN WANDERINGS .... BY M.
MOROCCO .... BY X. DURR
NIGER EXPLORATION .. BY T. J. HUTCHINS
THE ZULUS OF NATAL........ BY G. H. MAS

IN AMERICA.

BRAZIL.................. BY E. WILBERFOR
CANADA.................. BY A. M. JAMES
CUBA .... BY W. H. HURLB
NORTH AMERICAN WILDS .... BY C.

IN AUSTRALIA.

AUSTRALIAN COLONIES ...... BY W. HUG

ROUND THE WORLD.

A LADY'S VOYAGE.......... BY IDA PFEIFFE

HISTORY AND BIOGRAPHY.

MEMOIR OF THE DUKE OF WELLINGTON.
THE LIFE OF MARSHAL } BY THE REV. T. O.
   TURENNE............ COCKAYNE.
SCHAMYL .... BY BODENSTEDT AND WAGNER.
FERDINAND I. AND MAXIMI- } BY RANKE.
   LIAN II. ....
FRANCIS ARAGO'S AUTOBIOGRAPHY.
THOMAS HOLCROFT'S MEMOIRS.

CHESTERFIELD & SELWYN, BY A. HAYWAR
SWIFT AND RICHARDSON, BY LORD JEF
DEFOE AND CHURCHILL .... BY J. FORS
ANECDOTES OF DR. JOHNSON, BY MRS. PI
TURKEY AND CHRISTENDOM.
LEIPSIC CAMPAIGN, BY THE REV. G. R. GLEI
AN ESSAY ON THE LIFE AND } BY HENR
   GENIUS OF THOMAS FULLER } ROGERS.

ESSAYS BY MR. MACAULAY.

WARREN HASTINGS.
LORD CLIVE.
WILLIAM PITT.
THE EARL OF CHATHAM.
RANKE'S HISTORY OF THE POPES.
GLADSTONE ON CHURCH AND STATE.
ADDISON'S LIFE AND WRITINGS.
HORACE WALPOLE.
LORD BACON.

LORD BYRON.
COMIC DRAMATISTS OF THE RESTORATIO
FREDERIC THE GREAT.
HALLAM'S CONSTITUTIONAL HISTORY.
CROKER'S EDITION OF BOSWELL'S LIFE
   JOHNSON.
      —
MR. MACAULAY'S SPEECHES ON PARL
   MENTARY REFORM.

WORKS OF FICTION.

THE LOVE STORY FROM SOUTHEY'S DOCTOR.
SIR ROGER DE COVERLEY.... } FROM THE
             SPECTATOR.
MEMOIRS OF A MAITRE-D'ARMES, BY DUMAS.
CONFESSIONS OF A } ...... BY E. SOUVESTRE.
   WORKING MAN ..

AN ATTIC PHILOSO- } ...... BY E. SO
   PHER IN PARIS ..
SIR EDWARD SEAWARD'S NARRATIVE O
   HIS SHIPWRECK.

NATURAL HISTORY, &c.

NATURAL HISTORY OF } BY DR. L. KEMP.
   CREATION..............
INDICATIONS OF INSTINCT, BY DR. L. KEMP.

ELECTRIC TELEGRAPH, &c. BY DR. G. WILSO
OUR COAL-FIELDS AND OUR COAL-PITS.
CORNWALL, ITS MINES, MINERS, &c.

MISCELLANEOUS WORKS.

LECTURES AND ADDRESSES } BY THE EARL OF
                   CARLISLE.
SELECTIONS FROM SYDNEY SMITH'S

RAILWAY MORALS AND } .. BY H. SPENCE
   RAILWAY POLICY ......
MORMONISM

Wheeler (H. M.)—A Popular Harmony of the Bible, Historically and Chronologically arranged. By Henry M. Wheeler, Author of *Hebrew for Adults*, &c. Fcp. 8vo. 5s.

Wheeler (J.T.)—The Life and Travels of Herodotus in the Fifth Century before Christ: An imaginary Biography, founded on fact, illustrative of the History, Manners, Religion, Literature, Arts, and Social Condition of the Greeks, Egyptians, Persians, Babylonians, Hebrews, Scythians, and other Ancient Nations, in the Days of Pericles and Nehemiah. By J. Talboys Wheeler, F.R.G.S. 2 vols. post 8vo. with Map, 21s.

Wheeler.—The Geography of Herodotus Developed, Explained, and Illustrated from Modern Researches and Discoveries. By J. Talboys Wheeler, F.R.G.S. With Maps and Plans. 8vo. price 18s.

Whiteloeke's Journal of the English Embassy to the Court of Sweden in the Years 1653 and 1654. A New Edition, revised by Henry Reeve, Esq., F.S.A. 2 vols. 8vo. 24s.

Willich's Popular Tables for ascertaining the Value of Lifehold, Leasehold, and Church Property, Renewal Fines, &c. *Third Edition*, with additional Tables of Natural or Hyperbolic Logarithms, Trigonometry, Astronomy, Geography, &c. Post 8vo. price 9s. — Supplement, price 1s.

Wilmot's Abridgment of Blackstone's Commentaries on the Laws of England, intended for the use of Young Persons, and comprised in a series of Letters from a Father to his Daughter. A New Edition, corrected and brought down to the Present Day, by Sir John E. Eardley Wilmot, Bart. 12mo. price 6s. 6d.

Wilson (E.) — The Dissector's Manual of Practical and Surgical Anatomy. By Erasmus Wilson, F.R.S. Second Edition, corrected and improved; with 25 additional Woodcuts by Bagg. 12mo. 12s. 6d.

Wilson (W.)—Bryologia Britannica: Containing the Mosses of Great Britain and Ireland systematically arranged and described according to the Method of *Bruch* and *Schimper;* with 61 illustrative Plates. Being a New Edition, enlarged and altered, of the *Muscologia Britannica* of Messrs. Hooker and

Woods.—The Past Campaig of the War in the East, from of Lord Raglan to the Fall of By N. A. Woods, late Special dent to the *Morning Herald* at War. 2 vols. post 8vo. price 2

Yonge.—A New English-Greel Containing all the Greek W Writers of good authority. Yonge, B.A. *Second Edition,* corrected. Post 4to. price 21s.

Yonge's New Latin Gradus: Every Word used by the P authority. For the use of minster, Winchester, Harrow, and Rugby Schools; King's don; and Marlborough Co *Edition.* Post 8vo. 9s.—App thets classified according to Meaning, price 3s. 6d.

Youatt.—The Horse. By W With a Treatise of Draught. with numerous Wood Designs by William Har Longman and Co.'s Editior dered.) 8vo. price 10s.

Youatt.—The Dog. By W A New Edition; with numerous from Designs by W. Harvey.

Young.—The Christ of His Argument grounded in the F Life on Earth. By the Rev. Jo LL.D. Edin. Post 8vo. 7s. 6d.

Young.—The Mystery; or, Evil an the Rev. John Young, LL.D. E 8vo. 7s. 6d.

Young (E.) — Præ-Raffaelli Popular Inquiry into some new Principles connected with the I Poetry, Religion, and Revoluti By the Rev. Edward Young Trinity College, Cambridge; Au *its Constitution and Capacities.* P [Ju

Zumpt's Grammar of the La guage. Translated and adap use of English Students by Dr. I F.R.S.E.: With numerous Ad